T0305302

# Modelling Prices in Competitive Electricity Markets

# Wiley Finance Series

# Modelling prices in competitive electricity markets

*About the editor*

**DEREK W. BUNN** is currently Professor and
Chairman of the Decision Sciences subject area and
Director of the Energy Markets Group at the
London Business School, having held previous
appointments at Oxford and Stanford universities.
As a prominent international advisor on energy
economics, he has consulted for many global
energy companies and advised a number of
government agencies. Author of over 150 research
papers and 9 books in the areas of forecasting,
decision analysis and energy economics, he has also
been chief editor of the Journal of Forecasting since
1984. His research and practical involvement with
the electricity sector extends back over 25 years
experience.

# Modelling Prices in Competitive Electricity Markets

Edited by
**Derek W. Bunn**

John Wiley & Sons, Ltd

*Other Wiley Editorial Offices*

John Wiley & Sons Inc., 111 River Street, Hoboken, NJ 07030, USA

Jossey-Bass, 989 Market Street, San Francisco, CA 94103-1741, USA

Wiley-VCH Verlag GmbH, Boschstr. 12, D-69469 Weinheim, Germany

John Wiley & Sons Australia Ltd, 33 Park Road, Milton, Queensland 4064, Australia

John Wiley & Sons (Asia) Pte Ltd, 2 Clementi Loop #02-01, Jin Xing Distripark, Singapore 129809

John Wiley & Sons Canada Ltd, 22 Worcester Road, Etobicoke, Ontario, Canada M9W 1L1

Wiley also publishes its books in a variety of electronic formats. Some content that appears
in print may not be available in electronic books.

*Library of Congress Cataloging-in-Publication Data*

Modelling prices in competitive electricity markets / Derek W. Bunn, editor.
    p.   cm.—(Wiley finance series)
Includes bibliographical references and index.
ISBN 0-470-84860-X (Cloth : alk. paper)
1. Electric utilities—Rates—Mathematical models.   I. Bunn, Derek W.   II. Series.

HD9685.A2 M627 2004
333.793′231′01519—dc22

                                                    2003023105

*British Library Cataloguing in Publication Data*

A catalogue record for this book is available from the British Library

ISBN-10: 0-470-84860-X (H/B)
ISBN-13: 978-0-470-84860-9 (H/B)

Typeset in 10/12pt Times by TechBooks, New Delhi, India

This book is printed on acid-free paper responsibly manufactured from sustainable forestry
in which at least two trees are planted for each one used for paper production.

# Contents

# Contributors

**Ioannis Andreadis** is a lecturer in statistics at the European University of the Hague. His research interests are in differential geometry, nonlinear dynamics and financial time series. He has published 35 articles in mathematics, physics and nonlinear dynamics.

**Nicolas Audet** is currently Risk Manager at the European Bank for Reconstruction and Development in London, where he is working on model and market risks. He was previously working for the Bank of Canada. Nicolas holds an MSc from the Financial Engineering Program at the University of Michigan.

**David A. Bessler** is a Professor of Agricultural Economics at Texas A&M University. His recent interests include modelling observational data as directed acyclic graphs. He received his PhD in Agricultural Economics from the University of California at Davis.

**Svetlana Borovkova** is a lecturer at the Delft University of Technology in the Netherlands, having specialized in applying statistical methods to problems within the energy sector. She received her PhD from the University of Groningen, Netherlands in 1998 for analysis of nonlinear and chaotic time series.

**John Bower** is Senior Research Fellow at the Oxford Institute for Energy Studies (OIES) with primary responsibility for leading the electricity market research programme. His research interests are in the emergence and integration of international markets for electricity, generating fuels, emissions and cross-border transmission capacity.

**Derek W. Bunn** is Professor of Decision Sciences at the London Business School, where he has directed the energy markets research group for about 15 years. He is Editor-in-Chief of the *Journal of Forecasting* and has been a previous Chief Editor of *Energy Economics*.

**Agustín Martín Calmarza** obtained his Bachelor Degree in Electrical Engineering from Universidad Pontificia Comillas (UPCo), Madrid, 2001. His interest areas include power system control, time series analysis applied to energy bidding strategies and ancillary services topics. Now he is involved in risk analysis and risk management topics related to energy companies.

**Shi-Jie Deng** is an Assistant Professor in the School of Industrial & Systems Engineering at the Georgia Institute of Technology. He received a BSc degree in mathematics from Peking University (China) and a PhD degree in operations research from the University of

California, Berkeley. His research interests include financial modelling in deregulated energy markets and logistics. He received a CAREER Award from the US National Science Foundation in 2002.

**Julián Barquín Gil** obtained a Degree in Industrial Engineering (1988) and a PhD in Industrial Engineering (1993) at the Universidad Pontificia de Comillas, Madrid, and the Licenciado en Ciencias Físicas Degree in 1994. He belongs to the research staff at the Instituto de Investigación Tecnológica. His present interests include control, operation and planning of power systems.

**Javier Garcia Gonzalez** obtained his Industrial Engineering degree, specializing in electricity, from the Universidad Politecnica de Cataluña in 1996. He joined the Instituto de Investigacion Tecnológica (IIT) and obtained his PhD from the Universidad Pontifica Comillas in 2001 and the Spanish Royal Doctors Academy Award for the best thesis presented during that year in the scientific and technological area. Currently he belongs to the research staff of the IIT.

**Alicia Mateo González** obtained her Mathematics degree from the University of Málaga, Spain in 1996. She joined the Instituto de Investigación Tecnológica at the Pontificia Comillas University in 1997, where she is currently working on her PhD thesis. Her areas of interest include the application of Artificial Intelligence techniques and Hidden Markov Models to the modelling of competitive electricity markets.

**Chris Harris** took his PhD in metallurgy with the Central Electricity Generating Board, at Cambridge University. Positions at Innogy include Head of Asset Management and General Manager of Commercial Operations and Product Development in Operations and Engineering.

**Pirja Heiskanen** is Manager of Operative Market Analysis at Fortum Portfolio Management and Trading. Prior to Fortum she has been with Helsinki University of Technology (1994–1997), Delft University of Technology (1997–1998) and Helsinki School of Economics (1998–2000) from where she received her PhD in 2001.

**Udi Helman** is an Economist with the Office of Markets, Tariffs and Rates of the Federal Energy Regulatory Commission. He holds a PhD in Energy Economics from The Johns Hopkins University and an MA in Environmental Studies from the University of Toronto.

**Efraim Centeno Hernáez** obtained a Degree in Industrial Engineering (1991) and a PhD in Industrial Engineering (1998) at the Universidad Pontificia de Comillas, Madrid. He belongs to the research staff at the Instituto de Investigación Tecnológica. His areas of interest include planning and operation of power systems.

**Helen Higgs** is Lecturer in the School of Economics and Finance at the Queensland University of Technology. She is currently completing her doctorate and has held a previous academic appointment at the University of Queensland. Her research centres on the application of multivariate econometric techniques to financial and economic markets.

**Benjamin F. Hobbs** is Professor of Geography & Environmental Engineering and Mathematical Sciences, The Johns Hopkins University. He serves on the California ISO Market Surveillance Committee, and is Scientific Advisor to the ECN Policy Studies Unit. His PhD is in Environmental Systems Engineering from Cornell University.

**Christine A. Jerko** has been part of the Commercial and Trading Group at PacifiCorp since May, 2003. Her primary responsibility is the development of a long-run portfolio to supply their customers with least cost electricity while ensuring reliability. She holds a PhD in Agricultural Economics from Texas A&M University.

**Wenjiang Jiang** is Professor of Mathematical Finance and Mathematical Statistics in the School of Mathematical Sciences, Yunnan Normal University, where he teaches courses on mathematical finance, simulation, statistics and stochastic processes. He received an MS degree in mathematical statistics from Beijing Normal University and a PhD in mathematical finance from University of Aarhus.

**Jussi Keppo** received the Dr. Tech degree in Applied Mathematics from Helsinki University of Technology in 1998. He continued as a Post Doctoral Fellow in Columbia University and after that he started in the University of Michigan. His research interests include stochastic control and mathematical economics.

**Jacob Lemming** is employed in the System Analysis Department at Risoe National Laboratory. He holds a masters degree in mathematical modelling from the Technical University of Denmark (DTU) and has undertaken a PhD on the topic: Investments and Risk Management Strategies in Liberalized Electricity Markets.

**Angel León** is an Associate Professor in the Department of Financial Economics, University of Alicante (Spain), and lecturer at CEMFI in Madrid. He holds a PhD in Financial Economics from the University of Alicante. His current areas of interest focus on applied financial econometrics, derivatives and real options.

**José Ignacio de la Fuente León** obtained both his BS and PhD degrees in Electrical Engineering from Universidad Pontificia Comillas (UPCo), Madrid, in 1990 and 1997 respectively. He has been a staff researcher at the Instituto de Investigación Tecnológica (IIT-UPCo). His interest areas have included power systems control and optimization, energy markets and power quality issues. Nowadays, he works at Red Eléctrica de España, S.A.

**James W. Mjelde** is a Professor of Resource Economics in the Department of Agricultural Economics at Texas A&M University in College Station, Texas. His research interest is primarily focused on information forecasting systems. He holds a PhD in Agricultural Economics from the University of Illinois at Champaign-Urbana.

**Mariano J. Ventosa Rodríguez** obtained a PhD in Electric Energy Systems in 2001, from the Universidad Pontificia Comillas, Madrid, Spain. He is an Assistant Professor at the Instituto de Investigacion Tecnologica (IIT). His areas of interest focus on the application of operations research in electricity markets.

**Antonio Muñoz San Roque** obtained the Degree of Doctor Ingeniero Industrial in 1996, and the Degree of Ingeniero Industrial in Electrical Engineering in 1991 from the Universidad Pontificia Comillas, Madrid. He is now an Assistant Professor in the Engineering School (ICAI) of the Universidad Pontificia Comillas and Vice Director of the Industrial Systems Area of the Instituto de Investigación Tecnológica.

**Antonio Rubia** is an Associate Professor in the Department of Financial Economics, University of Alicante (Spain). He holds a PhD in Financial Economics from the University of Alicante. His current research focuses on several fields of applied financial econometrics.

**Apostolos Serletis** is Professor of Economics at the University of Calgary. His research focus is on financial economics, macroeconometrics, and nonlinear and complex dynamics. He is the author of five books and more than one hundred articles in refereed economics and finance journals.

**James W. Taylor** is a Lecturer in Management Studies at the Saïd Business School, University of Oxford. His research interests are in the area of forecasting and include exponential smoothing, prediction intervals, quantile regression, combining forecasts, volatility forecasting, electricity demand forecasting and weather ensemble predictions.

**Iivo Vehviläinen** has been with Fortum Portfolio Management and Trading, a unit of Fortum Group, since the electricity market deregulation in Finland in 1998. Presently he is managing the financial portfolio analysis of Fortum's generation business in the Nordic area. His research focuses on the application of financial theory to the deregulated electricity markets.

**Andrew C. Worthington** is Associate Professor in the School of Economics and Finance at the Queensland University of Technology. He holds his PhD from the University of Queensland and previously held an academic appointment at the University of New England. His research focuses on efficiency and productivity measurement and market interrelationships.

# Preface

Electricity markets have emerged out of the political enthusiasm for restructuring public utilities, which in turn was founded upon a belief in the ability of competitive forces to deliver innovation and efficiency gains. This widespread emergence has been a remarkable worldwide trend, and a considerable technical achievement. Electricity used to be viewed as one of the most natural of monopolies: an invisible, capital-intensive product that was totally dependent upon a network structure to provide an essential, instantaneous service to customers. When we operate a domestic appliance, a cooling fan, for example, its rotations are in harmony with those of the massive generating turbines in the many power stations, which provide a steady voltage and alternating current, interconnected across vast distances. To split up such a highly co-ordinated, technically complex, supply chain into separate operating companies, mutually competitive, with transparent, almost real-time markets, required not only brave economic vision, but also huge information processing capabilities.

The first decade of research on electricity markets, not surprisingly therefore, had an economic focus upon industry structure and market mechanism design. Model-based analysis in this context was developed either through stylised analysis or simulation. It was more normative than descriptive. As market liberalisations progressed, participants became gradually more exposed to the risks that competitive markets bring, and so the adaptation of financial models and techniques for price risk management then became high on the research agenda. It has taken a while for the accumulation of sufficient data for interesting and useful econometric work to be undertaken, but we are now in a position to look at the empirical data on wholesale power markets, their special characteristics, and assess the applicability of various methods of price modelling. That is the rationale for this book.

Within this volume we have a rich compilation of leading-edge research and innovative methods for modelling electricity prices. Each chapter should be a stimulus for further researchers, as well as for analysts and advanced modellers in the markets.

The special characteristics of electricity prices, that sets them apart from other commodities, are described in the first introductory chapter. Fundamental drivers of consumption, together with technical constraints in generation/transmission, for a product which consumers cannot store and which display almost negligible short-term elasticity create spot markets that have complex, but identifiable structures. Their stochastic behaviour is typically mean-reverting, spiky and with volatilities an order of magnitude higher than is commonly seen on the financial and other commodity markets. Furthermore, the markets are generally inefficient, high in regulatory risk and prone to persistent political interventions.

Part I of this volume therefore concentrates on this structural aspect. In Chapter 2, there is a compilation of several lines of work that the research group at the University Pontifica Comillas in Madrid have been pursuing in explicitly modelling the way that individual generators will formulate their offers to the market in the face of anticipated competitive behaviour. This framework for modelling competitive market behaviour is extended from the individual company perspective to that of equilibrium for the market as a whole, in Chapter 3 by Hobbs and Helman. They present the basic approach of complementarity for developing a realistic equilibrium model of prices across a power network, with an oligopoly of generators, and show how this has important applications for market power analysis in practice. Market power has indeed been a major factor determining the level of prices in many of the liberalised electricity markets. Just how this depends empirically upon the market structure, specifically generator concentration, is estimated in Chapter 4 by John Bower. This is an important piece of work, as part of the debate in the UK into whether the change of market rules in 2001, from a compulsory pool to an unadministed bilateral process, or the reduction in generator concentration, was the cause of the 40% reduction in wholesale prices over the following year. The regression models, which he develops, provide useful insights into the longer-term determination of prices.

Part II moves on from that structural perspective of fundamental drivers to analyse the stochastic properties of spot market data. One of the first investigations that time series analysts usually undertake is to establish the stationarity properties, the so-called "unit-root" tests. This is quite an intuitive procedure, although the testing set-up is rather precise, and so in Chapter 5, León and Rubia describe it in some detail, with application to Spanish daily prices. More advanced testing of the stochastic properties are presented in Chapter 6 by Serletis and Andreadis, where elements of multifractal and chaotic specifications are discussed in the context of peak prices in Alberta. Apart from specification tests for the levels of prices, the modelling of volatility presents special challenges. The standard assumptions of GARCH models do not hold up on electricity prices. In Chapter 7, Deng and Jiang discuss this and present the use of quantile-GARCH methods as a practical solution. Finally, Part II concludes with Chapter 8, in which the issue of intraday correlations in volatility is modelled, by León and Rubia, with a multivariate GARCH. This has practical application in situations where there is daily trading of blocks of prices.

Part III looks at the regional aspect of price correlations. Electricity networks often span several spot markets so that the dynamics of price discovery and the transmission of volatility become important questions for market efficiency analysis and trading. Jerko, Mjelde and Bessler in Chapter 9 present in detail an innovative use of time series analysis and directed acyclic graphs, whereas Worthington and Higgs in Chapter 10 present another example of the use of multivariate GARCH.

Part IV is about forward prices. Chris Harris in Chapter 11 provides a conceptual and practical basis for fundamental modelling of forward prices based upon real options and equilibrium analysis, from a generators' perspective. Chapters 12 and 13 seek to empirically estimate the characteristics of the forward curve. In Chapter 12, Audet, Heiskanen, Keppo and Vehviläinen model the foward curve dynamics with parameterised volatility and correlation structures, whilst Borovkova in Chapter 13 develops indicators to predict the basic changes in the shape of the term structure.

Finally, in Part V there are two chapters looking at broader aspects. Jacob Lemming in Chapter 14 considers the sensitivity of price risk management techniques to input values, and in effect emphasises the importance of accurate price modelling. It is a reminder, if one were needed, of the importance of developing better price modelling techniques. Furthermore, one of the greatest sources of short-term uncertainty, mainly for volume, but indirectly for price, is the weather. James Taylor, in Chapter 15, describes the use of quantile methods again, but this time in the context of estimating weather variable uncertainty, which could indirectly lead into weather derivative pricing.

Overall, I am grateful for the timely co-operation of all these contributors, for facilitating this compilation of the most important state-of-the-art modelling techniques, which are converging to provide the special set of approaches required to unravel and forecast the behaviour of electricity prices. There is clearly a lot more that needs to be done, and this will remain an active and rich area of financial econometrics for many years to come. I am also grateful to the publisher for their patience and good-natured support during the whole editorial process from concept to production.

*Derek Bunn*
London
July 2003

# 1

# Structural and Behavioural Foundations of Competitive Electricity Prices

## DEREK W. BUNN

*London Business School, Regents Park, London NW1 4SA, UK*

## ABSTRACT

This chapter provides an introductory background to the fundamental and strategic drivers of price formation in electricity markets. It does not go into detail on the various time-series and econometric models, which are beginning to be applied to electricity data, as a range of these are presented in later chapters. Alternatively, it seeks to provide a basic understanding of why electricity prices are quite different in their behaviour and properties to those in other financial and commodity markets. It is also an introduction to some aspects of power system economics and electricity market liberalisation, for readers coming to electricity with experience of modelling other financial markets.

## 1.1  INTRODUCTION

From a financial and commodity markets perspective, wholesale electricity prices can generally be viewed as the result of investors having created real options upon various underlying primary fuel commodities such as gas, oil or coal. Although a substantial amount of electricity is generated from hydro and nuclear sources in various parts of the world, the dominant production process is still the thermal conversion of fossil fuels such as gas, oil and coal. This is a very capital intensive process, with surprisingly few workers actually being employed at the power plants. Thus, as electricity is often traded on exchanges close to an hour before it is needed, in this short term, the variable cost of power generation is essentially just the cost of the fuel. Even in power systems with a substantial amount of hydro and nuclear, it is the fossil fuel plant that often sets the market prices.

Depending upon the age and technology of the generating plant, in general, around a half of the energy content of the primary fuel gets converted into electricity. It follows from this, that with knowledge of the spot and futures market prices for primary fuels, and relatively well-known efficiency ratings for individual power plants on the system, the short-run marginal cost of each power plant on the system can be reasonably well estimated as a simple conversion of the fuel price. Of course, the owners of power plants would also like to recover their overheads and produce a return on investment, and so the spread between the market prices for fuel and power, the so-called tolling margin, is the value of owning and operating a power plant. As a real asset, or a contract held by a trader, the tolling margin represents the optionality of converting fuel prices into power prices. From this perspective, the

Price £/MWh

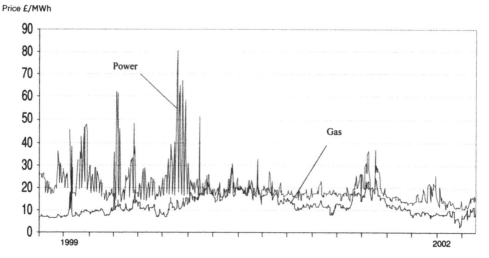

**Figure 1.1**   British daily average power and gas prices (50% gas to power efficiency assumed)
*Source:* Heren.

fundamental drivers of power prices should, it seems at first sight, be quite straightforward to understand.

In practice, however, whilst this fundamental concept is valid, its application has many complications. Take the case of gas, for example. This is now becoming the fuel of choice for electricity generation. The investment costs are lower than coal, or oil plant; it is cleaner and, depending upon location, the fuel costs are comparable. But with more and more of the gas resources being used for power generation, in some markets the issue of whether gas drives power prices, or *vice versa*, is not easily answered. Clearly, with convergence between two markets, they become partially co-determined. Figure 1.1 shows the daily average spot prices in the UK for gas and electricity. Clearly convergence was beginning to happen over this period, but at times, the relationship between the two is rather erratic.

Intuitively, the first reason that comes to mind, for the lack of an apparently better convergence with gas, is that gas may not be the only fuel source influencing prices. At some times it may be coal, oil or other plant that is dominant in setting the market prices. Just as the so-called "spark spread" refers to the spread between power and gas prices, the "dark spread" refers to the power–coal market price. As far as the British market has been concerned, gas has steadily been replacing coal as the dominant fuel since the mid-1990s, and there is evidence even in the few years shown in Figure 1.1 that the convergence with gas is improving. However, that is only part of the story.

Looking at Figure 1.1, the basic nature of the electricity time series does seem to be quite different to gas, even though there is a trend to an underlying convergence. As a time series, it is much more spiky, shows higher volatility and a stronger mean-reverting pattern. These, indeed, are the general stochastic characteristics of power prices, as observed in most markets around the world, and there is a fundamental structural reason for this.

The crucial feature of price formation in electricity spot markets is the instantaneous nature of the product. The physical laws that determine the delivery of power across a transmission grid require a synchronised energy balance between the injection of power at generating points

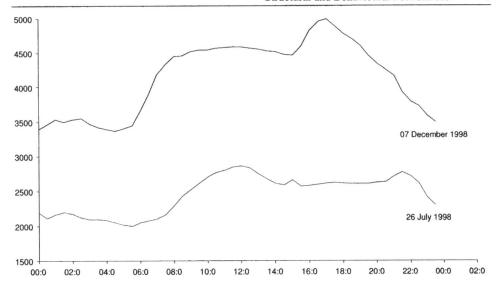

**Figure 1.2**    Summer and winter demand profiles
*Source:* NGC.

and the offtake at demand points (plus some allowance for transmission losses). Across the grid, production and consumption are perfectly synchronised, without any capability for storage. If the two get out of balance, even for a moment, the frequency and voltage of the power fluctuates. Furthermore, end-users treat this product as a service at their convenience. When we go to switch on a light, we do not re-contract with a supplier for the extra energy before doing so. We just do it, and there is a tendency for millions of other people to do likewise whenever they feel like it. Electricity may be produced as a commodity, but it is consumed as a service. The task of the grid operator, therefore, is to be continuously monitoring the demand process and to call on those generators who have the technical capability and the capacity to respond quickly to the fluctuations in demand. Figure 1.2 shows the annual range of daily demand profiles from England and Wales. Through a mixture of good forecasting and scheduling by the grid operator, together with a sufficient stock of flexible generating capacity, instantaneous production also follows these demand profiles.

Most spot markets for electricity are defined on hourly intervals (although the British market is half-hourly), and therefore it is clear that throughout the day and throughout the year, a wide variety of plant will be in action and therefore setting the prices at different times. Furthermore, we would expect a diversity of plant on the system for at least two reasons. The obvious one is obsolescence. With power plant lasting for some 40 years, new technologies will come in and be more efficient. So prices will be fluctuating because of the varying efficiencies of the set of plant being used for generation at any particular moment in time.

The more subtle, and second, reason for diversity is, however, again due to the instantaneous nature of the product. The most efficient plant, with the lowest marginal costs (the "baseload" plant), will operate most of the time, but during some of the peaks in demand, some of the power plants (the "peaking" plant) may only be operating for a few hours. The recovery of capital costs on peaking plant, through market prices, may have to be achieved over a relatively few hours of operation compared to the 8760 hours in a normal year for which a baseload plant,

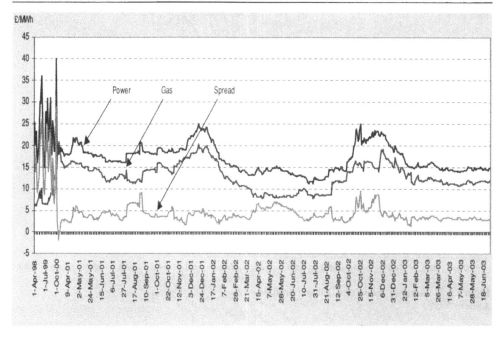

**Figure 1.3**  Monthly forward prices on the British power and gas markets
*Source:* Heren.

without maintenance breaks, could, in principle, serve. Indeed, if we were optimising our stock of power plant, we would invest in some capital-intensive, low-operating-cost plants to serve the baseload, and some relatively cheap to build, but relatively expensive to run, plant (e.g. small diesel generators) available for the peaks. This is, of course, what does happen in practice, with the consequence that prices are much higher in the peaks. We will go through, in more detail, some of the basic economic aspects of the capacity mix in the next section.

So, whilst the fundamental nature of fuel price convergence has a mean-reverting implication, the instantaneous production process of following a highly variable demand profile, with a diversity of plant costs, creates the high spot price volatility. Other factors also come into play in the short term. There may be technical failures with plant, causing more expensive standby generators to come online. The transmission system may become congested so that rather expensive, but locally necessary plant gets called upon. And, of course, there may be unexpected fluctuations in demand. All of these events show up in spot prices. Average forward prices, would, in contrast, be expected to be rather more attenuated than the spot prices. Figure 1.3 shows average month-ahead prices, and compared with Figure 1.1, the fundamental convergence with gas is indeed rather more stable.

There is one further important characteristic of electricity markets, with major implications for price behaviour, and that is their imperfect nature. Most power markets are characterised by a few dominant players, and even in those less common situations where there may appear to be sufficient competitors to achieve efficient prices, at particular times and in special locations, individual companies may have the ability to influence prices. Of the academic research on liberalised electricity markets, by far the bulk of work that has been published has been done on the analysis of, and strategies for the mitigation of, the abuse of market power by the generating companies. As a result of the presence of this market power, prices are generally much higher, and even more volatile, than the fundamentals suggest. In the third section of this chapter, we look at the strategic consequences on prices of imperfect market designs.

## 1.2   MARKET FUNDAMENTALS

An electricity system essentially provides capacity for immediate consumption, and we, as users, have acquired a call option, to exercise at our convenience, essentially unconstrained in volume up to the limit of our fuse-box. The total utilisation of this capacity by all customers on the system is referred to as the "load", and the basic unit of load is the "watt".

---

### Terminology and Calibration

As an aside, a typical bright domestic light bulb may use 100 W. A thousand watts is a kilowatt, and a typical domestic electric heating appliance may use 2 kW. A small commercial building may use 100 kW. A thousand kilowatts is a megawatt, and a small gas or diesel generating plant (rather like an aero-engine) would generate about 50 MW. Another thousand megawatts is a gigawatt, and some very large power stations may be 2 GW. Energy consumption is generally integrated over time and sold to retail customers in kilowatt-hours (kWh). Wholesale power prices, on the other hand, tend to be denominated in megawatt-hours (MWh).

---

In terms of analysing capacity, and the reasons for possible diversity in its composition, a basic construct is the load duration curve. Figure 1.4 shows an annual load profile of average

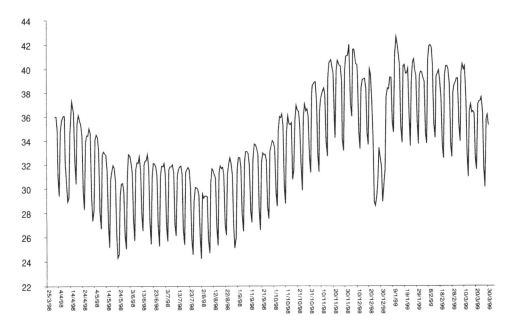

**Figure 1.4**   Daily average electricity demand UK 98/99
*Source:* NGC.

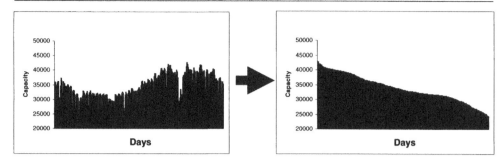

**Figure 1.5**    Re-sequencing the load profile to give the load duration curve

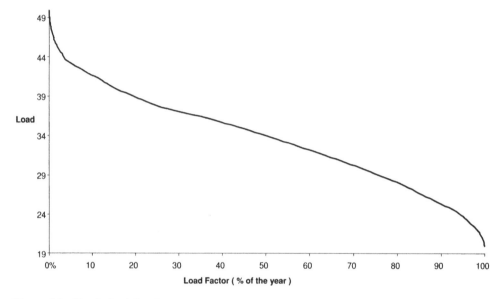

**Figure 1.6**    Hourly load duration curve

daily demands, and it is clear that the average daily demand seems to lie within the range 24–43 GW. In Figure 1.5, this same data series, expressed now in hourly intervals, is re-sequenced according to decreasing daily loads, to produce the load duration curve. This load duration curve displays the number of days of the year for which the daily average load is greater than a particular level. Within-day variation would of course display an even greater range of demand on an hourly basis. In Figure 1.6, this same data series, expressed now in hourly intervals, thus displays the hourly load duration curve (note the points on the horizontal axis are now re-expressed as a percentage of the 8760 hours in the year).

For example, it is apparent that for 5% of the year the hourly loads are greater than 43 GW. In other words, if you owned a peaking plant, the running costs of which were so inferior that there was 43 GW of capacity on the system that could be offered more cheaply to the market, then you would only expect to run 5% of the time, which is to say that the "load factor" of this plant is only 5%. Obviously, it is only worth keeping this as an investment if you can gain a substantial margin over the running costs. So, it is easy to see why, in an imperfect market, prices become spiky at the peaks.

**Table 1.1**  Technology choice for a simple example

| Technology | Investment cost (£/kW) | Marginal production cost (£/MWh) | Life-time years |
|---|---|---|---|
| Nuclear | 1300 | 2 | 40 |
| Coal | 600 | 10 | 40 |
| OCGT | 200 | 30 | 40 |
| CCGT | 350 | 13 | 30 |

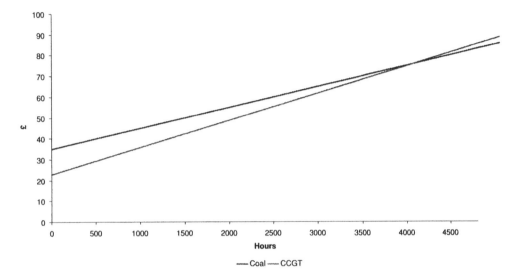

**Figure 1.7**  Annual cost of each plant for hours operated

In order to fix our understanding of the fundamental economics of the capacity mix, we proceed with a simple example. In Table 1.1, we have assumed a simple set of costs for four technologies, and let us presume an idealised situation where we can design the optimal capacity mix from these four alternatives in order to serve the above-mentioned load duration curve. We would expect nuclear to be baseload, and the open cycle gas turbines (OCGTs) to be peaking; coal and combined cycle gas turbines (CCGTs) will be somewhere in between ("mid-merit"); but how much of each we need is not obvious.

A simple concept is to look at the annual costs of owning and operating a unit (e.g. 1 kW) of each technology. The initial investment cost can be spread over the life of the plant by converting it into an annual annuity using the usual discounting formula, with an assumed cost of capital. This annual annuity value can then be considered the fixed cost of ownership per year. In other words, if you had to lease the plant from an owner, this is the annual rent that would just recover the owner's investment at its cost of capital.

The annual operating cost is the fuel cost multiplied by the number of hours the plant operates in the year. Thus, at a 5% cost of capital (which was the case for pre-liberalised, public sector utilities), for two technologies, we get the annual break-even functions shown in Figure 1.7. We can see from this break-even chart that, under the assumptions of Table 1.1, a coal plant needs to run for more than 4000 hours per year to be a better investment than a CCGT. So, if we were just using these two technologies, how much of each do we install?

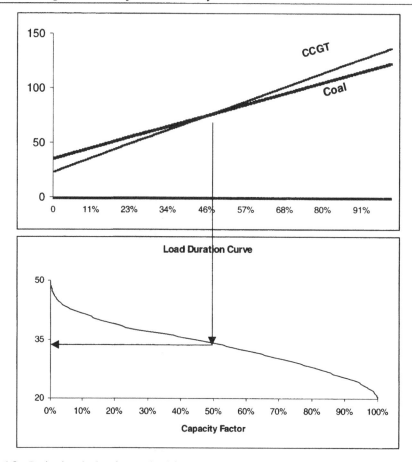

**Figure 1.8**   Projecting the break-even load factor

In Figure 1.8, we see how this break-even analysis can be projected onto the load duration curve to give the amount of each technology in the cost-minimising capacity mix. With just coal and CCGT, coal would be the baseload, to the extent of about 34 GW. With all four technologies, we get the break-even analysis of Figure 1.9. Thus, nuclear provides the baseload in an era of public ownership and access to low costs of capital (but if we went up to a "market" rate of 11%, there would be no nuclear or coal in the optimal mix, just gas CCGT and OCGT, as the higher cost of capital penalises the capital-intensive alternatives). However, staying with these 5% cost of capital results, for the purpose of illustration, after projecting these onto the load duration curve as above, we get a capacity mix of 65%, 4%, 16% and 15%, for the nuclear, coal, CCGT and OCGT technologies.

Figure 1.10 displays this capacity mix in terms of the stack of marginal costs, i.e. the supply function, which this simple system provides. The shape of the supply function is one of the most important fundamentals in understanding the behaviour of electricity prices. It displays the marginal cost of supplying power at a particular level of demand. Evidently, to the extent that market prices are efficient and reflect short-run marginal costs, this is a nonlinear driver of prices, depending upon demand in a particular hourly period. With demand being highly

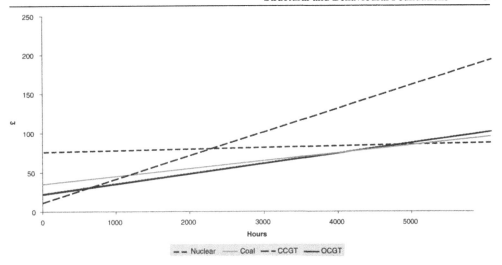

**Figure 1.9**  Break-even analysis

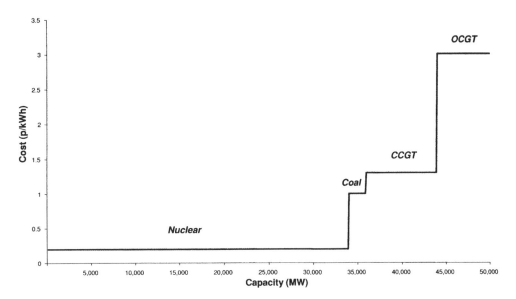

**Figure 1.10**  The marginal cost supply function for the optimised simple example

variable throughout the day, the translation of this into prices via such a steeply-increasing supply function has an amplification effect in producing the hourly price volatility.

The key lesson of this simple example is that, for purely economic investment reasons, there may be a diversity of plant on the system, with increasing marginal costs for supplying the higher load periods. Of course the example is ideal, in assuming we can have a complete stock of new plant. In practice the capacity stock reflects historical investments over 40 years or more, each made at times when the cost and resource perspectives were quite different. So, there is further cost diversity because of these evolving structural changes in the perceptions of investment and running costs.

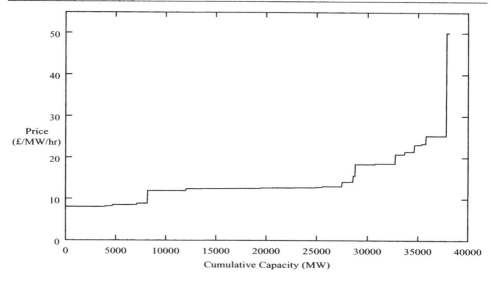

**Figure 1.11**   Marginal cost estimates for 1997 (for price-setting plant)

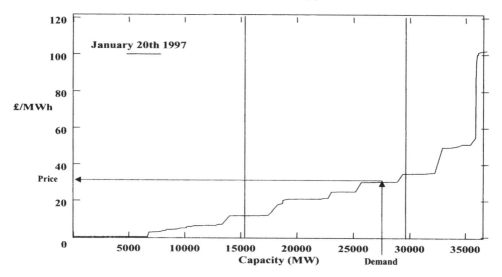

**Figure 1.12**   Price formation in 1997

In addition, the above example makes a purely economic point. For technical reasons, some types of plant can respond to changes in demand quicker than others. Some plant, such as nuclear, need to run to a constant load. Other plant, such as large coal plant, can follow the load, but need a long time to start-up and so would not be useful for serving short-duration peaks. For technical, dynamic reasons, therefore, there is also a need for highly responsive, yet possibly expensive, generating plant to be available in the stack comprising the supply function.

Figure 1.11 shows marginal cost estimates for the England and Wales supply function in 1997, as comprised by the three main generating companies who were setting prices at the time. This is esssentially the stack of plant above a baseload of some 20 GW, which was mostly nuclear plant and at the time would always be in merit. Compare this with Figure 1.12, which is the actual supply function, which was offered to the market on January 20 of that year. In those days, the England and Wales market operated a pool system whereby all generators had to make offers from each of their plant for the whole of the 48 half-hourly periods of the subsequent day. These were then effectively stacked into a supply function for the day, and as the half-hourly demand fluctuated thoughout the day, i.e. between the two vertical lines on the figure, a "system marginal price" (SMP), for each half hour, would be projected onto the vertical axis, as illustrated. Note that this SMP would then become the market price received by all generators in that half hour, such that the more efficient plant, with lower offers, received extra profit contributions from the differences between SMP and their offer prices. This is the uniform-price auction, characteristic of many pool-based markets, having the economic logic that the more efficient plant is likely to require a higher contribution to its investment costs. Even with less institutionalised markets, e.g. bilateral trading, price discovery should lead to the market price approaching that of the marginal producer's.

Three important differences should be noted between the marginal cost supply function of Figure 1.11 and the actual market supply function of Figure 1.12. Firstly, as expected, the generators' offers making up the market supply function are substantially above marginal cost. This is obviously the result of a lack of competitive pressure in the market, with the price-setting plant in 1997 being controlled by just three generators. The high prices therefore reflect a market structure issue, and perhaps also some tacit collusive market conduct. Secondly, we observe that not all of the plant was actually made available that day, so that the demand range extended into a steeper part of the supply function. In practice, in many parts of the world, capacity withholding by dominant players has been a constant issue for market surveillance. Because of the convexity of the supply functions, wholesale prices are very sensitive to the reserve margin between available supply and demand. Rather more subtle is the third observation that the slope of the supply function across the demand range is steeper in the market than marginal cost estimates would imply. This reflects the greater competition for load factor at lower levels of demand, and perhaps the greater ability of the generators to co-ordinate offers for the higher demand periods. All of these aspects together reflect a substantial strategic overlay to the fundamental economic drivers of price formation.

Furthermore, the strategic behaviour manifests a dynamic game, with the players repeatedly experimenting, learning and signalling through their daily offers. Figure 1.13 displays the series of subsequent weekday supply functions, from the three price-setting generators, following the day displayed in Figure 1.12. The evolutionary behaviour is quite evident.

Clearly, when it comes to analysing electricity spot price data, the challenge is to develop time-series models that are rich enough to capture both the nonlinear economic fundamentals and the stochastic behaviour induced by imperfect competition.

## 1.3 INSTITUTIONAL REFORM AND STRATEGIC EVOLUTION

Modelling and forecasting electricity prices is a totally new activity for the majority of companies in the energy business. Until recently, electricity was a monopoly in most countries, often government owned, and if not, highly regulated. As such, electricity prices reflected the government's social and industrial policy, and any price forecasting which was undertaken was really focussed on thinking about underlying costs. In this respect, it tended to be over the longer term, taking a view on fuel prices, technological innovation and generation efficiency. This changed dramatically, however, during the 1990s.

Ownership has generally become private rather than public, competitive markets (pools and power exchanges) have been introduced for wholesale trading and retail markets gradually

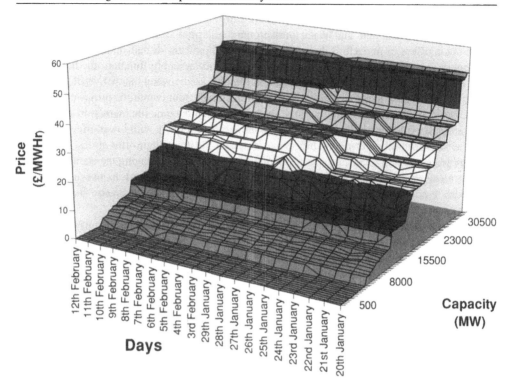

**Figure 1.13** Dynamic evolution of the supply function

liberalised to erode local franchises. Typically the industry has been split up into separate companies for generation, transmission, local distribution and retail supply. Transmission and distribution are network services and, as natural monopolies, are regulated. Generation is progressively deregulated as competition develops between a sufficient number of companies to promote an efficient wholesale market. Retail suppliers buy from the wholesale market and sell to customers. Industrial and commercial customers have generally been the first to receive full market liberalisation. The residential sector has been opened in many countries, but often quite slowly, and in some cases not at all.

All of this structural change has been motivated by a faith in the ability of competitive forces to create a more efficient and enterprising industry than either public sector or regulated monopolies could deliver. Thus, the most basic fundamental driver that we must keep in mind is *institutional intent*. Even in a privatised, apparently deregulated form, if the industry is not fulfilling government ideology and policy, it will be changed again. For example in the UK, there was a price cap imposed upon the pool during 1994–96, four years after its inception and a further two rounds of asset divestment required of the generators in 1996 and 1999 when it became apparent that their market power was not being sufficiently eroded by new competitive entry. Later in 2001, after a decade of accusations that the high pool prices were the result of market manipulations, the pool-based system was replaced by a fully decentralised bilateral trading system. These are clearly issues of what would normally be called regulatory risk. However, in the UK at least, they are essentially consequences of the strategic behaviour in the market creating a divergence from the institutional intent, which motivated the government. Markets may be liberalised, but such a sensitive industry as electricity continues to be more carefully monitored than others. Price rises, which are tolerated in other sectors, quickly become regional and national issues of concern. Similarly, any prospects of power shortages become a major social and economic threat. As Indira Ghandi is once attributed to have remarked, "no power costs more than no power".

One of the tragedies engendered by creating a new market by decree is that it is most likely to be incepted as an artefact of political compromise. Thus the privatisation processes of many countries are motivated by the fiscal objective of raising as much money as possible. Governments quickly realise that selling a few large companies will command higher prices than a large number of small entities. Companies operating in an imperfect market, where market power could be exercised and where the risk of bankruptcy is small, will sell at a premium and raise more money to offset government debt. Even if government revenue is not an issue, concerns about stranded assets or system security may prompt restructuring with more than the ideal amount of market power (e.g. Spain, California). So, even if efficiency via competition is the government rhetoric, we have seen new power markets persistently created with insufficient competition to drive prices down.

In seeking to understand electricity prices, we must first look at the fundamental economic drivers, and then assess this tension between regulatory tolerance and strategic opportunism. Thus, if we seek to relate the story of price behaviour in the England and Wales pool since the 1990s, it is one of strategic behaviour and regulatory reaction. Figure 1.14 shows the monthly average prices, alongside demand for the 1990–98 era of the pool. It is clear that despite demand being a fundamental driver of prices, this relationship does not have a high correlation during this period.

In 1990, the industry was restructured with the generation side of the market split up into only three main players, two of whom owned almost all of the price-setting plant. National Power was given about 48% of the fossil fuel capacity and Powergen 30%, with the remaining

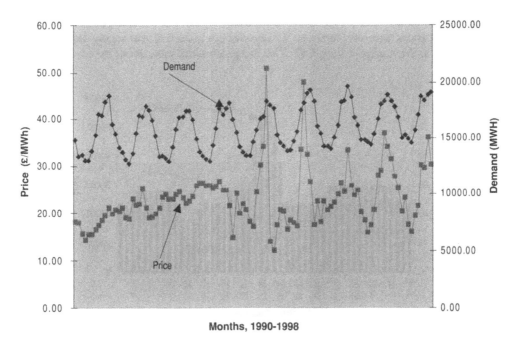

**Figure 1.14**   Monthly demand and wholesale prices in England and Wales, 1990–1998

22% consisting mostly of baseload nuclear and some imports from France and Scotland. A set of contracts to safeguard the coal industry was initially incorporated into the privatisation, the effect of which was to encourage National Power and Powergen to bid quite low into the pool. By the end of 1992, however, with prices settling around £21/MWh, the regulatory office suggested that this was inhibiting new entry (the new entry price for gas-fired plant was thought to be about £24/MWh at the time). Prices thereafter moved up. By spring of 1994, the regulatory office suggested that prices of around £28/MWh were too high, and imposed a two-year average price cap of £24/MWh. A condition for this price cap to be relaxed was the divestment of about 17% of their mid-merit (price-setting) plant.

It was a shrewd regulatory policy to set an average annual price cap. The generators could not risk the consequences of not appearing to comply, yet for the market price to come in precisely at an *annual average* of £24/MWh does vindicate the accusation that they were collectively in total control of the prices. The prices did indeed average exactly £24/MWh over those two years. Clearly, prices, which responded to regulatory suggestions in such a sensitive and precise way, hardly reflected competitive market forces in action.

However, regulatory controls stimulate strategic reactions. Note the increased volatility of prices during the 1994–96 period. The average was 24, but the standard deviation increased dramatically. For 94/95, the standard deviation of pool purchase price (which is what generators received) was 30.8, compared to 7.7 the year before. This presumably reflected the rather complex interrelationships with contract positions. Volatility would clearly encourage contracting and risk premia to the generators' benefit, at a time when average prices were being controlled. Price fluctuations, which were relatively higher during periods of the year where contract cover was relatively low, would also enhance generation revenues, despite the price cap. There was some evidence of generators being relatively over-contracted for the summer and under-contracted for the winter.

Figures 1.15 and 1.16 show the demand and price profile of the England and Wales pool for two very similar winter Wednesdays, separated by a year. The demand profile was almost the same, but prices were very different. The answer lies in the different supply functions that were offered to the market, Figure 1.17. Two things are remarkable about the comparison of

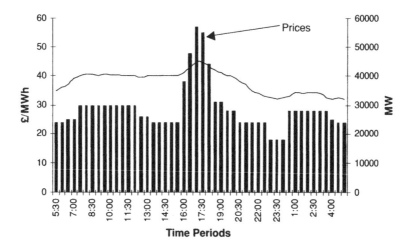

**Figure 1.15**   Pool prices and demand for Wednesday 19th January 1994

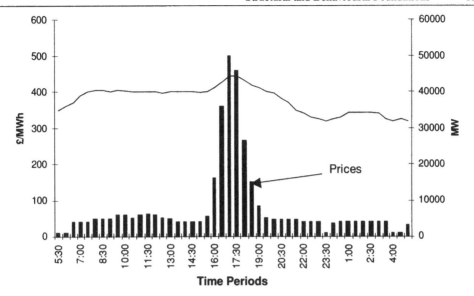

**Figure 1.16**    Pool prices and demand for Wednesday 18th January 1995

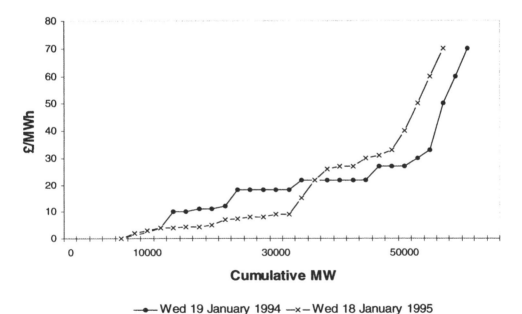

**Figure 1.17**    Supply functions for the two Wednesdays

these supply functions. The first is that there is less capacity available in 1995. This can be seen as a shift of the function to the left as some of the mid-merit plant was taken out. More important, however, is the subtle change in the convexity of the function. In 1995 it became steeper, with lower prices at the baseload and a steeper function in the peaking zone. The result of this is much higher price volatility.

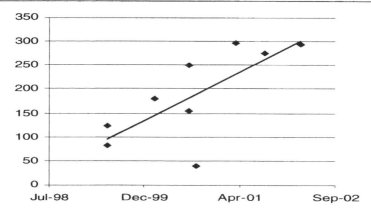

**Figure 1.18**    Increasing price of retail assets (£/customer)

Finally, the balance of strategic behaviour and institutional intent undertook a regime switch to a new type of equilibrium in 2000. The regulatory policy of the 1990s had been moulded by the imperfect privatisation of 1990 and the duopoly market that followed, with the consequent imperative to encourage lower generator concentration and increase new entry. By 2000, this had happened. There was excess capacity by this time, and the previously dominant generators were very much smaller in market shares. But with the advent of retail liberalisation, they had sold off generating assets and bought retail customers, to become much more balanced as vertically integrated energy companies. Figure 1.18 shows how the price per retail customer increased as retail supply companies were being acquired.

Furthermore, once the major players became balanced between generation and retail, the issue of supporting high wholesale prices, in the face of obvious regulatory intent to bring them down, became less relevant. Indeed, if wholesale prices fell, government objectives would be achieved, and to the extent that retail prices did not follow, the vertical players were not worse off. Between 1998 and 2002, the wholesale prices, remarkably, fell by about 40%.[1] The vertically integrated energy companies retained value in the retail market, as residential customers in particular did not prove to be active in switching suppliers, whilst most of the generation-only companies went into financial distress. Figure 1.19 shows how the price of generating assets fell during this period.

This chapter began with the observation that power plants are real options on the spread between power prices and the underlying fuel commodity. Clearly, the value of these options will decline with wholesale power prices, and that is what Figure 1.19 demonstrates. Within the supply chain, value moved to the least elastic part, the retail business. The strategic evolution will continue, however, and in 2003 there were already signs of the distressed assets being acquired and consolidated within the larger companies. These pro-cyclical market forces may well become an inherent feature of fully liberalised markets. To the extent that institutional reform of the sector was inspired by the ambition to make electricity rather more like other capital-intensive businesses, the extreme price sensitivity of the market to capacity margin, and the lead times in bringing in new capacity, would indeed appear to replicate the key ingredients for the emergence of business cycles, as we do see in other industries.

---

[1] In Chapter 4, John Bower presents a more thorough discussion and an explicit econometric model for this event.

Coal Resale  (£/kW)

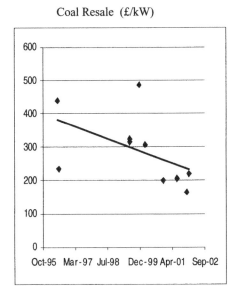

CCGT Resale (£/kW)

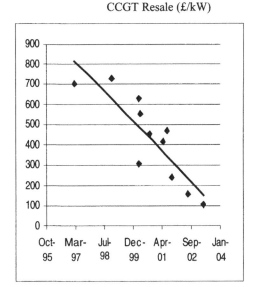

**Figure 1.19**    The declining value of generation assets

## 1.4   SUMMARY COMMENTS

This chapter has sought to provide a basic introduction to the fundamentals of price formation in the new electricity markets. In particular, the economic implications of synchronising the balance of demand and production creates a nonlinear, increasing supply function which translates demand variability into price volatility. The strong fundamental link to fuel commodity prices motivates convergence, and together with the seasonal regularities in demand, provides the source of mean reversion in the price series.

Electricity prices are politically sensitive and will ultimately reflect institutional intent. However, the strategic ambitions of companies are to make markets less efficient, and prices will emerge to reflect this delicate and transitory balance of regulatory control and strategic opportunism. Furthermore, the more liberalised the tolerance to market forces becomes, the more sensitive the system will become to the forces of cyclical behaviour.

From a modelling perspective, a consequence of understanding the microstructure of the price formation process is the realisation that there is a rich underlying structure which needs to be identified within the electricity spot price time series. The mean-reverting and volatility fundamentals are nonlinear, which together with structural nonstationarity, suggests that spot market behaviour may be better modelled from a set of adaptive regime-switching models, than from a single specification. The strategic opportunism and learning may induce a rich stochastic property to overlay these fundamentals. Forward price movements, however, to the extent that the markets become liquid and complete, may become well represented by models rather more similar to those seen elsewhere in financial markets. The ultimate interaction between forward and spot close to real time will, however, be quite different. Clearly, the research agenda for electricity market econometrics now becomes both timely and challenging.

# Part I
## Prices and Strategic Competition

# 2

# Competitors' Response Representation for Market Simulation in the Spanish Daily Market

EFRAIM CENTENO HERNÁEZ,[1] JULIÁN BARQUÍN GIL,[1] JOSÉ IGNACIO DE LA FUENTE LEÓN,[2] ANTONIO MUÑOZ SAN ROQUE,[1] MARIANO J. VENTOSA RODRÍGUEZ,[1] JAVIER GARCÍA GONZÁLEZ,[1] ALICIA MATEO GONZÁLEZ,[1] AND AGUSTÍN MARTÍN CALMARZA[1]

[1] Instituto de Investigación Tecnológica (IIT), University Pontificia Comillas (UPCO), Alberto Aguilera 23, 28015 Madrid, Spain
[2] Red Eléctrica de España, Paseo del Conde de los Gaitanes 177, 28109 La Moraleja (Madrid), Spain

## ABSTRACT

Since the 1998 liberalization, the Spanish daily electricity market has been based on an hourly auction process managed by a market operator, through which buyers and sellers submit their bids and offers. A common approach within companies for elaborating this is to model competitors' behaviour by means of past market public results. This chapter provides a detailed description of different techniques to address this problem.

## 2.1 INTRODUCTION

The objective of this chapter is to introduce some different techniques that can be used to characterize electricity bid-based markets when price is considered as an endogenous variable. This premise makes it necessary to represent, explicitly, the expected competitive behaviour. Two different groups of methods are described. The first group includes those that are based on a short-term competitors' response, represented by means of a detailed representation of residual demand function, based on historical bidding information. Once residual demand is estimated, the market can be simulated for different values of own firm's bids. The second group uses historical price information to establish the competitive bids' conjectural variations. In this case, the market is simulated by computing a market equilibrium. Detailed information about bidding is not necessary. Several real examples are presented, extracted from real and successful Spanish electricity market studies.[1]

---

[1] The authors would like to express their gratitude to the Spanish electrical utilities Endesa, Iberdrola and Union Eléctrica Fenosa for their cooperation in some parts of the models described herein.

---

**Table 2.1**   Spanish firms' market share at the end of the last intra-daily market (September 2002)

| Agent | Endesa | Iberdrola | Unión Fenosa | Hidrocantábrico | Viesgo | Others |
|---|---|---|---|---|---|---|
| Market share | 33.5% | 24.5% | 9.9% | 5.6% | 3.7% | 22.8% |

**Table 2.2**   Production by technologies (2001)

| Nuclear | Coal | Hydro | Fuel-gas | Special regime | Importations |
|---|---|---|---|---|---|
| 30% | 31% | 18% | 3% | 15% | 3% |

## 2.2   HOURLY BIDDING-BASED SPANISH ELECTRICITY MARKETS

This section introduces some basic concepts in order to understand and analyse hourly bid-based markets, with special emphasis on short and medium-term analysis. It uses the Spanish electricity market as an example, including a description of its distinctive features.

### 2.2.1   Structure of the Spanish electricity generation market

The Spanish electricity generation market was established in 1998 and since then, four firms have competed: Endesa, Iberdrola, Unión Fenosa and Hidrocantábrico. A fifth firm was added in 2001 as a result of the sale of part of Endesa's assets (Table 2.1). The system meets a maximum peak load close to 30 000 MW and a yearly energy demand of about 175 000 GWh, and the average hydro energy available is over 30 000 GWh (Table 2.2).

In Spain, the wholesale electricity business is organized in a sequence of different types of markets (daily, intra-day and ancillary services such as secondary and tertiary reserves, etc.). These markets are managed by two different operators, the market operator (MO) and the system operator (SO), which are responsible for receiving participants' offers to sell and to buy, and for determining the market clearing price (OMEL, 2001).

The daily market's purpose is the execution of the electric energy transactions for a scheduling horizon of the following day, divided into 24 consecutive hourly periods. The intra-day markets' purpose is to ensure adjustments to the result of the daily market, and they are currently convoked six times per day. These markets allow both the generation and the demand agents to react to unforeseen changes (unit total or partial outage, errors in forecasted demand, etc.) that arise after the daily market has closed. After daily and intra-day markets, some adjustments can be made due to network constraints, safety or reliability of the electrical system. Then, successive markets are convoked to ensure system reserve and other ancillary services. A deviation market can be convoked in case of extra energy requirements. As the major part of the total energy negotiation takes place in the daily market (96.7% in 2001), this chapter is devoted only to this main market. The average daily market energy price was 31.5€/MWh in 2001. Final wholesale energy price is formed by the daily market price (81.6%), technical operation (6.5%) and capacity payments (11.9%).

The Spanish electricity market presents some features that make it especially difficult to model. A strong horizontal and vertical concentration remains in place. A 10-year transition period was adopted in order to fully liberalize the market. During this period, a competition transition charge (CTC) will be collected in order to pay the stranded costs of the utilities (all private, except one that was more recently privatized). The CTC remuneration mechanism interferes with the market so that market prices and productions cannot be fully explained without them. A detailed review of the factors that condition the Spanish electricity market can be found in Kahn (1998).

### 2.2.2 Bidding structure

The daily market is based on a sealed-bid double auction. It is summoned once a day. Bids cannot be modified after they are submitted. Selling and buying offers (and bids) are sent simultaneously by every participant, so each participant's submissions are unknown to the others.

Daily market bids consist of a limited number of hourly blocks, with a different price for each one. Each selling block must be associated with a physical generation unit, but several blocks with different increasing prices can be submitted for a single unit. Thermal units are usually divided into two or more blocks, the cheaper one covers minimum unit power and the others the rest of the power to the maximum. Bidding blocks can be simple or complex. Simple blocks for one hour are independent of the other hourly blocks, while complex blocks can be affected by temporal conditions. For example, the matching of the first block of the sale offer for a single generating unit can be set to ensure that starting units are not stopped whilst their starting-up is in process. It is also possible to include an "income constraint", which sets a minimum daily income for a bid to be accepted, accompanying each generation unit bid. Other complex constraints may be added: inseparable bidding blocks and ramp-rates.

### 2.2.3 Clearing and price determination

Each single bid is defined by a pair $(q_i, p_i)$ where $p$ stands for price and $q$ stands for quantity. The market operator receives a set of single bids for each hour (inclusion of complex bidding will be treated later). They are divided into selling offers $S$ and buying biddings $B$. An aggregated supply function for each hour $h$ is built using this set. It represents the total amount of energy the generators are offering for a given price. Selling offers must be ordered increasingly to build this function:

$$S^{-1}(p) = \sum_{(p,q)\in S} \{q_i \,|\, p_i \le p\} \qquad (2.1)$$

An aggregated demand function for each hour $h$ is built in a similar way using buying bids. It represents the total amount of energy the buyers would buy for a given price. In this case, bids must be ordered decreasingly:

$$D^{-1}(p) = \sum_{(p,q)\in B} \{q_i \,|\, p_i \ge p\} \qquad (2.2)$$

Market clearing is obtained as the intersection of these two functions. The marginal price is determined by the point of intersection. Selling offers with a price lower than market clearing price are accepted and buying bids are accepted above this value. Additional rules must be stated to deal with offers that exactly match the clearing price.

Supply and demand functions can also be defined for each firm. They will be denoted as $S_f(q)$ and $D_f(q)$. Aggregated supply and demand functions can be obtained as:

$$S^{-1}(p) = \sum_f S_f^{-1}(p)$$

$$D^{-1}(p) = \sum_f D_f^{-1}(p) \qquad (2.3)$$

Supply and demand functions, as previously defined, are step-shaped functions. This kind of function is discontinuous and non-invertible. In order to make the analysis easier, they will be considered as continuous and strictly monotonic approximations of the defined functions. Under this assumption, the market clearing point $(q^*, p^*)$ can be expressed as:

$$p^* = D(q^*) = S(q^*)$$

$$q_f = S_f^{-1}(p^*) \qquad (2.4)$$

$$q_f = D_f^{-1}(p^*)$$

The previous expression must be replicated for each bidding hour. Complex bidding complicates the analysis, but it is usually possible to build up an equivalent single bidding that provides a good approximation for market clearing.

### 2.2.4  Residual demand

A generation firm $f$ can represent the other firms' bidding as a single function. It is the so-called residual demand. It is built from the aggregated demand function and the other offers (denoted as $-f$):

$$R_f^{-1}(p) = D^{-1}(p) - S_{-f}^{-1}(p) \qquad (2.5)$$

Residual demand represents the potential capacity of a single firm to modify the market price. Market clearing can be obtained from a generating firm's point of view, from residual demand and firm's offers, represented by means of the supply function:

$$p^* = R_f(q^*) = S_f(q^*) \qquad (2.6)$$

If a firm knows beforehand its residual demand function, it could determine the optimal quantity to be sold in the market to maximize profit. Remuneration of accepted offers is made at marginal price, so the profit function (assuming no contracts have been signed by the company) can be expressed as firm income minus firm cost $C_f(q_f)$. The problem to solve is to find the value of $q_f$ that maximizes firm profit $\Pi_f$:

$$\Pi_f = R_f(q_f)q_f - C_f(q_f) \qquad (2.7)$$

Short and medium-term market analyses differ from each other in the way they represent the residual demand functions as a consequence of their different scope and objectives, as well as the meaning given to marginal cost value.

### 2.2.5  Short-term market analysis

Short-term market analysis is commonly performed by generation companies with a scope of one or two weeks. These studies supersede traditional unit commitment studies in which a centralized operator decides the production schedule for every generating unit according to minimum cost and reliability criteria. In a competitive framework, each company has to forecast the part of demand that it wishes to supply as a result of the bidding and clearing process, and plan which units to run for this purpose. This kind of analysis uses information provided by the medium-term analysis, such as the quantity of hydro resources to be used and the marginal cost of these resources. The objective is to fulfil as much as possible these referential values, with a feasible operation of generation units.

The main result of these studies is the complete set of offers and bids that should be sent to the market to obtain, as a result of market clearing, the previously computed unit commitment. As a secondary result, useful information for subsequent markets, the availability and marginal cost of reserve, can be obtained. Furthermore, this provides the basis for short-term price forecasting.

A common method to address the short-term analysis is based on obtaining an accurate estimation of the firm's residual demand. It can be managed as a set of offers and bids, but it is also possible to use some kind of approximation as linear, linear piecewise or sigmoid functions. The use of continuous and strictly monotonic approximations of the real functions has some advantages. Firstly, they are easier to manage from a mathematical point of view: clearing algorithms can be expressed more easily and their derivatives can be obtained to provide sensitivity information. Secondly, they need less memory to be stored and manipulated in a computer.

Once the residual demand function has been built, alternative bidding sets for the particular firm are evaluated by obtaining the clearing result with a market clearing algorithm. Uncertainty in residual demand can be taken into account, by considering the result of the different bidding sets under different residual demand values.

The method to estimate the residual demand depends on information availability about previous market bids. Although every single hour is represented separately, some classification and characterization methodology is needed to deal with historic bidding information. Time series clustering techniques and neural networks are some of the most useful alternatives, as will be shown.

### 2.2.6   Bidding information availability

Residual demand estimation can be performed from historic information, if available. The Spanish market operator provided all of the bidding information during the first months of market, with the objective of allowing a fast learning of market rules operation. Every market agent could obtain the bidding of the rest of the agents with a delay of one day. This period was later extended to one month. From July 2001 to date, aggregated supply and aggregated demand functions are published, with a one-day delay, and complete agents' biddings are made public after three months.

Although transparency is a basic principle in any competitive market, there is no commonly accepted criterion about the desirability of publishing the agents' full submissions. On the one hand, historical data on bidding may help the market participants to understand the behaviour of their competitors, but on the other hand, transparency should be restricted to non-strategic features in order to avoid anti-competitive actions.

This controversy has demonstrated various levels of information availability in different countries. Thus, information is not available in Nord pool, for example. In contrast, the market operator published on its web page aggregated supply and demand functions for each hourly period in California, as in Alberta pool. The Australian market operator also makes public bidding information, distinguishing those made by each agent. In New Zealand, offers were originally anonymous, but they started to be identified from April 1999.

### 2.2.7   Medium-term market equilibrium analysis

Medium-term market analysis usually deals with market operation from the generating company's point of view with a yearly horizon. Maximum production capacity is fixed by previous long-term decisions including: new plant building, seasonal hydro operation and energy sales or fuel purchases under long-term contracts. The objective is to decide the firm's market share objective, fuel and hydro resources management (also known as water allocation). These studies can also be oriented to forecast prices and associated values (costs, incomes, taxes, etc.), to evaluate medium-term contracts and to assess risk coverage. In Spain, special attention must be paid to take-or-pay gas contract management and to the use of subsidized national coals.

Short-term methods are not suitable over this scope. The study of every hour in a year separately is not only complex and time-consuming but also difficult to understand at the end. An adequate hourly aggregation is required. Besides, the meaning of marginal cost from a medium-term point of view is different to the short-term focus. In the short term, marginal cost is closely related to the variable cost of the most expensive unit that has been committed for production by the firm. However, medium-term analysis includes such considerations as fulfilment of yearly production requirements (produced by coal subsidy quotas, take-or-pay contracts and/or market-share objectives, for example; see Reneses *et al.*, 1999 or Barquín *et al.*, 2004). Finally, another weak point of detailed hourly analysis is that it does not reflect properly firms' long-term strategies, as daily bidding is frequently distorted by transitory situations.

The concept of market equilibrium is very useful in the mid-term analysis. It represents an ideal point, defined by the value of firms' output such that there exists no possibility for any firm to improve its profit by means of a unilateral decision. Market dynamics are heavily affected by external and strategic factors and this equilibrium point is seldom reached when we analyse the daily market in the short term. However, in the mid-term approach, it can be considered as a good estimation of the average behaviour of market variables as well as facilitating sensitivity analysis. Market equilibrium is computed as the solution of the set of equations:

$$\frac{\partial \Pi_f}{\partial q_f} = 0 \qquad (2.8)$$

This derivative may be obtained from equation (2.7):

$$\frac{\partial \Pi_f}{\partial q_f} = R_f(q_f) + \frac{\partial R_f(q_f)}{\partial q_f} q_f - \frac{\partial C_f(q_f)}{\partial q_f} = 0 \qquad (2.9)$$

Assuming that the derivative of cost (marginal cost) is known, solving this set of equations requires some assumption about the residual demand function's shape. Considering that $R_f(q_f)$ represents price, only an assumption about $\partial R_f(q_f)/\partial q_f$ is needed. This function represents the variation of equilibrium price when one firm's output changes. A conjecture about price behaviour around market equilibrium is called a conjectural variation. A set of conjectural variations for every firm determines a mid-term market behaviour. Conjectural variations can be obtained without using competitors' bidding information.

### 2.2.8   Chapter overview

The next sections present four different methods devoted to managing the problem of obtaining a representation of competitors' behaviour by constructing a residual demand function (RDF) with the final objective of forecasting market behaviour. The first of them is based on a cluster procedure to group similar bid functions. The second model uses several time-series-based techniques. The third one utilizes input–output hidden Markov methods. Finally, the fourth example makes use of a market equilibrium representation. These methods use different focuses both in market behaviour analysis and RDF representation, and are designed for different time horizon market analysis. The chapter is completed with some conclusions and a comparison of the different approaches.

## 2.3 A TWO-PHASE CLUSTERING PROCEDURE FOR THE ANALYSIS OF BID FUNCTIONS

This section introduces a method for the analysis of bid functions (including RDF) based on a two-phase clustering technique. The first stage is to convert the original hourly step functions into piecewise linear approximations. Subsequently, the second stage performs a cluster analysis of the piecewise linear functions in order to discover some patterns along the temporal scope considered.

For the sake of simplicity, the term *bid function* (BF) will be used hereafter to refer to any of the following concepts: supply function $S(q)$, demand function $D(q)$ or residual demand function $R(q)$.

This section is organized as follows. Firstly, the proposed methodology to analyse historic offer data is presented. Then, the two-phase clustering algorithm is explained and finally, its application to a real case is presented.

### 2.3.1 Proposed methodology

The initial difficulty that appears when analysing historical offers data is that the quantity of available information can be extraordinarily high. There is no common agreement about the convenience of publishing the offers presented to the market by the different participants, as mentioned before. Nowadays, the aggregated supply and demand functions are published the day after the market clearing, allowing each participant to build its own residual demand functions. When this kind of information becomes public, it is necessary to have automatic procedures to extract outstanding information from all the stored data.

Given a particular hour, the offer stack $\{(q_1, p_1), (q_2, p_2), \ldots, (q_n, p_n)\}$ can be modelled as a stepwise process (increasing for supply functions and decreasing for demand or residual demand functions). As the number of submitted blocks of quantity–price can be very high, many steps with different sizes can be observed in the original stepwise functions.[2] The proposed analysis methodology consists of two stages.

The first stage is to convert the original hourly stepwise functions into piecewise linear approximations. Besides the advantage of summarizing the input data without losing relevant information, another important advantage is that piecewise linear approximations can be derived along the quantity axis. Therefore, instead of having just two possible first derivate values (0 for the horizontal steps and $\pm\infty$ for the vertical ones), the linear approximations provide intermediate values, reflecting the result after fitting consecutive steps by straight lines. The slopes of these segments will play a very important role in the equilibrium-based models, as will be shown.

---

[2] Notice that in the Spanish case each generating unit can present up to 25 blocks of quantity–price for every hour of the day. Therefore, the analysis of the offers of 100 generating units during a whole year could require managing up to $100 \times 365 \times 24 \times 25 = 21.9 \times 10^6$ offers.

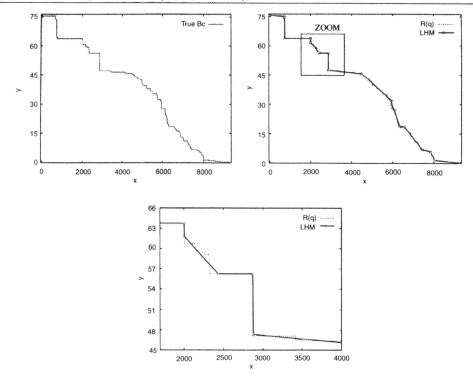

**Figure 2.1**   Fitting the original stepwise function by a piecewise linear approximation

In order to fulfil this stage, the *linear hinges model* (LHM) can be useful. Basically, the LHM is a very specialized algorithm to find piecewise linear approximations from scatter-plot data (Sánchez-Úbeda, 1999). Figure 2.1 shows an example where the LHM is applied to approximate a real BF. In the augmented zoom, it can be seen how one linear segment filters a set of small consecutive steps, where large ones are preserved.

The second stage of the proposed methodology is to make a cluster analysis of the piecewise linear functions in order to discover some patterns along the temporal scope considered. Hereafter, the clustering procedure is described in detail.

### 2.3.2   Cluster analysis of bid functions

The objective of the cluster analysis is to find natural groupings among a set of observations or samples, so that observations with similar characteristics are grouped in the same cluster whereas different or heterogeneous ones are grouped in different clusters. Each observation is normally represented by a vector with a dimension equal to the number of attributes characterizing it. Therefore, when this dimension is higher than 3, an inherent difficulty of cluster techniques is to check the goodness of the obtained results. In the case of BF, this difficulty does not appear since they are two-dimensional observations, on quantity–price, and thus a simple visual inspection could validate the correct operation of the algorithm. However, it is very important to highlight that the decision to group a pair of observations depends very much on the kind of study being carried out. This means that a subjective component always exists in this type of procedure, which it will be necessary to automate.

### 2.3.3 Two-phase procedure: hourly and daily clustering

A natural correlation exists among BF belonging to the same day. This empirical evidence can be justified because, when companies define their strategies, temporal horizons greater than one day are considered. As a consequence, given a particular day, the shapes of the supply functions for the same type of hours (off-peak, peak or medium load hours) are very similar, reflecting the fact that the underlying parameters used to build the functions (the load, the set of started-up generating units, the fuel costs, etc.) are analogous. It is possible to take advantage of this fact to facilitate the search of the clustering algorithm, diminishing notably its computational effort.

Let's assume that it is desired to analyse the BF of a whole month. Instead of defining the samples just as all the hourly BF simultaneously, it is proposed here to split the problem into two phases:

- **Hourly clustering.** For each day included in the studied period, perform a clustering of the 24 functions to obtain a small number (three to six) of clusters and their representatives, also called centroids.
- **Daily clustering.** Taking as samples the set of representatives obtained in the previous step, the daily clustering could reveal the pattern of the BF along the temporal scope considered. Moreover, the centroids of the new clusters formed during this phase can be stored in a library of historic "typical functions" which might be accessed later from some other forecasting models, scenario generators, etc.

In order to perform the clustering in whichever of the two phases, it is necessary first to define how to code each function, how to measure the dissimilarity between a pair of functions, and how to obtain a centroid representative of a set of functions.

### 2.3.4 BF codification

Usually, the observations used in cluster analysis are quantified as vectors $\mathbf{x} \in \mathbb{R}^p$, where $p$ denotes the number of attributes used to characterize each sample.[3] If the total number of samples is $N$, the objective of the clustering is to find a partition of the set $\{\mathbf{x}_i \in \mathbb{R}^p : i = 1, \ldots, N\}$, trying to maximize the dissimilarity among samples belonging to different clusters (between-cluster dissimilarity), and to minimize the dissimilarity among samples belonging to the same cluster (within-cluster dissimilarity).

In order to perform a clustering of bid functions, the first step would be the codification of each function as a vector. The selected components should express common attributes, as for instance the quantities related to a fixed set of prices. In the case of Figure 2.1, if the reference prices are $\{0, 15, 30, 45, 60, 75\}$, the vector representing that function should contain the quantities related to them, i.e. $\mathbf{x} = (9.1 \quad 7.0 \quad 6.0 \quad 4.4 \quad 2.1 \quad 0.6)$ [GWh]. In this case, each vector representing a BF could be viewed as a point in the multi-dimensional space $\mathbb{R}^6$. As all the functions are coded homogeneously, this approach allows the application of conventional cluster algorithms.[4] However, the necessity of selecting *a priori* the set of reference prices is a great disadvantage because wide steps could exist between them, and therefore, outstanding information on the function could be lost or filtered. Instead of increasing

---

[3] When these attributes measure different magnitudes, it is convenient to normalize and homogenize the data in order to avoid the influence of the units adopted.

[4] In Kauffman and Rousseeuw (1999), clustering algorithms are classified as "partitioning methods" and "hierarchical methods". For instance, distance-based methods such as **k**-means analysis, nearest-neighbour clustering, etc.

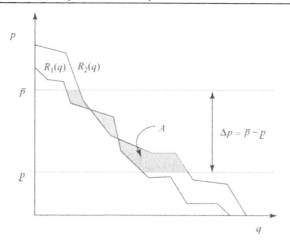

**Figure 2.2**  Defining the dissimilarity between a pair of BF as the area enclosed by them

the number of reference prices, i.e. the sampling density, here it is proposed to code each BF as the coordinates of every point in the quantity–price plane defining the continuous piecewise linear function. For instance, if the original function is a stepwise residual demand function $R(q)$, its piecewise linear approximation obtained with the LHM can be expressed as:

$$\hat{R}(q) \equiv \{(q_k, p_k) : k = 1, \ldots, K\} \tag{2.10}$$

where $K$ is the number of "knots", i.e. the joining points between consecutive linear segments. This number is determined automatically by the LHM, and each piecewise function would have a different one depending on the complexity of the original function. This heterogeneous codification makes traditional measures of dissimilarity non-applicable.[5]

### 2.3.5  Defining the dissimilarity between BF

The dissimilarity between a pair of observations $i$ and $j$ is defined as a positive number $d(i, j)$ which is very small for similar observations and very large for dissimilar ones. In García-González (2001) it is proposed to compute the dissimilarity between a pair of bid functions using the area enclosed by them: nearby functions in the quantity–price plane would enclose a small area, and accordingly, faraway functions a bigger one (Figure 2.2). Moreover, when the functions are very close, but their shapes are different, the area would be greater than for the case of similar shapes.

Although the functions could be defined for a wide range of prices, the cluster analysis might be interesting just for a particular price interval, $[\underline{p}, \overline{p}]$. This happens because the uncertainty faced by market participants can be bounded, and therefore, their strategic behaviour could be revealed only in the part of the function covering the most expected marginal prices. For that reason, the area should be computed along the price axis. For instance, let $R_1(q)$ and $R_2(q)$ be two residual demand functions. The area enclosed by them in the interval $[\underline{p}, \overline{p}]$ is obtained as:

$$A = \int_{\underline{p}}^{\overline{p}} \left| R_1^{-1}(p) - R_2^{-1}(p) \right| dp \tag{2.11}$$

---

[5] Given a pair of observations $i$ and $j$ coded as vectors $\mathbf{x}_i$ and $\mathbf{x}_j \in \mathbb{R}^p$, the dissimilarity can be computed using any measure of distance, such as for instance the Euclidean one $d(i, j) = \left\| \mathbf{x}_i - \mathbf{x}_j \right\|_2$.

where $R^{-1}(p)$ denotes the inverse function. Notice that as $R_1(q)$ and $R_2(q)$ are piecewise linear functions, the numeric integration can be achieved easily. In order to normalize the results, it is proposed to divide the mentioned area by the width of the price interval of interest. Therefore, the dissimilarity between functions $R_1(q)$ and $R_2(q)$ can be evaluated as:

$$d(R_1, R_2) = \frac{\int_{\underline{p}}^{\overline{p}} \left| R_1^{-1}(p) - R_2^{-1}(p) \right| dp}{\overline{p} - \underline{p}} = \frac{A}{\Delta p} \qquad (2.12)$$

### 2.3.6 Centroid calculation of a cluster of bid functions

In order to implement the two-phase clustering procedure, it is necessary to calculate the representative element, i.e. the centroid, of each formed cluster. The intuition behind the centroid is the averaging over all elements in the cluster. As the functions are coded heterogeneously, it is necessary to define how to average bid functions, as a traditional mean vector is not applicable. In García-González (2001) it is proposed to obtain the centroid by applying again the LHM. In this case, the scatter-plot data used to build the model is obtained by sampling the set of original functions belonging to the cluster (Figure 2.3).

### 2.3.7 Example case

The example case presented in this section shows how the proposed methodology can be successfully applied to analyse real offer data. In particular, observations used as input data were the Californian hourly supply functions of the whole system during the week from 6th to 12th September 1999. Similar analysis could be applied to bidding on the Spanish market.

Arbitrarily, it has been decided to study the similarity of the functions just within the price interval 5–60$/MWh.

#### 2.3.7.1  Hourly clustering

Among the different techniques available to perform a cluster analysis, an agglomerative linkage algorithm has been implemented. Each iteration of the algorithm, the two previously formed

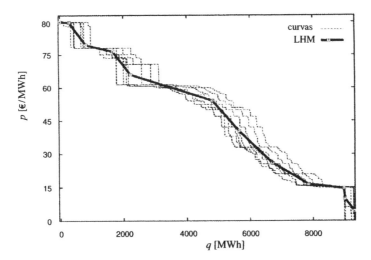

**Figure 2.3**  Centroid computation from the set of original functions belonging to the cluster

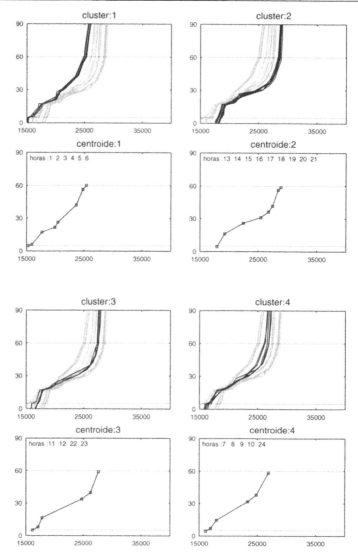

**Figure 2.4**    Obtained results for the 6th September hourly clustering

clusters with the lowest dissimilarity values (i.e. the most similar) are merged, continuing the process until the goodness of the partition satisfies a stop criterion.

Figure 2.4 shows the results of the hourly clustering of the 6th September. For each one of the four obtained clusters, two graphs are presented. In the superior ones, all the 24 offer functions used as observations are drawn, but only the functions belonging to the corresponding cluster are coloured in black. On the other hand, the inferior graphs present the representative centroid of each cluster, drawn and computed just for the interesting range of prices. The set of hours belonging to each cluster has also been indicated. For instance, the first cluster gathers the supply functions of hours 1, 2, 3, 4, 5, 6, i.e. off-peak hours.

Table 2.3 Number of centroids
obtained for each day

| Day | No. centroids |
| --- | --- |
| Monday | 4 |
| Tuesday | 5 |
| Wednesday | 6 |
| Thursday | 6 |
| Friday | 5 |
| Saturday | 6 |
| Sunday | 5 |
| Total | 37 |

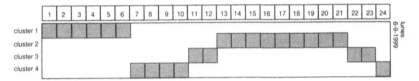

Figure 2.5  Obtained results for the 6th September hourly clustering

Another way to represent these results is shown in Figure 2.5, where hours (columns) belonging to each cluster (row) are shadowed. This chart can easily be interpreted, as the clustering results stem from a physical meaning: clusters 1 and 2 correspond to off-peak and peak hours respectively; clusters 3 and 4 correspond to medium hours, depending on whether they are close-to-peak or off-peak hours, respectively.

The same procedure described here should be repeated for every day included in the temporal scope in order to generate the representatives to be used as samples during the next phase.

### 2.3.7.2  Daily clustering

The number of samples in this phase is the sum of the number of centroids obtained after performing the hourly clustering for each day of the week (see Table 2.3).

The number of daily clusters has been preset to eight. Therefore, the set of 37 centroids obtained during the first phase is grouped on eight clusters. Note that in this case, the linkage algorithm finishes when this number of clusters is reached, without it being necessary to quantify the goodness of the partition at each iteration.

Similar plots to the ones shown in Figure 2.4 could also be generated here, where the centroids would now be the "representatives" of the "daily representatives". However, in order to capture some pattern along the temporal scope, it is proposed to show the clustering results in a *chromogram*, as presented in Figure 2.6.

For each day considered, a similar chart to the one shown in Figure 2.5 (6th September) can be obtained. In order to build the chromogram, it would be necessary to join all those daily charts in a consecutive order, but using the same colour for the rows (i.e. the centroids) that have been grouped within the same cluster during the second phase. In this way, a simple visual inspection of the chromogram allows us to:

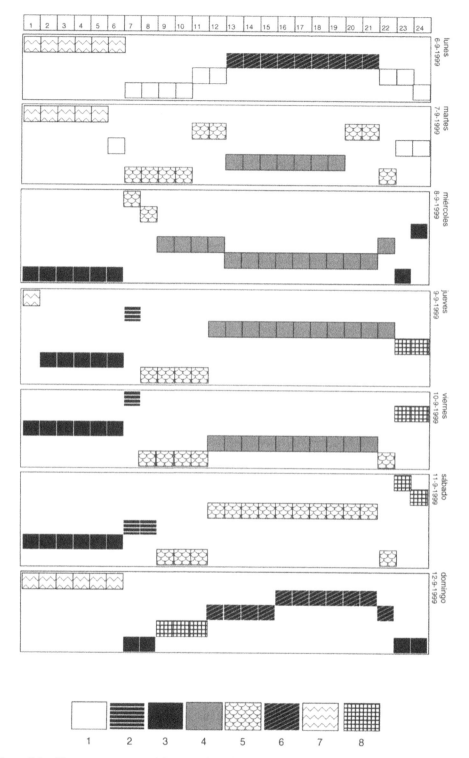

**Figure 2.6**   Chromogram summarizing two phases' results

- Represent the hourly clustering results for each day. This may help the user to easily identify the groups of similar hours belonging to the same day.
- Represent the daily clustering results. Hours belonging to different days, but sharing the same colour, would have a very similar BF. Therefore, if a pattern of behaviour along the time exists, it would be captured with the chromogram.

Figure 2.6 shows the obtained chromogram corresponding to the studied week. It can be seen how hours assigned to different clusters during the first phase are grouped later on during the second one. This is due to the fact that the hourly clustering is more refined than the daily clustering, as only the 24 functions of the day are considered each time. However, when considering the whole week, the differences among those functions are not big enough to separate them into different clusters, but rather they group together. For example, when making the Monday clustering, hours 11, 12, 22 and 23 form the cluster number 3 while hours 7, 8, 9, 10 and 24 form the cluster number 4. However, when carrying out the daily clustering, all those hours are grouped together with hours 6, 23 and 24 of Tuesday to constitute the "definitive" cluster labelled as 1 and marked with white frames.

The most significant conclusions from the inspection of the chromogram are the following:

- Cluster 1 contains off-peak hours of Monday and some medium-load hours of Tuesday.
- Cluster 3 contains off-peak hours of Wednesday, Thursday, Friday and Saturday.
- Cluster 4 contains peak hours of Tuesday, Wednesday, Thursday and Friday.
- Cluster 5 contains medium-load hours of Tuesday, Wednesday, Thursday and Friday as well as peak hours of Saturday.
- Cluster 6 contains peak hours of Monday and Sunday.
- Cluster 7 contains off-peak hours of Monday, Tuesday and Sunday.

From the previous analysis, operational optimization and bidding elaboration can be carried out avoiding the use of the whole set of bidding data (García-González, 2001). The description of these methods goes beyond the scope of this chapter.

The presented method performs a static analysis of bidding functions based on a linear piecewise approximation of residual demand functions, grouped by means of a clustering method. The next two sections are devoted to methods that are also oriented to short-term analysis and with a simpler RDF representation, but which deal with dynamic phenomena appearing in the daily market evolution.

## 2.4   FORECASTING METHODS FOR RESIDUAL DEMAND FUNCTIONS USING TIME SERIES (ARIMA) MODELS[6]

RDFs are important inputs in order to carry out the dispatch optimization, which every utility has to solve in order to maximize its expected profits. A wrong prediction of these functions may provide misleading results in the dispatch optimization process. An accurate forecasting of the day-ahead residual demand function can be carried out using *time series analysis*.

The present section is focused on the forecasting and estimation of the *hourly* RDFs. For generation agents of a moderate size, the shape of the RDFs can usually be approximated using a linear interpolation. Thus, the problem is reduced to the analysis of the time evolution of

[6] The authors gratefully acknowledge the contributions of the staff at *Centro de Gestión de la Energía* of *Unión Fenosa Generación, S.A.* for their work and collaboration in this research. Also we appreciate the helping hand of SCA company members William Lattyak and Professor Lon Mu Liu, who have provided great support and brilliant ideas.

two variables, the *slope and the intercept of the linearized RDFs*. Both of them can fluctuate sharply depending on the hour of the day and also the day of the week. Thus, hours with a strong demand for electricity tend to have greater values of slope and intercept than the rest, due to the higher level of demand served and the more expensive generation technologies dispatched. As the prediction's horizon is very short (day-ahead market or spot market), tools like ARIMA time series are useful to achieve a good RDF estimation. In particular this approach will allow the following analysis:

- Determining whether a unique time series model for each one of the variables is enough or whether more detailed models (i.e. distinction between labour days and weekends or between peak/valley demand hours) lead to more accurate results. In the latter case a weighted estimation will be developed in this section that allows us to obtain optimal parameters for each of the time zones considered. The study of data seasonality is considered as well.
- Evaluating the influence of some explanatory variables in the shape of the residual demand functions: expected system demand, expected level of run-of-the-river power or the expected amount of nuclear power in the system. This fact leads to the use of transfer function (TF) models.
- Classification/filtering of outliers that can come up in the data.
- Analysis of calendar variations (i.e. holidays like Easter or Christmas) and known disturbances (like a sudden increase in the run-of-the-river power level due to heavy rainfalls), which can distort the performance of the models used.

This section is structured as follows: in subsection 2.4.1 a first approach to the problem is carried out by performing a classical ARIMA analysis of both intercept and slope corresponding to the linearized RDFs. In subsection 2.4.2 a useful combination of explanatory variables is looked at in order to improve the performance of the original ARIMA model. Besides this, a weighted estimation method is presented that will allow the achievement of optimal models for each of the different time intervals that can be considered depending on the type of day (labour, weekend) and the hour (peak, valley, plateau). After this, subsection 2.4.3 shows a case study where each of the above model's (ARIMA, TF and weighted estimation) performance is compared. Finally, subsection 2.4.4 contains a summary of conclusions obtained by means of a detailed analysis of the models' performance.

### 2.4.1  Analysis using an ARIMA model

Firstly, it must be determined whether a transformation of the original series is required in order to deal with the conditions required to perform an ARIMA analysis. Standard ARIMA analysis relies on the assumption that the time series is stationary. This means that the mean and the variance of the data series are constant through time. The first of these (stationary mean) is usually solved by differencing the series and it is clearly visible in the pattern of the ACF (autocorrelation function). Possible modifications to induce a stationary variance must be applied (when needed) before any further analysis of the data. It is fairly common to find data series where the variance is proportional to its level. In this case a constant variance is induced by transforming the data, where the Box–Cox transformations are the most widely used (Pankratz, 1991; Liu, 2001).

An analysis of a typical two-month sample (Figure 2.7) of the linearized RDC intercept (a similar graph is obtained using the variable slope) shows that the variance tends to be

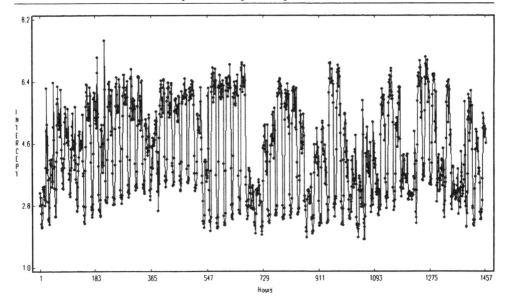

**Figure 2.7** Variable intercept (c€/KWh), hourly evolution during two months
*Source:* Association for Studies on the Quality of Electric Energy. Reproduced with permission.

more or less constant, regardless of the level reached. So a transformation in this case is not necessary. It should be noticed that if the data span is extended (i.e. a year or more instead of two months) there will be periods with higher volatility than the others, thus the variance would not be stationary. Nevertheless, up to three or four months the constant variance assumption is usually right, and there are enough data contained in this period to perform adequate analysis.

Once these previous steps have been accomplished, it is time to analyse the ACF and PACF (partial autocorrelation function) of the model, in order to identify the autoregressive (AR) and moving average (MA) parameters of the model. During the identification procedure the principle of parsimony is applied. According to this principle, models with as few coefficients as necessary to adequately explain the behaviour of the data will be selected.

When a tentative model is proposed, then it must be estimated and checked to verify if it complies with the conditions of stationarity (mean, variance and ACF are constant through time) and invertibility (which ensures that more recent data have more weight than the distant past). Our ACF/PACF graphs correspond to the variable intercept. The graphs obtained with the variable slope present the same kind of pattern and behaviour.

The remarkable features of the ACF shown in Figure 2.8 are a slow decay at the first seasonal lags (24, 48, 72) mixed with a slow growth during the following seasonal lags (96, 120, 144) until it reaches a local maximum at lag 168. Then the procedure repeats itself from lag 168 to lag 336 but with slightly lower values. So it seems that there is a double periodicity, one with a daily scope (this is the reason for the peaks of the ACF function at lags $t = 24k$, with $k = 1, 2, 3, \ldots$) and the other with a weekly horizon (ACF peaks at lags $t = 168k$, with $k = 1, 2, 3, \ldots$). Due to the ACF pattern at these seasonal lags, a double seasonal differencing is needed. Regular differencing (i.e. between adjacent values) is not necessary because the ACF decays fairly quickly at the first lags.

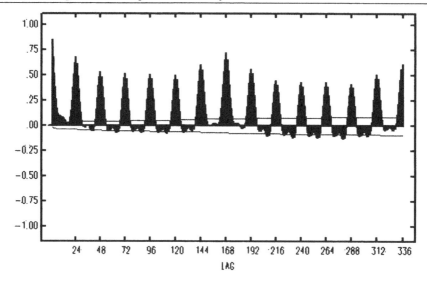

**Figure 2.8**   ACF for the variable intercept. 1 LAG = 1 hour
*Source:* Association for Studies on the Quality of Electric Energy. Reproduced with permission.

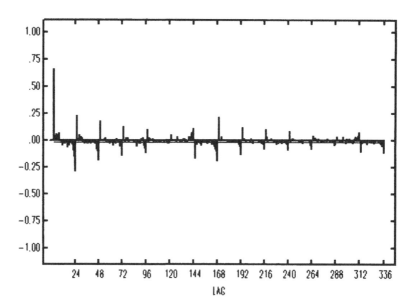

**Figure 2.9**   PACF for the variable intercept with double seasonal differencing. 1 LAG = 1 hour
*Source:* Association for Studies on the Quality of Electric Energy. Reproduced with permission.

Figure 2.9 shows a slow decay in the PACF pattern at the seasonal lags $t_1 = 24k$ and $t_2 = 168k$ ($k = 1, 2, 3, \ldots$). Figure 2.10 shows high spikes at lags $t = 24$ and $t = 168$ and a lower one at lag $t = 48$. This means that a moving average behaviour is present at these lags. In contrast, the first lags show a different pattern with a spike at lag $t = 1$ in the PACF (Figure 2.9) and a decay in the ACF (Figure 2.10), so a first-order autoregressive parameter looks adequate. Many of the other large autocorrelations (e.g. lags 144 and 192) observed

**Table 2.4**  SCA results for the variable intercept. ARIMA model

| Coefficients | Type | Order | Value | $t$-Value |
|---|---|---|---|---|
| $\theta_1$ | MA | 24 | 0.6379 | 67.81 |
| $\theta_2$ | MA | 48 | 0.1551 | 16.27 |
| $\theta_3$ | MA | 168 | 0.7708 | 118.26 |
| $\phi_1$ | AR | 1 | 0.7368 | 114.98 |
| $k$ | | 0 | $-0.0006$ | $-0.41$ |
| RSE | | | 0.82 | |

*Source:* Association for Studies on the Quality of Electric Energy. Reproduced with permission.

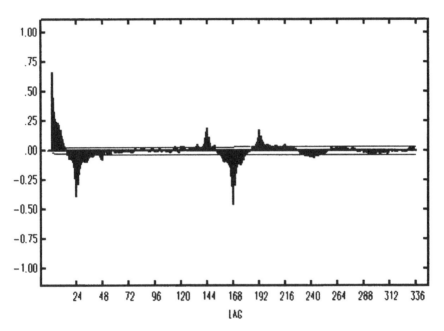

**Figure 2.10**  ACF for the variable intercept with double seasonal differencing. 1 LAG = 1 hour
*Source:* Association for Studies on the Quality of Electric Energy. Reproduced with permission.

in Figure 2.4 are probably a reflection of the weekly seasonality, thus it is not necessary to consider more differencing.

It is also very important to avoid over-differenced models, which always drive the identification process to pure moving average models (Box, 1976; Liu, 1997). Thus, a tentative model which complies with all the above characteristics is proposed:

$$\nabla_{24}\nabla_{168}Y = k + \frac{(1 - \theta_1 B^{24} - \theta_2 B^{48})(1 - \theta_3 B^{168})}{(1 - \phi_1 B)}a_t \qquad (2.13)$$

where $Y$ corresponds to the model output variable (either intercept [c€/kWh] or slope [c€/MW*kWh] of the linearized RDFs) and $k$ is a constant. $\nabla_x$ is a differencing operator of order $x$, $a_t$ is a white noise (random shock) and $B^x$ represents the backshift operator, that delays $x$ lags when applied to a given variable. SCA$^{TM}$ (the statistical software program used) provides particular values for the model given in equation (2.13): see Tables 2.4 and 2.5.

**Table 2.5**   SCA results for the variable slope. ARIMA model

| Coefficients | Type | Order | Value | $t$-Value |
|---|---|---|---|---|
| $\theta_1$ | MA | 24 | 0.6406 | 68.04 |
| $\theta_2$ | MA | 48 | 0.1455 | 15.24 |
| $\theta_3$ | MA | 168 | 0.8006 | 126.63 |
| $\phi_1$ | AR | 1 | 0.7208 | 109.75 |
| $k$ | | 0 | −0.0963 | −0.4 |
| RSE | | | 151.65 | |

*Source:* Association for Studies on the Quality of Electric Energy. Reproduced with permission.

The $t$-value indicates whether a parameter of the model is meaningful ($t$-value greater than two) or not by means of a Student-$t$ significance test. As was pointed out, both intercept and slope present the same characteristics (same periodicities and differencing). It is straightforward to check that both determined models deal successfully with the stationarity and invertibility conditions required for an ARIMA model – all the roots of the AR and MA polynomials lie outside the unit circle (Pankratz, 1991; Box, 1976; Box *et al.*, 1994). Once a tentative model is specified, it is mandatory to check if the residuals obtained are normally distributed. There are a great variety of tests to accomplish this task – e.g. the histogram of the residuals, the normal probability plot or the Box–Ljung test (Pankratz, 1991; Box, 1976; Box *et al.*, 1994).

The histograms of the intercept and slope variable residuals (not shown here) are quite symmetrical, suggesting that the residuals are normally distributed. The normal probability plot, not shown here (Pankratz, 1991; Liu, 1997), does not have large deviations from a straight line except from very large residuals, again suggesting that the residuals are normally distributed and also that an outlier test should be done to analyse the largest residuals (this task will be briefly commented on in subsection 2.4.2.3).

Finally, it was also checked that the ACF of the residuals series was non-significant (i.e. each residual autocorrelation falls well short of its two standard error limit), concluding that the model adequately captures the autocorrelation patterns in the data. The ARIMA models built in this section will be used as a baseline comparison for an improved model, which will be proposed in the following section.

### 2.4.2   Analysis using TF models and weighted estimation

In order to improve the performance of the above ARIMA model, further explanatory variables should be identified. In order for an explanatory variable to be useful, it should be easily available and, if possible, predictable with relatively little uncertainty. Three meaningful variables have been determined in order to explain the evolution (level and slope) of the linearized RDFs (results will only be shown for the variable intercept, but the interpretation with the variable slope is straightforward). For the sake of clarity *results are shown in weekly average values although real data are hourly values*. Thus, these explanatory variables are (in order of importance):

- **The national hourly electricity demand.**
  It is obvious that the higher the demand, the higher and more abrupt should be the RDFs. At present, existing demand forecasting models are very accurate, so the demand will be treated as a non-stochastic variable.

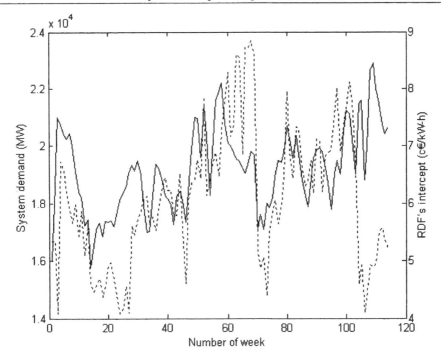

**Figure 2.11** Evolution of the variable system demand (continuous line) versus variable intercept (dashed line). Weekly average values
*Source:* Association for Studies on the Quality of Electric Energy. Reproduced with permission.

Although it can be seen in Figure 2.11 that there is a meaningful correlation between both variables, there are periods where the demand was high and the intercept low, and *vice versa*. So there are more factors involved in the RDF time evolution.

- **Run-of-the-river power.**
  There is always a fraction of the whole generation power available which is offered at the lowest prices. This portion of power (known as base generation) corresponds to the amount offered by both nuclear power plants and run-of-the-river units (hydro plants without regulating capacity, because they do not have dams). This base hydro generation remains rather constant through a day and it is easy to forecast, knowing the dam's hydro conditions and the weather forecast. Figure 2.12 shows the correlation between the variable intercept and the variable run-of-the-river power with a weekly average value basis.
  It can be observed that when there has been a sudden increase in the level of the run-of-the-river power (due to heavy rainfalls), the values of the variable intercept have fallen dramatically. Also in this situation the RDFs tend to be flatter so the values of the variable slope are lower than under normal conditions.

- **The level of nuclear power.**
  Nuclear power is also a base generation component. The scheduled maintenance of the nuclear power plants is often known in advance, so this variable becomes a useful explanatory variable. The effect of the level of this variable is quite similar to the run-of-the-river power.

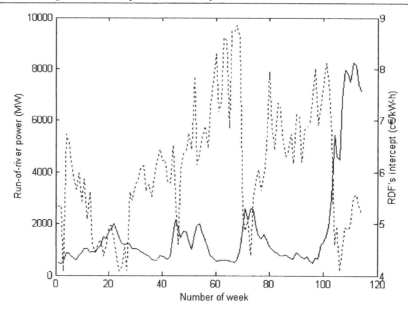

**Figure 2.12**   Evolution of the variable run-of-the-river power (continuous line) versus variable intercept (dashed line). Weekly average values
*Source:* Association for Studies on the Quality of Electric Energy. Reproduced with permission.

### 2.4.2.1   Aggregation with a single explanatory variable

If a TF model is tried using separately the above three explanatory variables, all the variables except from the electricity demand become considered as non-significant. The reason is clear, on the one hand the two output variables (intercept and slope) change greatly from hour to hour, but the variables run-of-the-river and nuclear power are rather constant during the whole day, so the estimated correlation between the output variables and these two input variables will be very small. On the other hand, if these variables are compared on a weekly basis (as in Figure 2.12), it is obvious that there exists a relationship between the output variables and the level of run-of-the-river power (or nuclear power).

Therefore an explanatory variable with an hourly scope and that takes into account all the above characteristics needs to be defined. If the sum of run-of-the-river power and nuclear power (nearly constants for the whole day) is subtracted from the hourly system demand, a useful explanatory variable is obtained. This can be expressed as the non-base demand. Formally, the proposed explanatory variable is defined for each hour $h$ as:

$$NBD_h = D_h - F_h - N_h \qquad (2.14)$$

where *NBD* stands for non-base demand, $D$ is the demand, $F$ is run-of-the-river power and $N$ is nuclear power. All the values in this expression must be interpreted as expected values.

This new explanatory variable covers all the possible cases. It will take high values if the system demand is high and/or there is a lack of base generation (due to low values of run-of-the-river power and/or nuclear power) and lower values if the system demand is low and/or there is a high level of base generation, so it presents an adequate hourly variation. For the sake

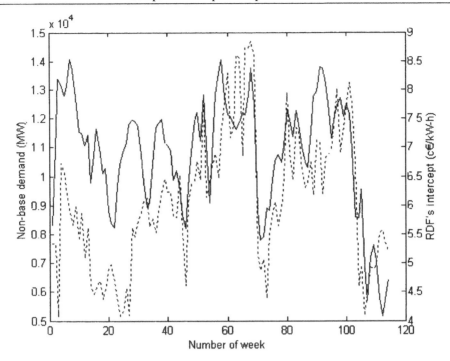

**Figure 2.13** Evolution of the variable non-base demand (continuous line) versus variable intercept (dashed line). Weekly average values
*Source:* Association for Studies on the Quality of Electric Energy. Reproduced with permission.

of clarity, Figure 2.8 shows in weekly values the relationship between the new explanatory variable and the variable intercept.

It is observed in Figure 2.13 that the peaks and valleys of the new explanatory variable evolution bear a strong resemblance with those of the variable intercept, and their correlation is much better than when only the variable demand (Figure 2.11) is considered. For example, focusing on the last weeks of Figure 2.11 and Figure 2.13, which corresponds with a period of both high levels of system demand and run-of-the-river power, the new explanatory variable is able to capture the sudden drop of the variable intercept, while if only the system demand is used the results will be poor, because higher prices are expected. The same result occurs with the variable slope of the linearized RDFs, which has low values (i.e. the RDFs are flatter) if the explanatory variable non-base demand also has low values, and *vice versa*.

### 2.4.2.2 TF models and a weighted estimation approach

Firstly, a non-weighted TF model with non-base demand as explanatory variable will be proposed. The LTF approach (Liu, 1996, 2001) has been applied to adjust the model stated in equation (2.15), because it presents some advantages with respect to the more classical prewhitening method (Box, 1976; Box *et al.*, 1994). Using this method and skipping the non-meaningful lags of the explanatory variable, the following structure results:

$$\nabla_{24}\nabla_{168}Y = \nu_0\nabla_{24}\nabla_{168}\,[NBD] + \frac{(1 - \theta_1 B^{24} - \theta_2 B^{48})(1 - \theta_3 B^{168})}{(1 - \phi_1 B)}a_t \qquad (2.15)$$

The TF model shown in equation (2.15) does not dramatically reduce the RSE (residual standard error) in comparison with the ARIMA model proposed in subsection 2.4.1, but when an outlier analysis is carried out, a great number of the outliers caused by changes in the input variable are explained, so its total amount is strongly reduced using the TF model. Regarding the model considered in equation (2.15), it has some serious drawbacks:

(a) If the terms containing differencing are fully developed, the model shows that the values of the output and input variables at current time and the values which took place 24 hours ago (the day before) and 168 hours ago (the week before) are related. In fact there are some more relations than these, but they are much less important.
(b) The fact stated above can give problems when one is focused on days like Mondays or Saturdays, when there are great differences between their RDFs pattern and those of the previous day (Sunday and Friday respectively). So it seems reasonable that Saturdays, Sundays and Mondays will follow a different model than that stated in equation (2.15), therefore a daily discrimination must be considered.
(c) The TF model shows a linear and unique relation between the output and the input variable – coefficient $v_0$ in equation (2.15) – regardless of the type of hour considered. This is not fundamentally true, because it is obvious that the ratio between the values of the output and input variables will change depending on the hour and the day of the week. Thus both daily and hourly discriminations should be taken into account.

The *weighted estimation method (WE)* provides a good and easy way to deal with problems like non-linear relations or saturations between the variables (Liu, 2001). In order to use the weighted estimation approach, a prior classification of the available data series divided in time ranges must be done:

**Daily discrimination.** One independent model for each of the following groups: (1) Saturday, (2) Sunday, (3) Monday and (4) Tuesday through Friday.
**Hourly discrimination.** One independent model for each of the following groups, according to the pattern of the system demand function: (1) from 2 a.m. to 7 a.m., (2) from 8 a.m. to 9 a.m., (3) from 10 a.m. to 2 p.m., (4) from 3 p.m. to 6 p.m., (5) from 7 p.m. to 10 p.m., and (6) from 11 p.m. to 1 a.m.

An example of the Spanish system electricity demand is provided in Figure 2.14. It can be seen that the hourly discrimination is based on grouping together those periods of time with approximately the same characteristics. Nevertheless, these properties should not be considered as fixed, due to the fact that they depend on seasonality (peak–valley hours are not exactly the same in summer as in winter, there is always a certain displacement). A clustering process could be used in order to obtain an adequate hourly discrimination regarding the current period of the year.

The weighted estimation method searches for the optimal values of the parameters which minimize the RSE at the time range considered (Liu, 2001). It is important to note that, despite the weights applied, the whole series is still considered, so the dynamic pattern of the data is not lost. The objective is to adequately represent the non-linear relationship between output and input variables as a group of linear models focused in different time intervals, taking advantage of the simplicity and clarity of linearity. The following model equations (2.16)–(2.18) and Tables 2.6–2.8 are focused on the time period 8 a.m.–9 a.m. and results are displayed for different days and for the variable intercept. Firstly, the adjusted model and its estimated parameters focusing on Saturdays are shown. The model has been adjusted using

**Table 2.6**   SCA results for time interval Saturday, 8 a.m.–9 a.m.
Weighted estimation. Model equation (2.16)

| Coefficients | Type | Order | Value | $t$-Value |
|---|---|---|---|---|
| $v_0$ | | 0 | 0.0002 | 14.62 |
| $\theta_1$ | MA | 1 | 0.5746 | 10.21 |
| $\phi_1$ | AR | 1 | 0.8962 | 32.16 |
| Differencing | None | | | |
| RSE (time zone) | | | 0.51 | |

*Source:* Association for Studies on the Quality of Electric Energy.
Reproduced with permission.

**Table 2.7**   SCA results for time interval Tuesday through Friday,
8 a.m.–9 a.m. Weighted estimation. Model equation (2.17)

| Coefficients | Type | Order | Value | $t$-Value |
|---|---|---|---|---|
| $v_0$ | | 0 | 0.0008 | 13.07 |
| $\theta_1$ | MA | 1 | 0.2802 | 3.04 |
| $\theta_2$ | MA | 24 | 0.7904 | 13.86 |
| $\phi_1$ | AR | 1 | 0.7426 | 11.01 |
| $\phi_2$ | AR | 24 | 0.4392 | 6.01 |
| Differencing | Yes | 24 | | |
| $\phi_3$ | AR | 168 | 0.1562 | 3.6 |
| RSE (time zone) | | | 0.9 | |

*Source:* Association for Studies on the Quality of Electric Energy.
Reproduced with permission.

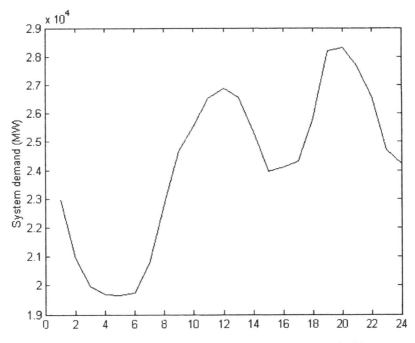

**Figure 2.14**   Hourly evolution of the Spanish system electricity demand (12/12/2001)

**Table 2.8**  SCA results for time interval Sunday, 8 a.m.–9 a.m.
Model equation (2.18)

| Coefficients | Type | Order | Value | $t$-Value |
|---|---|---|---|---|
| $v_0$ | | 0 | 0.0001 | 4.41 |
| $\theta_1$ | MA | 1 | 0.2285 | 2 |
| $\theta_1$ | AR | 1 | 0.848 | 14.43 |
| $\phi_3$ | AR | 168 | 0.1727 | 2 |
| Differencing | None | | | |
| RSE (time zone) | | | 0.59 | |

*Source:* Association for Studies on the Quality of Electric Energy. Reproduced with permission.

the SCA™ statistical software. As has been stated, $Y$ stands for the output variable (intercept or slope of the RDFs), the explanatory variable *non-base demand* is measured in MW, and $v_0$ is expressed either in [c€/(MW*kWh)] for the RDF intercept equation or [c€/(MW$^2$*kWh)] for the slope equation:

$$Y = v_0 \, [NBD] + \frac{(1 - \theta_1 B)}{(1 - \phi_1 B)} a_t \tag{2.16}$$

Next, the optimal model for the same hourly range (8 a.m.–9 a.m.) focusing on Tuesday through Friday is developed:

$$\nabla_{24} Y = v_0 \nabla_{24} \, [NBD] + \frac{(1 - \theta_1 B)(1 - \theta_2 B^{24})}{(1 - \phi_1 B)(1 - \phi_2 B^{24})(1 - \phi_3 B^{168})} a_t \tag{2.17}$$

Finally, the optimal model focused on Sundays with the previous hourly range (8 a.m.–9 a.m.) is expressed:

$$Y = v_0 \, [NBD] + \frac{(1 - \theta_1 B)}{(1 - \phi_1 B)(1 - \phi_{31} B^{168})} a_t \tag{2.18}$$

Tables 2.6–2.8 show a great variety in the structure of the models depending on the time interval considered. They should be interpreted in the following way: for instance, focusing on the row corresponding to parameter $\phi_2$ in Table 2.7, it means that a seasonal daily (order 24) autoregressive (AR) parameter labelled $\phi_2$, which takes a value of 0.4392 is considered in the model, because it is a meaningful parameter (its $t$-value is greater than two).

Although the base model used has always been the one stated in equation (2.15), the weighted estimation method focused on the time zone selected skips in each case the non-significant parameters and differencings or adds new parameters like $\phi_2$ and $\phi_3$ in Table 2.7, until an optimal parsimonious model which deals with the stationarity and invertibility conditions has been reached (Pankratz, 1991; Box, 1976; Box *et al.*, 1994).

It can be noted that Table 2.6 and Table 2.8, which correspond to weekend days, do not include any differencing, because due to the strong variation in the RDF pattern from Friday to Saturday and from Saturday to Sunday, there does not exist any relation between these days and previous days.

In order to avoid confusion, it is necessary to remark that the ARIMA model developed in subsection 2.4.1, which includes two seasonal differencings, did not discriminate the data series in time intervals, so a model, which minimizes the overall RSE, was obtained.

However, using the WE method, it is possible to see that depending on the time interval analysed, some of them do not need any differencing at all (like the ones detailed in Table 2.6 and Table 2.8), while others may need one (Table 2.7) or more differencings.

Each time zone model also includes its own RSE, whose magnitude will usually have a strong resemblance to the range of variation of the values of each time interval (i.e. the lower the output variable dispersion, the lower the value of the RSE). In contrast to the ARIMA model, where only one overall RSE was used, the WE method provides one different weighted RSE (calculated focusing only on the residuals of those observations belonging to the analysed time period, i.e. their weight equals one) for each one of the previously selected time periods.

The weighted RSE can be used to generate multiple RDF scenarios (instead of using only a base scenario for the dispatch optimization problem, upper and lower scenarios could also be generated. The separation between them would be proportional to the standard deviation of the weighted RSE. Thus, valley hour scenarios would tend to be less dispersed than the ones obtained for peak hours) in order to build up the 24 optimal bid functions as required by the MO.

### 2.4.2.3   A brief comment on outliers

The SCA™ software package provides the capability to detect the most common type of outliers (for example a level shift or a temporary change in the data series) and its deviation from the expected value (i.e. obtained under normal conditions) in order to evaluate their impact. The effects of outliers should always be considered, because they can bias the estimation of the parameters of the model. The problem is that the outlier detection procedure takes a lot of time if the data series has a big size, as is usually common with hourly data.

A possible approach to this topic would be to build auxiliary daily and weekly TF models, in which both input and output variables are the daily/weekly average values, so the size of the series is shortened. The daily model would detect those days where there has been an abnormal behaviour (usually non-labour days different from the weekends) and the weekly model would be suitable for more longer special pattern events like Easter or Christmas.

Finally, as the RDFs must be generated hourly, the average daily or weekly deviations should be converted into hourly deviations taking into account the different characteristics of each period of time.

### 2.4.3   Case study

In this case study the advantages of an accurate prediction of the variables slope and intercept corresponding to linearized RDFs are going to be shown. Firstly, a week of year 2001, with a step increase of run-of-the-river power with respect to the previous week, has been chosen. It is expected that the RDF forecasts of the classical ARIMA model without explanatory variables described in Section 1.2 will deviate greatly from the real RDF functions, while the more complex weighted estimation model which uses the explanatory variables described in Section 1.3 (denoted as WE in the next figures) should capture the change in the RDF pattern caused by the new hydro conditions. Figures 2.15–2.17 display the different performance of the forecasting models in three different types of hours of a Wednesday (one valley hour, one plateau hour and one peak hour).

As was expected, ARIMA model forecasts present big departures from the real RDF functions. In this case, forecasted RDFs tend to be higher and more abrupt, whereas weighted estimation model forecasts match better to the real pattern.

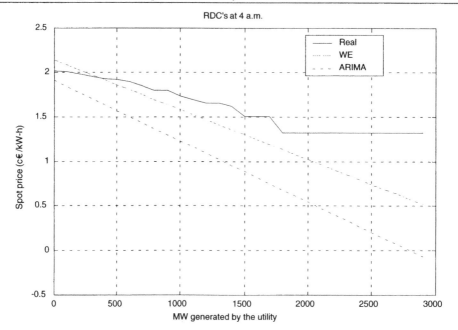

**Figure 2.15**   Real residual demand function (continuous line) versus WE forecast (dashed line) and ARIMA forecast (dotted line). Valley hour
*Source:* Association for Studies on the Quality of Electric Energy. Reproduced with permission.

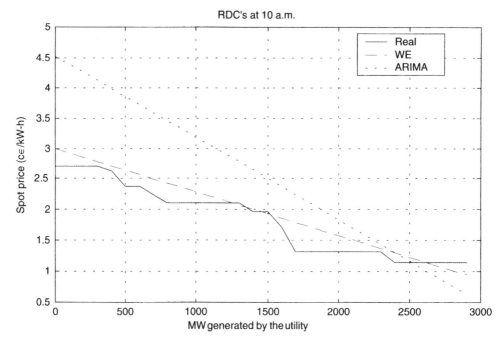

**Figure 2.16**   Real residual demand function (continuous line) versus WE forecast (dashed line) and ARIMA forecast (dotted line). Plateau hour
*Source:* Association for Studies on the Quality of Electric Energy. Reproduced with permission.

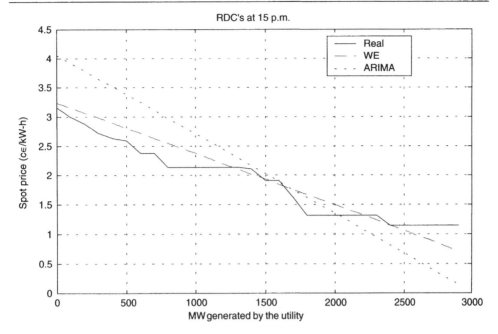

**Figure 2.17** Real residual demand function (continuous line) versus WE forecast (dashed line) and ARIMA forecast (dotted line). Peak hour
*Source:* Association for Studies on the Quality of Electric Energy. Reproduced with permission.

### 2.4.4 Section conclusions

In this section a method for an accurate prediction of the residual demand functions of a given utility has been shown. An adequate hourly explanatory variable has been defined which takes into account different situations of the national system. A weighted estimation method has been proposed in order to deal with the non-linear relationship between the explanatory and the input variables, depending on the time period (day and hour) considered. Finally, a case study has been carried out, showing the advantages of the weighted estimation using the proposed explanatory variable. The next section presents an alternative method to deal with the multi-regime aspect of the electricity price series.

## 2.5 DISCOVERING ELECTRICITY MARKET STATES FOR FORECASTING THE RESIDUAL DEMAND FUNCTION USING INPUT–OUTPUT HIDDEN MARKOV MODELS

In the previous section, the problem of forecasting the residual demand function has been approached from the point of view of time series analysis, with the primary aim of maximizing the accuracy of the forecasts. The model proposed in this section takes a step forward. The objective is not only to propose a successful model in terms of accuracy, but also to extract dynamical information about the market by identifying and characterizing different regimes in competitor's behaviour. Since market participants often apply the same strategy for several days, the residual demand time series can reflect a switching nature related to discrete changes in a participant's behaviour. This phenomenon gives rise to piecewise stationary time series where the series switches between different regimes (Weigend and Mangeas, 1995).

Two fundamental groups of switching models appear in the literature. The first one comes from the economic and financial fields, and their application to electricity markets has been focused mainly on the analysis of system marginal price time series. The most important model of this group for the purpose of this section was introduced by Hamilton (1990). In that paper, the time series is modelled by a Markovian algorithm for switching among autoregressive regimes, adapting to occasional discrete shifts in the level, variance and autoregressive dynamics of the series. The probability law governing these shifts is fixed, time-invariant and non-conditioned to exogenous variables. Therefore this model presents a serious shortcoming to capture the idiosyncrasy of electricity markets. In the model proposed in this section, a set of exogenous input variables are considered in such a way that both the distribution of the output variable in each regime and the transition probabilities among regimes are conditioned to them.

The second group is related to models based on artificial neural networks. The most relevant model in this group is the one presented in Weigend and Mangeas (1995). In that paper, the authors present a gated experts architecture in order to discover different regimes in the electricity load time series. This gated experts model consists of a non-linear gating network and several competing experts. Each expert learns to predict the conditional mean of the output variable and adapts its width to match the noise level in its corresponding regime. The gating network learns to predict the probability of each expert, given the input. Although in this approach exogenous variables are considered at each time step and therefore the probability of each regime is time-variant, the previous regime is not considered to forecast the next expert.

The model proposed in this section combines both, focusing on trying to solve their main drawbacks. The proposed model is a probabilistic model with a fixed number of states corresponding to different conditional distributions of the output variables given the input variables, and with transition probabilities between states that can also depend on the input variables.

### 2.5.1  Hidden Markov models and the analogy with electricity markets

2.5.1.1  Introduction to hidden Markov models

Hidden Markov models (HMM) were first introduced in the late 1960s (Baum and Petrie, 1966) as statistical methods extremely useful for modelling sequentially changing behaviours. A hidden Markov model (Levinson *et al.*, 1982; Rabiner, 1989) is a double embedded stochastic process:

1. An *underlying process* defined by a Markov chain with a finite number of states $S = \{S_1, S_2, \ldots, S_N\}$, which is hidden from observation.

   A Markov chain (Berger, 1993) describes a system which at any time step is in one of a set of mutually exclusive states. Let $\{Y_n\}_{n \geq 0}$ be a sequence of random variables taking values in a finite set $S = \{S_1, S_2, \ldots, S_N\}$. These random variables are said to be a Markov chain if there is no dependence between states that are not immediately consecutive (order 1). That is:

$$P(s_{t+1} = S_i | s_0 = S_j, \ldots, s_t = S_k) = P(s_{t+1} = S_i | s_t = S_k) \qquad (2.19)$$

   Equation (2.19) is known as the Markovian property, where $P$ stands for probability. The Markovian property implies that given the present state, the future probabilistic behaviour is independent of its past history.

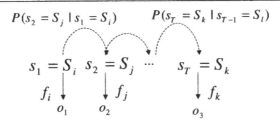

**Figure 2.18**   Hidden Markov model process

   The conditional probabilities $P(s_{t+1} = S_i | s_t = S_k)$ are referred to as the "transition prob-abilities", and when they are time-invariant, the Markov chain is said to be homogeneous.
2. An *observable process* which is determined by the underlying Markov chain. At each state a unique probability density function (*pdf*) governs the emission of observations.

Mathematically, a hidden Markov model is defined by the following four elements:

* The number of states in the model $N$.
* An initial state probability distribution:

$$\Gamma = (\gamma_i = P(s_0 = S_i)) \in [0, 1]^N \tag{2.20}$$

* The transition state probability matrix:

$$A = (a_{ij} = P(s_{t+1} = S_i | s_t = S_j)) \in [0, 1]^{N \times N} \tag{2.21}$$

* A set of $N$ emission probability density functions $(f_i)_{i=1,2,...,N}$.

   The HMM process of generating observations is as follows (Figure 2.18). The first state is selected according to the initial state distribution, which contains the probabilities of starting from each state $S_i$, $\forall i \in \{1, \ldots, N\}$. For each time step $t$ the system shifts from the state $s_{t-1} = S_k$ to the state $s_t = S_j$ according to the transition probability matrix. At this state $S_j$, a new observation $o_t^j$ is emitted using its corresponding *pdf* $f_j$. After that, the system evolves to time $t + 1$, and a new state $s_{t+1} = S_i$ is reached according again to the transition probability matrix. On that state, another observation $O_{t+1}^i$ is emitted according to the *pdf* $f_i$. This process evolves until the last stage $T$ is reached.
   When a sequence of length $T$ is generated, the result of the HMM process will be both the observations sequence $o_1, o_2, \ldots, o_T$ and the states sequence $s_1, s_2, \ldots, s_T$. However, whereas the observations sequence is visible, the states sequence remains hidden and no information about it is available for an observer.
   Given an observation sequence $o_1, o_2, \ldots, o_T$ (or several defined over the same temporal scope), the problem of adjusting the HMM is concerned with finding the set of parameters $\Theta = \{\Gamma, A, (f_i)_{i=1}^N\}$ which best fits all these training data. For this issue the expectation maximization algorithm (Dempster *et al.*, 1977; Geoffrey, 1997) and its simplified version, the Baum–Welch algorithm (Rabiner, 1989), are widely proposed in the related literature.
   At this point it is important to remark that in standard HMM the probability law governing the transitions between states is fixed, time-invariant and non-conditioned to exogenous variables. The *pdf* of the output variable is also non-conditioned to input variables. Therefore this model presents a serious shortcoming to capture the idiosyncrasy of electricity markets. As a generalization of HMM, IOHMM considers at each time step a set of input variables. The

**Table 2.9**   Analogy between IOHMM and electricity markets

| IOHMM | Electricity market |
|---|---|
| States $S = \{S_1, S_2, \ldots, S_N\}$ | "*Market states*" $M = \{M_1, M_2, \ldots, M_N\}$ |
| Observations $O_t$ | Residual demand functions *RDF* (slope $m$ and intercept $I$) |
| *pdf* at state $s_i$ (conditioned to a set of input variables) | Probability of generating a particular residual demand function from the *market state* $m_i$ given the current explanatory variables |
| Initial probability | Probability of selecting the market state $m_i$ at time $t = 1$ |
| Transition matrix (conditioned to a set of input variables) | Probability of market state $m_i$ at time $t$ given the market state $m_j$ at time $t - 1$ and the set of current explanatory variables |

main difference between HMM and IOHMM is that in IOHMM both the distribution of the output variable in each regime and the transition probabilities among regimes are conditioned to a set of explanatory variables. In this section IOHMMs are proposed to model electricity markets.

### 2.5.1.2   Applying IOHMMs to electricity markets

In the case of electricity markets, the observations and states of IOHMMs can be interpreted as follows.

*Observations:* Residual demand functions will be considered as the observations of the electricity market bidding process treated in this section.[7] In the Spanish daily electricity market, residual demand functions are published by the market operator after market clearance.

*Market states:* Each market state is characterized by a different residual demand function *pdf*, conditioned to a set of input variables such as load, hydro, thermal and nuclear resources, etc. In that sense, different states correspond to different functional relationships between input variables and residual demand functions. These functional relationships are associated with the interaction of competitors' strategies.

Table 2.9 shows the analogy between IOHMM and electricity markets.

### 2.5.2   Model description

#### 2.5.2.1   Architecture

IOHMMs were first introduced by Bengio and Frasconi (1996). The architecture is based on a traditional HMM including a set of input variables at each time step. Whereas HMMs are focused on estimating the *pdf* of the output sequence $f(o_1^T)$, IOHMMs are trained to fit the output sequence *pdf* $f(o_1^T|u_1^T)$ conditioned to the input variable sequence. Using the *Markovian*

---

[7] Instead of the residual demand function other variables to study the market, such as for example the market clearing price, participant market shares, etc., could also be used.

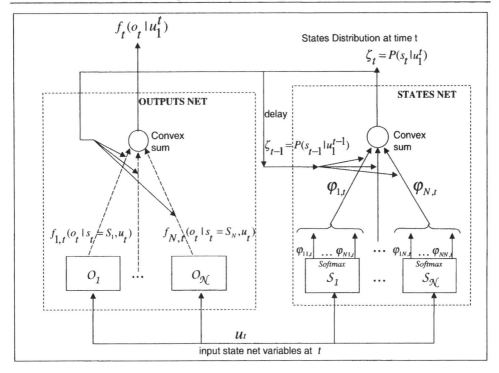

**Figure 2.19**   IOHMM architecture

*property* (2.19), the conditional distribution at each time step $t$ can be expressed as:

$$f\left(o_t|u_1^t\right) = \sum_{s=1}^{N} P\left(s_t = S_i|u_1^t\right) f(o_t|s_t = S_i, u_t) \qquad (2.22)$$

$$\text{where} \quad u_1^t = (u_1, \dots, u_t)$$

that is, sums of products of the conditional output distributions and the conditional states distribution.

The basic idea of the IOHMM architecture (Figure 2.19) relies on taking advantage of the above expression in order to distribute the learning tasks. In that sense, a modular architecture is composed of a states network and an outputs network. Both networks share the learning problem but each of them is specialized on estimating just one of the product factors in equation (2.22).

The *states network* is composed of a set of states subnetworks $\{S_j\}_{j=1}^{N}$, one for each state defined in the model. The aim of each state subnetwork $S_j$ is to propose a prediction of the next state distribution assuming that the previous state was its own state, and given the current input variables, i.e. $\varphi_{jt} = P(s_t|s_{t-1} = S_j, u_t)$. Hence, at each time step, every state subnetwork has $r$ inputs $u_t \in R^r$ and $N$ outputs (one for each state), $\varphi_{jt} = [\varphi_{1j,t}, \dots, \varphi_{Nj,t}]$ where $\varphi_{ij,t} = P(s_t = S_i|s_{t-1} = S_j, u_t)$.

In this application, each states subnetwork is implemented as a multilayer perceptron (Bishop, 1995) with a single hidden layer and sigmoidal activation functions (Bishop, 1995). As proposed in the original architecture, the softmax (Bishop, 1995) function has also been implemented at the output units as a normalization function, which guarantees that the outputs of states subnetworks are non-negative and sum to one. It is important to highlight on the one hand that the transition probabilities $\varphi_{ij,t}$ are estimated by the set of states subnetworks. On the other hand, combining the candidates of each subnetwork and the previous state distribution, the current state distribution is computed as $\zeta_t = [\zeta_{1,t}, \ldots, \zeta_{N,t}]$ where $\zeta_{j,t} = \sum_{j=1}^{N} \zeta_{j,t-1} \varphi_{j,t}$.

The *output network* is composed of a set of output subnetworks $\{O_j\}_{j=1}^{N}$ each associated with a unique state of $S$. The task of the output subnetworks is concerned with predicting the expected output value given the current state and the current input variables. For this issue a conditional *pdf* $f_j$ is implemented in each output subnetwork $O_j$. The output of $O_j$ is computed as the distribution expectation $f_{j,t} = E[f_j(o_t|, u_t)] \in \mathbb{R}^r$. Several distributions seem to be well suited (Lauzon, 1999) for the output subnetworks. In this application a conditional Gaussian distribution $G^j(\mu^j, \sigma^j)$ with diagonal covariance matrix has been adopted. The distribution expectation is modelled as a linear function of the input variables, $\mu = W u + b$, where $W \in \mathbb{R}^N \times \mathbb{R}^r$ and $b \in \mathbb{R}^N$.

The combination of the output subnetworks generates an output distribution $f(o_t|, u_t)$ which is a mixture of probabilities (Titterington *et al.*, 1985), where each component is conditional on a particular state and the mixing weights are the current state probabilities (states network outputs) conditioned to the input. That output can be expressed as follows: $f_t = \sum_{j=1}^{N} \zeta_{j,t} \eta_{j,t}$.

Concerning the learning algorithm, the expectation maximization algorithm has been implemented. A detailed description of this algorithm is presented in Bengio and Frasconi, 1996).

### 2.5.3  Example case

#### 2.5.3.1  Description

The problem of analysing the RDF is reduced in this case to the analysis of the time evolution of two variables, the slope and the intercept of the linearized RDF. In this section the studied period was from January 2001 to July 2001 divided into hourly intervals. The two time series of this study are represented in Figure 2.20.

A different IOHMM model has been adjusted for the slope $m$ and for the intercept $I$, but only the intercept variable analysis will be presented (similar results have been obtained for the slope variable). Concerning the explanatory variables, the model has to be restricted to public information. In that sense, past values of hourly production by technology, hourly system demand and marginal price have been used to generate the input variables. The set of explanatory variables for the IOHMM model is summarized in Table 2.10 and shown in Figure 2.21.

**Table 2.10**  Explanatory variables definition

| Variable | Description |
|---|---|
| $D_{d,h}$ | Load for the day $d$ and hour $h$ |
| $N_{d,h}$ | Nuclear generation for the day $d$ and hour $h$ |
| $H_{d,h}$ | Hydro generation for the day $d$ and hour $h$ |
| $P_{d,h}$ | Marginal price value for the day $d$ and hour $h$ |
| $NBD_{d,h}$ | Non-base demand for the day $d$ and hour $h$ |

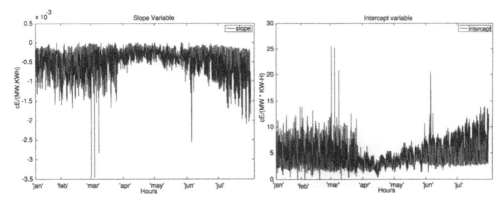

**Figure 2.20**    Slope and intercept for the linearized residual demand functions

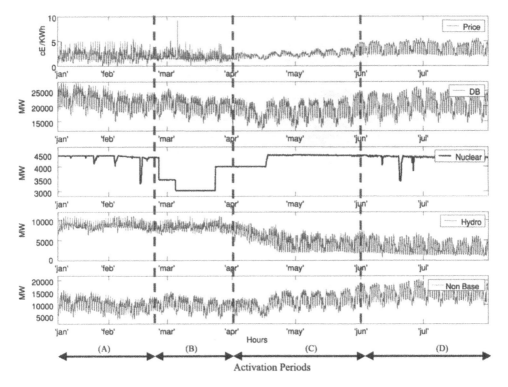

**Figure 2.21**    Explanatory variables for the studied period

At this point it is important to note that the original IOHMM proposed in Bengio and Frasconi (1996) considers the same input variables for the state and output networks. By contrast, in this application different variables for each type of network are allowed. This small improvement makes it easier to interpret and understand model results. For instance, states input variables capture the market states and switches among them, whereas input variables for output networks accurately fix the RDF intercept and slope values given the probability

**Table 2.11**   Input variables for each type of network

| Network | Input variables |
| --- | --- |
| States | $p_{d-1,h}$, $D_{d,h}$, $D_{d-1,h}$, $N_{d-1,h}$, $H_{d-1,h}$, $NBD_{d-1,h}$, $I_{d-1,h}$ |
| Output | $p_{d-1,h}$, $D_{d,h}$, $D_{d,h-1}$, $D_{d-1,h}$, $I_{d-7,h}$, $I_{d-1,h}$, $I_{d,h-1}$ |

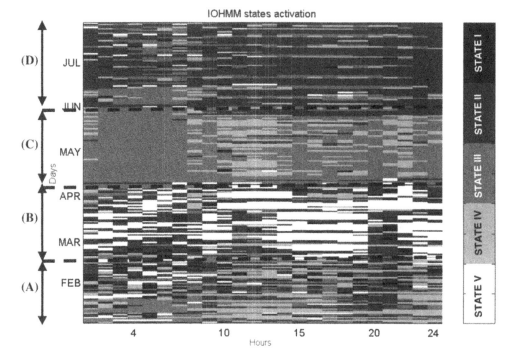

**Figure 2.22**   Activation of IOHMM states

states distribution. Under this approach, the user can intentionally split input variables using their knowledge and experience. Table 2.11 presents the input data used for state and output networks.

### 2.5.3.2   Discovering and analysing market states

The first step to apply the IOHMM is to select the number of states. In this example a five states model was selected according to accuracy and interpretability.

In Figure 2.22 the activation of the most probable state for each hour is represented. Each row corresponds to one day and each column to one hour. States are represented in different colours. This figure provides useful information since it can be interpreted from two standpoints:

1. The first analysis consists of fixing the $y$-axis values (days) and moving along the $x$-axis (hours). A first sight of Figure 2.22 reveals a state activation pattern related to off-peak, peak and medium-load hours. For instance, during the period April–May, hours from 2:00 to 7:00 are activated in most cases with state III. In the same period medium-load hours

from 11:00 to 13:00 are activated with state IV, and the 15:00 and 20:00 peak hours are also clearly identified with state III.

2. The opposite point of view consists of fixing the $x$-axis values and moving along the $y$-axis. In that analysis the evolution of the different market states along the temporal scope shows discrete changes related to the different patterns of a competitor's behaviour. This visual inspection provides mainly four activation periods. The first one (A) goes from January to mid-February. In this period states III and IV are mainly activated. The second period (B) is identified because state V is the most probable and goes from mid-February to the beginning of April. The third activation period (C) is characterized by state III, which is the most representative of this period. And finally, during June–July (D), state II seems to exhibit the higher activation probability. From this point of view, it may be observed that specific patterns are assigned to weekends. For example in the last period from 8:00 to 24:00, Saturdays and Sundays are activated with most probability with state III whereas workdays are activated with state II.

### 2.5.3.3   States and explanatory variables

The identification of four activation periods (A, B, C and D in Figure 2.22) is related to the occurrence of causal episodes in the states network input variables. In the first activation period (A), explanatory variables do not suffer abrupt changes. In the second fortnight of February (A→B), nuclear production is drastically reduced due to the maintenance of several units. The joint effect of this reduction of base production and the decreasing tendency of the load is reflected as a shift in the variance of the RDF intercept and slope time series. At the end of March (B→C), some of the nuclear units in maintenance are recovered but water resources present an important drop. This new situation results in an increase in thermal production (see Figure 2.21). Finally, at the end of May (C→D), a new market condition takes place due to an increase in the load while available production resources are stable.

On the other hand, Figure 2.23 provides information about the normalized significance of each explanatory variable in the outputs subnetworks. For this sake, coefficients of the regression model for the conditioned mean of the Gaussian model, as well as standard deviation values, are presented. The analysis of the signs of the coefficients (positive for $D_{d,h}$, negative for $D_{d,h-1}$ and $D_{d-1,h}$ and positive for $I_{d-7,h}$, $I_{d-1,h}$ and $I_{d,h-1}$) reveals an autoregressive integrated component of the form:

$$I_{d,h} - \alpha_1 I_{d,h-1} - \alpha_2 I_{d-1,h} - \alpha_3 I_{d-7,h} = \beta_1 D_{d,h} - \beta_2 D_{d,h-1} - \beta_3 D_{d-1,h} \quad \text{with} \quad \alpha_i, \beta_j > 0$$

$$(2.23)$$

The comparative analysis of the coefficients of each state reveals the similarities between states I and II, IV and V, and the specificity of state III. States I and II stand out for their first-order autoregressive component (coeff($I_{d,h-1}$) > 0.5). The difference between these two states comes from the daily and weekly autoregressive components (coeff($I_{d-1,h}$) and coeff($I_{d-7,h}$)). States IV and V are the only ones to consider the marginal price as a relevant input variable. The difference between them also comes from the daily and weekly autoregressive components. State III has been characterized by the high significance assigned to the load input variable.

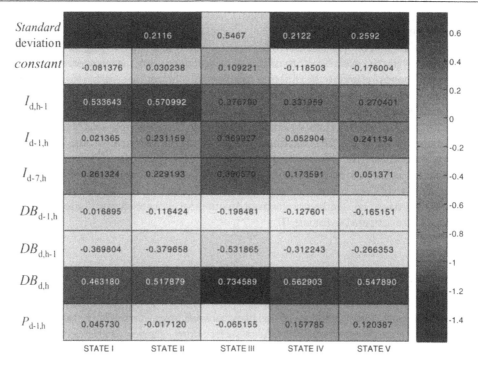

| | STATE I | STATE II | STATE III | STATE IV | STATE V |
|---|---|---|---|---|---|
| *Standard* deviation | 0.2116 | 0.5467 | 0.2122 | 0.2592 | |
| *constant* | -0.081376 | 0.030238 | 0.109221 | -0.118503 | -0.176004 |
| $I_{d,h-1}$ | 0.533643 | 0.570992 | 0.376790 | 0.331959 | 0.270401 |
| $I_{d-1,h}$ | 0.021365 | 0.231159 | 0.369927 | 0.052904 | 0.241134 |
| $I_{d-7,h}$ | 0.261324 | 0.229193 | 0.090570 | 0.173591 | 0.051371 |
| $DB_{d-1,h}$ | -0.016895 | -0.116424 | -0.198481 | -0.127601 | -0.165151 |
| $DB_{d,h-1}$ | -0.369804 | -0.379658 | -0.531865 | -0.312243 | -0.266353 |
| $DB_{d,h}$ | 0.463180 | 0.517879 | 0.734589 | 0.562903 | 0.547890 |
| $P_{d-1,h}$ | 0.045730 | -0.017120 | -0.065155 | 0.157785 | 0.120387 |

**Figure 2.23**   Explanatory variables coefficient for each state

### 2.5.3.4   Forecasting residual demand functions

Examples of slope and intercept forecasts for each activation period are presented in Figure 2.24. The mean absolute percentage error (MAE) defined as

$$MAPE = \frac{1}{N} \sum_{i=1}^{N} \frac{|y_i - \widehat{y_i}|}{y_i} \qquad (2.24)$$

was 0.85 for the intercept value and 0.57 for the slope.

Figure 2.25 shows examples of the residual demand function forecasts for each activation area for different types of hours in the four periods.

## 2.6   CONJECTURAL VARIATIONS APPROACH FOR MODELLING ELECTRICITY MARKETS

This section presents a fitting procedure designed for medium-term electricity markets unlike the previous sections that were oriented towards short-term analysis. It uses as input data only public information. This feature makes the model especially useful in situations when detailed bidding submissions are not available.

The method is based on the conjectural variations approach. This approach allows a more flexible representation of firms' behaviour and a more accurate price generation process than the more commonly applied Cournot equilibrium formulations (Vives, 1999). These improvements are achieved by means of modelling firms' residual demand functions, which provide information about the energy that firms are able to sell at each price. As we have seen in

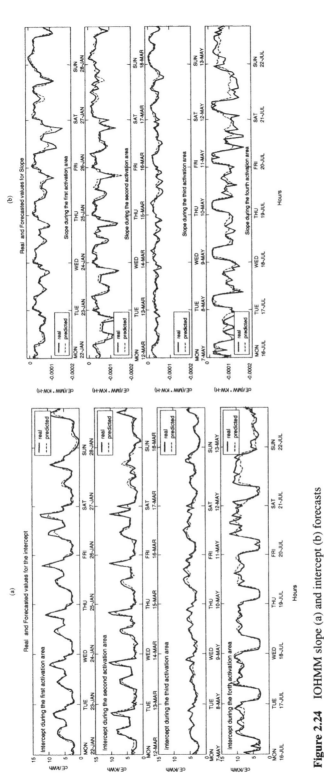

**Figure 2.24** IOHMM slope (a) and intercept (b) forecasts

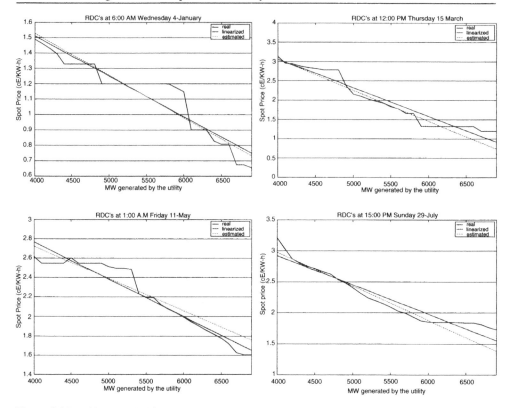

**Figure 2.25**   IOHMM RDF forecasts

previous sections, these residual demand functions are difficult to estimate because they are related to the other firms' supply functions.

The proposed methodology characterizes each residual demand function by its elasticity and estimates the implicit values of this parameter. Thereby, this procedure computes the long-term residual demand elasticity that each firm has been inferring when it has been bidding. The inference about firms' bidding perceptions is based on clearing market information provided by the market operator, instead of the real supply functions submitted by the firms. An estimation process based on short-term supply functions has been dismissed because they do not reflect properly firms' long-term strategies but just firms' short-term tactics.

### 2.6.1   Conjectural variations

There exist a number of long-term electricity market models based on Cournot competition (Scott and Read, 1996; Bushnell, 1998; Wei and Smeers, 1999; Hobbs, 2001). However, it is well known that these models provide very high, barely credible prices. These high prices are due to neglecting competitors' supply functions (Day *et al.*, 2002).

The conjectural variations approach considers the reaction of competitors when a firm is deciding its optimal production. This reaction comes out from firms' supply functions and demand function and can be modelled by means of the residual demand function.

### 2.6.1.1   Firms' optimization problem

In this section, the optimization problem of each firm is stated as its profit maximization program facing its own residual demand function. Thereby, conjectural variations are considered in the firms' strategic behaviour.

Since the system marginal price is set by the decisions made on the supply and demand sides, it is possible to relate this price to the aggregated production by means of the demand function $d$:

$$p = D\left(\sum_f q_f\right) \tag{2.25}$$

In order to calculate the $f$th firm optimal production, the derivative of the profit function (2.7) with respect to the decision variable ($q_f$) is equalized to zero:

$$\frac{\partial \Pi_f}{\partial q_f} = p + \frac{\partial p}{\partial q_f} q_f - MC_f\left(q_f\right) = 0 \tag{2.26}$$

The first two terms of the equation make up the firms' marginal revenue $MR_f$. The marginal revenue measures how a firm's revenue increases (or decreases) when the firm increases (or decreases) its production in one unit. Likewise, the firm's marginal cost can be defined as how a firm's cost increases (or decreases) when the firm increases (or decreases) its production in one unit. Therefore, a firm's optimal production is achieved when its marginal revenue is equal to its marginal cost.

A firm's marginal revenue can be expressed in terms of its residual demand elasticity $\varepsilon_f$ instead of the residual demand slope

$$MR_f(q_f) = p + \frac{\partial p}{\partial q_f} q_f = p\left(1 + \frac{1}{\varepsilon_f}\right) \tag{2.27}$$

where the residual demand elasticity is defined as the quotient between the unitary change in the firm's production caused by a unitary change in market price:

$$\varepsilon_f = \frac{\partial q_f / q_f}{\partial p / p} \tag{2.28}$$

Note that the residual demand elasticity is different for each firm. This parameter takes into account how the market price changes when each firm changes its production unilaterally.

To conclude, this parameter expresses the market conjecture of each firm. The variation of this parameter encompasses different types of competition, providing great flexibility of modelling.

### 2.6.1.2   Flexibility of modelling

Depending on the value of a firm's residual demand elasticity, a different assumption is made about how the firm's marginal revenue is conceived, and consequently, about how firms behave. In this way, some widely used market models can be stated in terms of the residual demand elasticity as follows.

*Perfect competition*: Perfect competition can be defined as a market situation where firms are not able to change the market price by modifying their production unilaterally. In terms of market modelling, each firm's residual demand function becomes horizontal. The elasticity

**Table 2.12**   Market conjecture

| Model | Market conjecture |
| --- | --- |
| Perfect competition | $\varepsilon_f = \infty$ |
| Cournot | $\varepsilon_f = \varepsilon_d/\alpha_f$ |
| Conjectural variations | $\varepsilon_f \neq \varepsilon_d$ |

value of a fixed-price residual demand function is infinity – see equation (2.28). From equation (2.26), the firm's marginal revenue is equal to the market price. As expected, the firm's optimal production takes place when its marginal cost reaches the market price.

*Cournot model*: The Cournot model is one of the most common approaches to represent competition amongst just a few firms. In contrast to perfect competition, these firms are able to modify the market price by means of changing their own production. The market model conjecture that states a Cournot equilibrium can be written in terms of a demand elasticity equal to every firm competing in the market scaled by its market share ($\varepsilon_f = \varepsilon_d/\alpha_f$), where $\varepsilon_d$ is the demand function elasticity and $\alpha_f$ is the $f$th firm market share. Cournot prices are usually far higher than real market prices.

The different values of the residual demand elasticity depending on the theoretical market model are summarized in Table 2.12.

### 2.6.2   Implicit elasticity estimation

In this subsection, a methodology suitable to estimate residual demand elasticity is presented. The resulting estimations will allow the fitting of medium-term, equilibrium, electricity market models.

#### 2.6.2.1   Estimation overview

The proposed methodology is based on fitting the residual demand elasticity by means of an evaluation of the conjectural variations model on past data. It is firstly supposed that firms behaved via a conjectural variations pattern during the fitting period. Therefore, the decisions – productions – they made can be assumed to be optimal. This optimal schedule can be expressed equalizing the firm's marginal revenue with its marginal cost – see equation (2.26).

Consequently, we can infer the past residual demand elasticity by using these decision variables as acknowledged values. This procedure is known as implicit valuation. Thus, the residual demand elasticity obtained is called *implicit elasticity*. It is important to remark that the implicit values of the elasticity measure firms' perception about their market positions in a conjectural variations context. In fact, this perception does not need to coincide with the real residual demand computed by the supply and demand functions submitted to the market by all the firms.

#### 2.6.2.2   Implicit elasticity

The procedure to obtain the implicit value of firms' residual demand in a conjectural variations context is stated along these lines. Let $p$ be the actual system market price and $MR_f$ be the marginal revenue of the firm $f$. The implicit value of the residual demand elasticity ($\widehat{\varepsilon_f}$) is derived from expression (2.27) and can be written as follows:

$$\widehat{\varepsilon_f} = \frac{p}{MR_f - p} \qquad (2.29)$$

The value of firm's marginal revenue is impossible to estimate from market data. However, it can be approximated to the firm's marginal cost through the assumption that each firm is generating optimally (2.26). The firm's marginal cost can then be approximated as the generation cost of the most expensive committed unit.[8] Therefore, the implicit expression of the residual demand elasticity can be stated in terms of the market price and firm's marginal cost as follows:

$$\widehat{\varepsilon_f} \simeq \frac{p}{MC_f - p} \qquad (2.30)$$

### 2.6.2.3 Estimation

By means of valuing the implicit residual demand elasticity, it is possible to infer firms' long-term behaviour. The estimation procedure uses public market information provided hourly – prices and production – and an estimation of the firms' marginal costs. Applying equation (2.30) to this information, the hourly time series of the implicit residual elasticity of each firm is directly assessed. These implicit values not only consider long-term behaviour, but also are very influenced by short-term uncertainty sources and short-term operational constraints.

Some relevant short-term uncertainty sources that have some bearing on the implicit demand elasticity are plant outages, hydraulic inflows, deviations from the forecasted demand and supply functions submitted by the rest of the firms. Short-term operational constraints such as plant ramps, minimum stable output, limited reservoir capacity and network constraints also have a significant effect on implicit values.

Therefore, the previous short-term issues must be sieved in order to properly estimate the implicit values that will model firms' long-term behaviour. It is necessary to process all the information about the implicit residual demand evolution looking for a long-term trend value. Statistics make available several data-analysis methodologies that are able to deal with long-term behaviour estimation from short-term data. Depending on the nature of the variables used to do so, statistical methods can be classified as follows.

*Relational models*: By means of these models, the implicit elasticity of the residual demand is related to one or several relevant variables – explanatory variables – whose long-term values are easy to infer. This relationship is expressed by a function among the variables. Having a long-term estimation of the set of explanatory variables – e.g. demand, hydraulic inflows – a trend value of the implicit elasticity can easily be obtained by evaluating the former function. Some of the statistical methods that can be defined as *relational models* are regression, neural networks and decision trees.

*Classification models*: In contrast to relational models, the set of values of implicit elasticities is categorized by the different levels of several discrete factors. The long-term value of the implicit elasticity for each factor combination – i.e. class – can be expressed as a statistical measure – average, median or mode – of the past data distribution. Variance analysis and clustering are some statistical methodologies based on classification processes.

---

[8] A more precise marginal cost estimation requires considering units' generation constraints (i.e. ramps and minimum stable output) and other relevant market issues (i.e. capacity payments).

**Table 2.13**   Spanish firms' production structure (1999)

| Type | # Units | Power (MW) | Iberdrola | Endesa | Unión Fenosa | Hidrocantábrico |
|------|---------|-----------|-----------|--------|--------------|------------------|
| Thermal | 82 | 32 107 | 29% | 54% | 13% | 5% |
| Hydro | 38 | 16 628 | 51% | 36% | 3% | 10% |

*Time series models*: These models consider implicitly the evolution of the elasticities and infer a trend value of the time series. Time series methodology generally precludes taking into account other variables or factors when estimating the long-term values of the implicit residual demand elasticity. Some of the time series methodologies that deal with long-term trends are time series decomposition and exponential smoothing methods.

### 2.6.3   Case study

A complementarity-based equilibrium model (Rivier *et al.*, 2001) in which firms compete in a Cournot manner has been adapted to consider conjectural variations (García-Alcalde *et al.*, 2002). This model has been applied to the Spanish electricity market to validate the estimation and fitting procedures detailed in previous subsections. A comparison with firms' Cournot behaviour is also shown.

#### 2.6.3.1   System description

Data used to fit this estimation model is based on the market results of the year 1999. The annual scope of the model has been divided into 12 periods – months – with five load levels for each one.

There are 82 thermal generators grouped into 42 thermal plants. The hydro units have been grouped into 28 equivalent units plus 10 pumped-storage units (Table 2.13).

All the information that has been used in this case study is public. Units of production and market prices have been obtained through the Spanish market operator. Fuel costs and unit thermal rates are respectively based on international fuel prices and standard technology rates.

#### 2.6.3.2   Numerical results

Two different Cournot scenarios have been considered by changing the aggregated demand's elasticity value. For the first one $\varepsilon_d$ is equal to 0.3, while for the second one $\varepsilon_d$ is equal to 0.5. A conjectural variations approach has also been implemented and fitted. The value of firms' residual demand elasticities has been estimated using a classification model where each value was labelled depending on the firm, demand level and the expected hydraulic inflows.

The model-obtained prices (€/MWh) and the real market results can be seen in Table 2.14. Note that conjectural variations provide a realistic estimation of the real market prices for every demand level. In contrast, the Cournot equilibrium gives deficient results when demand elasticity decreases.

For the first Cournot scenario, estimated prices are eight times higher than the real ones. It is important to remark that a demand elasticity value of 0.3 is very high in electricity markets.

**Table 2.14**  Model's average prices (€/MWh) for each demand level

| Model | On-on-peak | On-peak | Plateau | Off-peak | Off-off-peak |
|---|---|---|---|---|---|
| Cournot $\varepsilon_d = 0.3$ | 281.21 | 258.80 | 231.34 | 168.47 | 116.76 |
| Cournot $\varepsilon_d = 0.5$ | 79.09 | 74.24 | 68.45 | 54.61 | 39.99 |
| Conjectural variations | 43.92 | 38.01 | 31.59 | 19.56 | 13.77 |
| Market prices (2000) | 46.08 | 40.21 | 32.61 | 22.16 | 16.53 |

**Table 2.15**  Comparison of presented methods

| Method | RDF representation | Time scope for market behaviour representation | Analysis type |
|---|---|---|---|
| Clustering techniques | Linear piecewise functions | Short-term | Static |
| Time series (ARIMA models) | Linear function (slope and intercept) | Short-term | Dynamic |
| Input–output hidden Markov models | Linear function (slope and intercept) | Short-term | Dynamic |
| Market equilibrium | Conjectural variations (slope) | Medium-term | Static |

For instance, the average demand elasticity in the Spanish electricity market in 1999 was 0.03. Therefore, the use of a Cournot model in which its demand elasticity estimation is based on the submitted demand functions is completely inappropriate. Note that although only four firms compete in the Spanish electricity market, actual clearing prices are much lower than those provided by a theoretical Cournot model. In fact, price shocks as occurred in California have not been observed in the Spanish electricity market.

Regarding the results obtained from the case study, the conjectural variations approach and the proposed implicit estimation methodology of the residual demand elasticities provide a flexible and accurate tool to infer realistic firms' productions and market prices. The advantages with respect to Cournot-based models are notable.

## 2.7  CONCLUSIONS

Four different methods devoted to managing the problem of obtaining a representation of competitive behaviour by constructing an RDF have been presented (Table 2.15). The first one is based on a cluster procedure to group similar bid functions. The second method uses time series techniques. The third one utilizes input–output hidden Markov methods. Finally, the fourth approach makes use of a market equilibrium representation.

There are several differences between the four models that can be pointed out. RDF is approximated by means of a linear piecewise function in the first case, with a linear function in the second and third and using a conjectural variation in the fourth. As for the time scope, the first three approaches represent RDF from a short-term analysis point of view (however they can manage data for long time periods), while the fourth focuses on a medium-term market representation. This analysis is made from a static point of view in the first and fourth examples, while the other two address the dynamic behaviour of bidding processes.

# APPENDIX: NOMENCLATURE

| Subscript | Meaning |
|-----------|---------|
| $d$ | Day |
| $f, -f$ | Firm (generation company), all firms but $f$ |
| $h$ | Hour |
| $t$ | Time step |

| Symbol | Meaning |
|--------|---------|
| $a$ | Random shock (white noise) |
| $ACF$ | Autocorrelation function |
| $AR$ | Autoregressive term |
| $ARIMA$ | Autoregressive integrated moving average |
| $B$ | Backshift operator. It delays $x$ lags when applied to a given variable |
| $BF$ | Bid function (supply or demand) |
| $C$ | Cost |
| $d$ | Dissimilarity |
| $D$ | Demand |
| $F$ | Run-of-the-river power |
| $HMM$ | Hidden Markov model |
| $IOHMM$ | Input–output hidden Markov model |
| $LHM$ | Linear hinges model |
| $LTF$ | Linear transfer funcion. Method used to adjust TF (transfer function) models |
| $m$ | Slope of a linear function |
| $MA$ | Moving average term |
| $MC$ | Marginal cost |
| $MO$ | Market operator |
| $MR$ | Marginal revenue |
| $N$ | Nuclear power |
| $NBD$ | Non-base demand |
| $H$ | Hydro generation |
| $I$ | Intercept of a linear function |
| $p$ | Price |
| $pdf$ | Probability density function |
| $P$ | Probability |
| $PACF$ | Partial autocorrelation function |
| $q$ | Quantity (energy production) |
| $R, RDF$ | Residual demand function |
| $RSE$ | Residual standard error |
| $s$ | Markovian process state |
| $S$ | Supply function |
| $SCA^{TM}$ | Comercial software for time series analysis |
| $SO$ | System operator |
| $TF$ | Transfer function model |
| $WE$ | Weighted estimation method |
| $Y$ | Random variable |
| $\varepsilon$ | Elasticity |
| $\nabla$ | Differencing operator |
| $\Pi$ | Profit |

# REFERENCES

Barquín J., Centeno E. and Reneses J. (2004). "Medium-term Generation Programming in Competitive Environments: A New Optimisation Approach for Market Equilibrium Computing". *IEE Proceedings, Generation, Transmission and Distribution* **151**(1): 119–126.

Baum L.E. and Petrie T. (1966). "Statistical Inference for Probabilistic Functions of Finite States Markov Chain". *Annals of Mathematics and Statistics* **37**: 1554–1563.

Bengio J. and Frasconi P. (1995). "An Input–Output HMM Architecture". *Advances in Neural Information Processing Systems* **7**: 427–434.

Bengio J. and Frasconi P. (1996). "Input–Output HMM's for Sequence Processing". *IEEE Transactions on Neural Networks* **7**(5).

Bengio J., LeCun Y., Nohl C. and Burges C. (1995). "A NN/HMM Hybrid for On-line Handwriting Recognition". *Neural Computation* **7**(6): 1289–1303.

Bengio J., Lauzon V.P. and Ducharme R. (1999). "Experiment on the Application of IOHMMs to Model Financial Returns Series". *IEEE Transactions on Neural Networks* **7**(5).

Berger M.A. (1993). *An Introduction to Probability and Stochastic Processes*. Springer-Verlag, New York.

Binroth W., Burshstein I., Haboush R.K. and Hartz J.R. (1979). "A Comparison of Commodity Price Forecasting by Box–Jenkins and Regression-based Techniques". *Technological Forecasting and Social Change* **14**: 169–180.

Bishop C.M. (1995). *Neural Networks for Pattern Recognition*. Oxford University Press, Oxford.

Box G.E.P. and Jenkins G.M. (1976). *Time Series Analysis*. Holden-Day.

Box G.E.P., Jenkins G.M. and Reinsel G.C. (1994). *Time Series Analysis*. Prentice Hall, Englewood Cliffs, NJ.

Bushnell J. (1998). "Water and Power: Hydroelectric Resources in the Era of Competition in the Western US". *POWER Conference on Electricity Restructuring*. University of California Energy Institute, Berkley, CA.

Day C.J., Hobbs B.F. and Pang J.-S. (2002). "Oligopolistic Competition in Power Networks: A Conjectured Supply Function Approach". *IEEE Transactions on Power Systems* **17**(3): 597–607.

Dempster A.P., Laird N.M. and Rubin D.B. (1977). "Maximum Likelihood from Incomplete Data via EM Algorithm". *Journal of the Royal Statistical Society* **39**(1): 1–38.

Espasa A., Revuelta J.M. and Cancelo, J.R. (1996). "Automatic Modelling of Daily Series of Economic Activity". *Compstat 12th Proceedings in Computational Statistics*. Barcelona.

García-Alcalde A., Ventosa M., Rivier M., Ramos A. and Relaño G. (2002). "Fitting Electricity Market Models. A Conjectural Variations Approach". *Proceedings 14th PSCC Conference*. Seville; Session 12–3, pp. 1–8.

García-González J. (2001). "Short-term Operation Optimization and Bidding Elaboration in a Liberalised Electric System. Problem Analysis and Solution Methods". (Optimización de la explotación en el corto plazo y elaboración de ofertas en un sistema eléctrico liberalizado. Naturaleza del problema y métodos de solución.) Ph.D. Thesis.

Gelow M.E. (1993). "Economic Evaluation of Commodity Price Forecasting Models". *International Journal of Forecasting* **9**.

Granger C. (1998). "Forecasting Stock Market Prices: Lesson for Forecasters". *International Journal of Forecasting* **8**.

Hamilton J.D. (1990). "Analysis of Time Series Subject to Change in Regime". *Journal of Econometrics* **45**: 39–70.

Hobbs B.F. (2001). "Linear Complementary Models of Nash–Cournot Competition in Bilateral and POOLCO Power Markets". *IEEE Transactions on Power Systems* **16**(2): 194–202.

Ip W.H. (1995). "Integration of Simulation and Expert System through Intervention Modeling". *Computer Integrated Manufacturing, 3rd International Conference*. Singapore.

Kahn E. (1998). "Introducing Competition to the Electricity Industry in Spain: The Role of Initial Conditions". *Utilities Policy* **7**(1/4): 15–22.

Kauffman L. and Rousseeuw P.J. (1999). *Finding Groups in Data*. John Wiley & Sons, New York.

Lauzon, V.P. (1999). "Modèles Statistiques comme algorithmes d'appentissage et MMCC's. Prédiction de Séries Financières". Départament d'Informatiqué et de recherche opérationelle: Faculeté d'arts et sciences. University of Montreal, Montreal.

Levinson S.E., Rabiner L.R. and Sondhi M.M. (1982). "An Introduction to the Application of the Theory of Probabilistic Functions of a Markov Process to Automatic Speech Recognition". *The Bell System Technical Journal* **62**(4).

Liu L.M. (1996). *Multivariate Time Series Analysis using VARMA Models*. SCA Publications.

Liu L.M. (2001). "Effective Forecasting and Time Series Data Mining". *Course Material*. Madrid, December 13–15.

Liu L.M., Hudak G.B., Box G.E.P., Muller M.E. and Tiao G.C. (1997). *Forecasting and Time Series Analysis using the SCA Statistical System, Vols 1 and 2*, Scientific Computing Associates Corp.

Makridakis S., Wheelwright S.C. and Hyndman R.J. (1998). *Forecasting Methods and Applications*, 3rd edn. John Wiley & Sons, New York.

McLachlan G.J. and Krishnan T. (1997). *The EM Algorithm and Extensions*. John Wiley & Sons, New York.

OMEL (2001). "Electricity Market Activity Rules" (Electricity Market Operator). http://www.omel.es/es/pdfs/EMRules.pdf

Pankratz A. (1991). *Forecasting with Dynamic Regression Models*. John Wiley & Sons, New York.

Rabiner L.R. (1989). "A Tutorial on Hidden Markov Models and Selected Applications in Speech Recognition". *Proceedings of the IEEE* **77**(2): 257–286.

Reneses J., Centeno E. and Barquin J. (1999). "Computation and Decomposition of Marginal Costs for a GENCO in a Constrained Competitive Cournot Equilibrium". *Proceedings of 1999 IEEE International Conference on Electric Power Engineering Power Techniques*. Budapest.

Rivier M., Ventosa M. and Ramos A. (2001). "A Generation Operation Planning Model in Deregulated Electricity Markets based on the Complementarity Problem". In *Applications and Algorithms of Complementarity*, M.C. Ferris, O.L. Mangasarian and J.-S. Pang (eds). Kluwer Academic, Boston; pp. 273–298.

Sánchez-Úbeda E. (1999). "Data Analysis Oriented Models: Contributions to Example Based Knowledge". (Modelos para el análisis de datos: contribuciones al aprendizaje a partir de ejemplos.) Ph.D. Thesis.

Scott T.J. and Read E.G. (1996). "Modelling Hydro Reservoir Operation in a Deregulated Electricity Market". *International Transactions in Operational Research* **3**: 243–253.

Taylor S.J. (1988). "Forecasting Market Prices". *International Journal of Forecasting* **4**.

Titterington D.M., Smith A.F. and Markov U.E. (1985). *Statistical Analysis of Finite Mixture Distributions*. John Wiley & Sons, New York.

Vives X. (1999). *Oligopoly Pricing*. MIT Press, Cambridge, MA.

Wei J.-Y. and Smeers Y. (1999). "Spatial Oligopolistic Electricity Models with Cournot Generators and Regulated Transmission Prices". *Operations Research* **47**(1): 102–112.

Weigend A.S. and Mangeas M. (1995). "Nonlinear Gated Experts for Time Series: Discovering Regimes and Avoiding Overfitting". *International Journal of Neural System* **6**: 373–399.

------- 3 -------

# Complementarity-Based Equilibrium
# Modeling for Electric Power Markets

## BENJAMIN F. HOBBS[1] AND UDI HELMAN[2]

[1] *Department of Geography & Environmental Engineering, Whiting School of Engineering, The Johns Hopkins University, Baltimore, MD 21218, USA*
[2] *Federal Energy Regulatory Commission, Washington, DC 20426, USA*

## ABSTRACT

Complementarity-based power market models represent the constrained optimization problems of electricity generators, consumers, arbitragers and transmitters. These models directly solve a system of conditions that include each player's first-order optimality conditions plus market clearing. We introduce basic complementarity modeling concepts and a general energy model, and then compare alternative specifications of oligopolistic power markets subject to transmission constraints. Computational advances allow equilibria to be obtained for very large problems, such as the North American Eastern Interconnection case study described herein.

## 3.1  INTRODUCTION

Price simulation using computable network equilibrium market models is one promising approach to understanding the complexity of market power in electricity markets.[1] There is a rich literature on small-scale equilibrium analyses of this type. But while the regulated energy sector was a focus of large-scale modeling for many years, only recently has the availability of commercial software that includes efficient, robust algorithms for computation of equilibria allowed for growth in sophisticated large-scale simulation of deregulated national and multinational energy markets. In Europe and North America, modeling of regional electricity markets – using simulation, empirical analysis and types of concentration analysis – has been increasingly important in *ex ante* and *ex post* evaluation of market competitiveness and in resolving disputes over market outcomes.[2]

---

[1] In the USA and some European countries, electricity industry regulators generally have concluded that market power policy is necessary given the high concentration of supply in some markets, the lack of price-responsive (elastic) demand, and the market-narrowing effects of transmission constraints. There are two basic policy approaches: to require structural changes in the market or to impose behavioral restrictions, often called market power "mitigation", on a permanent or transitory basis. If the behavioral approach is chosen, then a great degree of sensitivity is required in implementation to ensure measures that limit prices, such as bid caps in the spot auction markets, are set at levels that allow for both short-term and long-term efficiency. These measures should also be consistent with other elements of the market design, for example, markets of ancillary services such as installed capacity or operating reserves.

[2] Until recently, most *ex ante* market power simulations of regional US markets included little network detail (e.g., Borenstein *et al.*, 2000). Helman (2003) undertakes a simulation of the eastern part of the US electricity grid with a more detailed DC load flow network model, as discussed in Section 3.5. Examples of detailed *ex post* empirical analysis to measure market power in US markets with different market designs include Borenstein *et al.* (2003) and Joskow and Kahn (2002) on the California market, Bushnell and Saravia (2002) on the New England market and PJM (2001) for the Pennsylvania–Maryland–New Jersey interconnection (the PJM reports are available for every year of market operation). Such analyses often compare observed market prices with a competitive (marginal-cost pricing) "benchmark", constructed with the help of simulation models.

---

*Modelling Prices in Competitive Electricity Markets.* Edited by D.W. Bunn.
© 2004 John Wiley & Sons, Ltd. ISBN 0-470-84860-X.

Simulation has the advantage of permitting a more realistic representation of the various types of market participants and their decision variables while accounting for physical generation and transmission constraints that are crucially important in the determination of market prices (e.g., Amundson *et al.*, 2001; Bushnell, 2003; Day *et al.*, 2002; Helman, 2003; Hobbs, 2001; Hobbs *et al.*, 2004; Smeers, 1997; Wei and Smeers, 1999). Further, once basic data are gathered, simulation can be used to study interactions between elements of market design and market power to assess alternative policies. To the extent that regulators and other policy-makers become comfortable with simulation, it can also be incorporated into standard regulatory or market oversight procedures, such as ongoing market power monitoring and merger screening.[3]

The purpose of this chapter is to provide a tutorial on an increasingly popular framework for formulating and solving equilibrium electricity market models: complementarity.[4] Because the first-order optimality conditions for mathematical programs are a special case of complementarity conditions, complementarity is a natural way to cast equilibrium problems among market players whose profit maximization problems are stated as constrained optimization problems. Further, because it is practical to solve very large complementarity problems (having tens or even hundreds of thousands of variables) (Dirkse and Ferris, 1995), much detail concerning generation options, demand variation and transmission constraints can be captured. Finally, there is a rich body of theory that allows one to analyze such models for properties such as solution existence and uniqueness (Cottle *et al.*, 1992). These advantages of complementarity models have motivated applications to a wide variety of engineering and economic problems (Ferris and Pang, 1997). The focus of this chapter is on how this approach can be applied to energy markets, with an emphasis on electric power markets.

Section 3.2 begins the tutorial by defining two building blocks: complementarity and the Karush–Kuhn–Tucker (KKT) conditions for an optimal solution of an optimization problem. The KKT conditions are one particular instance of a complementarity problem. Then in Section 3.3 we present a general complementarity framework for modeling market interactions of supply, demand, transportation and transformation of energy commodities. Both competitive and Cournot market formulations are summarized.

In Section 3.4, we turn to the more specific situation of electricity generators competing on an electric power network. We consider and compare two different formulations of Cournot power market models. In the first, simpler version (Section 3.4.1), generators are assumed to be

---

[3] A common alternative to price simulation for *ex ante* analysis of potential market power is market concentration analysis. Examples are the Herfindahl–Hirschman Index (HHI, equal to the sum of squared market shares) and identification of "pivotal" suppliers who by withdrawing supply could create shortages. The HHI is widely recognized as being only weakly correlated with the actual potential for exercise of market power in electricity markets (e.g., Borenstein *et al.*, 1999; Helman, 2003, compares HHIs to simulated equilibrium market prices). In the United States, the Federal Energy Regulatory Commission has expressed interest in market price simulations as possible alternatives (or complements) to HHI calculation in merger policy; see FERC (1998). Helman (2003) suggests an approach to equilibrium merger analysis using the market models discussed in Sections 3.4.1 and 3.5.

Meanwhile, pivotal supplier methodologies are being developed for use in several regional US markets. For instance, market monitors identify generators in large networks that could exert market power by congesting key transmission elements, such as lines. This is done by determining the amount of their power flowing over particular transmission elements in a simplified load flow model and then determining whether any generators have a pivotal impact on the congestion of that element – that is, a sufficient amount of their power flows over the element that they can congest it through their own actions under certain loadings (e.g., MISO IMM, 2003). The objective in this analysis is not to predict market power by simulating prices but rather to identify generators whose output (and the resulting market prices) should be monitored under certain system conditions. The relationship between this type of analysis and the transmission-constrained price simulations of the type described in Sections 3.4 and 3.5 remains to be examined.

[4] Daxhelet and Smeers (2001) and Day *et al.* (2002) review complementarity applications in electric power modeling. An example of a complementarity model of another energy sector is GASTALE, a model of the EU gas market (Boots *et al.*, 2004). Complementarity is also the basis of PRIMES, the most widely used comprehensive EU energy sector model (Capros *et al.*, 2000), and has also been proposed as a framework for improved integration and solution for NEMS, the US Department of Energy comprehensive energy model (Gabriel *et al.*, 2001).

price-takers with respect to the price of transmission services. This results in an efficient allocation of transmission capacity, in which the marginal valuations of the same transmission
service by different generation companies are equalized (Wei and Smeers, 1999). This simpli-
fication allows for the formulation of the equilibrium as a mixed complementarity problem. As
a result, equilibrium prices and profits are unique and, furthermore, easy to calculate. There is
a price to pay, however: it is necessary to assume that generators are naïve with respect to how
their generation choices will affect transmission congestion and prices.

In the second power market formulation (Section 3.4.2), strategic generators can manipulate transmission prices by actively seeking to congest, or decongest, transmission lines.
Previous studies have found that strategic congestion can increase generator profits in energy
markets (e.g., Cardell *et al.*, 1997; Cunningham *et al.*, 2002). The formulation belongs to a
class of models known as an equilibrium problem with equilibrium constraints (Daxhelet and
Smeers, 2001). This model structure provides more realism but it also limits the size of the
model because the generator models are non-convex and difficult to solve. Furthermore, there
may either be no equilibrium or multiple equilibria in pure strategies, rather than a unique
equilibrium.

In Section 3.4.3, we apply the two formulations to a simple two-node problem to highlight
their theoretical and practical differences. For a duopoly problem, they yield distinctly different
solutions. On the other hand, if only one of the two generators exercises market power, the
equilibria are the same under the particular assumptions made here.

We conclude the chapter by presenting sample results from a large-scale application of the
Cournot complementarity model of Section 3.4.1 to the North American Eastern Interconnection (Section 3.5). That model includes hundreds of transmission constraints and generating
companies, permitting detailed comparison of opportunities to exercise market power in different parts of the eastern USA.

## 3.2  DEFINITIONS

The complementarity problems and KKT conditions defined in this section are the basis of the
market models of Sections 3.3 and 3.4.

### 3.2.1  Complementarity

A *complementarity condition* between a non-negative variable $x_i$ and a function $G_i(x)$ of a
vector of variables $x = \{x_i\}$ can be defined as:

$$x_i \geq 0; \quad G_i(x) \leq 0; \quad x_i G_i(x) = 0$$

This can be written more compactly as:

$$0 \leq x_i \perp G_i(x) \leq 0$$

In general, complementarity conditions can have inequalities in either direction (e.g.,
$G_i(x) \geq 0$). A *complementarity problem* is:

$$CP: \quad \textit{Find } x \textit{ such that}: \quad 0 \leq x \perp G(x) \leq 0$$

where $G(x) = \{G_i(x)\}$ and $0 \leq x \perp G(x) \leq 0$ is read "$x \geq 0; G(x) \leq 0; x^T G(x) = 0$". This
complementarity problem is *square* in that the number of individual conditions equals the

number of variables in $x$. If all the $G_i(x)$ are affine functions, then CP is termed a *linear complementarity problem* (LCP).

More general is the *mixed complementarity problem* (MCP). Let $y$ be a second vector of variables, and $H(x, y)$ be a vector-valued function with the same dimension as $y$. An MCP can be stated as:

$$MCP: \quad Find\ x, y\ such\ that: \quad 0 \le x \perp G(x, y) \le 0\ and\ H(x, y) = 0$$

### 3.2.2   Karush–Kuhn–Tucker conditions

Let a constrained optimization problem be stated as:

$$CO: \underset{\{x\}}{MAX}\ F(x)$$

$$subject\ to\ (s.t.): \quad G(x) \le 0$$
$$x \ge 0$$

where $F(x)$ is an objective function to be maximized.[5] We assume that $F(x)$ is smooth and concave, and each $G_i(x)$ is smooth and convex. These assumptions imply that $CO$'s feasible region $\{x: G(x) \le 0, x \ge 0\}$ is convex and, further, any local optimum of $CO$ is a global optimum.

The KKT conditions are a set of complementarity conditions whose solution $\{x, \lambda\}$ is also a local (and thus global) optimal solution to CO, and *vice versa* (i.e., the KKT equations are necessary and sufficient for optimality under the above assumptions). The KKT conditions for problem $CO$ are:

$$0 \le x_i \perp \partial F / \partial x_i - \Sigma_j \lambda_j \partial G_j / \partial x_i \le 0 \quad \forall i$$
$$0 \le \lambda_j \perp G_j \le 0 \quad \forall j$$

(Note that $F$, $G_j$ and the partial derivatives $\partial G_j / \partial x_i$ are all functions of $x$; here and in the rest of the chapter, we will often omit the arguments of functions for simplicity.) Each element of a vector of dual variables $\lambda = \{\lambda_j\}$ is associated with one constraint $G_j \le 0$ in the KKT conditions.[6]

## 3.3   A GENERAL COMPLEMENTARITY-BASED MODEL OF ENERGY COMMODITY MARKETS

The purpose of this section is to show how complementarity can be used to simulate markets, and to illustrate a model structure that underlies several energy market models. Our general complementarity-based model considers trade in several energy commodities. Figure 3.1 shows the structure of the model: consumers buy the commodity, suppliers provide it, and

---

[5] Note that a more general statement of an optimization problem would allow some constraints $G_j(x) = 0$ while some variables could be unrestricted in sign. However, there is no lack of generality here: an equality constraint can be rephrased as two inequalities $[G_j(x) \le 0$ and $-G_j(x) \le 0]$, while an unrestricted variable $x_i$ can be expressed as the difference between two non-negative variables $x_i^+$ and $x_i^-$ $(x_i = x_i^+ - x_i^-)$.

[6] One interpretation of these conditions is as follows. The condition on $G_j$ says that if the constraint is slack, then the marginal worth of increasing the right-hand side of the constraint $(\lambda_j)$ must be zero. The condition on $x_i$ says that if $x_i$ is positive, then its marginal benefit (in terms of the objective) equals the marginal cost of the constrained resources it uses (the marginal worth of each constraint times the marginal effect of $x_i$ on the amount of the resource used).

The KKT conditions for the more general optimization problem of footnote 5 will also be more general than these. For instance, if $G_j$ is an equality constraint $(G_j = 0)$, then its dual $\lambda_j$ is unrestricted in sign. The KKT condition associated with $G_j$ then just becomes the equality $G_j = 0$. Conversely, if $x_i$ is unrestricted, then its associated net benefit condition is an equality $(\partial F / \partial x_i - \Sigma_j \lambda_j \partial G_j / \partial x_i = 0)$.

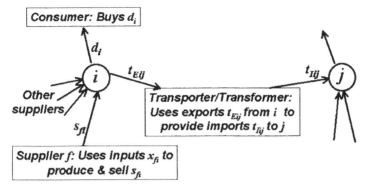

**Figure 3.1** Schematic of model of two commodity markets $i$ and $j$

transporters/transformers convey or convert energy from one market or to another. All energy variables should be expressed in appropriate and compatible units, such as GJ, MBTU or MWh. We assume that only energy commodities are traded, but of course other types of commodities (water, limestone for scrubbers, etc.) could be represented, and would have appropriate units. Section 3.3.1 defines the notation used in the general model. Then the competitive version of the general model is introduced in Section 3.3.2, followed by a Cournot version in Section 3.3.3.

### 3.3.1 Notation

Below we introduce the notation we use in the model, including indices, primal decision variables, dual variables, prices and functions.

Indices

$i,j$ Indices for nodes in the network. The nodes on the network can represent distinct points in space, connected by energy transportation links (pipelines, transmission lines). They can also represent distinct commodities (e.g., oil, natural gas, refined products, electricity), where the links among nodes represent transformations of products (e.g., refining of crude oil to produce oil products, or burning of coal to produce electricity). Consumption in different time periods could also be defined as different nodes $i$. Flows between nodes are referred to as "transformations".

$f$ Index for supply firms.

$I(i)$ The set of nodes $j$ that can receive imports that originate as exports from node $i$. (For example, other locations that are directly linked to $i$ on a transmission grid.) "Imports" and "exports" are interpreted loosely, referring not only to transportation, but also to transformation (e.g., $i$ = natural gas to $j$ = electricity) and storage (e.g., storage of gas from one period to the next).

$E(j)$ The set of nodes $i$ that can supply exports that are transported/transformed into imports to node $j$.

Note that in general we could also index everything by time period $t$ if demand/supply conditions vary over time, and storage is unavailable. If storage is available, then a storage firm could be defined that buys energy in one period and sells it, perhaps net of losses, in another. This is precisely what pumped storage plants do in the UK deregulated electricity system.[7] If the optimization is taking place over multiple years, then the optimizations discussed below would have to discount future benefits and costs using appropriate interest rates.

Decision variables (lowercase Latin letters)

$s_{fi}$  Amount of energy sold by supply firm $f$ at node $i$.

$d_i$  Amount of energy demanded by consumers at node $i$. (One could also have multiple consumers with separate demand functions at node $i$. It is also possible to have $d_i$ be the result of an optimization process in which the consumer chooses $d_i$ as well as other decision variables to maximize profit or net benefit – in a manner analogous to the supply optimization model below.)

$t_{Eij}$  Exported energy: amount of energy demanded at $i$ or removed from $i$ by transformers, which will ultimately be delivered to $j$. (This could be energy exports, e.g., oil, from $i$ which is shipped to another location $j$. Or it could be a transformation process in which energy from $i$, say coal, is transformed into energy at $j$, say electricity. This could also be a storage function, transferring energy from an earlier time $i$ to a later time $j$.) In this model, we assume there is only one company that transforms commodities at $i$ into commodities at $j$, and that this company is by some miracle a price-taker, perhaps because it is subject to regulation. Equivalently, there might be many competitive firms whose aggregate behavior in the market is summarized by this one hypothetical firm. Multiple companies who compete to transport/transform energy from $i$ to $j$ could of course be modeled.

$t_{Iij}$  Imported energy: amount of energy supplied at $j$, or transported to $j$ by transporters/transformers, which originated as an export from $i$. More generally, a single transformer could use inputs from one or more $i$ to produce outputs for one or more $j$ – such as a refinery producing both light and heavy oil products from crude oil.

$x_{fi}$  Other decision variable(s) for supplier $f$ at node $i$. Examples could include capacity, resources, intermediate products and fuels used to produce $s_{fi}$; e.g., variables indicating the capacity of power plants, whether or not sulfur scrubbers are installed, or the amount of natural gas burned at power plants.[8]

Dual variables (Greek letters) and price

$p_i^*$  Price of energy at node $i$ [\$/unit]. Under the pure competition assumptions of Section 3.2, each optimizer (supplier, consumer, transformer) treats $p_i^*$ as fixed (or "exogenous") to its optimization problem. That is, they believe they have no market power. For this reason, we put an asterisk (*) on the variable. However, from the market's point of view, $p_i^*$ will

---

[7] Large pumped storage units can have significant market effects in certain regions. If static market simulations are conducted for a sequence of short time frames – e.g., hours, or daily peaks and off-peaks – the dynamic price effects of pumped storage can be captured roughly by modeling them as demand in the off-peak hours when they are typically pumping and as supply during the peak hours when they are typically releasing (as in Helman, 2003). More rigorously, an explicitly dynamic CP could be defined with separate sets of variables for each period, and appropriate storage variables and constraints linking decisions in different periods (as in Bushnell, 2003).

[8] Fuel inputs can be modeled in this framework in two ways: as an input to a producer model or as an export from the fuel market that is then converted into a different energy form and imported into an energy product market. In the former case, the fuel is represented by $x_{fi}$ in a supplier model with an exogenous cost. In contrast, in the latter case, fuel use is instead given by $t_{Iij}$ in a transformer/transporter model, and the price of fuel is solved for endogenously.

adjust in order to balance supply and demand (satisfy the "market clearing" condition). On the other hand, in a model with market power, price will be "endogenous" to some players' profit maximization problem; i.e., it is a decision variable for them. An example is the Cournot model of Section 3.3.

$\mu_{fi}$    Marginal cost associated with $f$'s supply model constraint at node $i$ [\$/unit of constraint]. (If there is more than one constraint in the supply model, this would instead represent a vector of dual variables.)

$\theta_{ij}$    Marginal cost associated with the constraint for transport/transformer $ij$. (Again, this could be a vector.)

Functions (uppercase letters)

$C_{Sfi}(x_{fi})$    Total cost of using $x_{fi}$ to produce $s_{fi}$ at node $i$. (For example, this might be the cost of building generation capacity for a utility producing electricity $s_{fi}$.) This is assumed to be smooth and convex (so $-C_{Sfi}(x_{fi})$ will be concave, as required in order to ensure that local optima are also global optima).

$C_{Tij}(t_{Eij}, t_{Iij})$    Total cost of transforming export $t_{Eij}$ from $i$ to import $t_{Iij}$ to $j$ – excluding the expense of buying $t_{Eij}$ at $i$. This function could be the cost of building transmission or refining capacity, for instance. Again, smoothness and convexity is assumed.

$B_i(d_i)$    Total benefit to consumer at node $i$ of consuming $d_i$. This is approximated by the integral of the demand curve $P_i(d)$ from $d = 0$ to $d = d_i$; the demand curve can therefore be viewed as the marginal benefit that consumers receive from consuming more of the commodity. $B_i(d_i) - p_i^* d_i$ is therefore the consumer surplus for consumers at $i$. If the demand curve is downward sloping, then $B_i(d_i)$ has the required concavity. We assume that the quantity demanded $d_i$ depends only on $p_i$, and on no other price. However, cross-price elasticities can be considered in this framework, representing, e.g., the fact that the price of natural gas does affect the demand for electricity.

$G_{Sfi}(x_{fi}, s_{fi})$    Constraint set for supplier $f$ at node $i$. This may represent one or several inequalities. As an example of this type of constraint, for a power producer, generation at a given power plant cannot exceed its capacity ($s_{fi} - x_{fi} \leq 0$), or fuel use equals sales times heat rate ($HR_{fi}s_{fi} - x_{fi} = 0$). This function is assumed to be smooth and convex.

$G_{Tij}(t_{Eij}, t_{Iij})$    Constraint set for transporter/transformer $ij$. This may be a single inequality, or a set. An example could be a power line with a fixed loss rate $L_{ij}$: $t_{Iij} - (1 - L_{ij})t_{Eij}$. Or, for a refinery, this might represent a very complicated set of constraints describing the options available to produce gasoline $t_{Iij}$ from crude oil $t_{Eij}$. Again, smoothness and convexity are assumed.

### 3.3.2  The competitive market model

The basic conditions for a pure competition market equilibrium are that:

1. all players – suppliers, consumers, transporters/transformers – make their decisions subject to the perhaps naïve belief that they cannot affect prices, and
2. markets clear, i.e., supply equals demand at each node, net of imports and exports.

Below are listed optimization models for the players and their KKT conditions, along with market clearing conditions. An MCP that implements these conditions can be built by first defining an optimization problem for each player, then obtaining the KKT conditions for each problem, and finally bringing all those conditions together with the market clearing conditions.

**Supplier $f$ at $i$:** Its optimization problem is to maximize its revenue from selling power at $i$ minus its cost, given the price which it (naïvely) believes is fixed:

$$SUPPL_{Comp,fi}(p_i^*): \underset{\{s_{fi}, x_{fi}\}}{\text{MAX}} \ p_i^* s_{fi} - C_{Sfi}(x_{fi})$$

$$\text{s.t. } G_{Sfi}(s_{fi}, x_{fi}) \leq 0 \text{ (dual variable } \mu_{fi})$$

$$x_{fi}, s_{fi} \geq 0$$

Under the concavity/convexity and smoothness assumptions we made above, the following KKT conditions will define an optimal solution to this problem:

For $s_{fi}$:    $0 \leq s_{fi} \perp (p_i^* - \mu_{fi} \partial G_{Sfi}/\partial s_{fi}) \leq 0$

For $x_{fi}$:    $0 \leq x_{fi} \perp (-\partial C_{Sfi}/\partial x_{fi} - \mu_{fi} \partial G_{Sfi}/\partial x_i) \leq 0$

For $\mu_{fi}$:    $0 \leq \mu_{fi} \perp G_{Sfi} \leq 0$

**Consumer at $i$:** In its optimization, it strives to maximize the value it receives from consumption minus what it pays for that consumption, assuming it cannot affect the price:

$$CONS_i(p_i^*): \underset{\{d_i\}}{\text{MAX}} \ B_i(d_i) - p_i^* d_i$$

$$\text{s.t. } d_i \geq 0$$

The associated KKT is:

For $d_i$:    $0 \leq d_i \perp (P_i(d_i) - p_i^*) \leq 0$

Remember that $P_i(d_i)$ is both the demand function and the first derivative of $B_i(d_i)$.

**Transporter/transformer for nodes $i$, $j$:** Its optimization problem is formulated as:

$$TRANS_{ij}(p_j^*, p_i^*): \underset{\{t_{Eij}, t_{Iij}\}}{\text{MAX}} \ p_j^* t_{Iij} - p_i^* t_{Eij} - C_{Tij}(t_{Eij}, t_{Iij})$$

$$\text{s.t. } G_{Tij}(t_{Eij}, t_{Iij}) \leq 0 \text{ (dual variable } \theta_{ij})$$

$$t_{Eij}, t_{Iij} \geq 0$$

Its KKTs become:

For $t_{Eij}$:    $0 \leq t_{Eij} \perp (-p_i^* - \partial C_{Tij}/\partial t_{Eij} - \theta_{ij} \partial G_{Tij}/\partial t_{Eij}) \leq 0$

For $t_{Iij}$:    $0 \leq t_{Iij} \perp (+p_j^* - \partial C_{Tij}/\partial t_{Iij} - \theta_{ij} \partial G_{Tij}/\partial t_{Iij}) \leq 0$

For $\theta_{ij}$:    $0 \leq \theta_{ij} \perp G_{Tij} \leq 0$

**Market clearing:** The mass balance at each $i$ is:

$$d_i - \sum_f s_{fi} - \sum_{j \in I(i)} t_{Iji} + \sum_{j \in E(i)} t_{Eij} = 0$$

If we gather together the KKT conditions for problems $SUPPL_{Comp,fi}(p_i^*)$ for all $fi$, $CONS_i(p_i^*)$

for all $i$, and $TRANS_{ij}(p_j^*, p_i^*)$ for all $i$ and all $j \in I(i)$, and then add the market clearing condition to the pile, we will have a square MCP. That is, there will be one condition for each primal, price, and dual variable $\{d_i, s_{fi}, x_{fi}, t_{Eij}, t_{Iij}, p_i^*, \mu_{fi}, \theta_{ij}\}$. Under the smoothness and convexity/concavity assumptions made above, this MCP can be solved for the equilibrium values of those variables.[9]

### 3.3.3   The Cournot market model

The above model can be modified to represent a *Cournot game* ("game in quantities") among commodity suppliers. In this game, rather than taking the market price $p_i^*$ as exogenous, a supplier can exercise market power and alter the price by changing the amount it sells. In a Cournot game, the supplier $f$ is modeled as if it (1) correctly anticipates the reactions of consumers to changes in price but (2) expects that other suppliers (and the transformers) will not alter their sales in reaction to $f$'s sales decisions.[10] To do this, we substitute the consumer's demand function for the exogenous price in the supplier's objective, resulting in the following profit maximization problem:

$$SUPPL_{Cournot, fi}: \quad \underset{\{s_{fi}, x_{fi}\}}{\text{MAX}} \quad P_i \left( \sum_g s_{gi} + \sum_{j \in I(i)} t_{Iji} - \sum_{j \in E(i)} t_{Eij} \right) s_{fi} - C_{Sfi}(x_{fi})$$

$$\text{s.t. } G_{Sfi}(s_{fi}, x_{fi}) \leq 0 \text{ (dual variable } \mu_i)$$

$$x_{fi}, s_{fi} \geq 0$$

Notice that instead of $d_i$ in the demand function, we instead show total supply to the market (net of imports/exports), which equals $d_i$ due to the market clearing condition. Notice too that quantities controlled by others (including $s_{gi}$ for $g \neq f$, $t_{Iji}$ and $t_{Eij}$) are *not* decision variables in this problem. Instead, they are exogenous to $f$, consistent with the Cournot assumption.

The KKTs for model $SUPPL_{Cournot, fi}$ are the same for model $SUPPL_{Comp, fi}(p_i^*)$, except for $s_{fi}$'s condition, which becomes:

$$\text{For } s_{fi}: \quad 0 \leq s_{fi} \perp [(P_i + s_{fi} \partial P_i / \partial s_{fi}) - \mu_{fi} \partial G_{Sfi} / \partial s_{fi}] \leq 0$$

The Cournot supplier's marginal revenue $P_i + s_{fi} \partial P_i / \partial s_{fi}$ has been substituted for the exogenous price $p_i^*$. For $s_{fi} > 0$, marginal revenue is less than price (since the partial price term is negative); this provides an incentive for the supplier to reduce sales. In the classic Cournot oligopoly, total equilibrium supply is less than in the competitive model, and prices are higher. (However, when there are multiple markets with transmission constraints, prices can actually

---

[9] It is also sometimes possible to solve complementarity problems by formulating and solving a single optimization model whose KKTs are identical to the original CP. This allows one to apply standard nonlinear or quadratic programming software instead of specialized complementarity algorithms. In the case of the competitive model of this section, an equivalent optimization model would have an objective equal to the familiar welfare measure of consumer plus producer surplus (equal to consumer benefits minus all resource costs):

$$WO_{comp}: \quad \underset{\{d_i, s_{fi}, x_{fi}, t_{Eij}, t_{Iij}\}}{\text{MAX}} \quad \sum_i B_i(d_i) - \sum_{fi} C_{Sfi}(x_{fi}) - \sum_{ij} C_{Tij}(t_{Eij}, t_{Iij})$$

plus the constraints $G_{Sfi}(s_{fi}, x_i) \leq 0, \forall f, i; G_{Tij}(t_{Eij}, t_{Iij}) \leq 0, \forall i, j \in I(i); d_i - \sum_f s_{fi} - \sum_{j \in I(i)} t_{Iji} + \sum_{j \in E(i)} t_{Eij} = 0, \forall i$; and non-negativity for the decision variables. Its KKTs are the same as the KKTs for the individual supplier, consumer and transformer problems, plus the market clearing condition. The dual variable for the market clearing condition will be the price $p_i^*$.

[10] The Cournot game is a classic economic representation of strategic interaction between two or more firms and has been widely used to simulate electricity markets. In a modern game theoretic framework, the mathematical properties of this game have been researched extensively. For overviews of the Cournot and other games, see Tirole (1988) and Vives (1999).

decrease in some markets; see Section 3.5, *infra*.) The Cournot equilibrium is calculated in the same way as the competitive model, except that this new KKT condition for $s_{fi}$ is used rather than the competitive one.[11]

## 3.4  A COMPARISON OF TWO APPROACHES TO MODELING COURNOT GENERATORS ON A TRANSMISSION NETWORK

In this section, we apply some of the above principles of the complementarity approach to the modeling of power markets. We start by summarizing a complementarity-based model of network-constrained power markets in which generation firms have market power but do not consciously manipulate transmission prices. We then contrast it to a more realistic, but computationally more challenging model in which generators do anticipate how the price of transmission would be affected by their decisions. Each approach has advantages and disadvantages, which we will explore with the help of a small example.

In these models, we assume a somewhat different network arrangement than the general modeling approach of the previous section. We assume that individual firms can generate and sell power in several markets $i$ simultaneously, representing different locations on a network, and that they can pay a transmission system operator (TSO) to convey power from the generators to the consumers. The TSO also acts as a PJM-style POOLCO or Nord Pool-style market splitter, in that it can also purchase power at locations with excess supply and sell it where there is a deficit. In a sense, such a TSO is an arbitrager in addition to a provider of transmission services. This is how the northeastern US TSOs work: generators have the choice of selling power bilaterally to customers, or can sell their power to the TSO in day-ahead or real-time auctions.[12]

Another assumption is that power flows on the TSO's network can be adequately approximated by a linearized "DC" load flow, in which linear equations constrain those flows to conform to the "DC" versions of Kirchhoff's current and voltage laws (Schweppe *et al.*, 1988). The DC model is an increasingly common representation of transmission flows in power market models (see the survey in Day *et al.*, 2002).

### 3.4.1  MCP power market model: generators Cournot in sales, Bertrand in transmission

This model is similar in many ways to those proposed by Smeers and Wei (1997) and Hobbs (2001).

---

[11] If the demand functions are affine ($\partial P_i / \partial s_{fi}$ is constant), then a nonlinear optimization problem can be used to solve for the Cournot equilibrium. The problem has the same constraints as the nonlinear program of footnote 9, but the objective is altered to:

$$WO_{Cournot}: \quad \max_{\{d_i, s_{fi}, x_{fi}, t_{Eij}, t_{Iij}\}} \sum_i B_i(d_i) + \sum_{fi} (s_{fi}^2/2) \partial P_i / \partial s_{fi} - \sum_{fi} C_{Sfi}(x_{fi}) - \sum_{ij} C_{Tij}(t_{Eij}, t_{Iij})$$

After some algebra, the KKTs of this problem can be shown to be equivalent to the Cournot complementarity problem just posed. The second summation, when differentiated, adjusts price (the derivative of the first summation) so that it equals the Cournot supplier's marginal revenue (Hashimoto, 1985).

[12] The arbitrage function can also be performed by marketers or other entities who are distinct from the TSO. See Hobbs (2001) and Metzler *et al.* (2003) for models based on that assumption. However, if arbitrage is perfect, whether the TSO or other parties perform the arbitrage will not affect the price equilibrium.

### 3.4.1.1    MCP generating company model

The Cournot generating company's optimization problem is given below. The variables $s_{fi}$ and $x_{fi}$ represent the firm's power sales and generation, each in MW:

$$GEN_{MCP,f}\left(w_i^*, a_i + \sum_{g \neq f} s_{gi}, \forall i\right):$$

$$\underset{\{s_{fi}, x_{fi}\}}{\text{MAX}} \sum_i P_i\left(a_i + \sum_g s_{gi}\right) s_{fi} - \sum_i C_{Sfi}(x_{fi}) - \sum_i w_i^*(s_{fi} - x_{fi})$$

$$\text{s.t.}\quad G_{Sfi}(x_{fi}) \leq 0 \quad \forall i$$

$$\sum_i (s_{fi} - x_{fi}) = 0$$

$$x_{fi}, s_{fi} \geq 0 \quad \forall i$$

The new notation is:

$a_i$  The MW flow from the hub node into $i$ provided by the TSO performing an arbitrage function. This flow can be negative (in which case the arbitrager moves power from $i$ to the hub). Consistent with the Cournot assumption, these TSO sales, like sales by rival firms $\sum_{g \neq f} s_{gi}$, are treated as exogenous by $f$. An important feature of the DC load flow model is that its linear form means that the principle of superposition applies, so it is unnecessary to have separate $a_{ij}$ variables for every possible pair of nodes $i, j$. This is because that principle implies $a_{ij} = 100$ MW would have the same impact on flows in the network as the pair of arbitrage transactions $\{a_i = -100$ MW, $a_j = +100$ MW$\}$. Consequently, all arbitrage can be modeled as occurring through an arbitrary hub node.

$w_i^*$  The price charged by the TSO for transporting power from a hub node to $i$ (i.e., for allowing 1 MW to be injected at the hub and withdrawn at $i$). Its negative $(-w_i^*)$ is charged for reverse transactions (1 MW injected at $i$ and withdrawn at the hub). This pricing model is based on the notion of congestion pricing, in which flows that lessen congestion are paid the shadow prices on the constraints that they ease, while flows that aggravate congestion do the opposite (Schweppe *et al.*, 1988). Again, the principle of superposition means that a power transaction between two nodes $i$ and $j$ can be modeled as a pair of transactions between each of those nodes and an arbitrary hub. Consequently, transmission prices are only needed between the hub and other nodes, and not between all possible pairs of nodes.

We note four differences between this and the general Cournot model of Section 3.3. First, the firm can generate and sell at all nodes. Second, the import and export variables have been simplified to a single variable $a_i$ representing the MW flow into $i$ provided by arbitrage.

Third, any surplus in the firm's production ($x_{fi} - s_{fi} > 0$) at a node can be transported to a so-called "hub node", from where it can then be retransmitted to other nodes where the firm has a deficit ($x_{fi} - s_{fi} < 0$). The price of bringing power from the hub to $i$ is $w_i^*$. The model is called "Bertrand" in transmission because the generator is modeled as being a price-taker with respect to transmission prices $w_i^*$. However, those prices are endogenous to the market model as a whole, which is why that price is shown in lowercase; the asterisk indicates that the supplier (naïvely) views it as exogenous to its own optimization problem.

Fourth, the constraint set $G_{Sfi}(s_{fi}, x_{fi}) \leq 0$ has been broken into two parts: a set of constraints on generation $G_{Sfi}(x_{fi}) \leq 0$ (e.g., capacity, ramp rates, fuel use), and a sales balance that forces the net amount transported to the hub to be zero ($\sum_i (s_{fi} - x_{fi}) = 0$).

## 3.4.1.2  Consumer model

This model is the same as $CONS_i(p_i^*)$, the consumer model in the general model of Section 3.3.

## 3.4.1.3  Transmission provider model

Turning to the TSO, we assume that it operates the network as a disinterested, but efficient entity. For example, it might be a non-profit firm that operates but does not own network or generation assets (similar to the Independent System Operator concept in the United States), or an incentive-regulated firm that owns and operates the network but does not own generation (often called a "Transco"). Its objective is to determine the maximum transmission capacity that can be scheduled and to allocate that capacity to maximize the value that the market receives from those assets. We represent this behavior here by modeling the TSO as a price-taker.

The TSO's model has two categories of variables: accounting variables for services it provides, and physical power flows on the network. There are, in turn, two types of accounting variables. One is the transmission service it sells to power suppliers: in particular, $y_i$ is the MW of transmission from the hub to each $i$ (i.e., the injection of $y_i$ MW at the hub and the withdrawal of an equal amount at $i$). Once again, the linearized DC load flow model and the principle of superposition means that all transmission services can be represented as being routed through an arbitrary hub. The second type of accounting variable is the TSO's purchase of power in one location and resale of it in another, which can be viewed as spatial arbitrage. Such power movements are represented by the arbitrage variables $a_i$. The other category of variables controlled by the ISO represents physical MW flows $t_{ij}$ on transmission lines that directly connect nodes $i$ and $j$. Constraints in the TSO model ensure that the accounting variables are consistent with these physical flows.

The TSO's model is a version of the transformer/transporter's model modified to reflect the above assumptions and allowing it to operate at all nodes $i$.[13]

$$TSO(p_i^*, w_i^*): \quad \underset{\{a_i, y_i, t_{ij}\}}{\text{MAX}} \sum_i p_i^* a_i + \sum_i w_i^* y_i$$

$$\text{s.t.} \quad \sum_i a_i = 0$$

$$a_i + y_i + \sum_{j \in J(i)} (t_{ij} - t_{ji}) = 0 \quad \forall i$$

$$\sum_{ij \in IJ(v)} R_{ij}(t_{ij} - t_{ji}) \quad \forall v \in V$$

$$t_{ij} - t_{ji} \leq T_{ij} \quad \forall ij$$

$$t_{ij} \geq 0 \, \forall ij$$

---

[13] An alternative but equivalent formulation for the MCP model would instead combine the TSO and consumer equilibrium models as follows. The TSO chooses the values of $\{d_i, a_i, y_i, t_{ij}\}$ that maximize the net benefits of demand plus the value of bilateral transmission services, subject to the fixed quantities (sales and generation) provided by generators. That is, the TSO maximizes $\sum_i B_i(d_i) + \sum_i w_i^* y_i$. The constraint set includes the constraints of the TSO model in the text, plus the energy market clearing constraint set $a_i + \sum_f g_{fi} - d_i = 0$, $\forall i$. A separate consumer model is then no longer necessary, nor is a separate statement of the clearing condition. This alternative model can be viewed as a restricted POOLCO who is choosing which demand-side bids to accept, given the transmission constraints and fixed values of generator sales and output. Basically, the POOLCO adjusts demand and its arbitrage variables so that the transmission constraints are met and consumer welfare is maximized. (This is also equivalent to the more general POOLCO model in which the POOLCO maximizes the benefits of demand-side bids minus the cost of generator bids, where it is assumed that the generator bids a large negative value for generation it wants dispatched and a large positive value for generation it prefers not to supply.)

The new (or revised) notation is as follows:

$v$   Index associated with a loop in the transmission network.

$J(i)$   The set of nodes $j$ directly connected to node $i$ by a transmission link.

$IJ(v)$   The ordered set of transmission links $ij$ on voltage loop $v$ in the linearized DC load flow approximation. The links are ordered so that the nodes on the loop are encountered in clockwise (or counterclockwise) order. For instance, if loop $v = 7$ connects nodes 1, 2 and 3 in the following order 1–2–3–1, then $IJ(7) = \{12, 23, 31\}$.

$V$   The set of independent voltage loops in the network used in the linearized DC load flow approximation. In a network with $I$ nodes and $N$ transmission links, there are $N - I + 1$ of these loops.[14]

$t_{ij}$   The positive component of the MW flow on the transmission link from $i$ to $j$. Thus, $(t_{ij} - t_{ji})$ is the net flow from $i$ to $j$, and can be negative.

$R_{ij}$   The reactance (inductance minus capacitance) of the transmission line from $i$ to $j$. In a true DC circuit, current $\times$ resistance = voltage drop from one end of a conductor to another; the analogy in the linearized DC load flow approximation is that the change in the AC voltage angle between two buses is proportional to the product of reactance (assumed to be much larger than resistance) and power flow between the two buses.

$T_{ij}$   The MW capacity of the link from $i$ to $j$. In this congestion pricing model, only when transmission capacity is binding can the transmission prices $w_i^*$ be non-zero.

The TSO model differs from the simpler transporter/transformer model of Section 3.3.2 in several important ways:

1. The TSO imports to and exports from all nodes in the network.
2. The TSO buys and sells at different nodes $(a_i)$ based on the local nodal prices $p_i^*$, and also provides transmission services $(y_i)$, receiving price $w_i^*$ for their provision.
3. Flows among nodes are constrained by the linearized DC versions of Kirchhoff's laws. The second set of constraints is the analogue to Kirchhoff's current law (mass balance), while the third set is the analogue to the voltage law. (See footnote 14, *supra*.)
4. Variables $t_{Eij}$, $t_{Iij}$ have been replaced by a single net flow variable $t_{ij} - t_{ji}$.[15]

### 3.4.1.4   Market clearing conditions

These include the following two sets of conditions:

$$d_i - a_i - \sum_f s_{fi} = 0 \quad \forall i$$

$$y_i - \sum_f (s_{fi} - x_{fi}) = 0 \quad \forall i$$

The first market clearing condition is for energy at each node $i$: quantity demanded equals sales

---

[14] A linearized DC load flow model defines a unique set of flows on $N$ transmission lines, given injections at the $I$ nodes, by defining $N$ independent equations (Schweppe *et al.*, 1988). The equations are as follows: (1) $I - 1$ Kirchhoff's current law equations (nodal energy balances), which is the second set of constraints in the TSO model (excluding $i = HUB$); and (2) $N - I + 1$ independent Kirchhoff's voltage law equations, in which the net voltage drop around a loop $v$ is set equal to zero (the TSO's third set of constraints). As an example, consider a network with $I = 4$ nodes, and $N = 4$ links connecting nodes 1 with 2, 1 with 3, 2 with 3, and 3 with 4. If the hub node is, say, node 3, then three nodal energy balances (for nodes 1, 2 and 4) and one voltage loop ($IJ(1) = \{12, 23, 31\}$) comprise the necessary set of equations.

[15] However, if resistance losses are represented on the network, then the amount exported from one node can differ from the amount imported at the other end of the line. Quadratic resistance losses can be modeled in more complicated versions of the DC load flow model (Schweppe *et al.*, 1988).

by the TSO/arbitrager and suppliers. The second market clearing condition is for transmission services: the total quantity to be delivered on behalf of suppliers from the hub to $i$ equals the transmission services provided by the TSO.

### 3.4.1.5  Solution properties

A market equilibrium is obtained by deriving the KKT conditions for problems $GEN_{MCP,f}(\cdot)$, $CONS_i(\cdot)$ and $TSO(\cdot)$, adding the market clearing conditions, and then solving for the primal variables $\{a_i, d_i, s_{fi}, x_{fi}, t_{ij}, y_i\}$, prices $\{p_i^*, w_i^*\}$ and dual variables for all constraints. In addition to numerical results for particular sets of assumptions, general properties for the market model can be derived. One important general property is that with the TSO acting, in effect, as a price-taking arbitrager, the equilibrium price of transmission services will be based on the locational marginal pricing model of Schweppe *et al.* (1988) and Hogan (1992). That is, the price of transmission from $i$ to $j$ (i.e., from $i$ to the hub, and then the hub to $j$) equals the price difference between the nodes:

$$-w_i^* + w_j^* = -(p_i^* - p_{HUB}^*) + (p_j^* - p_{HUB}^*) = p_j^* - p_i^*$$

Furthermore, if $G_{Sfi}(x_{fi})$ consists merely of generation capacity limits and linear relationships between generation and sales and $C_{Sfi}(x_{fi})$ is a piecewise linear convex function, then under very mild conditions, it can be shown that an equilibrium exists and has unique prices, consumption $d_i$ and profits for each $f$ (Metzler *et al.*, 2003). It can also be demonstrated that a much-reduced version of this model can be derived in which generators sell power just to the TSO/arbitrager (i.e., a POOLCO). The reduced model dispenses with the sales variables $s_{fi}$ and transmission service variables $y_i$, and yet yields the same prices, consumption and profits (Metzler *et al.*, 2003). It is this model for which we present some results for the Eastern Interconnection of North America in Section 3.5, *infra*.

### 3.4.2  EPEC power market model: generators Cournot in sales, Stackelberg in transmission

A justifiable criticism of the MCP model proposed above is that it assumes that generators are strategic (Cournot) with regard to other firms' sales, but are naïve (price-taking) with respect to transmission prices. Other more sophisticated models have been proposed in which a generating firm correctly anticipates how the TSO will adjust transmission prices and its arbitrage in response to changes in the firm's outputs. Such models represent *Stackelberg* games between generators (Stackelberg leaders) and the TSO (a Stackelberg follower). For instance, in a two-node market with a single generator at each node, a clever firm at node 2 will realize that if it expands its output, at some point it will congest the line in the direction 2 to 1. Further expansion beyond that point will result in no further exports to 1, no further change in $p_1^*$ and accelerated decreases in $p_2^*$, which will precisely equal the increases in the price of transmission from 2 to 1 $(-w_2^* + w_1^* = p_1^* - p_2^*)$. On the other hand, if the firm at 2 decreases output enough, eventually the line will become congested in the other direction, which will result in a different set of price responses. In contrast, the MCP model of Section 3.4.1 instead has firm 2 anticipating (incorrectly) that changes in its output would leave the price of transmission unaffected.

The more sophisticated model of this section has the following structure: each generating firm maximizes its profit subject to (1) the sales of the other suppliers and (2) the response of the TSO and consumers, represented by the market clearing conditions together with the

KKT conditions of problems $TSO(\cdot)$ and $CONS_i(\cdot)$. The generator "sees" the hard transmission constraints, knows how the TSO will react to them, and can take advantage of congesting or decongesting them. Unfortunately, the generator's problem becomes an MPEC: a *mathematical program with equilibrium constraints* (Luo *et al.*, 1996). The constraint set defines a non-convex feasible region, creating the possibility of local optima for the supplier's problem that are not globally optimal. Consequently, it is not possible to define KKT conditions that will necessarily yield the generator's profit-maximizing solution. Unlike the MCP model, nothing in general can be said about the existence or uniqueness of an equilibrium among generators with MPEC profit maximization problems. The problem of finding such an equilibrium is called an EPEC (*equilibrium program with equilibrium constraints*). In addition to the inability to establish analytical conclusions about the nature of an EPEC solution, EPECs are also much more difficult to solve numerically than MCPs.

Below we outline the formulation of an EPEC that allows generators to anticipate transmission price changes for the type of market considered in the MCP model above.[16] This EPEC can readily be extended so that large generators also anticipate the response of a competitive "fringe" of small suppliers to changes in price.[17] In Section 3.4.3, we apply both the below EPEC and the MCP of Section 3.4.1 to the same simple example, and compare the solutions.

The MPEC describing supplier $f$'s profit maximization problem is as follows:

$$SUPPL_{MPEC,f}(s_{gi}^*, x_{gi}^*, \forall g \neq f, \forall i):$$

$$\underset{\{s_{fi}, x_{fi}, t_{ij}, a_i, y_i, p_i, w_i, \lambda\}}{\text{MAX}} \sum_i P_i(d_i) s_{fi} - \sum_i C_{Sfi}(x_{fi}) - \sum_i w_i(s_{fi} - x_{fi})$$

s.t.: (1) *Generator's internal constraints:*

$$G_{Sfi}(x_{fi}) \leq 0 \quad \forall i$$

$$\sum_i (s_{fi} - x_{fi}) = 0$$

$$x_{fi}, s_{fi} \geq 0 \quad \forall i$$

---

[16] There are several models that adopt this EPEC structure, or something closely related to it. Two models that considered transmission networks of moderate size (dozens of nodes) are Cardell *et al.* (1997) and Hobbs *et al.* (2000). The Cardell *et al.* (1997) model is a Cournot model in which generation amounts are the strategic variables, and each generator's MPEC accounts for how the RTO prices transmission. The Hobbs *et al.* (2000) model instead defines the generator's strategic variables as supply bids from its power plants submitted to a POOLCO. Ralph *et al.* (2002) analyze the properties of the solution of the latter model in some detail. London Economics (2002) is also a supply bid-type model with much more detail on generation, but a much simpler transmission grid. Simple 2–4 node models have been analyzed extensively for Cournot producers (Borenstein *et al.*, 2000; Oren, 1997; Stoft, 1999), and also for suppliers who are instead playing a game in supply functions (Berry *et al.*, 1999).

Smeers and Daxhelet (2002) describe an EPEC for a different problem: that of utility regulators from different countries (Stackelberg leaders) who can redistribute fixed costs among generators and consumers, and who attempt to do this in a way that maximizes their country's net benefits from the electricity market. In each regulator's model, equilibrium constraints represent the response of the electricity market (so the market is a Stackelberg follower). Meanwhile, each of the regulators assume that the other regulators' decisions won't change (Nash game among regulators).

[17] This extension addresses another criticism of our model: that suppliers are Cournot players with respect to all other suppliers. In reality, there may be a competitive fringe of smaller suppliers whose reaction to price is predictable by the larger suppliers. The large suppliers could then net out the fringe's supply from demand in their model, rendering the effective demand more elastic. Thus, there is a Stackelberg game between leaders (large suppliers) and followers (the fringe). However, since the fringe's exact response (a step function) would be represented by the fringe's KKT conditions, modeling that response would also convert the larger generator's problem into MPEC. Then the equilibrium problem for several large suppliers would become an EPEC.

An alternative approach is to approximate the large suppliers' anticipation of the fringe's response using a smooth supply function. This reduces the MPEC to a convex optimization problem, which in turn simplifies the EPEC to a CP. This is the approach taken by Day *et al.* (2002), in which each supplier can have a conjecture about the response of the rest of the suppliers to price changes. This conjecture can be modeled either as a fixed slope for the rest-of-market supply, or a fixed intercept. However, in the Day *et al.* model, the actual response of the rest of the market is governed, as it should be, by profit-maximizing decisions by the other generators. In other words, large generators might anticipate a smooth response by the fringe or their larger rivals to price, but the model allows the actual response to be non-smooth (e.g., step functions if fringe generators have constant marginal costs and fixed capacity).

(2) *Optimal solution to consumers' problem $CONS_i(\cdot)$:*

$$0 \le d_i \perp (P_i(d_i) - p_i) \le 0 \quad \forall i$$

(3) *Optimal solution of problem $TSO(p_i^*, w_i^*)$, defined by its KKT conditions*
(4) *Market clearing conditions:*

$$d_i - a_i - \sum_f s_{fi} = 0 \quad \forall i$$

$$y_i - \sum_f (s_{fi} - x_{fi}) = 0 \quad \forall i$$

The new symbol is $\lambda$, which is the vector of dual variables to the TSO's optimization problem.

There are several things worth noting about this problem. As mentioned, the feasible region is non-convex, because of the complementarity nature of the KKT conditions for the consumers' problems (shown) and the TSO's problem (not shown). Also, with important exceptions, *all* the market's primal decision variables and prices are now decision variables in the generating firm's model, not just its own sales and generation. Thus, we have removed the asterisk that designates exogeneity from the prices. The exceptions are the sales and generation from rival firms $g \ne f$; consistent with the Cournot oligopoly assumption, firm $f$ treats those as fixed in its optimization problem. To highlight this assumption, we add asterisks to rivals' generation and sales in the above problem.

We can then define an equilibrium solution as occurring when each and every generating firm's problem yields the same value of all the variables. In that case, firm 1's optimal sales response to firm 2's sales decisions are the same sales that firm 2 assumed when it optimized its response. For very simple cases (e.g., the three-node model in Oren, 1997), $SUPPL_{MPEC,f}(\cdot)$ can be reduced in size to the point that equilibrium solutions can be analytically identified. For situations in which there are two or three firms and only one strategic variable for each (e.g., total output), reaction functions can be calculated and plotted that show each firm's optimal response to the decisions of the other firms (e.g., Cunningham *et al.*, 2002). If the reaction functions intersect, then there is a solution. If they do not (as in Cunningham *et al.*, 2002), then no pure strategy equilibrium exists, although Nash's theorem guarantees existence of a mixed strategy equilibrium under certain circumstances.[18]

### 3.4.3  A simple numerical example

Figure 3.2 shows the example that we will use to compare the results of the MCP and EPEC models. Although this example is extremely simple, it highlights the differences in results and computational difficulty of these two approaches to representing transmission constraints in strategic market models.

The example has two markets ($i = 1, 2$), each having one power plant along with consumers with a linear demand curve. The hub node is arbitrarily assigned to $i = 1$. There are two generating firms ($f = A, B$), with A owning the plant at $i = 1$ and B owning the plant at $i = 2$. As a result of the technological innovations motivated by liberalization of the power sector, each plant has zero marginal cost and no capacity limit. A transmission line with 50 MW capacity connects the two markets.

---

[18] A mixed strategy for a firm is its choice of a set of probabilities that it will use to choose randomly from among possible values of its strategic variables.

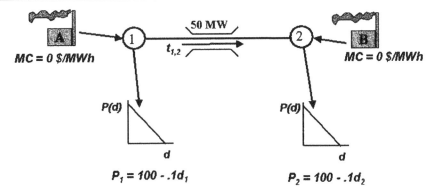

**Figure 3.2**   A two-node example

### 3.4.3.1   EPEC model formulation and results

We present the models in reverse order, with the EPEC first. There are two separate problems $SUPPL_{MPEC,f}(\cdot)$ that comprise the EPEC model, one for each supplier. Using several of the equality conditions in constraint sets (2)–(4) of $SUPPL_{MPEC,f}(\cdot)$, we are able to eliminate some of the variables, resulting in much simpler models.[19] For firm A:

$$SUPPL_{MPEC,A}(s^*_{B1}, s^*_{B2}): \underset{\{d_1,d_2,s_{A1},s_{A2},t_{12'},\lambda_{12},\lambda_{21}\}}{\text{MAX}} P_1(d_1)s_{A1} + P_2(d_2)s_{A2} - [P_2(d_2) - P_1(d_1)]s_{A2}$$

subject to: (1) *Generator's internal constraints:*

$$s_{A1}, s_{A2} \geq 0$$

(3) *Optimality of reduced problem* $TSO_{EPEC}(\cdot)$:

$$\underset{\{t_{12'}\}}{\text{MAX}}[P_2(d_2) - P_1(d_1)]t_{12'}$$
$$\text{s.t.: } t_{12'} \leq 50 \text{ (dual variable } \lambda_{12})$$
$$-t_{12'} \leq 50 \text{ (dual variable } \lambda_{21})$$

(4) *Market clearing conditions:*

$$-t_{12'} + s_{A1} + s_{A2} - d_1 = 0$$
$$t_{12'} + s^*_{B1} + s^*_{B2} - d_2 = 0$$

where $P_i(d_i) = 100 - 0.1 \, d_i$ (Figure 3.2). Notice that A's problem is conditioned on B's sales. Firm A's objective is to maximize revenue from sales minus the cost of transmitting power from 1 to 2 (equal to the price difference times its sales at 2). When actually solving this problem, the TSO's KKT conditions replace its optimization problem in constraint set (3)

---

[19] First, the transmission services price $w_i$ can be eliminated as in equilibrium $w_1 = 0$ (as node 1 is the hub) and $w_2 = p_2 - p_1$. Then, assuming that the demand variables $d_i$ are basic, the function $P_i(d_i)$ can be substituted for the price $p_i$, and constraint set (2) is eliminated. Also, the primal variables $x_{fi}$, $y_i$ and $a_i$ can be eliminated. The generation variable is eliminated by noting that each firm's generation equals the sum of its sales. The $y_i$ and $a_i$ can be eliminated using the market clearing constraints, so all that the TSO controls is $t_{ij}$. Finally, we define the unrestricted net transmission flow $t_{12'} = t_{21} - t_{12}$.

above:

$$[P_2(d_2) - P_1(d_1)] - \lambda_{12} + \lambda_{21} = 0$$
$$0 \le \lambda_{12} \perp (t_{12'} - 50) \le 0$$
$$0 \le \lambda_{21} \perp (-t_{12'} - 50) \le 0$$

It is these constraints that render $SUPPL_{MPEC,A}$'s feasible region non-convex, and make it an MPEC.

Meanwhile, generator B's problem is:

$$SUPPL_{MPEC,B}(s^*_{A1}, s^*_{A2}): \quad \underset{\{d_1, d_2, s_{B1}, s_{B2}, t_{12'}, \lambda_{12}, \lambda_{21}\}}{\text{MAX}} \quad P_1(d_1)s_{B1} + P_2(d_2)s_{B2} - [P_1(d_1) - P_2(d_2)]s_{B1}$$

subject to: (1) *Generator's internal constraints:*

$$s_{B1}, s_{B2} \ge 0$$

(3) *Optimality of* $TSO_{EPEC}(\cdot)$:

$$[P_2(d_2) - P_1(d_1)] - \lambda_{12} + \lambda_{21} = 0$$
$$0 \le \lambda_{12} \perp (t_{12'} - 50) \le 0$$
$$0 \le \lambda_{21} \perp (t_{21'} - 50) \le 0$$

(4) *Market clearing conditions:*

$$-t_{12'} + s^*_{A1} + s^*_{A2} - d_1 = 0$$
$$t_{12'} + s_{B1} + s_{B2} - d_2 = 0$$

A pure strategy equilibrium, if it exists, solves the following problem:

   *EPEC:*   Find a set of values for $\{d_1, d_2, s_{A1}, s_{A2}, s_{B1}, s_{B2}, t_{12'}, \lambda_{12}, \lambda_{21}\}$ such that:

(1) $\{d_1, d_2, s_{A1}, s_{A2}, t_{12'}, \lambda_{12}, \lambda_{21}\}$ solves $SUPPL_{MPEC,A}(s_{B1}, s_{B2})$, and
(2) $\{d_1, d_2, s_{B1}, s_{B2}, t_{12'}, \lambda_{12}, \lambda_{21}\}$ solves $SUPPL_{MPEC,B}(s_{A1}, s_{A2})$

It turns out that *no* such set of values for the variables exists under Figure 3.2's demand and cost assumptions. This can be most readily seen by examining the two firms' reaction functions and noticing that they do not intercept. To do this, we first note that the above formulations imply that A's total sales ($s_A \equiv s_{A1} + s_{A2}$) and profit are unique given a value of total sales by B ($s_B \equiv s_{B1} + s_{B2}$), and *vice versa*. Therefore, we can simply plot A's optimal reaction to B's sales as $s_A = s_A(s_B)$, while B's optimal reaction to A's sales is $s_B = s_B(s_A)$. We show these functions in Figure 3.3.

To interpret these functions, consider for instance a situation in which B has chosen $s_B = 475$ MW. The dotted line in the figure shows that A's optimal reaction is to sell 575 MW. At that point, $p_1 = p_2 = 47.5$ \$/MWh and $t_{12'} = 50$ MW. The sales $\{s_{A1}, s_{A2}, s_{B1}, s_{B2}\} = \{525$ MW, 50 MW, 0 MW, 475 MW$\}$. It is precisely at this level of A's sales that the line becomes congested. Although the flow is at its upper bound, there is no economic congestion, as the price difference is zero.[20] If A sells less, the line becomes uncongested and the price falls at both locations 1 and 2. But if A sells more, the congestion means that node 1 must absorb all the additional sales, which rapidly decreases the price there.

---

[20] Oren (1997) notes that Cournot firms in his model also choose outputs so that lines are just barely congested, and no revenues are received by the TSO.

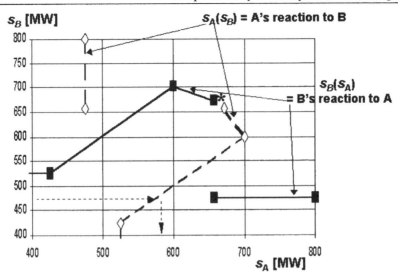

**Figure 3.3** Reaction functions for EPEC model in which generators anticipate transmission price changes (*Note*: asterisk indicates location of MCP solution)

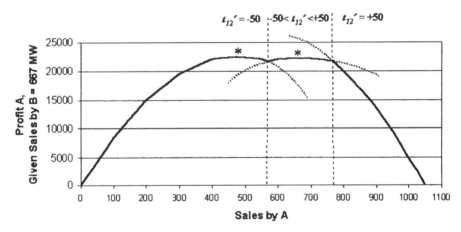

**Figure 3.4** Firm A's profit, given $s_B = 667$ MW, showing two local optima

Now consider the situation where B has instead picked $s_B = 667$ MW. A's reaction function indicates that it should sell only 475 MW, which results in 50 MW of flow from node 2 to node 1. Thus, it is optimal for A to concede market 2. Figure 3.4 shows the profit for A as a function of its total sales decision. This profit function is neither convex nor concave, as a result of the non-convex feasible region of $SUPPL_{MPEC,A}(s_B = 667)$. There are three concave sections of the profit function, each corresponding to a different resolution of the complementarity conditions in constraint set (3) of $SUPPL_{MPEC,A}(\cdot)$. The leftmost region occurs when the TSO flows the maximum possible amount from 2 to 1, while the rightmost region is the opposite case. The middle region corresponds to when transmission flows are between the two bounds. The borders of the region correspond to when a complementarity condition for the TSO "flips", in that which

**Table 3.1**   Comparison of two-node solutions

| Solution | $s_A$ [MW] | $s_B$ [MW] | $p_1$ [$/MWh] | $p_2$ [$/MWh] | Consumer surplus [$/hr] | Profit [$/hr] | Welfare [$/hr] |
|---|---|---|---|---|---|---|---|
| Cournot EPEC1 | 475 | *575* | 47.5 | 47.5 | 27 563 | 49 875 | 77 438 |
| Cournot EPEC2 | *675* | 575 | 37.5 | 37.5 | 39 063 | 46 875 | 85 938 |
| Cournot EPEC3 | 675 | *475* | 37.5 | 47.5 | 33 313 | 47 875 | 81 188 |
| Cournot EPEC4 | *575* | 475 | 47.5 | 47.5 | 27 563 | 49 875 | 77 438 |
| Cournot EPEC5 | 575 | *675* | 37.5 | 37.5 | 39 063 | 46 875 | 85 938 |
| Cournot EPEC6 | *475* | 675 | 47.5 | 37.5 | 33 313 | 47 875 | 81 188 |
| Average Cournot EPEC | 575 | 575 | 42.5 | 42.5 | 33 313 | 48 208 | 81 521 |
| Cournot MCP | 666.7 | 666.7 | 33.3 | 33.3 | 44 444 | 44 444 | 88 889 |
| Competitive | 1000 | 1000 | 0 | 0 | 100 000 | 0 | 100 000 |
| A Cournot, B Competitive | 475 | 1050 | 47.5 | 0 | 63 781 | 22 563 | 86 344 |

*Note:* Underlined italicized $s_f$ values are the optimal $SUPPL_{MPEC, f}(\cdot)$ reaction to the other firm's sales.

inequality is binding changes. The asterisks show two local optima, one at $s_A = 475$ MW (A's profit = 22563$/hr) and the other at $s_A = 667$ MW (A's profit = 22 222$/hr). The lower sales figure represents the global optimum. The existence of a local optimum that is not the global optimum implies that traditional gradient-based optimization techniques could find the wrong local optimum when attempting to solve $SUPPL_{MPEC, A}(\cdot)$.

When $s_B$ instead equals 656.5 MW, the middle curve in Figure 3.4 shifts upwards enough so that the profits from the two local optima are precisely equal. This is the point corresponding to the gap in A's reaction function in Figure 3.3. At that level of $s_B$, firm A would be indifferent between $s_A = 475$ MW or 671.75 MW. However, any level of sales that falls strictly between those levels would yield a lower profit for A, which is the reason for the gap in Figure 3.3.

The gaps in these two reaction functions are located such that there is no intersection. This implies that there is no Cournot pure strategy equilibrium; i.e., there is no point at which neither firm wishes to adjust its sales unilaterally. If we attempted to find an equilibrium by a "diagonalization" approach,[21] the process would never converge.[22]

Table 3.1 demonstrates this diagonalization procedure, showing a sequence of six solutions of the MPEC (labeled "EPEC1" through "EPEC2"). Starting with an assumption of relatively low sales by A ($s_A = 475$ MW), EPEC1 shows that the optimal solution to B's problem $SUPPL_{MPEC, B}(s_A = 475)$ is $s_B = 575$ MW (the underlined value in that row). EPEC2 then shows A's response to that $s_B$; solving $SUPPL_{MPEC, A}(s_B = 575)$ gives $s_A = 675$ MW. In both of these solutions, the supplier is reacting to relatively low generation by its rival (and thus high prices) by expanding its supply, cutting prices and exporting 50 MW to its rival's

---

[21] The diagonalization method, which is a variant of the Gauss–Seidel method for numerical solution of simultaneous equations, starts with an initial set of values for the firms' sales, and then allows one firm at a time to adjust their sales optimally in response to the other firm's previous decision. This repeats until convergence, or until it is evident that convergence is not possible. Relaxation methods (setting the latest value of sales equal to a convex combination of the previous sales and the last solution) can accelerate convergence. Diagonalization was used by Cardell *et al.* (1997), Hobbs *et al.* (2000) and London Economics (2002), and sometimes successfully achieved convergence, and on occasion not.

[22] For a much simpler two-node Cournot case, Borenstein *et al.* (2000) found that a pure strategy did not exist, while this also occurred in Berry *et al.* (1999), who describe a case in which the firm's strategic variable is either the intercept or slope of a bid curve submitted to a POOLCO. Each of these are EPEC models in which the generator anticipates how a TSO will adj-st transmission and nodal energy prices to clear the markets.

market. However in EPEC3, the reverse happens; B reacts to A's sales of 675 MW by cutting production and conceding part of its home market at node 2, allowing A to export 50 MW. Table 3.1 shows the first six iterations; EPEC7 turns out to be identical to EPEC1, and the cycle starts again. There is no convergence.

Of course, this lack of a pure strategy equilibrium may indeed be the reality in power markets; there is no reason *a priori* that one should expect such an equilibrium. For instance, in Day and Bunn's (2001) autonomous agent simulations of the UK market, there often was no convergence. But a challenge facing the analyst using this model is how to characterize the market outcomes. One way is to describe the range and distribution of prices that occur during iterations of the diagonalization (London Economics, 2002), and calculate averages over that distribution. For instance, in the seventh row of Table 3.1, we show the average sales, prices, consumer surplus, profit and welfare (the sum of profit, consumer surplus and transmission revenue) over the six-solution cycle EPEC1–6. A practical difficulty of this procedure is that the computational cost of doing enough iterations to characterize the distribution of prices may be prohibitive.

Meanwhile, a conceptual difficulty with the diagonalization approach is that the range and distribution of prices it yields will in general differ from the probability distribution that would result if a true Nash (mixed strategy) equilibrium for the game was calculated. Therefore, if practical, it is preferable to calculate the mixed strategy equilibrium. There are various approaches to doing this; e.g., Stoft (1999) shows how an LCP can be formulated to solve for the probability that each firm assigns to different values of its strategic variables for a simple two-firm case. However, calculating mixed equilibria is a daunting task even for simple problems, and cannot be contemplated for more realistic problems.

Even if distributions of prices and other market outcomes can be described for the EPEC, there is still the practical challenge of communicating the results concisely and clearly. If no pure strategy exists (or, alternatively, several exist), then it becomes difficult to present the results of comparative statics, such as the price impacts of alternative market designs or structures. The ability of policy-makers and other "consumers" of market simulations to understand the results and the methodology lying behind them becomes harder if they cannot be reassured that model solutions exist and are unique.

### 3.4.3.2 MCP formulation and results

Instead of calculating and communicating EPEC results, an alternative is to instead use the MCP approach of Section 3.3.1. This method poses none of the practical difficulties just described; there is generally a solution, it is easily calculated, and it is unique in terms of market prices and profits. Its key assumption (that generators do not anticipate how their actions might affect congestion and the price of transmission) is clearly hard to defend in the case of simple transmission systems in which only one firm lies on one side or another of critical transmission constraints. Such firms will readily notice and should be able to predict how their outputs and bids affect transmission prices.[23] However, in a more complex network with multiple transmission paths where there are a number of firms using the network, the calculation of congestion-based prices will be more opaque and such predictions may be more difficult. (For instance, our case study in Section 3.5 involves several hundred firms, and an equally large number of transmission constraints.) In that circumstance, the Bertrand assumption

---

[23] Although, as shown below, the EPEC and MCP approaches can sometimes still yield the same results in that case.

(that generators treat transmission prices as being exogenous) becomes more credible as a basis for an analysis.

We now apply the MCP method to the same simple two-node case just analyzed with the EPEC. We first present a version of the model that, like the EPEC, is much reduced in size by taking advantage of some of the equality conditions in the MCP to eliminate variables. We then compare its outcome with the EPEC model.

First, we state the optimization problems for the generator and TSO, and along with the market clearing conditions:

$$GEN_{MCP,A}(a_2, s_{B1}, s_{B2}, w_2^*):$$
$$\underset{\{s_{A1},s_{A2}\}}{\text{MAX}} \ P_1(-a_2 + s_{A1} + s_{B1})s_{A1} + P_2(a_2 + s_{A2} + s_{B2})s_{A2} - w_2^* s_{A2}$$
$$\text{s.t.: } s_{A1}, s_{A2} \geq 0$$

$$GEN_{MCP,B}(a_2, s_{A1}, s_{A2}, w_2^*):$$
$$\underset{\{s_{B1},s_{B2}\}}{\text{MAX}} \ P_1(-a_2 + s_{A1} + s_{B1})s_{B1} + P_2(a_2 + s_{A2} + s_{B2})s_{B2} + w_2^* s_{B1}$$
$$\text{s.t.: } s_{B1}, s_{B2} \geq 0$$

$$TSO_{MCP}(d_1, d_2, w_2^*): \ \underset{\{a_2,y_2\}}{\text{MAX}}[P_2(d_2) - P_1(d_1)]a_2 + w_2^* y_2$$
$$\text{s.t.: } a_2 + y_2 \leq 50 \text{ (dual variable } \lambda_{12})$$
$$-a_2 - y_2 \leq 50 \text{ (dual variable } \lambda_{21})$$

*Market clearing conditions*:

$$-a_2 + s_{A1} + s_{B1} - d_1 = 0$$
$$a_2 + s_{A2} + s_{B2} - d_2 = 0$$
$$-y_2 + s_{A2} - s_{B1} = 0$$

The MCP that results from concatenating the KKTs for the optimization problems with the market clearing conditions is:

*MCP*:    Find $\{a_2, d_1, d_2, s_{A1}, s_{A2}, s_{B1}, s_{B2}, Y_2, w_2^*, \lambda_{12}, \lambda_{21}\}$ that satisfy:

$$0 \leq s_{A1} \perp (P_1 + s_{A1}\partial P_1/\partial s_{A1}) \leq 0$$
$$0 \leq s_{A2} \perp (P_2 + s_{A2}\partial P_2/\partial s_{A2} - w_2^*) \leq 0$$
$$0 \leq s_{B1} \perp (P_1 + s_{B1}\partial P_1/\partial s_{B1} + w_2^*) \leq 0$$
$$0 \leq s_{B2} \perp (P_2 + s_{B2}\partial P_2/\partial s_{B2}) \leq 0$$
$$[P_2(d_2) - P_1(d_1)] - \lambda_{12} + \lambda_{21} = 0$$
$$w_2^* - \lambda_{12} + \lambda_{21} = 0$$
$$0 \leq \lambda_{12} \perp (a_2 + y_2 - 50) \leq 0$$
$$0 \leq \lambda_{21} \perp (-a_2 - y_2 - 50) \leq 0$$
$$d_1 + a_2 - s_{A1} - s_{B1} = 0$$
$$d_2 - a_2 - s_{A2} - s_{B2} = 0$$
$$-y_2 + s_{A2} - s_{B1} = 0$$

where $\partial P_i / \partial s_{fi}$ in all cases equals $-0.1$ (Figure 3.2). The solution is:

$$\{a_2, d_1, d_2, s_{A1}, s_{A2}, s_{B1}, s_{B2}, y_2, w_2^*, \lambda_{12}, \lambda_{21}\}$$
$$= \{0, \ 667 \text{ MW}, 667 \text{ MW}, 333 \text{ MW}, 333 \text{ MW}, 333 \text{ MW}, 333 \text{ MW}, 0, 0, 0, 0\}$$

The equilibrium price at each node is the same, $p_1 = p_2 = 33.3\$/\text{MWh}$. Each firm splits each market and there is no transmission congestion. We compare this MCP solution to the EPEC reaction functions in Figure 3.3. It lies close to the gap between the two functions. Because there is no congestion, the MCP solution is identical to the Cournot duoply solution for a single market with a demand curve equal to the horizontal sum of the two nodal demand curves. Table 3.1 compares the market outcomes of the Cournot MCP with the average results of the EPEC model. We see that the Cournot MCP model yields lower prices and profits, and higher consumer surplus and welfare than the EPEC approach. Intuitively, this is because in the MCP model, generators are price-takers regarding transmission constraints, rather than strategic; less strategic behavior leads to less market power.

However, relative to the competitive solution, in which both generators are price-takers in the energy market rather than Cournot, the two Cournot models indicate the same qualitative result: market power will significantly raise prices and harm consumers.

The symmetry assumptions we used in this numerical comparison of the MCP and EPEC models, however, tend to maximize their apparent differences. If instead congestion tends to follow predictable patterns, then we anticipate that their results would be more similar. For instance, if costs or demands are asymmetric or if some nodes have less market concentration than others, then congestion is likely to occur in which the net flow is from the node with the lowest costs, lowest demands or most competition to the other node. As an example, the last row of Table 3.1 shows a case in which the MCP and EPEC approaches give *identical* results.[24] There, supplier A is a monopolist at node 1, while the suppliers at node 2 are competitive (price-takers). As a result, transmission flows will be from the aggressive suppliers at node 2 to the less competitive market in node 1. This convergence gives some reason to suspect that the EPEC and MCP approaches will give fairly similar results in situations in which there are consistent patterns of congestion. A systematic comparison of the results of these models for a wider range of cases would be useful to confirm or refute that conjecture.

An alternative approach that combines the computational and analytical convenience of MCP formulations with greater realism concerning generator manipulation of congestion is proposed in Hobbs *et al.* (2004). Their model explicitly hypothesizes conjectures that generators hold concerning how transmission prices respond to changes in demand for transmission services. These conjectures can be modeled as exogenous parameters that might state, for instance, that increasing a firm's demand for services between Germany and Belgium by 100 MW would increase the price of the constrained interface by, say, 1\$/MWh. These conjectures can then be varied parametrically to gauge the effect of those expectations on competition on prices, as was done for northwestern Europe (Hobbs *et al.*, 2004).[25]

---

[24] The EPEC and MCP models also give identical results in the less interesting pure competition case (next to last row, Table 3.1).

Interestingly, the MPC model indicates that net welfare is worse in the more competitive scenario (only A is strategic) than in the less competitive case (both A and B are strategic) (Table 3.1). In contrast, the EPEC model gives the anticipated result of higher welfare when there is more competition. However, this is not necessarily evidence that the MPC model is somehow flawed; transmission constraints often can result in counterintuitive outcomes. For example, both EPEC- and MCP-based models have shown cases where increasing competitiveness at one node relative to others can actually worsen welfare and raise average prices (Berry *et al.*, 1999; Borenstein *et al.*, 2000; Hobbs *et al.*, 2003). This occurs because the competitive producers expand their production and cause congestion that can distort production decisions and prices.

[25] These conjectured transmission price responses are analogous to the parameters that describe the conjectured supply response of rival suppliers in the model of Day *et al.* (2002). See footnote 17, *supra*.

## 3.5    A LARGE-SCALE APPLICATION: THE NORTH AMERICAN EASTERN INTERCONNECTION

To illustrate how the complementarity framework can be useful for analyzing large-scale power markets, we summarize an application of a variant of the MCP model of Section 3.4.1 to the US portion of the North America Eastern Interconnection (Figure 3.5) (Helman, 2003). The model has approximately 100 nodes, 75 of which represent different control areas in the region, while the rest represent boundary locations with Canadian provinces, the Western US grid and Texas (for the period examined, imports and exports across these boundaries were fixed at their average hourly levels). There are over 300 utilities and larger merchant generating companies modeled, as well as a number of small non-utility generators. To reduce the model size, only the largest 100 or so firms are treated as strategic Cournot firms, and the rest are modeled as price-takers. (Price-taking firms tend to be very small in size; in the model, they were firms that owned up to 1000 MW, with firms larger than this treated as Cournot.) About 600 GW of generation capacity is modeled, divided into 2725 units (multiple identical units at a single location were generally aggregated, but multiple ownership of a generator was modeled in its ownership shares).

The analysis also assumes that generation has been completely decoupled from local distribution, so that no generator is tied into a particular load (this parallels the actual operations of a centralized spot energy auction, but does not account, at this point, for forward contracts that might mitigate spot market power). Demand is represented at the control area level and is assumed to be linear; sensitivities can be conducted on different demand elasticities (the results shown below assume an elasticity of $-0.1$). Twenty-four different demand periods are modeled representing the actual hourly loads of an average June 2000 day. Flows between nodes are constrained by 814 transmission constraints representing NERC

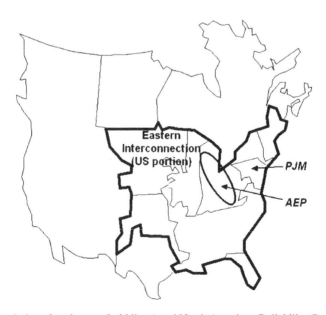

**Figure 3.5**    Boundaries of study area (bold lines) and North American Reliability Councils (thin lines)

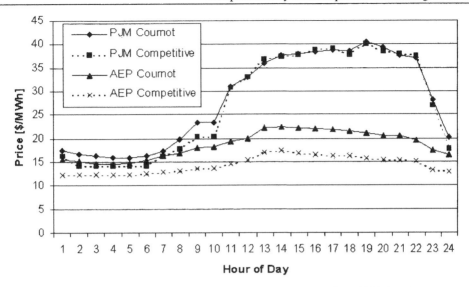

**Figure 3.6** Simulated hourly competitive and Cournot prices, average June 2000 day, for two control areas

flowgates in a linearized DC load flow model.[26] The resulting MCP has approximately 12 000 variables and conditions (but can be much larger depending on the market modeling assumptions).

Sample results from the model are shown for two large and geographically close control areas in Figure 3.6. The upper pair of lines represent prices in the Pennsylvania–Maryland–New Jersey Interconnection (PJM) in the competitive and Cournot cases, while the lower pair are from the same runs, but for the American Electric Power (AEP) control area.[27] There is a clear difference in results: assuming, as we do, that firms' market power is related to their total operable capacity (rather than only to their capacity net of forward contractual obligations), conditions are more competitive in PJM than in AEP. The reason why Cournot prices are approximately one-third higher than competitive prices in AEP is that the East-Central Area Reliability (ECAR) Council area in which AEP sits has just a few very large firms, with less than 10% of the capacity being provided by small price-takers. AEP itself is a giant, with 38 GW of capacity. Since AEP is among the lowest cost utilities in the US portion of the Eastern Interconnection, the seemingly ample transmission capacity in the region does not elicit sufficient imports to temper market power in that region.[28]

---

[26] The North American Electric Reliability Council (NERC) is a utility body that sets the standards for identification and monitoring of the subset of transmission elements in the network that are typically subject to congestion. These are called flowgates.

[27] The simulated competitive prices in these regions were compared to the actual average hourly prices where available (Helman, 2003). PJM operates a regional spot market, and the simulated prices for the period modeled were a few $/MWh over or under the actual price for most hours except for the peak hours, where the model was up to $7/MWh below the actual. This would be expected given that cost data are only estimates, and the competitive market model does not represent factors such as local transmission constraints within PJM, unit commitment constraints on generators, environmental emission limits on generators, and actual market power. In AEP, the competitive model prices were compared to reported utility system lambdas (the shadow price that results from the utility least cost dispatch) and generally remained within $2–3/MWh of the lambdas.

[28] This is one of the first attempts to model generation market power in ECAR, under the assumptions given above. In anticipation of the Midwest ISO spot market, which encompasses ECAR, some preliminary market analysis has been done (MISO IMM, 2003). This analysis confirms that transmission constraints can be a source of market power in the region, but does not offer price modeling.

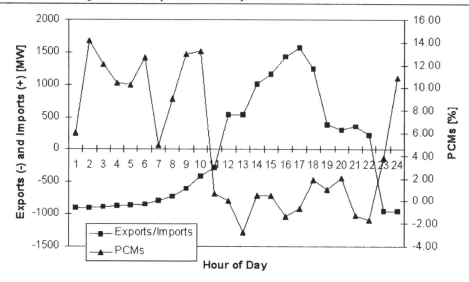

**Figure 3.7**   Simulated imports and exports and price-cost margins in PJM, average June 2000 day

In contrast, PJM is relatively unconcentrated. As modeled, 12 Cournot firms have plants in the region and up to 15% of the capacity is provided by price-takers. PJM can also import (or export) up to about 4–5% of its hourly load during the period modeled. Interestingly, PJM is a net exporter during the off-peak hours of the day, when its firms' generation costs are lower than those in neighboring New York, and a net importer during the peak hours of the day, when generation in ECAR is cheaper than that in PJM. The imports in the peak hours dilute the market power of the incumbent PJM firms, yielding the relationship shown in Figures 3.6 and 3.7 of higher Cournot prices relative to the competitive price in the off-peak hours than in the peak hours. Rather than the prices shown in Figure 3.6, Figure 3.7 plots the price–cost margin (PCM), which is calculated as ((Cournot price − competitive price)/Cournot price).[29] Note that this simulated result needs further analysis, because withholding significant capacity from the base-load generation that is operating off-peak may be harder to accomplish in practice than in the model. Nonetheless, the general relationship between market structure, network flows and price mark-ups shown by this model is plausible and does not appear in less detailed simulations.[30]

## 3.6   CONCLUSION

Complementarity is a natural way to phrase economic equilibrium problems that need to recognize hard constraints such as transmission and generation capacity limits. It is also a convenient framework for analyzing and calculating solutions. Thus, its increasing use in energy and

---

[29] The range of a PCM is typically between 0–1, or in percentage terms, between 0–100. As shown in Figures 3.6 and 3.7, in a few afternoon hours, the PCMs in PJM are actually slightly negative. While the Eastern Interconnection load-weighted average Cournot price is always higher than the associated competitive price, there are locations in the network where Cournot prices may be actually lower in some hours than competitive prices due to network effects and patterns of withholding.

[30] An analysis of actual market power in PJM during 2000 can be found in PJM (2001). That study confirms that the market was fairly unconcentrated and that the actual average monthly PCM was only 4%, with June being an average month. For an assumed demand elasticity of −0.1, the simulation discussed here finds an average mark-up of 4.96% although the PCM varies over the day as shown in Figure 3.7. This hourly variation has not been confirmed.

especially electric power market modeling is no surprise. However, there are different ways to model how generating companies view transmission prices and constraints, with different computational and theoretical characteristics. We have presented models and applications to illustrate how complementarity problems can be used to model energy markets, and especially transmission-constrained electricity markets. We have also illustrated how important the differences among alternative formulations may be in practice.

# ACKNOWLEDGMENTS

B.F. Hobbs was supported by NSF Grants ECS 0080577 and 0224817, and by the Energy Research Center of the Netherlands (ECN). An earlier version of this paper was presented at the Third International Conference on Complementarity Problems, July 2002. We thank G. Zwart of the Netherlands Energy Regulatory (DTe) and F. Rijkers of ECN for stimulating conversations that motivated the model comparison in Section 3.4, and for comments they and M. Boots provided on the manuscript. Our Hopkins colleagues C. Metzler and J.-S. Pang have provided many theoretical insights, without which this paper would not have been possible. The simulation results presented here are intended only to demonstrate a market modeling methodology; they do not reflect the official views of the Federal Energy Regulatory Commission on the potential exercise of generation market power in the regions discussed.

# REFERENCES

Amundsen E.S., Bergman L. and Andersson B. (2001). "Demand Variation and Market Power in the Norwegian–Swedish Power Market". WP 38, Foundation for Research in Economics & Business Administration, Bergen, Norway.

Berry C.A., Hobbs B.F., Meroney W.A., O'Neill R.P. and Stewart Jr. W.R. (1999). "Analyzing Strategic Bidding Behavior in Transmission Networks". *Utilities Policy* **8**(3): 139–158.

Boots M.G., Rijkers F.A.M. and Hobbs B.F. (2004). "Modeling the Role of Trading Companies in the Downstream European Gas Market: A Successive Oligopoly Approach". *Energy Journal*, in press.

Borenstein S., Bushnell J. and Knittel C.R. (1999). "Market Power in Electricity Markets: Beyond Concentration Measures". PWP-059r, University of California Energy Institute, Berkeley, CA.

Borenstein S., Bushnell J. and Stoft S. (2000). "The Competitive Effects of Transmission Capacity in a Deregulated Electricity Industry". *Rand Journal of Economics* **31**(2): 294–325.

Borenstein S., Bushnell J. and Wolak F. (2002). "Measuring Market Inefficiencies in California's Restructured Wholesale Electricity Market". *American Economic Review*, **92**(5): 1376–1405.

Bushnell J. (2003). "Water and Power: Hydroelectric Resources in the Era of Competition in the Western US". *Operational Research* **51**(1): 80–93.

Bushnell J. and Saravia C. (2002). "An Empirical Assessment of the Competitiveness of the New England Electricity Market". Analysis for ISO New England, CSEM WP-101, University of California Energy Institute, Berkeley, CA.

Capros P. *et al.* (2000). The *PRIMES Energy System Model: Reference Manual*. National Technical University, Athens, Greece.

Cardell J., Hitt C.C. and Hogan W.W. (1997). "Market Power and Strategic Interaction in Electricity Networks". *Resource and Energy Economics* **19**(1–2): 109–137.

Cottle R.W., Pang J.S. and Stone R.E. (1992). *The Linear Complementarity Problem*. Academic Press, New York.

Cunningham L.B., Baldick R. and Baughman M.L. (2002). "An Empirical Study of Applied Game Theory: Transmission Constrained Cournot Behavior". *IEEE Transactions on Power Systems* **17**(1): 166–172.

Daxhelet O. and Smeers Y. (2001). "Variational Inequality Models of Restructured Electric Systems". In *Applications and Algorithms of Complementarity*, M.C. Ferris, O.L. Mangasarian and J.-S. Pang (eds). Kluwer Dordrecht.

Day C.J. and Bunn D.W. (2001). "Divestiture of Generation Assets in the Electricity Pool of England and Wales: A Computational Approach to Analyzing Market Power". *Journal of Regulatory Economics* 19(2): 123–141.

Day C.J., Hobbs B.F. and Pang J.-S. (2002). "Oligopolistic Competition in Power Networks: A Conjectured Supply Function Approach". *IEEE Transactions on Power Systems* 27(3): 597–607.

Dirkse S.P. and Ferris M.C. (1995). "The PATH Solver: A Non-Monotone Stabilization Scheme for Mixed Complementarity Problems". *Optimization Methods and Software* 5: 123–156.

FERC. (1998). "Notice of Request for Written Comments and Intent to Convene a Technical Conference". Inquiry Concerning the Commission's Policy on the Use of Computer Models in Merger Analysis, Docket No. PL98-6-000, Federal Energy Regulatory Commission, April 16.

Ferris M.C. and Pang J.S. (1997). "Engineering and Economic Applications of Complementarity Problems". *SIAM Review* 39(4): 669–713.

Gabriel S.A., Kydes A.S. and Whitman P. (2001). "The National Energy Modeling System: A Large-Scale Energy-Economic Equilibrium Model". *Operational Research* 49(1): 14–25.

Hashimoto H. (1985). "A Spatial Nash Equilibrium Model". In *Spatial Price Equilibria: Advances in Theory, Computation, and Application*, P.T. Harker (ed.). Springer-Verlag, Berlin.

Helman U. (2003). "Oligopolistic Competition in Wholesale Electricity Markets: Theory, Large-Scale Simulation and Policy Analysis using Complementarity Models". Ph.D. Thesis, The Johns Hopkins University, Baltimore, MD.

Hobbs B.F. (2001). "Linear Complementarity Models of Nash–Cournot Competition in Bilateral and POOLCO-Based Power Markets". *IEEE Transactions on Power Systems* 16(2): 194–202.

Hobbs B.F., Metzler C. and Pang J.-S. (2000). "Calculating Equilibria in Imperfectly Competitive Power Markets: An MPEC Approach". *IEEE Transactions on Power Systems* 15(2): 638–645.

Hobbs B.F., Rijkers F.A.M. and Wals A.F. (2004). "Modeling Strategic Generator Behavior with Conjectured Transmission Price Responses in a Mixed Transmission Pricing System". *IEEE Transaction on Power Systems*, in press.

Hogan W.W. (1992). "Contract Networks for Electric Power Transmission". *Journal of Regulatory Economics* 4: 211–242.

Joskow P.L. and Kahn E. (2002). "A Quantitative Analysis of Pricing Behavior in California's Wholesale Electricity Market During Summer 2000". *The Energy Journal* 23(4): 1–35.

London Economics. (2002). "Final Methodology: Proposed Approach for Evaluation of Transmission Investment". Prepared for the California ISO, Folsom, CA, January. www2.caiso.com/thegrid/planning/

Luo Z.Q., Pang J.S. and Ralph D. (1996). *Mathematical Programs with Equilibrium Constraints*. Cambridge University Press, Cambridge.

Metzler C., Hobbs B.F. and Pang J.S. (2003). "Nash–Cournot Equilibria in Power Markets on a Linearized DC Network with Arbitrage: Formulations and Properties". *Networks & Spatial Theory*, 3(2): 123–150.

MISO IMM. (2002). "2002 State of the Market Report, Midwest ISO". Potomac Economics, Fairfax, VA, April. www.midwestiso.org

Oren S.S. (1997). "Economic Inefficiency of Passive Transmission Rights in Congested Electricity Systems with Competitive Generation". *Energy Journal* 18(1): 63–83.

PJM. (2001). "State of the Market Report, 2000". Market Monitoring Unit, PJM Interconnection, L.L.C., Valley Forge, PA, June. www.pjm.com

Ralph D., Hu X. and Ralph E.K. (2002). "Modelling Bilevel Games in Electricity Markets". Presented at the Third International Conference on Complementarity Problems, Cambridge, UK, July 29–August 1.

Schweppe F.C., Caramanis M.C., Tabors R.E. and Bohn R.E. (1988). *Spot Pricing of Electricity*. Kluwer, Norwell, MA.

Smeers, Y. (1997). "Computable Equilibrium Models and the Restructuring of the European Electricity and Gas Markets". *Energy Journal* 18(4): 1–31.

Smeers Y. and Daxhelet O. (2002). "Modelling Market Power and Regulation within the Florence Regulatory Forum Framework". 3rd International Conference on Complementarity Problems, Cambridge, UK, July 29–August 1.

Smeers Y. and Wei J.-Y. (1997). "Spatially Oligopolistic Model with Opportunity Cost Pricing for Transmission Capacity Reservations – A Variational Inequality Approach". CORE Discussion Paper 9717, Université Catholique de Louvain, February.

Stoft S. (1999). "Using Game Theory to Study Market Power in Simple Networks". In *Game Theory Tutorial*, H. Singh (ed.). IEEE Power Engineering Society, Parsippany, NJ.

Tirole J. (1988). *The Theory of Industrial Organization*. MIT Press, Cambridge, MA.

Vives X. (1999). *Oligopoly Pricing: Old Ideas and New Tools*. MIT Press, Cambridge, MA.

Wei J.-Y. and Smeers Y. (1999). "Spatial Oligopolistic Electricity Models with Cournot Generators and Regulated Transmission Prices". *Operations Research* **47**(1): 102–112.

# 4

# Price Impact of Horizontal Mergers in the British Generation Market[†]

JOHN BOWER

*Oxford Institute for Energy Studies, Oxford OX2 6FA, UK*

## ABSTRACT

Horizontal mergers in the electricity generation sector have become commonplace as a result of the process of deregulation and market liberalisation that took place in the 1990s. However, established quantitative measures of the competitive impact of such mergers, for example the Herfindahl–Hirschman Index (HHI), Lerner Index and SSNIP Test widely used by competition authorities, do not reflect the impact of factors such as demand elasticity, style of competition, forward contracting and market definition. These factors are particularly critical in whole-sale electricity markets where demand elasticity is virtually zero, supply function bidding is common, geographic market definition is determined by transient transmission constraints and product market definition is determined by time of day and the technical characteristics of generation plant operations. In practice, the established methods of measuring the impact of mergers are ill equipped to perform the true task of competition authorities – namely to produce an accurate forecast of post-merger market prices which can then be compared against known pre-merger market prices to determine the competitive impact of a proposed merger. A methodology is presented that estimates coefficients for a series of Capacity Concentration Indices (CCI) using a backward stepwise multiple regression procedure that relates historic changes in the ownership structure of generating plant to changes in wholesale prices. This econometric approach has been applied to analysis of wholesale day-ahead market prices, and a range of regulatory variables, from the England and Wales wholesale electricity market. The CCI are used to forecast the price impact of a series of proposed mergers in the generation sector.

## 4.1  INTRODUCTION

The introduction of competition into the global electricity industry through deregulation and price liberalisation has proved a much more difficult task than its early proponents imagined. While it is broadly accepted that the transmission and distribution sectors must remain regulated natural monopolies, with prices controlled by regulatory fiat, competition between firms in the generation and supply sectors is the preferred mechanism for controlling prices in the wholesale and retail markets. However, given that many countries begin the deregulation process with

---

[†] The views expressed in this chapter are those of the author, and do not necessarily reflect those of OIES.

*Modelling Prices in Competitive Electricity Markets.* Edited by D.W. Bunn.
© 2004 John Wiley & Sons, Ltd. ISBN 0-470-84860-X.

a monopoly or near monopoly state electricity board, the question of how to restructure the generation and supply sectors into a sufficiently large number of firms to ensure a competitive outcome is a crucial one. Even where this has been achieved successfully, subsequent mergers and acquisitions leading to horizontal mergers of firms (e.g. when one generating firm takes over another generating firm) have become commonplace and increasingly so across national borders. In some cases this has led to a rapid increase in industry concentration in the generation and supply sectors that may ultimately lead to a position of market dominance if left unchecked. This could ultimately result in wholesale and retail electricity prices that are as high or even higher than they were before the industry was deregulated.

The difficulty facing competition (antitrust) authorities analysing horizontal mergers in any industry is to decide which should be allowed to proceed on the grounds that they will increase overall economic efficiency, for example by reducing costs and removing redundant and inefficient management, and which should be blocked or modified because of the potential risk that the newly merged firms will exercise market power and raise prices to the detriment of consumers and overall economic efficiency. Fundamentally, the task that competition authorities face in analysing horizontal mergers is a forecasting problem. If the forecast post-merger price for a particular good or service is not significantly higher than the current pre-merger price, and assuming that the industry in question is starting from a competitive position, then there is little reason for the merger to be blocked or modified. However, if a significant post-merger price increase is forecast then either a complete reversal, or significant modifications including asset disposals from the merged firm, may be required.

### 4.1.1  Difficulties in applying current merger analysis tools to electricity markets

To bring consistency to their judgments competition authorities have adopted a range of well-established quantitative measures to assess the likely competitive effect of a proposed horizontal merger such as the Herfindahl–Hirschman Index (HHI) which is calculated by summing the squared market shares of firms in an industry with a maximum of 10 000 for a monopoly and zero for a perfectly competitive industry. Similarly, the Lerner Index compares the current market price with the short-run marginal production cost of the industry by subtracting the marginal cost from market price and dividing through by market price to produce a theoretical maximum index value of one and a minimum of zero. The US Department of Justice Horizontal Merger Guidelines use benchmark HHI levels to categorise the competitiveness of different industry structures as follows:

 (i) Post-merger HHI < 1000 are defined as unconcentrated markets and unlikely to have adverse competitive effects.
 (ii) Post-merger 1000 < HHI < 1800 are defined as moderately concentrated but mergers producing a change of 100 HHI points or more in such a market are likely to have adverse competitive consequences.
(iii) Post-merger HHI > 1800 are regarded as highly concentrated markets and mergers producing a change of 50 HHI points or more in such a market are likely to have adverse competition consequences.

However, despite the precise nature of the HHI there is no direct link between say an HHI of 1800 and any particular percentage mark-up on short-run marginal cost, nor indeed a method for calculating what impact a change in the HHI from 1800 to say 2500 due to a horizontal merger would have on post-merger prices. Indeed, Stoft (2002) argues against applying the

HHI to the electricity industry because it ignores four key factors that are crucial in determining the extent of market power: demand elasticity, style of competition, forward contracting and geographical extent of the market, each of which he suggests can affect market power by an order of magnitude.

More explicitly Stoft takes issue with the DOJ benchmarks themselves, noting "standard wisdom holds that HHIs below 1000 are certainly safe – (when) they are not". Given that short-term elasticity of demand is virtually zero for electricity, this explains why even in a relatively unconcentrated industry prices can quickly reach 10 times the level of short-run marginal cost. Moreover, Cournot is not the only style of competition and typically electricity generators bid upward sloping supply functions composed of price–quantity pairs rather than quantities alone. Forward contracting, he suggests, reduces market power by a factor of 10. Finally, he takes issue with the DOJ invention of the "hypothetical monopolist" as a means defining the boundaries of an electricity market. This so-called SSNIP Test attempts to define both the geographic and product market boundary, in the absence of price discrimination, as one in which a product or group of products such that a hypothetical profit-maximising firm that was the only present and future seller of those products ("monopolist") likely would impose at least a "small but non-transitory increase in price".

On the face of it, electricity is the archetypal homogenous commodity product but in practice the time of day at which it is supplied and the type of plant that generates it defines at least three product categorisations:

(i) *Baseload* covers power supplied at a constant rate throughout all demand periods of the year and usually produced by plant with little operational flexibility running at very low marginal cost (e.g. nuclear).

(ii) *Mid-merit* usually covers normal day-time load throughout the majority of the year and usually produced from flexible thermal (e.g. coal and gas) plant with higher marginal costs.

(iii) *Peak load* covers a relatively small number of hours in the year when demand is highest and usually met by flexible but very high marginal cost plant.

Electricity may be further categorised into separate submarkets in terms of the firmness of supply that defines the circumstances in which supply may be curtailed, for how long and at what time of day. Forward, day-ahead, balancing and ancillary service markets also define electricity as separate products in terms of the amount of notice required between contracting and physical plant dispatch that is related in part to the operational flexibility of the plant producing it. Finally, electricity may be defined in terms of the service it provides either in meeting load (energy service) or in guaranteeing supply quality through reliability reserves, voltage support, reactive power and black start (ancillary service). Finally, the geographic market that a generating plant supplies is defined by the degree to which transmission capacity between locations is congested, that may limit the degree to which supplies may enter from other locations. The question of which firms own what type of plant, with what operational characteristics, marginal production costs, and whether it is located within a transmission constrained region are crucial determinants of market power that HHI does not address.

Stoft also criticises the Lerner Index as being unreliable, citing the example of a generator withholding a small amount of capacity to dramatically reduce marginal production costs during a period of high demand, but only inducing a 5% increase in price which will appear to be exercising almost infinite market power compared with a generator withholding capacity during a normal demand period, without reducing marginal production costs which will appear to be exercising only a moderate amount of market power even if prices rise by 25%. As a tool for forecasting what the price impact of a horizontal merger might be the Lerner Index is also useless. Although the market price and marginal cost under the current industry structure is relatively easy to calculate from observable prices, the value which is of absolutely critical interest, namely what the level market prices will be after a merger has taken place, is an input to the Lerner Index, not an output. In other words the Lerner Index may be readily used for assessing the current state of competitiveness in a market but can only be used to assess the post-merger competitiveness of an industry if a forecast of future market prices has already been made.

In the remainder of this chapter an alternative mechanism for forecasting the price impact of a horizontal merger in the electricity generation sector is presented and used to forecast the impact of proposed mergers in the UK electricity generation sector. This is based on an econometric approach that analyses how small changes in the historic ownership pattern of different types of plant in the generation sector, whether induced by new entry, decommissioning, mothballing and divestment, impacted on prices in the past. In the next section, the structure of the England and Wales electricity market and the range of regulatory interventions, including mandatory plant divestment, that have been imposed since 1990 aimed at controlling generator market power are summarised. In the third section, the methodology is illustrated by analysing wholesale day-ahead prices drawn from the England and Wales electricity market in the period 1 April 1990–31 March 2002. Forecasts are produced in the fourth section of the post-merger price change that is likely to occur if a series of proposed generation asset mergers were to be authorised by the relevant competition authorities and conclusions drawn.

## 4.2  ENGLAND AND WALES WHOLESALE ELECTRICITY MARKET

The England & Wales Electricity Pool ("the Pool") began trading on 1 April 1990 and was the centrepiece of UK electricity market deregulation and price liberalisation. Operationally the Pool was a mandatory uniform price auction, repeated on a daily basis, into which generators submitted price–quantity bids to provide bulk wholesale supplies of electricity in each half-hour of the next day ("day-ahead").

### 4.2.1  Market power in the Pool

Economic theory had predicted that Bertrand price competition would quickly cause Pool prices to fall to short-run marginal generation costs, however, as Figure 4.1 shows, time-weighted mean annual Pool prices rose by 40% (nominal) in the first four years of its operation, and remained well above marginal generation costs up to and including 2000/01. The assumption that competition in the wholesale market would be sufficient to hold retail prices paid by consumers at or below pre-privatisation levels proved false. As a result, the Office of Gas and Electricity Markets[1] (Ofgem), which regulates the UK electricity and gas markets, was only able to

---

[1] Ofgem was created by merging the *Office of Electricity Regulation* (Offer) and the *Office for Gas Regulation* (Ofgas) in 1999 but for simplicity Ofgem will be used throughout.

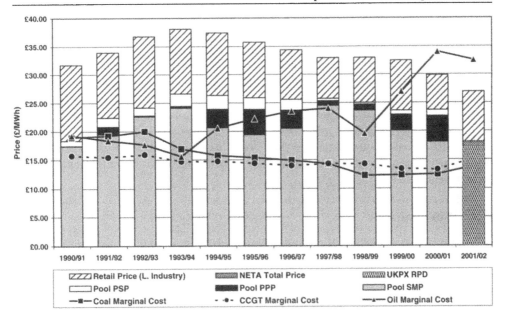

Retail Price = *DTI Quarterly Energy Prices*, Table 3.1.2 Prices of fuels purchased by manufacturing industry (www.dti.gov.uk/energy/inform/energy_prices/) with quarterly price for Large consumers in £/MWh calculated from formula p/kWh *10 then averaged over Q2, Q3, Q4, plus Q1
Marginal Cost = *DTI Quarterly Energy Prices*, Table 3.2.1 Average prices of fuels purchased by the major UK power producers (www.dti.gov.uk/energy/inform/energy_prices/) with quarterly marginal costs in £/MWh calculated from formula p/kWh *10 / Thermal Efficiency (coal 33%, CCGT 45%, oil 30%) then averaged over Q2, Q3, Q4 plus Q1
Pool Price = *Statistical Digest* (www.elecpool.com) with prices in £/MWh averaged over Month 4–12 plus Month 1–3
NETA Total Price = *UKPX RPD* (www.ukpx.co.uk) plus Balancing Mechanism Costs (from anonymous correspondent) with prices in £/MWh averaged over Month 4–12 plus Month 1–3

**Figure 4.1**    England and Wales arithmetic mean annual electricity prices and costs 1990–2002

deliver promised reductions in retail electricity prices to household/commercial consumers by imposing real-term reductions in the operating margins of the transmission, distribution and supply sectors where formal price controls were still in place. For large industrial consumers, many of whom had enjoyed subsidised tariffs prior to price liberalisation, rising Pool prices had a more immediate impact because price controls did not apply to electricity supplied to sites with peak demand above 1 MW after 1990/91.

Opinion had always been divided over whether day-ahead prices had remained high because of weaknesses in the complex market mechanism that underlay the Pool or because of the exercise of market power by the dominant duopoly of National Power and Powergen. Initially, Ofgem had been unconvinced that replacing the Pool trading mechanism with a mechanism where each generator got paid their own bid (Pay Bid), rather than a uniform marginal price (Pay SMP), would have a beneficial effect. Indeed, an Ofgem consultation on trading outside the pool in 1994 concluded that:

In sum, paying generators their bid prices would represent a major change which seems likely to have disadvantages in terms of increasing risks, particularly to smaller generators, without a strong likelihood that prices will be lower. In the longer term it could lead to higher prices. (Ofgem, July 1994)

The UK Government in the form of the Treasury, Competition Commission,[2] DTI and Ofgem intervened at various times, to modify the way that the wholesale electricity market operated in England and Wales from 1990 onwards. As a result, the Pool never really operated as a truly free market. In the absence of effective competition Ofgem was particularly active in controlling wholesale, and retail, prices through a series of regulatory interventions that had the implicit or explicit objective of placing a cap on prices. As Figure 4.2 shows, from 1996/97 onwards the frequency and duration of these regulatory interventions increased dramatically as compared with the previous six years. Eventually, at the request of the DTI, Ofgem reversed its earlier decision and announced that the Pool would have to be replaced by a bilateral trading mechanism similar to a traditional commodity market, called the New Electricity Trading Arrangements (NETA).

## 4.2.2  Coal contracts

On 31 March 1990, all of the coal-fired and oil-fired generating plant in England and Wales that had previously been under the control of the state-owned Central Electricity Generating Board (CEGB) were allocated ("vested") to two new companies, National Power and Powergen, in a 60:40 ratio.[3] The Regional Electricity Companies (RECs)[4] also had matching vesting contracts imposed upon them that obliged them to buy fixed amounts of electricity from the generators at a price that would provide a guaranteed margin to the generators and RECs. These vesting contracts, which lasted from 1 April 1990 to 31 March 1993, therefore effectively subsidised the UK coal industry by passing the cost of its deep-mined coal, which was higher than world prices, through to end users. Generators and RECs were therefore insulated from both the impact of high input prices as well as volatility in the Pool price.

During the term of these contracts the combined contractual volume of UK deep-mined coal consumed by UK generators was 70 million tonnes per year, in 1990/91 and 1991/92, then 65 million tonnes for 1992/93. Despite direct intervention by the DTI in the negotiations, generators were unwilling to continue contracting for large tonnages of UK coal after 31 March 1993 because of the prospect of coal plants increasingly being displaced by new entrant IPPs running CCGT plant. The deal that was eventually agreed saw contracted UK coal fall to 40 million tonnes for 1993/94 and 30 million tonnes for the following four years (Parker, 2000). Thereafter, the UK coal industry essentially had to compete with imported supplies at world market prices and much of the remaining deep-mine capacity closed as a result. In 2000/01, total UK deep-mined coal production fell to 18 million tonnes, as compared to 34 million tonnes of imports (DTI, 1990–2002a,b). Newbery (1995) argued that if a generator has sold forward contracts equal to the amount dispatched in a given period then its income is determined by the strike price of the forward contract not by the Pool price, and therefore it would have no incentive to raise SMP as this would not affect its revenue. Indeed the firm could do no better than bidding at short-run marginal cost.

---

[2] Formerly the Monopolies and Mergers Commission (MMC).

[3] For a chronology of the key events in the legislation, deregulation, privatisation, regulation of the UK electricity industry between 1988 and 2002 see *Electricity companies in the United Kingdom – a brief chronology* at http://www.electricity.org.uk/services_fr.html

[4] RECs were vertically disintegrated from generation at vesting, as was the National Grid Company (NGC) that owned and operated the transmission system. Initially each REC operated exclusively in one of 12 regions, where it had monopoly control of the distribution system and monopoly rights to supply household and commercial consumers with peak demand below 1 MW, the so-called "franchise market". After 31 March 1993, the franchise market threshold was reduced to 100 kW, and the RECs finally lost their remaining supply monopolies in 1998/99 when domestic and small commercial consumers were allowed to choose their own supplier.

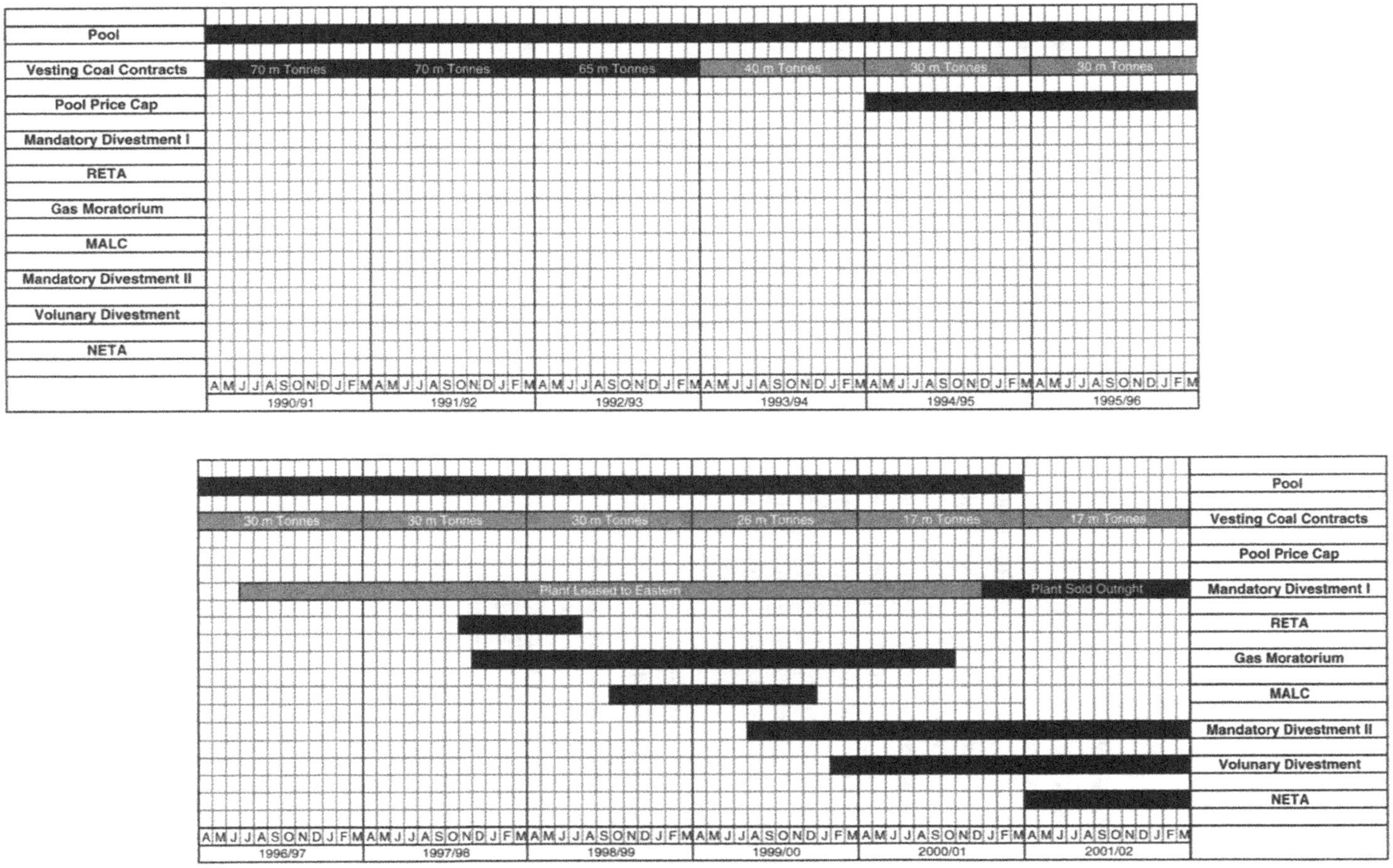

**Figure 4.2** Major regulatory interventions in the wholesale electricity market 1990–2002

Vesting contracts had a pro-competitive effect as they encouraged all generators to bid their plants as if the market were perfectly competitive. Thus vesting contracts reduced the incentive for mid-merit generators to exercise market power. As the volume of vesting contracts declined, the incentive for mid-merit generators to exercise market power in order to raise Pool prices increased. Indeed, as each anniversary of vesting approached pool prices did rise and the consensus view was that the duopoly generators used this as a signal to buyers that forward prices in the next contracting round would be above previous levels.

### 4.2.3   Pool price cap

As Pool prices had consistently risen since 1990, Ofgem had little choice but to place an explicit cap on them.[5] By threatening to refer the matter to the Competition Commission, Ofgem had extracted an undertaking from National Power and Powergen that they would bid their plant in such a way as to ensure that mean annual demand-weighted prices did not rise above £24.00/MWh on a time-weighted and £25.50/MWh on a demand-weighted basis (in October 1993 prices) for two years between 1 April 1994 and 31 March 1996. Although Pool prices did slightly exceed the target level in 1994/95 on a demand-weighted basis, they were a few percent below the cap on a time-weighted basis and no punitive action was taken. However, as plant owned by National Power and Powergen had set SMP over 90% of the time throughout the duration of the cap, and outturn price levels had so precisely matched the level agreed with the regulator some two years earlier, this suggests that they had exercised an extraordinary degree of control over the level of prices.

### 4.2.4   Plant divestment

The Pool price cap was only ever intended to be a temporary measure and integral to a wider agreement reached by Ofgem with National Power and Powergen that they would respectively divest 4000 MW and 2000 MW of capacity in the intervening period. Eventually, all the capacity was leased, but not sold, to Eastern Electricity, an REC, in mid-1996. The terms of these deals meant that Eastern paid a fixed charge, at the beginning of each year, plus a variable charge of around £6/MWh of output, that effectively raised its marginal production cost, and so prevented it being used to undercut the remaining National Power, and Powergen, plant portfolio.

It was hoped that the plant divestment, to create a third mid-merit generating firm, would increase competition sufficiently to keep prices under control once the price cap was removed. However, despite the divestment of plant to Eastern, arithmetic mean annual PSP only fell by about £1/MWh over the next four years. Though prices had on average been lower in 1997/98 than under the Pool price cap, severe price spikes in winter of that year promoted a further round of investigations into the price-setting behaviour of the duopoly generators which carried on for most of 1998. This was quickly followed by yet another investigation into the price spikes that occurred in January 1999. Almost as soon as this review had finished in May 1999 further spikes occurred in July, reported on in October of that year. Prior to the imposition of the price cap there had been a similar litany of investigation beginning as early as 1991, and it quickly became clear that this first round of plant divestment had only reduced mean annual prices slightly. Not only that, prices had become significantly more volatile, especially during the

---

[5] Key documents relating to the regular inquiries into price levels, and interventions such as the imposition of a price cap, are listed in the References section of this chapter under "Ofgem" and can be downloaded at http://www.ofgem.gov.uk/public/adownloads.htm#pool

winter months. Green and Newbery (1992) had argued that five price-setting (i.e. mid-merit) generators would be sufficient to ensure a competitive market. Green (1996) extended the work to show that although there would be an increase in competitiveness of the market due to the partial divestiture it would not be as large as if the duopolists had been split into several much smaller firms. Fundamentally, the creation of a third, relatively small generator left the market substantially more concentrated than it would have been had five equal sized generators been created and the empirically observed price response to the divestment is not surprising.

Ofgem and the DTI came under further pressure to take action and, simultaneous to the RETA public consultation process, they entered into a joint negotiation with National Power and Powergen over further plant divestment. Eventually it was agreed that each firm would be allowed to vertically reintegrate its generation businesses with the supply business of an REC in return for further divestment of around 4000 MW of plant. As a result, Powergen bought the retail supply business of East Midlands Electricity in July 1998 and National Power bought the retail supply business of Midlands Electricity Board (MEB) in June 1999. Subsequently, Powergen completed the sale of their Fiddlers Ferry (1960 MW) and Ferrybridge (1956 MW) plants in July 1999 to Edison Mission Energy. National Power likewise sold its Drax plant (3870 MW) in November 1999 to AES. In each case the divestments amounted to approximately 40% of their respective coal-fired plant portfolios. In addition, it was agreed that all of the lease arrangements on Eastern plant that had previously been divested were to be cancelled in exchange for a one-off lump sum payment. Despite the public pronouncements about the likely effectiveness of NETA, the Ofgem/DTI actions to force further plant divestment suggest they were less than wholly confident that reforming the electricity trading arrangements would be sufficient to reduce prices to a competitive level.

After the second mandatory round of divestment, National Power and Powergen management teams appear to have concluded that, in light of the prices that potential new entrants were willing to pay for existing coal plant, and in order to avoid further regulatory confrontation, it would be in the best interests of their shareholders to make further voluntary plant divestments. Over the next three years Powergen reduced its capacity share of the coal generation sector down to 13% by divesting further plant to British Energy and the French utility EDF. Eventually, the entire firm was taken over by E.ON, a German utility in July 2002. National Power reduced its coal generation capacity share to a similar level and then separated its now vertically integrated UK business from its international business to form two new companies, Innogy that was subsequently taken over by the German utility RWE in May 2002, and International Power. Eastern Electric also divested coal plant and a wave of generation asset trading, including CCGT plants, took place throughout 2000/01 to 2001/02. The result was that, by the time NETA began trading, the coal-fired generation sector became fragmented between eight firms. The industry structure of the mid-merit coal-fired generation sector that prevailed during the first year of NETA was therefore starkly different to that over the life of the Pool, as shown in Figure 4.3.

### 4.2.5   Replacement of the Pool with NETA

Beginning in May 1998, the Review of Electricity Trading Arrangements (RETA) was launched, with the stated aim of developing an entirely new wholesale market mechanism to replace the Pool.

Trading in the wholesale electricity market, under both the Pool and NETA, can be broken down into three sequential phases, forward trading, day-ahead trading and on-the-day trading.

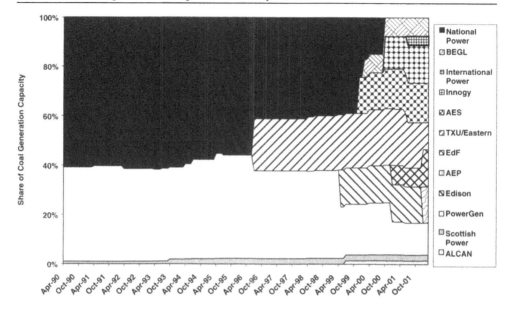

**Figure 4.3**   Coal-fired generation capacity ownership structure 1990–2002

Only day-ahead trading is dealt with here but for a more detailed analysis of the Pool mechanism see Electricity Pool of England and Wales (1994a,b, 1998) and for NETA see the key Ofgem documents separately listed in the Reference section at the end of this chapter.

Essentially, the Pool day-ahead market was a series of mandatory uniform price auctions, one for each half-hour of the day-ahead, operated by a centralised auctioneer with the objective of producing an optimal schedule of generating plant to meet demand. NETA replaced this process with decentralised voluntary bilateral contracting which could take place directly be-tween generators, suppliers and traders with generating plant self-dispatched by each generator according to its contractual commitments.

The primary purpose of the day-ahead price-setting process in the Pool was to produce a least-cost schedule of plants that would be dispatched by the National Grid Company (NGC) who operated the transmission system, to meet forecast demand in each half-hour of the next day. The deadline for submission of bids by generators was 10.00 a.m. on the day before dispatch with each generator submitting a nine-part bid made up of three price–quantity pairs plus a price that was intended to cover the fixed cost of starting the plant, a no-load price and a must-run flag that was used to indicate inflexible plant. Having received all the bids NGC then created a supply curve by "stacking" the bids low-to-high to produce an optimal unconstrained schedule of plant for dispatch. The bid price at which the supply function intersected with NGC's forecast demand schedule for each half-hour of the next day set the System Marginal Price (SMP).

After SMP had been set, NGC also calculated an additional capacity payment that reflected the probability of supply failing to meet demand, the Loss of Load Probability (LOLP) and the estimated marginal value of that unserved load, the Value of Lost Load (VOLL) as follows:

$$\text{capacity payment} = \text{LOLP} \times (\text{VOLL} - \text{SMP})$$

Capacity payments were therefore an entirely administered charge calculated from a formula that was intended to compensate generators for retaining marginal plant on the system, which they might have otherwise closed. To provide the appropriate signal, LOLP had been designed to increase exponentially as demand approached total available system capacity. As VOLL was set at £2000/MWh in 1990, with increases in subsequent years in line with Retail Price Inflation (RPI), this meant that capacity payments could potentially become a significant percentage of the total wholesale price, especially during the winter months when demand was highest. The capacity payment was added to SMP during each half-hour to produce the Pool Purchase Price (PPP) as follows:

$$PPP = SMP + \text{capacity payment}$$

All generators included in the unconstrained schedule received PPP for their output, comprising SMP plus capacity payments where applicable, regardless of what bids they had actually submitted. This "Pay SMP" approach resulted in those generators operating low-cost, but inflexible, nuclear and CCGT capacity consistently bidding zero in order to ensure their plant(s) were called to run. For more than half of the Pool's existence (until 1996/97) this effectively left the setting of SMP, and therefore PPP, under the control of a duopoly of firms, National Power and Powergen, which owned or controlled almost all of the mid-merit[6] coal-fired generation capacity.

Withdrawing capacity in the day-ahead market also had the effect of driving up LOLP, and as Bunn and Larsen (1992) show, since LOLP is an extremely convex function strategically withdrawing capacity to increase capacity payments would substantially increase the revenues earned by generators. Patrick and Wolak (1997) note that a more high powered and difficult to detect strategy than just bidding high prices to set a high SMP would be to bid each plant at close to marginal cost and then declare capacity available in different periods throughout the day.

Under NETA, day-ahead trading continues right up to gate closure, which is three hours before the relevant half-hour dispatch period.[7] As NGC is no longer responsible for producing a day-ahead dispatch schedule all generators, suppliers and traders must notify NGC of the quantity of electricity they intend to physically inject or withdraw from the transmission system in the relevant half-hour. The first notification is only indicative, known as Initial Physical Notification (IPN), and must be submitted by 11.00 a.m. on the day before dispatch. A subsequent firm Final Physical Notification (FPN) must then be submitted by gate closure. Although vertically integrated firms that operate both as generators and suppliers, they must submit separate notifications for their generation and supply business, not an aggregate net production or consumption figure. In other words, for operational purposes, NGC still regards a vertically integrated generator with a supply business as if it were two legally separate firms with each making an independent decision about the quantity of electricity they will contract for, as well as inject or withdraw, in any given period.

To facilitate day-ahead, and longer-term, trading two rival market operators (APX and UKPX) began operating screen-based exchange market places where bids and offers could be anonymously posted. Despite this, most trading migrated to an informal over-the-counter market, operated on the telephone and bulletin boards via brokers, and the liquidity and transparency of the day-ahead market is lower under NETA than the Pool. However, the

---

[6] Mid-merit plant usually only run during daylight hours when demand is relatively high, as opposed to baseload plant run continuously both day and night, or peaking plant that only run infrequently during periods of unusually high demand.

[7] This was reduced to one hour in July 2002, which is after the period considered in this chapter.

UKPX publishes a Reference Price Day-Ahead (RPD) index that facilitates the comparison of day-ahead prices under NETA with those in the Pool. Given its relative transparency, RPD has been used in this chapter as an indicator of the actual level of day-ahead prices under NETA.

In practice generators, suppliers and consumers under both the Pool and NETA did not rely on the day-ahead market to determine the price they paid or received. Instead, they hedged most (>90%) of their output and consumption via forward contracts signed months or often years ahead of dispatch. Despite the volume of electricity that was covered by contracts, forward markets were highly illiquid and largely limited to semi-annual contracting rounds, held in April and October. Forward market liquidity only improved as the number of consumers eligible to choose their own supplier gradually increased, the element of cost pass-through reduced and the ownership of generation fragmented.

In both the Pool and NETA, forward trading occurred on a bilateral basis through private over-the-counter (OTC) contracts. The main difference being that under the Pool forward contracting was restricted to trading in contracts for difference (CFDs) and exchange traded forward agreements (EFAs) that were not for physical delivery but settled in cash by reference to PPP on the relevant delivery day(s). All physical delivery took place through the Pool and contracted plant usually bid zero prices to ensure they were included in the unconstrained schedule. Under NETA, almost all forward contracts are for physical delivery rather than financial settlement. The bilateral nature of the NETA day-ahead market, with so-called "what-you-bid-is-what-you-get" (WYBIWYG or Pay Bid) pricing, meant that baseload generators could no longer bid zero and allow marginal generators to set the price as they had in the Pool.

### 4.2.6   Gas moratorium

Demand-weighted average prices for coal bought by UK generators fell as volumes of low-cost imported coal took an increasing share of the UK market. However, the guaranteed generation margin that vesting contracts provided had the unintended effect of encouraging incumbent generators, the RECS and new entrants to build new CCGT plant. These early CCGT entrants were able to undercut small and medium-sized coal plant, on a short-run marginal cost basis, and also displaced more efficient large coal plant from the baseload segment of the load duration curve. A combination of new entry by CCGT, and rising oil prices, also meant that much of the conventional oil-fired generation capacity was closed or mothballed under the Pool. Increasing thermal efficiency through rapidly advancing turbine technology, falling gas prices, falling capital costs and relatively short construction times for CCGT led to the "dash for gas" that resulted in 22 500 MW of new capacity being commissioned by 2002. Figure 4.4 shows the capacity share of each generation technology throughout the life of the Pool and first year of NETA. The technologies have been sorted according to their approximate marginal production costs and this shows how coal plant was displaced by the rapid entry of CCGT.

By the mid-1990s, the DTI was becoming alarmed at the increasing dependence of the UK on gas-fired generation capacity and in November 1997, coincident with launching RETA, it imposed a moratorium on issuing of new CCGT plant construction licences. This was designed to provide a breathing space during which energy policy could be reviewed, especially in relation to UK coal, and a final decision be made about whether to reform or replace the Pool trading arrangements. When the DTI published its final report in June 1998 (DTI, 1998), it concluded that the growth in CCGT capacity, and depletion of gas reserves in the North Sea, meant that the UK was likely to become a net importer of gas by 2010. Moreover,

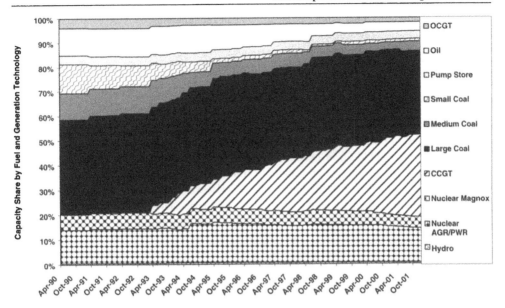

**Figure 4.4**   Capacity share by fuel and generation technology 1990–2002

growth projections to 2020 suggested gas could account for 60% of total UK primary energy consumption, and 75–90% of electricity generation fuel by 2020 (DTI, 2000).

The main proposal coming out of the review was that the gas moratorium should continue until the electricity market had been reformed, on the grounds that if no action was taken "the country could effectively lose a coal option". The intention was to allow NETA sufficient time to reduce wholesale prices to a level that would make further CCGT investment unattractive and preserve the remaining coal-fired generation capacity. However, Ofgem disagreed with the gas moratorium policy and publicly stated that:

> The policy of restricting new entry into generation is now the main obstacle to a more competitive electricity market. A continuing threat to incumbents from new entrants is of the utmost importance in preventing collusion, and in ensuring that reforms to trading arrangements are successful and deliver benefits to consumers, particularly in the form of lower prices. (Ofgem, 1999)

In practice, little could be done to increase the amount of UK coal contracted for by generators after 31 March 1998, even if all the existing coal-fired capacity remained open. Facing intense lobbying from foreign firms who wished to enter the UK electricity market with new CCGT plant, and without the support of Ofgem, the DTI had little choice but to abandon its policy. Once RETA had been completed, and the DTI and Ofgem had agreed the structure of NETA in October 1999, the gas moratorium was formally lifted in November 1999. As it did not cover plants already under construction, or that had already been licensed, the moratorium's impact was limited to delaying the construction of a few plants by a matter of a year to 18 months.

Even if the gas moratorium had not been lifted, it is likely that compensating mechanisms in the fuel and capital markets would have rendered it unnecessary anyway. As Figure 4.1 showed, the artificial cost advantage that CCGT enjoyed due to the coal vesting contracts had already been eroded by 1997/98 as the quantity of imported coal increased. Short-run marginal costs for coal and CCGT converged, which meant that in the later years of the Pool and first year of NETA coal and gas were competing head-to-head for fuel share of the electricity market. Under NETA, the BM rewarded flexible plant that could run at short notice and generators reinstated oil plants to take advantage of occasional very high SBP, displacing lower-cost but relatively inflexible CCGT and coal plants in the merit order.

### 4.2.7 Market abuse licence clause

In the intervening period, between the completion of RETA and the introduction of NETA, Ofgem attempted to control the wholesale price of electricity by introducing a new market abuse licence clause (MALC) in generation licences.[8] The objective was to limit the scope for generators to exercise market power throughout the remaining life of the Pool, and for at least the first year after the introduction of NETA. However, there was no definition of what price level, or trading activity, would constitute market abuse. Indeed, Ofgem explicitly stated that it was against the introduction of any form of price regulation because it was "likely to stifle innovation, have harmful effects on competition by limiting the incentives on new entry into the market and, additionally, have a detrimental effect on the development of the forward contract market". However, the proposal effectively gave Ofgem absolute discretion to determine a maximum permissible level for wholesale market prices, and define any trading activity as market abuse. By introducing MALC, it appears that Ofgem was attempting to signal to generators that wholesale market prices would either be reduced to competitive levels by competition or, if necessary, by regulatory intervention.

In effect, Ofgem gave generators little option but to accept MALC and reduce Pool prices. Only two generators refused to accept the modification to their generation licences, AES and British Energy, and both were immediately referred to the Competition Commission. However, the findings of the subsequent inquiry did not support Ofgem. The Competition Commission concluded that MALC was unnecessary in the context of the plant divestment that had taken place already, and further divestments that were likely to take place in future, as well as new entry by CCGT plant operators. It also noted the 17% fall in real terms in Pool prices that had already occurred in the five years up to 1999/2000 (Competition Commission, 2001). In the particular case of AES and British Energy, the Competition Commission noted that the behaviour of the two firms in forward contracting almost all of their output on a long-term basis made it virtually impossible for them to exercise market power either by withdrawing capacity or raising the price at which they offered that capacity to the market.

In view of the Competition Commission decision, Ofgem was forced to remove MALC from all the generator licences that had already agreed to its introduction. However, the Ofgem Director General's comments in response to the decision reveals that he was far from certain that the plant divestment that had already taken place, and/or the introduction of NETA in a few months' time, would be sufficient to deliver lower prices without MALC:

> I regard this as a substantial loss of measures needed by Ofgem to do our job. This is to the detriment of consumers whose protection is Ofgem's primary objective under the law. Ofgem will continue to look at other ways of tackling market abuse although none of these is likely to be as effective as the licence condition which we have now had to withdraw. (Ofgem, 2001)

With the backing of the DTI, Ofgem attempted to reintroduce MALC by producing fresh proposals in August 2001 but in a form that might be more acceptable to the Competition

---

[8] Key documents relating to the introduction of MALC and the Ofgem response to the Competition Commission decision are listed in the References section of this chapter under "Ofgem" and can be downloaded at: http://www.ofgem.gov.uk/public/pubframe.htm

Commission. However, as wholesale prices continued to fall throughout 2001/02, it became increasingly untenable to argue that MALC was needed in any form and the matter was quietly dropped.

# 4.3  ANALYSIS

In the first six years of the Pool's existence, up to the end of 1995/96, regulatory interventions fell into two distinct sequential phases. The first phase was the vesting contracts that were essentially driven by the UK Treasury's need to facilitate privatisation of the electricity industry and provide support to UK coal without recourse to public funds. The second phase was the imposition of the Pool price cap beginning on 1 April 1994. However, in the period from 1996/97 onwards, covering the last five years of the Pool and the first year of NETA, Ofgem and the DTI appear to have abandoned the earlier incremental approach to regulation in favour of a more aggressive multi-layered approach that manifested itself in a continuous stream of overlapping interventions. Against this background, the claims and counterclaims about the relative effectiveness of NETA in reducing wholesale prices, versus any of the other regulatory interventions that occurred over the same period, are difficult to assess.

## 4.3.1  Analytical method

In the remainder of this section an attempt is made to measure precisely the significance, and quantify the impact on day-ahead prices, of each of the major regulatory interventions described above. To achieve this, dependent variables representing different functionally equivalent components of the wholesale price under the Pool and NETA are regressed on a range of independent (explanatory) variables representing each of the major regulatory interventions, as well as external factors such as weather and plant investment. The method and results presented here are drawn from a larger and more comprehensive study (Bower, 2002) but the objective is to measure the impact of each of the regulatory interventions, especially changes in plant ownership patterns, on year-on-year wholesale price changes over the period 1 April 1990–31 March 2002. Table 4.1 summarises the data sources, units and time periods covered by each of the dependent and independent variables.

A backward linear least squares multiple regression procedure was applied to the variables in which the initial regression run contains all the candidate independent variables. The independent variable with the highest $p$-value (i.e. statistically least significant) is then eliminated and the regression repeated. The sequential elimination of insignificant independent variables is repeated until the $p$-values of all the remaining variables are equal to or less than 0.10. In other words, the final regression model only contains independent variables that have coefficients that are statistically significant at the 90% confidence level. Wolfram (1998) analysed time series of Pool prices with a multiple regression approach to measure the impact of regulatory interventions on Pool price mark-up over short-run marginal generation costs. From the results, she was able to conclude that generators were not taking full advantage of their ability to exercise market power, given the inelastic demand for electricity, but that they were modifying their behaviour in response to regulatory interventions, and that generators were restraining prices either to deter entry or stave off substantial regulatory action. Although the approach proposed in this paper does not attempt to replicate these results, this earlier study does indicate that it is feasible to detect the response of generators to regulatory interventions from an analysis of price time series and provides support for the choice of analytical approach. The construction

**Table 4.1** Dependent and independent variables

| Name | Underlying time series[1] | Frequency[2] | Units[3] | Data source | Utilised |
|---|---|---|---|---|---|
| | | Dependent variable | | | |
| PPPRPD | PPP concatenated with RPD | Daily | £/MWh | PPP: Statistical Digest at www.elecpool.com, RPD: UKPX at www.ukpx.co.uk | Y |
| | | Independent variables | | | |
| COALMC | (Mean price of coal purchased by UK generators in p/KWh/33%) ×1000 | Quarterly | £/MWh | DTI Quarterly Energy Prices at www.dti.gov.uk/energy/inform/energy-prices/ | Y |
| CCGTMC | (Mean price of gas purchased by UK generators in p/KWh/45%) ×1000 | Quarterly | £/MWh | DTI Quarterly Energy Prices at www.dti.gov.uk/energy/inform/energy-prices/ | Y |
| OILMC | (Mean price of oil purchased by UK generators in p/KWh/30%) ×1000 | Quarterly | £/MWh | DTI Quarterly Energy Prices at www.dti.gov.uk/energy/inform/energy_prices/ | Y |
| NUCLEARCCI | Sum of squared % coal plant capacity owned by each firm | Monthly | Index | CEGB Statistical Year Book 1988/89, NGC Seven Year Statements at www.nationalgrid.co.uk/library/ | Y |
| COALCCI | Sum of squared % coal plant capacity owned by each firm | Monthly | Index | CEGB Statistical Year Book 1988/89, NGC Seven Year Statements at www.nationalgrid.co.uk/library/ | Y |
| CCGTCCI | Sum of squared % CCGT plant capacity owned by each firm | Monthly | Index | CEGB Statistical Year Book 1988/89, NGC Seven Year Statements at www.nationalgrid.co.uk/library/ | Y |
| OILCCI | Sum of squared % oil plant capacity owned by each firm | Monthly | Index | CEGB Statistical Year Book 1988/89, NGC Seven Year Statements at www.nationalgrid.co.uk/library/ | Y |
| OCGTCCI | Sum of squared % OCGT plant capacity owned by each firm | Monthly | Index | CEGB Statistical Year Book 1988/89, NGC Seven Year Statements at www.nationalgrid.co.uk/library/ | N |
| HYDROCCI | Sum of squared % hydro plant capacity owned by each firm | Monthly | Index | CEGB Statistical Year Book 1988/89, NGC Seven Year Statements at www.nationalgrid.co.uk/library/ | N |
| PSTORECCI | Sum of squared % pump storage plant capacity owned by each firm | Monthly | Index | CEGB Statistical Year Book 1988/89, NGC Seven Year Statements at www.nationalgrid.co.uk/library/ | N |
| INDCCI | Sum of squared % total plant capacity owned by each firm | Monthly | Index | CEGB Statistical Year Book 1988/89, NGC Seven Year Statements at www.nationalgrid.co.uk/library/ | N |

| Variable | Description | Frequency | Units | Source | |
|---|---|---|---|---|---|
| PMARGIN | (Plant capacity – annual peak demand)/annual peak demand | Monthly | % | CEGB Statistical Year Book 1988/89, NGC Seven Year Statements at www.nationalgrid.co.uk/library/ | Y |
| TEMPMEAN | Mean monthly air temperature | Monthly | Celsius | DTI Digest of UK Energy Statistics at www.dti.gov.uk/energy/energystats/ | N |
| TEMPHEAT | MAX (monthly air temperature – 15, 0) | Monthly | Celsius | DTI Digest of UK Energy Statistics at www.dti.gov.uk/energy/energystats/ | Y |
| TEMPCOOL | MAX (15-mean monthly air temperature, 0) | Monthly | Celsius | DTI Digest of UK Energy Statistics at www.dti.gov.uk/energy/energystats/ | N |
| TEMPDEV | Mean monthly air temperature – long-term mean (1961–1990) | Monthly | Celsius | DTI Digest of UK Energy Statistics at www.dti.gov.uk/energy/energystats/ | N |
| COALCONR | Publicly reported estimates | Annual | 1000 tonnes | Parker (2000) *Thatcherism and the Fall of Coal* and Press archives searches | Y |
| COALCONI | Supply of UK deep-mined coal | Annual | 1000 tonnes | DTI Digest of UK Energy Statistics at http://www.dti.gov.uk/energy/inform/energy_stats/coal/ | N |
| CAP | Dummy variable (April 1994–March 1996) | Monthly | 0.1 | Ofgem Publications (www.ofgem.gov.uk/public/pubframe.htm) and press archive searches | Y |
| EASTLEASE | Dummy variable (July 1996–December 2000) | Monthly | 0.1 | Ofgem Publications (www.ofgem.gov.uk/public/pubframe.htm) and press archive searches | Y |
| GASMORAT | Dummy variable (December 1997–October 2000) | Monthly | 0.1 | Ofgem Publications (www.ofgem.gov.uk/public/pubframe.htm) and press archive searches | Y |
| RETA | Dummy variable (November 1997–July 1998) | Monthly | 0.1 | Ofgem Publications (www.ofgem.gov.uk/public/pubframe.htm) and press archive searches | Y |
| MALC | Dummy variable (October 1999–December 2000) | Monthly | 0.1 | Ofgem Publications (www.ofgem.gov.uk/public/pubframe.htm) and press archive searches | Y |
| NETA | Dummy variable (April 2001–March 2002) | Monthly | 0.1 | Ofgem Publications (www.ofgem.gov.uk/public/pubframe.htm) and press archive searches | Y |

*Notes*: 1. All underlying time series were transformed by calculating year-on-year monthly changes to produce the dependent and independent variables.
2. Frequency corresponds to that in underlying time series that were converted to a common monthly frequency before producing the dependent and independent variables.
3. Units correspond to those in the dependent and independent variables.

of the variables, their analysis and the results are discussed in detail throughout the remainder of this section.

### 4.3.2   Variables

The starting point for the analysis was the construction of Pool day-ahead wholesale price time series. Monthly arithmetic mean PPP values were collected from the period 1 April 1990 to 26 March 2001 (Electricity Pool of England and Wales, 1990–2002). NETA wholesale price time series were calculated for the period 1 April 2001 to March 2002[9] in the form of monthly arithmetic means for the day-ahead RPD calculated from hourly data supplied by UKPX. A raw wholesale price time series for the period 1 April 1990 to 31 March 2002 (144 monthly observations) covering the entire history of the Pool and first year of NETA was constructed by concatenating the PPP and RPD series. This was transformed to produce the dependent variable (PPPRPD) consisting of a series of 132 monthly year-on-year price changes, using the following formula:

$$P_{\text{differenced}} = P_{\text{current month}} - P_{\text{month 12}}$$

The independent variables were constructed in the same way by initially collecting raw time series consisting of 144 monthly observations for the period 1 April 1990–31 March 2002.

To capture the impact of changes in ownership of generation capacity, the fuel source, registered capacity and ownership of every power plant connected directly to the transmission system of England and Wales[10] was tracked on a monthly basis using publicly available data published by CEGB (1989), NGC (1991–2002), Electricity Association (1991–2001), Power UK (1994–2002), as well as press archive searches. In the absence of contradictory data, plant closures were assumed to take place on 31 March, the deadline imposed by NGC on generators to declare plant as transmission contracted for the following year. Commissioning of new plant, especially CCGT, is assumed to take place on the first day of the month following that in which plant testing and final hand-over from the contractor to the generator were completed. The evolution of capacity on interconnector transmission circuits that allow imports from France and Scotland into England and Wales was tracked from the same sources as for plant capacity.

A Capacity Concentration Index (CCI) was then calculated on a monthly basis for coal, CCGT, nuclear and oil plant, by summing the squared capacity share of each firm for each plant type. A CCI for the entire industry was also calculated by summing squared shares of total capacity owned by each firm, regardless of plant type. However, as changes in the industry CCI essentially tracked the change in CCI of the underlying plant technologies this variable was not used in the final analysis in order to avoid multicollinearity between variables. The open cycle gas turbine (OCGT) CCI was not used because these small auxiliary plants were generally operated from the same site as coal plant and changes in OCGT CCI were therefore highly correlated with changes in coal CCI. The CCIs for hydro and pump storage plant were also calculated but, as both were constant throughout, they were not used. Interconnector capacity from France was included in the nuclear CCI, and interconnector capacity from Scotland was split on a pro-rata basis between hydro and coal capacity to reflect the interconnector shares and generation capacity held by the two Scottish generators, Scottish & Southern Energy and

---

[9] Pool prices for March 2001 are calculated up to 26 March 2001 when the Pool ceased trading. NETA began trading on 27 March 2001, but April 2001 monthly average RPD is calculated from 1 April 2001.

[10] This transmission contracted plant excludes the embedded generation capacity connected directly to local distribution systems, which was excluded from the obligation to submit bids into the Pool.

Scottish Power respectively. Any dual fuel plant on the system was assumed to be burning coal and included in the coal CCI.

The CCI is non-linear with a theoretical maximum of 10 000 if one firm owns all of the capacity of a given type and zero if that capacity is spread between an infinite number of firms. It is therefore identical in concept to the HHI, the only difference being that the sum of squared market shares has been replaced with the sum of squared capacity shares in the CCI. At the inception of the Pool in 1990, National Power and Powergen owned all the coal-fired generation capacity in an approximate 60:40 ratio, corresponding to a coal CCI of around 5200. By 2001/02 the coal CCI had fallen to around 1400 because of plant divestment. By comparison, an industry with coal capacity split equally between five firms, as proposed by Green and Newbery (1992), would have resulted in a coal CCI of 2000. As the first CCGT plant in existence did not become fully operational until around November 1991, the CCGT CCI is assumed to be 10 000 before this date and thereafter until the second CCGT plant came on stream in April 1993 when the CCGT CCI begins to fall rapidly.

Short-run marginal generation costs were calculated for coal, CCGT and oil plants based on the average cost of each fuel used in UK power stations, and the estimated thermal efficiency for a marginal plant of each type, as reported in DTI statistics (DTI, 1990–2002a,b) using the following formula:

$$\text{marginal generation cost} = [\text{fuel price (p/kWh)} / \text{thermal efficiency (\%)}] \times 1000$$

Average thermal efficiencies have gradually increased for the entire fleet of UK coal plant from 34% to 36% and for CCGT from 43% to 50%, over the period 1990–2001, but marginal thermal efficiency data were not reported. For simplicity, it has been assumed that they remained constant at 33% for coal, 45% for CCGT and 30% for oil.

Data on annual tonnages of UK deep-mined coal production were also collected from DTI statistics (DT1, 1990–2002a,b) in an attempt to estimate annual contracted volumes of UK coal sold to power generators. However, after some preliminary testing it was found that contracted tonnages reported by Parker (2000), and drawn from searches of press archives, were a relatively more powerful explanatory variable.

The impact of new entry was modelled by estimating the plant margin for each month. As data on total system demand, and the quantity of plant available to the system after outages were not available, a proxy was estimated from total plant capacity and annual peak demand (NGC, 1991–2002; Electricity Association, 1991–2001) as follows:

$$\text{plant margin}_{\text{mthly}} = (\text{plant capacity}_{\text{mthly}} - \text{ACS peak}_{\text{yrly}})/(\text{plant capacity}_{\text{mthly}} \times 100)$$

The final quantitative variable considered was temperature. To capture its effect on prices, mean monthly temperature data as well as deviations from the long-term mean were collected. Mean heating degree and mean cooling degree parameters were also calculated from the following formulas:

$$\text{mean heating degrees} = \text{Max} (15 - \text{mean monthly temperature}, 0)$$

$$\text{mean cooling degrees} = \text{Max} (\text{mean monthly temperature} - 15, 0)$$

After preliminary analysis, it became apparent that mean heating degrees was the only significant temperature variable, and the others were discarded. This is consistent with UK peak electricity demand occurring in the winter, but this variable captures any increase in electricity demand above and beyond that normal winter seasonal pattern. As UK winter temperatures are

**Table 4.2**  PPPRPD regression output

| Variable | Coefficient | Std. error | $t$-Statistic | $p$-Value |
|---|---|---|---|---|
| CCGTCCI | 0.0014 | 0.0005 | 2.8566 | 0.0050 |
| COALCCI | 0.0018 | 0.0011 | 1.7313 | 0.0859 |
| COALCONR | −0.0003 | 0.0001 | −2.3563 | 0.0200 |
| GASMORAT | 3.4807 | 1.3090 | 2.6592 | 0.0089 |
| OILCCI | 0.0036 | 0.0013 | 2.7613 | 0.0066 |
| TEMPHEAT | 0.6348 | 0.3528 | 1.7995 | 0.0744 |
| C | 0.9804 | 0.8037 | 1.2198 | 0.2248 |
| $R$-squared | 0.2082 | Mean dependent variable | | −0.0213 |
| Adjusted $R$-squared | 0.1702 | S.D. dependent variable | | 6.5336 |
| S.E. of regression | 5.9515 | Akaike information criterion | | 6.4568 |
| Sum squared residual | 4427.6119 | Schwarz criterion | | 6.6096 |
| Log likelihood | −419.1456 | $F$-statistic | | 5.4794 |
| Durbin–Watson statistic | 1.6710 | Prob($F$-statistic) | | 0.0000 |

generally higher than for similar north European latitudes, periods of unusually cold temperatures tend to have a disproportionate effect on demand for electricity, and hence price. Though
the majority of UK space heating is from gas-fired and oil-fired boilers, relatively inefficient
electrical appliances are often used to meet incremental heating demand above normal winter
levels, especially for domestic and small commercial users.

Regulatory interventions including the Pool price cap, RETA, MALC, gas moratorium and
NETA are modelled as qualitative factors with dummy variables taking a value 1 for each
month that an intervention was in place, and 0 in months where it was not. For example, NETA
is represented by a dummy variable taking a value 1 in the 12 months from 1 April 2001 to 31
March 2002, and 0 in all preceding months. The period covered by the lease arrangements on
the plant divested to Eastern was also modelled with a dummy variable but the concentration
effect of the disposal was also separately accounted for in the coal CCI. As with the dependent
variables, all of the raw time series described above were transformed to construct a set of
independent variables, each consisting of a time series of 132 monthly year-on-year changes.

### 4.3.3   Results

The relationship between year-on-year monthly price changes in the PPPRPD price series and
the independent variables was analysed using backward stepwise regression. A summary of
the resulting coefficients and selected test statistics is set out in Table 4.2.[11]

The most immediate conclusion that can be drawn is that the lack of a significant NETA
variable suggests that the introduction of NETA had no effect on curtailing the exercise of market power and/or reducing PPP but that changes in the concentration of ownership in different
types of plant appear to be significantly important. The COALCCI variable is statistically
significant at the 90% level ($p$-value of 0.0859) and also has a magnitude and direction that are
consistent with a fall in day-ahead prices brought about by divestments. Over the entire period 1
April 1990 to March 2002 the coal CCI fell by 3856 which, when multiplied by the COALCCI

---

[11] The results were generated using *Eviews 4.0* software. As a crosscheck for accuracy and consistency the analysis was repeated
using *StatPro* software that produced identical results to two decimal places.

coefficient value of 0.0018, represents a price fall of £6.94. The COALCONR coefficient is also statistically significant and shows that there was a reciprocal (negative) relationship between the tonnage of UK coal that generators contracted for and day-ahead prices. As these coal contracts were matched by matching forward contract sales of electricity this result supports the empirical observation that vesting contracts made the market more competitive with Pool prices rising as contract volumes decreased.

Taken together, the significance, magnitude and direction of the COALCCI and COAL-CONR confirm the widely held view that the coal-fired generation duopoly of National Power and Powergen was able to exercise a considerable amount of market power in the Pool. This was especially so after 31 March 1993 when the vesting coal contracts expired. Furthermore, the results suggest that without the ameliorating effects of the Pool price cap, followed by the multiple rounds of plant divestment from 1996 onwards, the two firms would have continued to exercise significant market power and raise SMP significantly above the levels that were actually observed.

The CCGTCCI and GASMORAT variables also confirm that actual or threatened entry by new gas-fired plant also curtailed the duopolists' market power although clearly left them free to exercise it to a considerable degree. In the early days of the Pool CCGT normally ran as baseload plant but in later years and under NETA the convergence of coal and gas marginal generation costs may have had a more significant impact on prices than has previously been acknowledged since coal and CCGT plant were effectively competing head-to-head in the mid-merit. The GASMORAT coefficient indicates that the gas moratorium allowed generators to raise PPP by £3.48/MWh. Although it was only a temporary intervention, given that the moratorium was imposed shortly after coal and gas marginal generation costs had converged, this result supports the Ofgem view that the threat of new entry by CCGT helped to curtail the exercise of market power by the duopoly generators. The coal-fired duopoly appears to have responded rationally to the initial DTI announcement that it intended to leave the moratorium in place for an extended period by raising prices.

For oil plant, the CCI remained almost constant throughout the life of the Pool, though the rise in oil prices limited its use to peak load hours only. The inherent flexibility of oil-fired plant may have made it an important factor in the operation of market once NETA was introduced and statistically significant. This may have been encouraged by NGC because of the way in which it changed its contracting strategy for reserve capacity that allowed oil-fired plant to cover their fixed costs associated with ramping up their boilers to operating temperatures.[12] The unexpected reinstatement of partially mothballed oil plant also effectively increased total available generation capacity, especially on a day-ahead and on-the-day basis, which may have put further downward pressure on prices in 2001/02. However, this is a transient effect and unusually cold weather does not appear to have significantly increased generator market power.

The inclusion of the TEMPHEAT coefficient is consistent with the operation of the LOLP calculation that increased the capacity payment component of PPP as plant margin fell. The direction and magnitude of the coefficient reflects the short-term impact of unusually cold weather on electricity demand for heating in winter and suggests that PPP rose by approximately £0.63/MWh for each 1°C that mean monthly temperatures fell below the normal winter level. However, the impact is relatively small as the unusually warm weather in the months December–February of 2001/02 appears to have only contributed a £0.60/MWh reduction in RPD below the PPP of the previous year.

---

[12] That is the cost of fuel burnt in the initial heating stage before electricity can be produced.

Overall the PPPRPD result appears to be robust because all of the significant variables included in the model, as well as their magnitude and direction, are consistent with economic theory and empirical observation. In addition, the Durbin–Watson statistic indicates that there is no significant serial correlation in the residuals and that the process of differencing the variables to estimate year-on-year monthly price changes was sufficient to make both the dependent and independent time series stationary.

Overall, the results confirm that the introduction of NETA alone, in the absence of other regulatory interventions, would not have resulted in a statistically significant reduction in wholesale prices. The principal causes of falling prices in the last year of the Pool, and first year of NETA, were reductions in the concentration of ownership in coal-fired generation capacity, combined with new entry by CCGT that increased competition in the mid-merit market. Certainly the inclusion of the GASMORAT variable suggests that removing the threat of continuing entry by significant amounts of CCGT increased the duopolists' willingness to exercise market power and bid in such a way as to raise PPP above the competitive level.

## 4.4  PRICE FORECAST

The results presented above show that regulatory interventions that had resulted in a reduction in the concentration of the mid-merit sector both from divestment of coal plant and new entry by gas that initially undercut and then competed head-to-head with coal were the main reason why wholesale prices fell in the period 1 April 1990–31 March 2002. However, the industry continued to evolve after the end of the period of this study and in the remainder of the chapter, the CCI coefficients estimated previously are used to forecast the price impact of a series of generation asset mergers in England and Wales as well as Scotland that were proposed and partly implemented during the final quarter of 2002.

### 4.4.1  Events in 2002/03

By the time that NETA completed its first year of operation, in 2001/02, it began to be criticised by both the DTI and the industry, because of the very low level of wholesale prices. Fears began to grow about system security as nuclear plants were no longer able to cover their fixed costs, and a number of coal and CCGT plant were withdrawn from production and mothballed. In summer 2002, the DTI suggested that NETA would have to be reformed in some unspecified way to allow operators of inflexible nuclear or inherently unreliable capacity combined heat and power (CHP) plants to get a fair price for their output. Already alarmed by the growing UK dependency on gas, the DTI saw nuclear energy following the same declining path as coal. As an interim measure, the DTI intervened to save British Energy from bankruptcy by granting it a short-term £410m credit line, later raised to £650m and extended until March 2003, while a long-term solution could be considered including putting the company into administration, taking it back into state ownership and/or restructuring its debts and decommissioning liabilities, and asset sales.

Meanwhile, in October 2002, TXU Europe, which owned the Eastern supply business as well as some generation assets that were originally acquired as a result of the first round of mandatory divestment, was pushed into insolvency after its US parent company withdrew its support due to continuing low prices. The supply business was sold for £1.6bn to Powergen in a matter of a week, who additionally took control of the 3000 MW of TXU Europe generation capacity at close to zero cost. The collapse of TXU Europe had a domino effect because it also triggered a default on long-term supply contracts that it had purchased at above-market prices from AES Drax. With these contracts now void the US parent of AES Drax announced in November 2002 that it had negotiated a standstill agreement on its senior debt and that it intended to effectively default on its junior debt with immediate effect.

Ironically, most of the generation assets that TXU Europe had sold to Powergen were those coal-fired generation assets that it had acquired in the first round of divestment in 1996 from National Power and Powergen. Furthermore, the fate of the AES Drax plant that National Power had sold in the second round of divestment was now effectively in the hands of bondholders and banks which raised speculation that it might eventually be sold back to Innogy (the divested UK arm of National Power). Finally, the Eggborough coal-fired plant, bought by British Energy from Innogy in the wave of voluntary divestment in 2000, was also likely to be sold to pay down debt and either Powergen or Innogy were possible buyers. Although it was by no means certain that these transactions would take place, or over what timescale, it remained a possibility that a significant proportion of the coal plant originally divested by Powergen and National Power might once again be concentrated in the hands of the original duopoly.

Simultaneous with the reconsolidation of the generation sector in England and Wales rumours also began to circulate in early 2003/04 that the vertically integrated duopoly of firms that dominated the Scottish wholesale and retail markets, namely Scottish Power and Scottish & Southern, may also consider entering into a generation asset merger. Electricity market deregulation in Scotland had followed a different path to that in England and Wales and consumer prices remained under regulatory price control until the end of 2003/04 with the level set by Ofgem by reference to prices in England and Wales. As for England and Wales, the biggest regulatory problem that Ofgem faced in introducing a competitive market to Scotland was the presence of a duopoly. The proposal to introduce NETA to Scotland as well as England and Wales in the form of the British Electricity Trading Arrangements (BETTA)[13] was predicated on the belief that by introducing open access to the Scottish transmission (and distribution) systems by generators and suppliers in England and Wales, combined with an increase in the total available transmission capacity over the England–Scotland border to 2200 MW would dilute the concentration of the industry in Scotland from 2004/05. However, with the generation sector consolidating rapidly in England and Wales, a single generator controlling the entire baseload and mid-merit plant output in Scotland, and without the necessary legislation still to be put in place to introduce BETTA, the outlook for competition was less clear.

By early December 2002, the UK electricity industry had therefore entered a new phase with the most likely scenario being that the generation sector would eventually coalesce around five large vertically integrated firms: Powergen, Innogy, Centrica, a single Scottish Company, EDF-London Electricity and finally a merged British Energy–BNFL supplying baseload power under long-term contracts to the other four vertically integrated firms. By the beginning of 2003/04, this scenario had begun to play out and the competition implications had already been the subject of some investigation. In its consultation paper (Ofgem, 2002), issued before making its recommendations to the Director General of Fair Trading on the merger of Powergen and TXU assets, Ofgem focussed mainly on the competition implications of the supply businesses in gas and electricity. However, while noting that the merger would leave Powergen with 10 000 MW of generation capacity accounting for a 15% share of capacity in England and Wales, up by about 4%, and a somewhat lower share by output, it considered that the transaction did

---

[13] For key Ofgem documents relating to BETTA see the separate section of References at the end of the chapter.

not raise concerns with respect to concentration in electricity generation and limited its entire comment on the impact on the wholesale market to one short paragraph without presenting any analysis:

> Competition within the generation sector has developed well and concentration is relatively low within the sector. There are more than 40 companies currently active, and the transaction does not significantly increase the degree of concentration in electricity generation. (Ofgem, 2002)

In the remainder of the chapter, the CCI coefficients for coal and CCGT plant estimated previously are used to test this Ofgem conclusion by producing a forecast of the price impact of the proposed merger of TXU Europe generation assets with those of Powergen. The further incremental impacts of a potential acquisition of the Drax plant by Innogy, and perhaps the purchase of Eggborough from British Energy, followed by a merger of Scottish Power and Scottish & Southern duopoly in Scotland.

### 4.4.2  Estimating the price impact of proposed mergers

For the purposes of this analysis the mean CCI for each generation technology and the mean UKPX RPD for 2001/02 are taken to be the base case. The change in COALCCI and CCGTCCI has been estimated assuming that each of the following short-term scenarios is completed for the England and Wales market for 2002/03 onwards:

Scenario 1: Powergen–TXU Europe merger authorised
Scenario 2: Powergen–TXU Europe merger authorised and Innogy buys Drax
Scenario 3: Powergen–TXU Europe merger authorised and Innogy buys Drax and Eggborough

The implications of the merger of the two Scottish firms are considered in two further scenarios. Scenario 4 considers the price impact in 2003/04 before the Scotland–England transmission interconnector is increased and scenario 5 estimates the impact after the increase to 2200 MW capacity. In both cases it is assumed that generators in England and Wales will have access to capacity on the interconnector.[14] No scenario has been included involving the merger of nuclear plant operators since the NUCLEARCCI coefficient is statistically insignificant in all of the regression models produced. Since the CCI change would be multiplied by a coefficient of zero any change in nuclear CCI, even up to a nuclear monopoly, would therefore produce a forecast price impact of zero.

The COALCCI and CCGTCCI under each of these five scenarios as well as the base case is presented in Table 4.3 along with the original regression coefficients estimated from the PPPRPD series regression model. Since the OILCCI and GASMORAT do not change in any scenario, the direction of COALCONR is uncertain and the TEMPHEAT variable is a small but purely random factor these four variables are not considered further.

In Table 4.4 the change in the relevant CCI between the base case in England and Wales and each of the five scenarios is multiplied by the relevant COALCCI and CCGTCCI coefficient to produce a forecast of the price impact.

---

[14] It is assumed that the 500 MW Moyle interconnector between Ireland and Scotland would not result in competitive entry by competitive coal capacity because Northern Ireland generating plant is dominated by coal and gas.

**Table 4.3**  Summary CCI for merger scenarios and regression coefficients

| Merger scenarios | Scenario CCI | | PPPRPD coefficients | |
|---|---|---|---|---|
| | COALCCI | CCGTCCI | COALCCI | CCGTCCI |
| Base case | 1373 | 812 | 0.0018 | 0.0014 |
| 1: Powergen–TXU Europe merge | 1534 | 795 | 0.0018 | 0.0014 |
| 2: Powergen–TXU Europe merge and Innogy buy Drax | 2253 | 795 | 0.0018 | 0.0014 |
| 3: Powergen–TXU Europe merge and Innogy buy Drax and Eggborough | 2560 | 795 | 0.0018 | 0.0014 |
| 4: Scotland 2003/04 | 2442 | Not applicable | 0.0018 | 0.0014 |
| 5: Scotland 2004/05 | 3516 | Not applicable | 0.0018 | 0.0014 |

**Table 4.4**  Changes in CCIs and forecast price impact

| Merger scenarios | CCI change versus base | | Forecast price imapact £/MWh | | |
|---|---|---|---|---|---|
| | COALCCI | CCGTCCI | COALCCI | CCGTCCI | Total impact |
| Base case | 1373 | 812 | Mean 2001/02 price | | £17.21 |
| 1: Powergen–TXU Europe merge | 161 | −17 | £0.29 | −£0.02 | £0.27 |
| 2: Powergen–TXU Europe merge and Innogy buy Drax | 880 | −17 | £1.58 | −£0.02 | £1.56 |
| 3: Powergen–TXU Europe merge and Innogy buy Drax and Eggborough | 1187 | −17 | £2.14 | −£0.02 | £2.11 |
| 4: Scotland 2003/04 | 5643 | Not applicable | £10.16 | Not applicable | £10.16 |
| 5: Scotland 2004/05 | 4036 | Not applicable | £7.26 | Not applicable | £7.26 |

### 4.4.3  Discussion

The impact of the proposed mergers in England and Wales would be to increase mean annual prices by some £2.11/MWh if they were all allowed to proceed. That is a 12.5% increase over the mean 2001/02 SMP–RPD level of £17.21/MWh. In practice, the bulk of this increase is likely to be due to increases in winter prices and virtually none in summer. Assuming that the price increase was spread over just the four winter months (November–February) this means a winter price increase of around £6.00/MWh in England and Wales.

If the Scottish duopoly were allowed to merge but access to the Scottish market were prevented over the England–Scotland interconnectors then the COALCCI for Scotland would be 10 000 with a dramatic increase in market power and hence market prices. A more realistic scenario is that the duopoly will merge but before the capacity of the England–Scotland interconnector has been increased from 1200 MW to 2200 MW by 2004/05. Assuming that the two Scottish coal plants of Cockenzie (1152 MW) and Longannet (2304 MW) are owned by one firm, and the five large generators in England and Wales can potentially enter the Scottish market with equal shares of the 1200 MW interconnector, the COALCCI for Scotland would be much higher than in England and Wales during 2003/04 and still well above it in 2004/05 even after interconnector capacity has increased. As a result wholesale prices in Scotland would be much higher than in England and Wales and the transmission capacity would be heavily constrained in the direction England to Scotland in all but the lowest demand period because of the large and persistent price differential between the two regions. The threat of entry from marginal coal capacity, by virtue of exports from England and Wales, would not be sufficient to curtail the exercise of market power if the two Scottish firms merged. Scottish consumers would not see the 1–2% retail price reductions forecast by Ofgem. Indeed, the forecast price rise over the 2001/02 England and Wales base case of £7.26, or a premium of 42%, suggests that the merger of the Scottish generators should be blocked unless price controls are to be extended beyond 2003/04.

### 4.4.4 Conclusion

The analysis in this chapter has tested the impact of proposed mergers in a more rigorous way than have traditional measures used by competition authorities. The coefficients estimated here are based on a long history of wholesale price responses to changes in industry concentration and sufficiently robust to make it possible to produce an unbiased forecast of how prices will respond to future changes in industry concentration. In this case, the backward regression procedure allowed changes in ownership for different types of plant technology to be isolated from the broader aggregate changes in industry concentration and also from the impacts of other changes in the regulatory environment such as the introduction of NETA. Given that most of the plants divested during the period 1996–2002 are still in existence, albeit traded to a new owner for the second or even third time in a few years, the quality of the price forecast for future periods is likely to be significantly better than a qualitative assessment of the likely price impact based on HHI or SSNIP.

The results support the preliminary conclusions of Ofgem, which were that a firm owning 15% of total England and Wales capacity would not make a significant difference to prices. Furthermore, it also suggests that the creation of five or six large generators owning all of the coal and CCGT plant would not have a significant impact on prices either. In this case, the forecast mean annual post-merger increase in the day-ahead wholesale price would amount to around 12.5% over the level in 2001/02. This would be sufficient for all but the most marginal coal plant to cover their fixed costs and perhaps encourage some mothballed plant to be reopened during the winter months but not sufficiently high to encourage further new investment. The regression results show that the nuclear CCI coefficient was insignificant and therefore that nuclear capacity had had little impact on prices. Nuclear plant operators are constrained to run their plant at near full capacity because of high fixed costs, and cannot therefore exercise market power by withdrawing plant even if they supply a significant amount of total output. Likewise, coal plant that is covered by forward contracts, as in the case of AES Drax, must also produce at full capacity. Only plant that can be operated flexibly, so that its capacity can be rapidly but temporarily withdrawn from the market, even if that threat is never actually implemented, can be used to exercise market power and induce a price rise.

The post-merger price forecasts produced here address the weakness identified in the established measures typically used by concentration authorities in that the CCI coefficients that have been estimated not only take account of the impact of broad industry concentration on prices but also the microstructure of capacity ownership, the near-zero short-run demand elasticity and the impact of forward contracting. The impact of horizontal mergers in the two geographically separate markets of England and Wales and Scotland, potentially isolated by a constrained transmission line, have also been examined.

Whether an increase of 12.5% in the mean annual price over the existing competitive price level in England and Wales, or indeed an increase of 42% in Scotland, would be sufficient grounds for the UK Competition Commission to block or modify any of the potential proposed mergers is unknown. However, the precise and unbiased nature of the price forecasting method produced here provides a much more satisfactory basis for making those decisions than using broad HHI benchmarks and/or attempting to make a qualitative assessment of the likely impact of a merger on the mark-up of market price over marginal cost without taking account of demand elasticity or forward contracting.

## GENERAL REFERENCES

Bower J. (2002). "Why Did Electricity Prices Fall in England & Wales: Market Mechanism of Market Structure". *OIES Working Paper* (ELO2), September 2002, pp 56. ISBN 1-091795-22-5.

Bunn D.W. and Larsen E. (1992). "Sensitivity of Reserve Margin t Factor Influencing Investment Behaviour in the Electricity Market of England & Wales". *Energy Policy* **May**: 420–429.

CEGB. (1989). *CEGB Statistical Yearbook 1988/89*, Central Electricity Generating Board.

Competition Commission. (2001). *AES and British Energy: A report on references made under section 12 of the Electricity Act 1989*. CC No. 453. HMSO www.competition-commission.org.uk/reports/453elec.htm#full

DTI (1990–2002a). *Digest of United Kingdom Energy Statistics*, Department of Trade and Industry. HMSO. ISBN 0 11 515486 8. www.dti.gov.uk/energy/inform/dukes/dukes2002/index.shtml

DTI (1990–2002b). *Energy Trends: A Statistical Bulletin*, Department of Trade and Industry. HMSO. ISSN 03081222. www.dti.gov.uk/energy/inform/energy_trends/index.shtml

DTI (1998). *Conclusions of the review of energy sources for power generation and Government response to 4th and 5th reports of the Trade and Industry Committee*, Department of Trade and Industry. HMSO Cm 4071. ISBN 0 10 140712 2.

DTI (2000). *Energy Paper 68: Energy projections for the UK : energy use and energy-related emissions of carbon dioxide in the UK, 2000–2020*, Department of Trade and Industry. HMSO. ISBN 0115154965. www.dti.gov.uk/energy/inform/energy_projections/index.shtml.

DTI (2001). *Press release: New electricity market goes live: Wholesale prices down 30%. 27 March 2001*. http://www.nds.coi.gov.uk/coi/coipress.nsf/gti/

Electricity Association. (1991–2001). *Electricity Industry Review* (superseding *UK Electricity*). The Electricity Association, 30 Millbank, London SW1P 4RD. http://www.electricity.org.uk/services_fr.html

Electricity Pool of England and Wales. (1994a). *An Introduction to the Pool Rules: Issue 2.00*. The England and Wales Electricity Pool, 338 Euston Road, 10th Floor, Regent's Place, London NW1 3BP.

Electricity Pool of England and Wales. (1994b). *A Users Guide to the Pool Rules: Issue 2.00*. The England and Wales Electricity Pool, 338 Euston Road, 10th Floor, Regent's Place, London NW1 3BP.

Electricity Pool of England and Wales. (1998). *Pooling and Settlement Agreement for the Electricity Industry in England and Wales: Schedule 9: The Pool Rules*. The England and Wales Electricity Pool, 338 Euston Road, 10th Floor, Regent's Place, London NW1 3BP.

Electricity Pool of England and Wales. (1990–2002). *Statistical Digest* (various issues). The England and Wales Electricity Pool, 338 Euston Road, 10th Floor, Regent's Place, London NW1 3BP.

Green R.J. (1996). "Increasing Competition in the British Electricity Spot Market". *The Journal of Industrial Economics*. **XLIV**(2): 205–216.

Green R.J. (1999). "Draining the Pool: The Reform of Electricity Trading in England & Wales". *Energy Policy* **27**(9): 515.

Green R. and Newbery D.M. (1992). "Competition in the British Electricity Spot Market". *Journal of Political Economy* **100**(5): 929–953.

Newbery D. (1995). "Power Markets and Market Power". *Energy Journal* **16**(3): 39–66.

Newbery D. (1997). "Lectures on Regulation Series VII: Pool Reform and Competition in Electricity". The Institute of Economic Affairs, 2 Lord North Street, London SW1P 3LB.

Newbery D. (2001). "British Electricity Restructuring: From the Pool to NETA". Paper presented to the *MIT Energy and Environmental Policy Workshop* held on 6 December 2001 (see especially p. 17). http://www.econ.cam.ac.uk/dae/people/newbery/MIT2001R-slides.pdf

Newbery D. (2002). "England's Experience with NETA". Paper presented at the conference *International Experience with Energy Liberalization: Lessons for Europe* held in Oviedo, Spain on 5 July 2002 (see especially p. 31). http://www.econ.cam.ac.uk/electricity/news/oviedo/newbery.pdf

NGC. (1991–2002). *Seven Year Statement* (various issues), National Grid Company plc.

Parker M.J. (2000). *Thatcherism and the Fall of Coal.* Oxford University Press for the Oxford Institute for Energy Studies. ISBN 0-19-730025-1.

Patrick R.H. and Wolak F.A. (1997). "Estimating the Customer-Led Demand for Electricity Under Real-Time Market Prices" (preliminary draft). Available from http://www.stanford.edu/~wolak/

Power UK. (1994–2002). *Power Station Tracker* (various issues). Published by Platts, a division of McGraw Hill Companies, Inc. www.platts.com/

Stoft S. (2002). *Power System Economics: Designing Markets for Electricity.* IEEE Press, Piscataway, NJ/Wiley-Interscience. ISBN 0-471-15040-1.

Wolfram C.D. (1998). "Strategic Bidding in a Multi-unit Auction: An Empirical Analysis of Bids to Supply Electricity in England and Wales". *NBER Working Paper.* http://www.economics.harvard.edu/~cwolfram/papers/auctions.pdf

# OFGEM REFERENCES

Ofgem. (2002). *Powergen plc's completed acquisition of the UK assets of TXU Europe Limited: A consultation paper. November 2002.* Office of Gas and Electricity Markets, 9 Millbank, London SW1P 3GE.

## Review of Electricity Trading Arrangements (RETA)

The key RETA documents can be downloaded from: www.ofgem.gov.uk/elarch/aback.htm, further subsidiary documents, including inquiry terms of reference, conference presentations and third party submissions to the inquiry are available at: http://www.ofgem.gov.uk/public/adownloads.htm#retabm

*Review of electricity trading arrangements: a consultation paper. 5 November 1997.*

*Review of electricity trading arrangements: Background paper 1: electricity trading arrangements in England and Wales. February 1998.*

*Review of electricity trading arrangements: Background paper 2: electricity trading arrangements in other countries. February 1998.*

*Review of electricity trading arrangements: working paper on trading inside and outside the pool. 24 March 1998.*

*Review of electricity trading arrangements: a possible common model for trading arrangements: a discussion note by Offer. 1 May 1998.*

*Review of electricity trading arrangements: interim conclusions. June 1998.*

*Review of electricity trading arrangements: proposals. August 1998.*

*Review of electricity trading arrangements: framework document. November 1998.*

## New Electricity Trading Arrangements (NETA)

The key NETA documents can be downloaded at: www.ofgem.gov.uk/elarch/anetadocs.htm. Many more technical papers relating to the systems development can be downloaded at: http://www.ofgem.gov.uk/elarch/reta_contents.htm

*The new electricity trading arrangements: Volumes 1 and 2. July 1999.*

*The new electricity trading arrangements: Volume 2. July 1999.*

*The new electricity trading arrangements: a draft specification for the balancing mechanism and imbalance settlement. July 1999.*

*The new electricity trading arrangements: Ofgem/DTI conclusions document. October 1999.*

*An overview of the new electricity trading arrangements V1.0: A high-level explanation of the new electricity trading arrangements (NETA). 31 May 2000.*

*The new electricity trading arrangements: Ofgem/DTI further conclusions. August 2000.*

*The review of the first year of NETA: A review document Volumes 1 and 2. 24 July 2002.*

## British Electricity Trading Arrangements (BETTA)

Key documents relating to interim administrative wholesale pricing arrangements in Scotland after implementation of NETA, as well as plans to include transmission pricing in NETA and eventually extend it to Scotland can be downloaded at: www.ofgem.gov.uk/projects/betta_index.htm

*Transmission Access and Losses under NETA: A Consultation Document. May 2001.*

*Scottish administered wholesale pricing arrangements: A review of the present arrangements and consultation on prices to apply from 1 April 2002. 13 December 2001.*

*The Development of British Electricity Trading and Transmission Arrangements (BETTA): A consultation paper. 12 December 2001.*

*Application for a reservation of pre-upgrade capacity on the Scotland–England interconnector to Scottish Power Generation Ltd: Consultation Document. 25 October 2001.*

*Scotland–England Interconnector: Access & Charging Principles to apply in the transmission area of SP Transmission Limited for the period to 31 March 2002: A Consultation Document. 25 October 2001.*

*Interim Administered Access Arrangements on Scotland–England Interconnector: Final proposals. 6 March 2001.*

*Scotland–England Interconnector: Access Criteria to 31 March 2004 Summary of responses and next steps. 21 December 2001.*

*Decision by the Authority on an application for a reservation of pre-upgrade capacity on the Scotland–England interconnector to Scottish Power Generation Ltd Decision document. 25 January 2002.*

*Scotland–England Interconnector: Access & Charging Principles to 31 March 2002 and Access Principles to 31 March 2004. 21 December 2001.*

*Scottish administered pricing arrangements from 1 April 2002 Ofgem proposals document. 25 January 2002.*

*Transmission access and losses under NETA: Revised proposals. 26 February 2002.*

*The Development of British Electricity Trading and Transmission Arrangements (BETTA): Ofgem/DTI report on consultation and next steps (plus appendices). 20 May 2002.*

*BETTA Seminar Presentation Slides. 20 June 2002.*

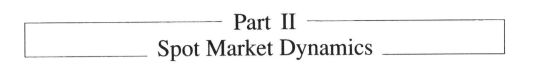

# Part II
## Spot Market Dynamics

# 5
# Testing for Weekly Seasonal Unit Roots in the Spanish Power Pool

ANGEL LEÓN AND ANTONIO RUBIA

*Departamento de Economía Financiera, University of Alicante, C.P. 03690, Spain*

## ABSTRACT

This chapter is concerned with the stationarity of the daily electricity price series in the Spanish pool. We review and apply several seasonal unit root testing procedures in order to determine whether the evidence of covariance-stationarity is fulfilled, not only at the zero frequency but also at the weekly seasonal frequencies. The main conclusion is that the data-generating process of the electricity prices in the Spanish pool during the period analysed includes a stochastic seasonal term which could be properly modelled by a weekly random walk.

## 5.1 INTRODUCTION

Recent years have witnessed the steady deregulation of the electricity industry through economic policy in several countries. This process has had a great impact on the traditional characteristics of the industry. Power generation is now regarded as an activity open to competition, and electricity is traded and priced in its own wholesale market as a new commodity. Unlike most traditional commodities, however, electricity is special because it is a non-storable good. This characteristic, coupled with the economic fundamentals of the pool market, is a key factor in the complex dynamics that electricity prices display over time. The stylised features of these time series include large levels of volatility (generally over 300% and often higher) and a tendency to exhibit dramatic and unforeseeable jumps (the so-called spikes), which typically disappear as rapidly as they arise. Furthermore, both electricity price and power demand time series include overwhelming seasonal components related to the intradaily, weekly and monthly patterns of power consumption over time.

Most of the recent economic literature concerned with power markets presents empirical applications based on observations of electricity prices quoted on a daily basis (De Vany and Walls, 1999; Byström, 2000; Robinson, 2000; Lucia and Schwartz, 2002; among others). In an empirical framework based on discrete observations of a stochastic process, one of the key elements to consider is whether the time series in question are covariance-stationary (i.e., second-order stationary), or whether their data-generating processes (DGP) include autoregressive unit roots. In spite of the strong seasonal nature of daily data from electricity markets, researchers have tested the required evidence of stationarity by means of standard unit root testing procedures. For instance, De Vany and Walls (1992) and Helm and Powell (1992) found evidence of a unit root in the long run of several daily time series of electricity prices from the US and the UK deregulated markets by using the well-known ADF test (Dickey and Fuller, 1979).

Standard unit root testing procedures, however, say nothing about the stability of the time processes at the seasonal frequencies. So, given the importance of the long run and the seasonal components in time series from power markets, it could also be possible that they contain stochastic trends in their seasonal dynamics. Since the intradaily seasonality of electricity prices and demand disappears when the time series are sampled on a day-to-day basis, the most recurrent cyclical pattern is the weekly seasonality. It should therefore be interesting from a methodological point of view to verify whether the stationarity property in daily electricity series is really fulfilled not only in the long term, but also at the weekly frequencies.[1]

The main aim of this chapter, therefore, is to present a statistical procedure for determining the stochastic nature of the weekly seasonal component in a time series of electricity prices, although it can be applied straightforwardly on the power demand series (see Rubia, 2001). Following the suggestion of Hylleberg (1995), we employ two statistical tests with interchanged hypothesis, as is often done in the empirical literature of standard unit roots. On the one hand, we consider the testing procedure of Hylleberg et al. (1990) (the so-called HEGY test), with the null hypothesis of non-stationarity. This method is a generalisation of the ADF test for seasonal series, and it has been extended to the case of weekly seasonality on a basis of daily observations in Rubia (2001). The HEGY test is also applied in this chapter in terms of the prewhitening procedure of Psadarakis (1997), more suitable than the standard procedure under certain conditions. On the other hand, we use the testing procedure of Canova and Hansen (1995) (CH test), with the null hypothesis of stationarity at the seasonal frequencies, as a counterpart of the HEGY test. It is assumed that if both tests give the same results there would be strong evidence for the underlying hypothesis. Finally, we conducted these tests on the daily electricity spot prices quoted on the Spanish wholesale electricity market during the early years of the electricity pool. We find significant evidence of unit roots at both the zero frequency and all the seasonal non-zero frequencies. Such evidence suggests that the daily price in the Spanish market over the period analysed could be parsimoniously described through a DGP that includes a weekly seasonal random walk.

The remainder of this chapter is organised as follows. Section 5.2 briefly describes the main characteristics of the Spanish electricity sector and the nature of the time series. Section 5.3 presents and applies the seasonal unit root tests on the daily average of electricity prices. Finally, concluding remarks are given in Section 5.4.

## 5.2   DATA

The set of data used in this chapter was collected from the Spanish electricity wholesale market.[2] This market began its trading activity on 1 January 1998, as a result of the deregulation process stipulated in the Law on the Electric Sector (No. 54/1997). The Spanish wholesale electricity market is organised as a competitive pool, where generators sell their production to purchasers (distributors, retailers and qualified end-use consumers).[3] Price and volumes are

---

[1] The applications of the techniques for inference of long-run dependence in time series include data description, forecasting, multivariate modelling and inference involved in the variables of interest. See Stock (1994) for an overview of the main topics concerning stochastic trends in time series.

[2] Data are available at http://www.mercaelectrico.comel.es

[3] A Market Operator manages the economic features of the power market, whereas a System Operator manages the technical aspects of the transmission grid.

fixed in an organised spot market (Hourly Market) through the equilibrium between the supply and demand functions for each of the 24 hours of the day.[4] The clearing price hence represents the system marginal price, i.e. the bid price of the most expensive power plant available at each period of time. The final price of the load supplied for each hour is determined by adding to the respective marginal system prices the costs of line losses, ancillary services, capacity guarantee and Market Operator fees.

One of the most important factors affecting the evolution of electricity prices in this power exchange is the strong horizontal concentration in the generation and distribution industries.[5] Practically all power that is traded on the Hourly Market is generated and then distributed by four large groups. Since 1998 the largest electricity company (Endesa) has generated about 47% of total production, Iberdrola has produced about 28% and Union Fenosa and Hidrocantabrico together have generated about 18% of total production. The degree of horizontal concentration that results from this production structure is the greatest among the countries in which a deregulation process of the electricity industry has been carried out. Obviously, the actual result of the deregulation process in Spain in terms of the effective competitive behaviour achieved seems to be quite limited by this feature, since the larger companies can find incentives to exercise market power and to influence prices in this oligopolistic environment.

The time series analysed in this chapter has been constructed as the arithmetic average of the 24 series of hourly system marginal prices (measured in pesetas per kilowatt-hour, Ptas/kWh) quoted on the spot market. The sample period analysed is from 1 January 1998 to 31 October 2000, and comprises 1035 daily observations of hourly prices. The daily average electricity price is the underlying asset in some hedging contracts, and has usually been taken as a reference in the economic and empirical framework of power markets. It should be noted that this series represents the average price on the spot market, and hence the average marginal cost of generation, so does not include other components of the final price (e.g. ancillary costs) that are not generated under competitive equilibrium.

We denote the natural logarithm of the daily average of the hourly price series by $y_t$, i.e., $y_t = \log(\bar{P}_{it})$, $t = 1, \ldots, T$, $i = 1, \ldots, 24$. The graphics of this series over the period analysed is displayed in Figure 5.1. The strong weekly seasonal behaviour of this series is quite clear from the graphics of the autocorrelation function (also in Figure 5.1), showing significant correlations at lags that are multiples of seven. This sort of seasonal pattern is due to the systematic decrease of industrial power consumption at weekends. It is interesting to note that, although annual seasonality is a remarked feature of electricity prices in some countries, such as those in Scandinavia, it seems to be rather weaker in the Spanish pool.

## 5.3 TESTING FOR SEASONAL UNIT ROOTS

A time series $\{x_t\}$ is said to be seasonally integrated if it is necessary to take seasonal differences to achieve a process with a stationary and invertible ARMA representation, i.e., if $x_t$ needs to be linearly filtered with $(1 - B^d)$, where $B$ denotes the usual back-shift operator $(B^j x_t \equiv x_{t-j})$ and $d$ is an integer greater than one. Note that $(1 - B^d)$ can be factorised as $(1 - B)S(B)$, with $S(B) = \sum_{j=1,d} B^{j-1}$ denoting the seasonal moving average filter, so that $x_t$ has a single unit root at the zero frequency (i.e. the long run), as well as $d - 1$ unit roots at the seasonal

---

[4] Although prices are settled in a spot market, they are actually day-ahead prices, since they usually refer to the following day after the market session.

[5] As in the case of any other deregulated markets, another important factor in the Spanish market is the occurrence of large stranded costs that have to be recovered by the electricity sector.

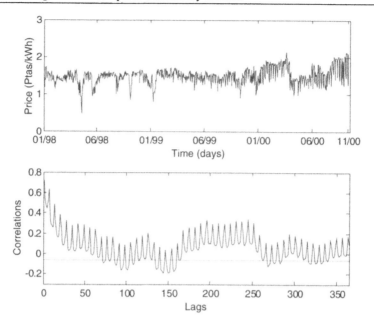

**Figure 5.1**    Daily electricity prices and autocorrelation function

frequencies. If we consider weekly seasonality on a daily basis of observations, then $d = 7$ and the roots of $(1 - B^d)$ are $\{1, e^{\pm \omega i}, e^{\pm 2\omega i}, e^{\pm 3\omega i}\}$ where $\omega = 2\pi/7$ is the elemental Fourier frequency of the weekly period. Hence, the former polynomial has both a single real root at the zero frequency and three pairs of conjugate complex seasonal unit roots on the harmonic frequencies $\{k\omega, \ k = 1, 2, 3\}$.

### 5.3.1 HEGY weekly seasonal unit root test

The HEGY testing procedure is undoubtedly the most popular method to check for stationarity in seasonal univariate series. The main advantage of the HEGY test over other alternatives (e.g. Hasza and Fuller, 1982 (HF); Dickey, Hasza and Fuller, 1984 (DHF); among others) is that it allows one to test the unit root hypothesis separately at each frequency. By contrast, the HF and DHF tests provide results that are difficult to interpret, since a rejection of the null hypothesis cannot be considered as evidence of stationarity in all frequencies, whereas a failure to reject does not indicate the precise location of the integrated frequencies. Furthermore, empirical research has revealed statistical drawbacks in these tests, such as low power and serial autocorrelation in residuals.

As previously mentioned, the HEGY test assumes under the null hypothesis that the series of interest, say $y_t$, is seasonally integrated against a stationarity alternative. This test is based on the following auxiliary regression:

$$\Delta_7 y_t = \alpha + \beta t + \sum_{j=2}^{7} \eta_j D_{jt} + \sum_{j=1}^{7} \pi_j z_{j,t-1} + \sum_{r=1}^{p} \phi_j \Delta_7 y_{t-r} + \varepsilon_t,$$

$$\varepsilon_t \sim \text{i.i.d.} \left(0, \sigma_\varepsilon^2\right) \tag{5.1}$$

where the $D_{jt}$ terms are dummy variables for each day of the week, and the $z_{j,t}$ regressors are properly defined on the zero and seasonal frequencies $\{k\omega, \ k = 1, 2, 3\}$ as follows:

$$z_{1,t} = \sum_{j=1}^{7} \cos(0j\omega) B^{j-1} y_t = S(B) y_t$$

$$z_{2k,t} = \sum_{j=1}^{7} \cos(jk\omega) B^{j-1} y_t$$

$$z_{2k+1,t} = -\sum_{j=1}^{7} \sin(jk\omega) B^{j-1} y_t \qquad (5.2)$$

In the same way as for the ADF test, the auxiliary regression of the HEGY test might include deterministic regressors in order to obtain power against relevant alternatives, such as an intercept, seasonal dummies or a linear trend; or it might have none of these. Hence, all such alternative specifications can be viewed as constrained models of equation (5.1). Moreover, as in the case of the ADF procedure, a number of lags of the dependent variable should be included in the auxiliary regression to ensure serial uncorrelation in the error term. Regressors in (5.2) are specifically designed on each frequency to remove all the possible unit roots from the original variable except for the one related to the specific regressor. The analytic form of these regressors is justified in Rubia (2001).

Applying ordinary least squares (OLS) to equation (5.1) or to a deterministic-constrained model, we obtain the estimations of the $\pi_j$ parameters. The series has a single unit root at zero frequency if the null hypothesis $\pi_1 = 0$ cannot be rejected with a $t$-test against a one-sided alternative ($\pi_1 < 0$). The assumption of conjugate complex unit roots at each seasonal frequency requires the non-rejection of the hypothesis that both coefficients associated with this frequency are zero, i.e. $\pi_{2k} \cap \pi_{2k+1} = 0$, which suggests an $F$-test (Ghysels *et al.*, 1994). If this test cannot reject the null hypothesis, then the series has the complex roots $e^{k\omega i}$ and $e^{-k\omega i}$. Neither the $t$-statistics nor the $F$-statistics have standard distributions; furthermore, they both depend on the set of deterministic variables included in the auxiliary regression, so they should be simulated by Monte Carlo experiments.[6] These tables are partially reproduced in Appendix B.

As in the ADF test case, the choice of the adequate number of autoregressive terms to be included in the auxiliary regression is a key element in this procedure, since it implies, in practice, a trade-off in the statistical properties of the test. On the one hand, too short an augmentation lag implies important departures from the nominal size of the test. On the other hand, the power of the test is significantly reduced when too many lags are included in the regression. So the lag-augmentation should apply the minimum number of parameters necessary to render the errors a white-noise process. Unfortunately, there is no unanimous agreement on the best way of choosing the proper number of lag coefficients. Initially we follow the method suggested in Ng and Perron (1995), which entails fixing a maximum augmentation lag and then successively removing those lags that fail to pass a significance test.

After a preliminary analysis, we selected 28 lags of the dependent variable as a maximum augmentation lag and conducted the test against both stationary alternatives, which included (i) a drift, seasonal dummies and a linear time trend, and then (ii) a drift and seasonal dummies. The relevant statistics of these tests are reported in Table 5.1. The outcomes show significant

---

[6] The asymptotic distributions of these statistics are non-standard random variables that can be expressed as rational functions on Brownian motion integrals.

**Table 5.1**  Results of the HEGY tests for seasonal unit roots in the log-price series

| Frequency | Statistics | HEGY(1) | HEGY(2) |
|---|---|---|---|
| 0 | $\pi_1$ | −2.81(*) | −3.72(**) |
| $2\pi/7$ | $\pi_2$ | −2.29 | −2.33 |
| | $\pi_3$ | 1.66 | −1.65 |
| $4\pi/7$ | $\pi_4$ | −2.63 | −2.65 |
| | $\pi_5$ | 2.67(b**) | −2.66(**) |
| $6\pi/7$ | $\pi_6$ | −5.35(***) | −5.37(***) |
| | $\pi_7$ | 1.31 | 1.30 |
| $2\pi/7$ | $F_{2,3}$ | 4.04 | 4.12 |
| $4\pi/7$ | $F_{4,5}$ | 7.06(***) | 7.11(***) |
| $6\pi/7$ | $F_{6,7}$ | 15.23(***) | 15.31(***) |
| Residuals | Q(200) | 224.67(0.11) | 227.24(0.09) |

*Note:* The auxiliary regressions include 28 lags of the dependent variable and (1) a drift and seasonal dummies; (2) a drift, seasonal dummies and a trend. The last row shows the Ljung–Box statistic of uncorrelation up to the $k$th autocorrelations ($p$-value in brackets). Significance levels: 1% (***), 5% (**), 10% (*).

evidence of complex seasonal unit roots at the frequency $2\pi/7$. The hypothesis of unit roots is rejected at the remaining frequencies at the 1% level, while the null hypothesis is weakly rejected at the 10% level at zero frequency. The results do not seem to be qualitatively different when the time trend is not included in the auxiliary regression, although a higher significance in rejecting the null seems to be achieved in the case of the zero frequency test.

The need to include so many lags in the auxiliary regression is due to the presence of a first-order seasonal moving average term, namely SMA(1), with a root near the unit circle, as is quite apparent when the partial autocorrelation function of $\Delta_7 y_t$ is examined. It is well known that this sort of term has severe repercussions in the size of seasonal unit root tests, as also occurs with the ADF test when the DGP includes an MA(1) process with a large root. Even though the size distortions can be reduced when the number of lags included in the auxiliary regression is high enough, the bias is still significant (Schwert, 1989). As an alternative to the lag-augmentation method, Psadarakis (1997) suggested a procedure based on prewhitening the data, which allows the exact size to be (asymptotically) close to the nominal significance level. On the other hand, this is achieved through a heavy burden on the methodology and expected reductions in the power of the test. This method is further discussed and applied in the following section.

## 5.3.2  Prewhitening method

The alternative procedure suggested by Psadarakis (1997) consists, basically, in prewhitening (filtering) the original time series to eliminate the effects of the SMA(1) term (see Appendix A for further details on the technical aspects of this method), and then applying the HEGY test on the filtered series without adding any lags. Where the series also follows an ARMA($r$, $q$) process in the non-seasonal component, the procedure then becomes more complicated and involves a two-stage estimation to eliminate all the annoying patterns. The standard time series analysis shows that $\Delta_7 y_t$ seems to follow an SMA(1) process, as well as an autoregressive process in its regular component.[7] The prewhitened series, say $\breve{y}_t$, could, therefore, be represented as follows:

$$\breve{y}_t = \left(1 - \sum_{j=1}^{r} \hat{\phi}_j B^j\right) \hat{\delta}(B) y_t, \qquad \hat{\delta}(B) = \left(1 - \sum_{j=1}^{k} \hat{\varphi}_j B^{7j}\right) \tag{5.3}$$

where $r$ and $k$ denote, respectively, the order of the AR process and the order of the seasonal autoregressive structure that approaches the SMA(1) process through its invertible representation (see Appendix A). We summarise, below, the two-stage estimation procedure:

(i)  First, the coefficients $\{\phi_i\}$, $i = 1, \ldots, r$ of the AR process are estimated by regressing $\Delta_7 y_t$ on $(\Delta_7 y_{t-1}, \ldots, \Delta_7 y_{t-r})$. This estimation is performed through the generalised method of moments (GMM), as it is more efficient than the instrumental variable method. The instruments selected are lags of the dependent variable of an order higher than seven. The optimal number of instrumental variables used in the GMM estimation was determined by the method suggested in Newey and West (1987b), resulting in 14 instruments. Finally, the GMM regression highlighted an autoregressive pattern with $r = 4$. It is noteworthy that the $p$-value of the Ljung–Box statistic up to the first six residual autocorrelations is 0.184, implying that the estimation process employed in the first stage was successful in removing the AR pattern entirely from the series. On the other hand, the Q statistic strongly rejected the uncorrelation hypothesis when at least seven autocorrelations were considered, because of the serial correlation that the seasonal moving average process induces through its invertible representation.

(ii)  We now need to eliminate the effect of the SMA(1) structure on the series. The coefficients $\{\varphi_i\}$, $i = 1, \ldots, k$ are estimated at this stage by an OLS autoregression of the residuals from (i) on several seasonal lags. A good way of choosing the lag-order $k$ is by adding successive seasonal lags of the dependent variable to the regression, as they prove to be statistically significant (Psadarakis, 1997). We used this method and found that up to eight seasonal lags were required. Such a relatively high number reflects quite clearly the strong influence of the SMA(1) process on the time series. It is worth noting that the $p$-value of the Wald test on the eighth seasonal lag was 0.00, whereas the corresponding $p$-value of the ninth seasonal lag was 0.29, thereby implying the non-significance for this coefficient.

Once the $\breve{y}_t$ series has been determined, the HEGY test can then be applied to it. The mean of the auxiliary regression under the alternative hypothesis is defined in the same terms as before. In other words, the test is performed against both a trend-stationary and a drift-stationary alternative. The relevant statistics from the auxiliary regressions are shown in Table 5.2. Note that the null hypothesis of a unit root cannot be rejected in either the zero frequency or the seasonal frequencies in this case, so the conclusion is that the series is seasonally integrated. As expected, the HEGY tests were performed without including any lag of the dependent variable. It is noteworthy that the $p$-value of the Ljung–Box statistic for up to the 200th-order autocorrelations in the residuals was 0.18 when considering a trend, and 0.22 when only a drift was considered; so the null hypothesis of a white-noise structure cannot be rejected at the usual confidence levels.

---

[7] These results are not reported here, but they are available upon request from the authors.

**Table 5.2**  Results of the HEGY tests for seasonal unit roots in the prewhitened series

| Frequency | Statistics | HEGY(1) | HEGY(2) |
|---|---|---|---|
| 0 | $\pi_1$ | −2.25 | −3.03 |
| $2\pi/7$ | $\pi_2$ | −0.89 | −0.90 |
| | $\pi_3$ | −0.35 | −0.33 |
| $4\pi/7$ | $\pi_4$ | −0.93 | −0.94 |
| | $\pi_5$ | 1.90 | 1.89 |
| $6\pi/7$ | $\pi_6$ | −2.62 | −2.62 |
| | $\pi_7$ | 1.19 | 1.18 |
| $2\pi/7$ | $F_{2,3}$ | 0.46 | 0.46 |
| $4\pi/7$ | $F_{4,5}$ | 2.23 | 2.25 |
| $6\pi/7$ | $F_{6,7}$ | 4.14 | 4.16 |
| Residuals | Q(200) | 214.61(0.22) | 218.41(0.18) |

*Note:* The auxiliary regressions include 28 lags of the dependent variable and (1) a drift and seasonal dummies; (2) a drift, seasonal dummies and a trend. The last row shows the Ljung–Box statistic of uncorrelation up to the $k$th autocorrelations ($p$-value in brackets). Significance levels: 1% (***), 5% (**), 10% (*).

This procedure avoids distortion in the test size by incurring a plausible reduction in the power of the test. Thus, the rejection of the null hypothesis cannot be interpreted as clear evidence of a seasonal random walk in the data. Therefore, Psadarakis (1997) recommends combining this method with a test that includes a stationary null hypothesis when the non-stationary null hypothesis cannot be rejected. This alternative is further analysed in the following section.

### 5.3.3  Canova–Hansen seasonal stationarity test

The CH test (Canova and Hansen, 1995) is the generalisation of the KPSS test (Kwiatkowski *et al.*, 1992) to the seasonal case. These tests have the hypothesis of stationarity as null, since sometimes this hypothesis seems to be more likely than the more frequently used hypothesis of unit root non-stationarities. As the KPSS procedure, the CH test is based on a Lagrange multiplier (LM) statistic. The test is conducted in general terms on the time series by means of the following regression model:

$$(1 - B)^\alpha y_t = \mu + f_t' \gamma + \varepsilon_t \tag{5.4}$$

where $\alpha$ is the order of integration of the long run of the series and $f_t'$ is a term that fits the deterministic seasonal component of the time series by means of trigonometric functions on the weekly harmonics.[8] Specifically, this term is defined as:

$$f_t' = [\cos(\omega t), \sin(\omega t), \cos(2\omega t), \sin(2\omega t), \cos(3\omega t), \sin(3\omega t)] \tag{5.5}$$

---

[8] The assumptions of this test method require no trends in the long run of the series, either deterministic or stochastic. We carried out the KPSS test on the log-price series in a preliminary analysis not presented here and found a strong rejection of the null hypothesis of stationarity. We have therefore differenced the original series just once (i.e. $\alpha = 1$), as all the tests rejected the hypothesis of a double unit root at the zero frequency.

It is assumed under the alternative hypothesis that the coefficients of the seasonal regressors are time-variant. Specifically, they follow a random walk process:

$$\Delta_\alpha y_t = \mu + f_t' \gamma_t + \varepsilon_t$$
$$\gamma_t = \gamma_{t-1} + \xi_t \tag{5.6}$$

where $\xi_t$ is an i.i.d. process independent of $\varepsilon_t$ with a zero mean and a constant variance. The strategy of the CH test is based on determining whether the covariance matrix of this process is equal to zero, as it should be under the null hypothesis of stability in the seasonal coefficients. The stationary hypothesis is rejected for large values of the following LM statistic:

$$L = T^{-2} \sum_{t=1}^{T} \hat{F}_t' \Gamma (\Gamma' \hat{\Omega} \Gamma')^{-1} \Gamma' \hat{F}_t \tag{5.7}$$

where $\hat{F}_t = \sum_{j=1,t} f_j \hat{\varepsilon}_j, \hat{\varepsilon}_j$ are the OLS residuals from equation (5.4) and $\Gamma$ is a $6 \times a$ matrix with $1 \leq a \leq 6$. If we want to test the stationary alternative simultaneously at all seasonal frequencies, then $a = 6$ and $\Gamma = I_6$. When we want to test the stability hypothesis at a specific frequency $k\omega$ where $k = 1, 2, 3$, then $a = 2$ and $\Gamma$ can be either $\Gamma \equiv (I_2, \tilde{0}, \tilde{0})$ with $k = 1$, or $\Gamma \equiv (\tilde{0}, I_2, \tilde{0})$ with $k = 2$, or $\Gamma \equiv (\tilde{0}, \tilde{0}, I_2)$ with $k = 3$, where $\tilde{0}$ denotes a $2 \times 2$ null matrix. The asymptotic distribution of the L statistic under the null hypothesis is characterised by an integral over Brownian bridge variables that generalises the Von Mises distribution with $a$ degrees of freedom.[9] Finally, note that this test employs a semi-parametric heteroskedasticity and autocorrelation-consistent covariance estimator, denoted as $\hat{\Omega}$, of the long-run variance of the process. This estimator is defined as:

$$\hat{\Omega} = T^{-1} \sum_{k=-h}^{h} w(k/h) \sum_{t=1}^{T} f_{t+k} \hat{\varepsilon}_{t+k} f_t' \hat{\varepsilon}_t \tag{5.8}$$

where $w(\cdot)$ is any kernel function that produces positive semi-definite covariance matrix estimations. Andrews (1991) and Newey and West (1994) documented that the quadric spectral kernel has optimal asymptotic mean squared error properties and Monte Carlo performance in small samples, so we estimated using this kernel.

Since the CH test includes a robust estimation to white-noise departures, the problem of selecting the optimum augmentation-lag in the ADF-type methodology is circumvented, but the complication that now arises concerns the proper calibration of the bandwidth parameter. If this parameter is too large, the long-run variance is overestimated and the test could have little or no power in finite samples. On the other hand, if the bandwidth parameter selected is too small, the test could suffer from size distortion. Newey and West (1987a) show that this parameter can be consistently estimated as a function of the sample size. This method is further discussed in Schwert (1989) and Newey and West (1994). Following these authors, we determine $h$ as the integer part of $[4(T/100)^{2/25}]$. Alternatively, Andrews (1991) and Newey and West (1994) suggested an automatic data-dependent selection method to estimate the optimal bandwidth parameter, which has also been used here.

The last element to be considered in this testing methodology is whether to include lags of the dependent variable in the regression (5.4). Canova and Hansen (1995) claim that a single lag reduces the autocorrelation and does not affect the roots of the seasonal pattern of the series, but Hylleberg (1995) questions this. The relevant statistics of this test are presented in Table 5.3.

---

[9] See the original paper of Canova–Hansen (p. 241) for the critical values of this distribution.

**Table 5.3** CH statistics of stationarity at each individual frequency and joint test

| | Automatic selection | | Sample size selection | |
|---|---|---|---|---|
| Frequency | CH-0 | CH-1 | CH-0 | CH-1 |
| $2\pi/7$ | 4.60(***) | 5.07(***) | 3.77(***) | 7.67(***) |
| $4\pi/7$ | 3.98(***) | 3.77(***) | 4.57(***) | 5.11(***) |
| $6\pi/7$ | 2.39(***) | 2.74(***) | 3.27(***) | 3.42(***) |
| Joint test | 5.63(***) | 5.68(***) | 8.18(***) | 9.48(***) |

*Note:* The auxiliary regressions include (i) no lags of the dependent variable (CH-0) and (ii) a single lag of the dependent variable (CH-1). The bandwidth parameter has been selected through an automatic selection method and as a function of the sample size (see main text).
Significance levels: 1% (***), 5% (**), 10% (*).

The outcome of the CH test shows a strong rejection of the null hypothesis in all cases, independently of the inclusion of a lagged regressor in the regression. Furthermore, we checked the robustness of these results by performing the CH test with different estimations and using the Bartlett kernel as an alternative kernel function, and found strong rejections of the null in all cases. Hence, these results agree strongly with the findings of the HEGY tests and, indeed, are consistent in suggesting the presence of a seasonal random walk process in the DGP of the Spanish electricity prices over the period analysed.

## 5.4  CONCLUDING REMARKS

Determining whether or not a time series is covariance-stationary is a key element in most econometric applications relevant for economic and financial analysis. In this paper we have reviewed the main testing procedures concerning seasonal weekly unit roots – like those of Hylleberg *et al.* (1990) and Psadarakis (1997) with the null hypothesis of non-stationarity, and Canova and Hansen (1995) with the null hypothesis of stationarity. We have applied these tests on the logs of the daily average electricity prices taken from the Spanish electricity pool. To the best of our knowledge, this is the first published work concerning the stochastic nature of electricity price time series. The main finding from the joint use of these tests is that a model with a unit autoregressive root at zero frequency, as well as unit roots at all of the weekly frequencies, could approximate reasonably well the weekly seasonal stochastic component of this series. The evidence of a unit root at zero frequency has also been found in other empirical works concerned with electricity prices by applying standard unit root tests, although these methods do not seem to be the most appropriate in seasonal series.

The instability of the mean to which the process reverted during the early years of trading is not necessarily a strange result, since during that period there were continuous changes in the composition of both the supply and the demand functions, as new players were steadily incorporated into the market. Furthermore, the rules of the market did not remain unchangeable over time, especially in the early years, and all of these elements have significant repercussions in the dynamics of prices. The fluctuations in electricity prices are due mainly to the effect of various local factors and features that characterise the background of each power market. The early years of the Spanish pool are actually considered a transition period from an oligopolistic, imperfect environment to a fully competitive market. It is thought likely that electricity prices display a stable performance around a mean that is representative of the marginal cost of the system, as the power market will be fully normalised.

Nevertheless, it is well known that unit root tests are sensitive to certain anomalies in data. Two different factors may well cause some form of bias in the results when the HEGY test is applied to electricity price time series. First, electricity prices often show extreme values (spikes) that are due mainly to technical problems in the system, leading to high prices.[10] It is known that such extreme values might bias the test for non-stationarity towards a too-frequent rejection of the null hypothesis. The HEGY procedure may be easily extended to cope with such anomalies by including dummy variables associated with the outlying observations in the auxiliary regression, as suggested in Franses and Haldrup (1994). This does not affect the asymptotic distribution of relevant statistics, provided that any extreme values are correctly identified. In the present case, some extreme values leading to low levels in prices were observed for 1998. Nevertheless, all the tests applied here are quite consistent in highlighting the non-stationarity of the time series involved.

Lastly, electricity prices display a remarkable structure of time-variant conditional volatility which can be fitted by GARCH-type models (see Bollerslev et al., 1994 for a review of this topic). It is also known that conditional volatility in data could lead the ADF-like test to accept the null hypothesis too frequently, since the relevant statistics would be based on consistent but inefficient OLS estimations. Although some procedures based on the likelihood ratio test (e.g. Boswijk, 2000) have been developed for testing standard unit roots in such a case, it has been shown that they do not offer significant gains over Dickey–Fuller tests when the volatility is quite persistent and, at the same time, has short-run variations. This, unfortunately, is the characteristic case with financial series and also seems to be the case of electricity prices, so that testing for unit roots in such high-volatile data seems to be quite problematic.[11] In any case, the different tests that we applied overwhelmingly support the evidence of seasonal unit roots. Finally, to the best of our knowledge, there is no published work concerned with seasonal unit root tests when the data include time-variant volatility. This is not very surprising, considering that in quarterly or monthly data, as in the relevant cases of seasonality analysed so far in the literature on unit roots, there is normally only very weak evidence, if any, of GARCH-type volatility. An interesting topic for further research in the framework of power markets would be to extend the methods presented in this chapter towards testing for seasonal unit roots in the presence of time-variant volatility, since this is specially relevant in data from those markets.

## APPENDIX A: PREWHITENING PROCEDURE

The prewhitening procedure is designed to ensure whitened residuals in the auxiliary regression of the HEGY test method through the preliminary filtering of the time series. Psaradakis (1997) claims that the relevant HEGY statistics on the prewhitened series converge to the same asymptotic distribution as the statistics based on an augmented regression with lagged variables. The prewhitening procedure, however, seems to have better statistical properties when certain white-noise departures appear in residuals. Several cases concerned with quarterly seasonality

---

[10] As electricity cannot be stored, the demand always has to be balanced with the available supply, resulting in great variations in the price.

[11] In an earlier version of this chapter, we estimated an ARIMA–GARCH time series model on the electricity prices after taking evidence of the non-stationary behaviour of the series involved. The time-varying volatility of the process was accurately fitted through an EGARCH process. The conditional mean was described through a SARIMA$(3, 0, 0) \times (0, 1, 1)_7$ model. These results are available upon request from the authors.

are studied in the original paper. We take as our background weekly seasonality, and present only those relevant cases for the purpose of this chapter.

## Case I

Let the following DGP for the time series $\{y_t\}$ be the stochastic difference equation:

$$(1 - B^7)y_t = u_t \tag{5A.1}$$

where $u_t$ follows a weekly SMA(1) process:

$$u_t = (1 - \theta B^7)\varepsilon_t, \quad \varepsilon_t \sim \text{i.i.d.}(0, \sigma_\varepsilon) \tag{5A.2}$$

If the SMA(1) structure is strictly invertible (i.e. $|\theta| < 1$), expression (5A.2) can be alternatively represented as:

$$\varepsilon_t = (1 - \theta B^7)^{-1}u_t = \left(1 - \sum_{j=1}^{\infty} \varphi_j B^{7j}\right)u_t \tag{5A.3}$$

where $\varphi_j = -\theta^j$. In combining (5A.2) with (5A.1) we now obtain:

$$\left(1 - \sum_{j=1}^{\infty} \varphi_j B^{7j}\right)(1 - \theta B^7)y_t = \varepsilon_t \tag{5A.4}$$

As $|\theta| < 1$ and $\varphi_j = -\theta^j$, the succession $\{\varphi_j\}$ converges geometrically to zero, so that it is possible to approximate $\varphi_j = 0$ for some $j > k$, given a value large enough for the truncation-lag parameter $k$. Note that through this approach, the latter equation can be written as $\bar{y}_t = \bar{y}_{t-7} + \bar{\varepsilon}_t$, where $\bar{y}_t = \delta(B)y_t$, with $\delta(B) = (1 - \sum_{j=1,k} \varphi_j B^{7j})$ and $\bar{\varepsilon}_t = \delta(B)\varepsilon_t$ for a fixed $k$.

Since $\bar{y}_t$ depends on the unknown parameters $(\varphi_1, \ldots, \varphi_k)$, the strategy of the Psadarakis procedure is to estimate these parameters through an OLS regression of $\Delta_7 y_t$ on $(\Delta_7 y_{t-7}, \ldots, \Delta_7 y_{t-7k})$. The original series is hence filtered with the resulting estimations $\hat{\delta}(B) = (1 - \sum_{j=1,k} \hat{\varphi}_j B^{7j})$, thereby building a new series $\bar{y}_t = \hat{\delta}(B)y_t$. It is verified that $\bar{y}_t = \bar{y}_{t-7} + \bar{\varepsilon}_t$, where the error term $\bar{\varepsilon}_t = \hat{\delta}(B)\varepsilon_t = \varepsilon_t + \sum_{j=k+1,\infty} \hat{\varphi}_j u_{t-7j}$ is approximately a white-noise process for a high enough value of $k$. The HEGY test is then performed on the prewhitened series without adding any lag of the dependent variable in the auxiliary regression.

## Case II: AR $(r)$ and SMA (1)

A generalisation of the previous case is considered when the proper DGP includes a stationary AR$(r)$ model in the long run together with an SMA(1) process in the disturbance term, that is:

$$\left(1 - \sum_{j=1}^{r} \phi_j B^j\right)\Delta y_t = u_t \tag{5A.5}$$

$$u_t = (1 - B^7)\varepsilon_t, \quad \varepsilon_t \sim \text{i.i.d.}\left(0, \sigma_\varepsilon^2\right)$$

In this case, the prewhitening process is developed in two stages.

(a) First, the AR$(r)$ coefficients $(\phi_1, \ldots, \phi_r)$ are estimated by regressing $\Delta_7 y_t$ on $(\Delta_7 y_{t-1}, \ldots, \Delta_7 y_{t-r})$. Since the error term is not serially uncorrelated, as it actually includes a seasonal MA structure, the OLS estimation of parameters on lagged variables is not consistent. The most suitable procedure, therefore, would be the instrumental variable method (IV), rather than OLS. The variables that verify the suitable orthogonality conditions are lags of the dependent variable of an order higher than seven, i.e. $\Delta_7 y_{t-m}$ with $m > 7$, since they are uncorrelated with the noise term. This stage yields both the estimated coefficients $(\hat{\phi}_1, \ldots, \hat{\phi}_r)$ and a vector of residuals, which is employed in the second stage.

(b) The IV residuals from the above regression are necessarily free of low-order autocorrelation, but still include the serial autocorrelation induced by the invertible representation of the SMA(1) process. The parameters $(\varphi_1, \ldots, \varphi_k)$ are then estimated (similarly to Case I) from an appropriate autoregression on the instrumental-variable residuals from stage (a).

Finally, the HEGY test is applied to the double-filtered series $(1 - \sum_{j=1,r} \hat{\phi}_j B^j)\hat{\delta}(B) y_t$ without adding any lags of the dependent variable in the auxiliary regression, as is done in the main text.

# APPENDIX B: CRITICAL VALUES OF THE HEGY TEST

Critical values of the usual percentiles for the relevant HEGY statistics from an auxiliary regression including either a drift and seasonal dummies (model [1]), or a drift, seasonal dummies and a time trend (model [2]). The $'t' : \pi_{2k}$ and $'t' : \pi_2$ distributions are respectively related to the individual $t$-statistics on the $\pi_{2k}$ and $\pi_{2k+1}$ parameters $(k = 1, 2, 3)$. The $'F'_{2k,2k+1}$ distribution is related to the joint $F$-statistic of conjugate complex roots at a given seasonal frequency. Note that, as a result of the orthogonality properties of the HEGY procedure, this distribution does not depend on the targeted frequency.

| | | Probability of a smaller value | | | | | | | |
|---|---|---|---|---|---|---|---|---|---|
| | | $'t' : \pi_1$ | | | | $'t' : \pi_{2k}$ | | | |
| | $T$ | 0.01 | 0.025 | 0.05 | 0.1 | 0.01 | 0.025 | 0.05 | 0.1 |
| | 240 | −3.36 | −3.04 | −2.78 | −2.47 | −3.83 | −3.52 | −3.25 | −2.95 |
| [1] | 480 | −3.39 | −3.10 | −2.81 | −2.51 | −3.86 | −3.54 | −3.30 | −2.99 |
| | 1000 | −3.41 | −3.10 | −2.85 | −2.56 | −3.88 | −3.58 | −3.33 | −3.03 |
| | 240 | −3.91 | −3.57 | −3.31 | −3.03 | −3.84 | −3.52 | −3.25 | −2.95 |
| [2] | 480 | −3.93 | −3.61 | −3.35 | −3.06 | −3.86 | −3.55 | −3.29 | −2.98 |
| | 1000 | −3.98 | −3.67 | −3.41 | −3.12 | −3.89 | −3.58 | −3.33 | −3.03 |

| | | $'t' : \pi_{2k+1}$ | | | | | | | |
|---|---|---|---|---|---|---|---|---|---|
| | $T$ | 0.01 | 0.025 | 0.05 | 0.1 | 0.90 | 0.95 | 0.975 | 0.99 |
| | 240 | −2.62 | −2.21 | −1.86 | −1.45 | 1.48 | 1.89 | 2.24 | 2.63 |
| [1] | 480 | −2.67 | −2.25 | −1.90 | −1.48 | 1.52 | 1.92 | 2.28 | 2.69 |
| | 1000 | −2.70 | −2.29 | −1.93 | −1.52 | 1.54 | 1.95 | 2.29 | 2.70 |
| | 240 | −2.60 | −2.21 | −1.85 | −1.45 | 1.45 | 1.85 | 2.21 | 2.63 |
| [2] | 480 | −2.66 | −2.26 | −1.91 | −1.50 | 1.49 | 1.89 | 2.24 | 2.65 |
| | 1000 | −2.70 | −2.30 | −1.93 | −1.51 | 1.51 | 1.94 | 2.31 | 2.71 |

*Source:* Rubia (2001).

| | | Probability of a smaller value | | | |
|---|---|---|---|---|---|
| | | $'F'_{2k,2k+1}$ | | | |
| | T | 0.90 | 0.95 | 0.975 | 0.99 |
| [1] | 240 | 5.25 | 6.25 | 7.18 | 8.33 |
| | 480 | 5.43 | 6.40 | 7.35 | 8.50 |
| | 1000 | 5.54 | 6.53 | 7.48 | 8.63 |
| [2] | 240 | 5.24 | 6.23 | 7.16 | 8.32 |
| | 480 | 5.40 | 6.37 | 7.30 | 8.60 |
| | 1000 | 5.56 | 6.59 | 7.54 | 8.69 |

*Source:* Rubia (2001).

# ACKNOWLEDGEMENTS

The authors are indebted to Julián López and Alfonso Novales for comments and suggestions. Support from the Spanish Department of Science and Technology through project 2002-03797 is acknowledged. An earlier version of this chapter appeared in the working paper series of the Instituto Valenciano de Investigaciones Económicas (IVIE), which is acknowledged. All the contents are the sole responsibility of the authors.

# REFERENCES

Andrews D.W.K. (1991). "Heteroskedasticity and Autocorrelation Consistent Covariance Matrix Estimation". *Econometrica* **59**: 817–858.

Bollerslev T., Engle R.F. and Nelson D.B. (1994). "ARCH Models". In *Handbook of Econometrics*, Vol. 4, R.F. Engle and D.C. McFadden (eds). North Holland, Amsterdam, pp. 2961–3038.

Boswijk P.H. (2000). "Testing for a Unit Root with Near-integrated Volatility". Working Paper, Department of Quantitative Economics, Universiteit van Amsterdam.

Byström H.N. (2000). "The Hedging Perfomance of Electricity Futures on the Nordic Power Exchange Nord Pool". Working Paper 2000:15, Lund University, Department of Economics.

Canova F. and Hansen B.E. (1995). "Are Seasonal Patterns Constant over Time? A Test for Seasonal Stability". *Journal of Business & Economic Statistics* **13**: 237–252.

De Vany A.S. and Walls W.D. (1999). "Cointegration Analysis of Spot Electricity Prices: Insights on Transmission Effiency in the Western US". *Energy Economics* **21**: 435–448.

Dickey D.A. and Fuller W.A. (1979). "Distribution of the Estimators for Autoregressive Time Series with a Unit Root". *Journal of the American Statistical Association* **74**: 427–431.

Dickey D.A., Hasza D.P. and Fuller W.A. (1984). "Testing for Unit Roots in Seasonal Time Series". *Journal of the American Statistical Association* **79**: 355–367.

Franses P.H. and Haldrup N. (1994). "The Effects of Additive Outliers on Tests of Unit Roots and Cointegration". *Journal of Business & Economic Statistics* **12**: 471–478.

Ghysels E., Lee H.S. and Noh J. (1994). "Testing for Unit Roots in Seasonal Time Series". *Journal of Econometrics* **62**, 415–442.

Hasza D.P. and Fuller W. (1982). "Testing for Nonstationary Parameters Specifications in Seasonal Time Series Models". *Annals of Statistics* **10**: 1209–1216.

Helm D. and Powell A. (1992). "Pool Prices, Contracts and Regulation in the British Electricity Supply Industry". *Fiscal Studies* **13**: 89–105.

Hylleberg S. (1995). "Test for Seasonal Unit Roots. General to Specific or Specific to General?". *Journal of Econometrics* **69**: 5–25.

Hylleberg S., Engle R.F., Granger C.W.J. and Yoo B.S. (1990). "Seasonal Integration and Cointegration". *Journal of Econometrics* **44**: 215–238.

Kwiatkowski D., Phillips P.C.B., Schmidt P. and Shin Y. (1992). "Testing the Null Hypothesis of Stationarity against the Alternative of a Unit Root". *Journal of Econometrics* **54**, 159–178.

Lucia J. and Schwartz E.S. (2002). "Electricity Prices and Power Derivatives, 2002, Evidence from the Nordic Power Exchange". *Review of Derivatives Research* **5**(1): 5–50.

Newey W. and West K. (1987a). "A Simple Positive Semi-Definite, Heteroskedasticity and Autocorrelation Consistent Covariance Matrix". *Econometrica* **55**: 703–708.

Newey W. and West K. (1987b). "Hypothesis Testing with Efficient Method of Moments Estimation". *International Economic Review* **28**: 777–787.

Newey W. and West K. (1994). "Automatic Lag Selection in Covariance Matrix Estimation". *Review of Economic Studies* **61**: 631–653.

Ng S. and Perron P. (1995). "Unit Root Tests in ARMA Models with Data-dependent Methods for the Selection of the Truncation Lag". *Journal of the American Statistical Association* **90**: 268–281.

Psaradakis Z. (1997). "Testing for Unit Roots in Time Series with Nearly Deterministic Seasonal Variation". *Econometric Reviews* **16**: 421–439.

Robinson T.A. (2000). "Electricity Pool Prices: A Case Study in Nonlinear Time-Series Modelling". *Applied Economics* **32**: 527–532.

Rubia A. (2001). "Testing for Weekly Seasonal Unit Roots in Daily Electricity Demand: Evidence from Deregulated Markets". Instituto Valenciano de Investigaciones Económicas, WP-2001–21 (www.ivie.es).

Schwert G.W. (1989). "Tests for Unit Roots: A Monte Carlo Investigation". *Journal of Business and Economic Statistics* **7**: 147–159.

Stock J.H. (1994). "Unit Roots, Structural Breaks and Trends". In *Handbook of Econometrics*, Vol. 4, R.F. Engle and D.C. McFadden, (eds). North Holland, Amsterdam, pp. 2740–2841.

--- 6 ---

# Nonlinear Time Series Analysis of Alberta's Deregulated Electricity Market

APOSTOLOS SERLETIS[1] AND IOANNIS ANDREADIS[2]

[1]*Department of Economics, University of Calgary, Calgary, Alberta T2N 1N4, Canada*
[2]*European University of the Hague, Center of Management Studies, Nassauplein 25, 2585 EC The Hague, The Netherlands*

## ABSTRACT

This chapter uses daily on-peak electricity prices for Alberta, Canada over the deregulated period after 1996, and various tests from dynamical systems theory, such as for example the Vassilicos *et al.* multifractal structure test, the Ghashghaie *et al.* turbulent behavior test and the Nychka *et al.* chaos test, to support a stochastic origin for this series.

## 6.1 INTRODUCTION

Electricity is considered to be one of the most volatile non-storable commodities in the world with limited transportability. In fact, transmission constraints, in the form of capacity limits in the transmission lines and their associated losses, make the transmission of electricity between certain regions impossible if not uneconomical. As a result, arbitrage across time and space is seriously limited and electricity prices are largely dependent on temporal and local demand and supply conditions.

The main objective of this chapter is to use tools from dynamical systems theory to explain the fluctuations in electricity prices in Alberta, Canada using daily data over the deregulated period from 1996 to 2002. In particular, we use average prices for the on-peak hours (generally 06:00 to 22:00 hours, Monday through Saturday) from 1 January 1996 to 10 May 2002 (a total of 2117 observations). Our principal concern is to distinguish between deterministic and stochastic origin for electricity prices.

The chapter is organized as follows. In Sections 6.2 and 6.3 we test for a random multifractal structure in on-peak electricity prices and in Section 6.4 for turbulent behavior. In Sections 6.5 and 6.6 we test for deterministic chaos using the Nychka *et al.* (1992) Lyapunov exponent estimator and its limit distribution. The final section provides a brief conclusion.

## 6.2 A NOISE MODEL

In recent years, a significant volume of research supports the existence of nonlinear dynamics in most economic and financial time series. Nonlinearity, however, is a necessary but not

*Modelling Prices in Competitive Electricity Markets.* Edited by D.W. Bunn.
© 2004 John Wiley & Sons, Ltd. ISBN 0-470-84860-X.

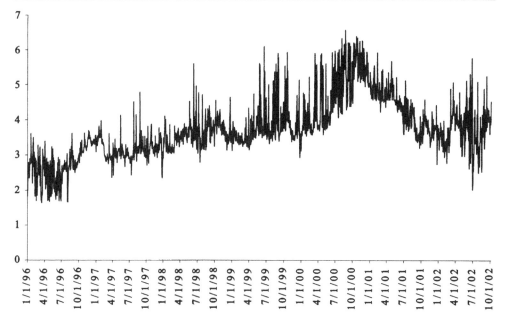

**Figure 6.1**    (Logged) daily Alberta prices

sufficient condition for chaos, since nonlinearity may be either deterministic or stochastic – see, for example, Barnett and Hinich (1992), Barnett and Serletis (2000) and Barnett *et al.* (1995, 1997). In this section, we provide evidence that the nonlinearity in electricity prices may have a noise origin.

### 6.2.1    The power spectrum

As we have a time series with a finite number of data points (see Figure 6.1), we follow Li (1991) and calculate its power spectrum $P(f)$, using the following discrete Fourier transform:

$$P(f) = N \| A(f) \|^2$$

where $\| A(f) \|$ is the module of the complex number

$$A(f) = \frac{1}{N} \sum_{j=1}^{N} x_j e^{\frac{i2\pi f j}{N}}$$

We present the power spectrum of the electricity price time series in Figure 6.2. We find behavior of the type $1/f^\alpha$, where $\alpha = 1.14$. This behavior is strictly related to the self-critical phenomena reported by Bak and Chen (1991). It is also consistent with the evidence reported in Andreadis (2000) for the S&P 500, in Andreadis and Serletis (2001) for the US federal funds rate, and Andreadis and Serletis (2002) for the Dow Jones Industrial Average.

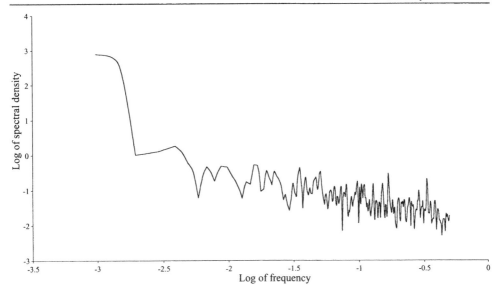

**Figure 6.2**    The power spectrum

### 6.2.2    The structure function test

Next we apply the structure function test, developed by Provenzale *et al.* (1992), in order to support and extend the results obtained so far indicating a fractal noise model. The structure function test was originally developed as a tool for distinguishing between a deterministic and a stochastic origin of time series whose power spectrum displays a scaling behavior.

We consider a time series $T$ with a finite length equal to $N$. For every $n$, $1 \leq n \leq N$, the structure function associated with $T$ is defined as follows:

$$\Sigma(n) = \sum_{i=1}^{N-n} [T((i+n)\Delta t) - T(i\Delta t)]^2$$

where $\Delta t$ denotes the sampling rate of $T$. According to Mandelbrot (1982), for a time series $T$ with a power-law spectrum $P(f) \propto f^{-\alpha}$, where $\alpha$ is positive real, one expects a scaling behavior of the form $\Sigma(n) \propto n^{2H}$ at small values of $n$, where $H$ is called the scaling exponent. In the case of a fractional Brownian motion, it holds (see Provenzale *et al.*, 1992) that:

$$\alpha = 2H + 1$$

When the signal is a fractal noise, the graph of $\log(\Sigma(n))$ versus $\log(n)$ displays an extended scaling regime and it is closely approximated by a straight line. On the other hand, if the time series corresponds to the motion of a strange attractor whose fractal structure is due to close returns in phase space, the graph of $\log(\Sigma(n))$ versus $\log(n)$ is closely approximated at small values of $n$ by a straight line with slope $2H = 1$. At intermediate $n$, $\Sigma(n)$ has an oscillatory behavior, due to orbit occurrence in phase space. Finally, for high values of $n$, $\Sigma(n)$ approaches a constant, due to the limited phase space visited by the system.

In Figure 6.3 we show the graph of $\log(\Sigma(n))$ versus $\log(n)$ for the electricity price series. We find that $2H = 0.32$ which gives a value of $\alpha = 2H + 1$ different from the one we found

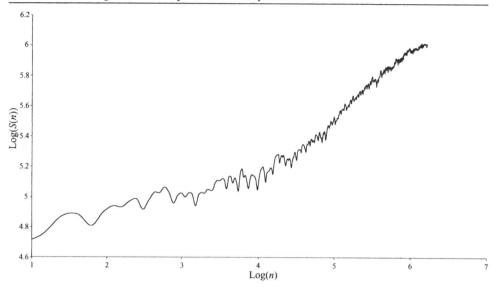

**Figure 6.3**  The structure function test

by calculating the scaling behavior of the power spectrum. Therefore the relation between the power spectrum and the structure function test does not support a fractional Brownian motion for this series.

### 6.2.3  The Hurst test

Here we apply the Rescale Range (R/S) analysis, or Hurst test – see Mandelbrot (1982) and Papaioannou and Karytinos (1995) – which can be described as follows. Consider the time series $T(i), i = 1, \ldots, N$ and for every $n$, $2 \le n \le N$, denote by $M_n$ the mean value of the truncated first $n$ elements. Then we define a new time series $X(j)$ representing the cumulative deviation over the $n$ periods, with elements

$$X(j) = \sum_{j=1}^{n} [T(j) - M_n], \quad j = 1, 2, \ldots, N$$

The range of the cumulative deviation from the average level, $R_n$, is the difference between the maximum and minimum cumulative deviations over $n$ periods:

$$R_n = \max_{1 \le j \le n} X(j) - \min_{1 \le j \le n} X(j)$$

The function $R_n$ increases with $n$. Finally, we denote by $S_n$ the standard deviation of the first $n$ elements of the time series $T(i)$. According to the Hurst law, in the case of a fractional Brownian motion, the following should hold, in the limit of large $n$:

$$\frac{R_n}{S_n} \propto \left(\frac{n}{2}\right)^{\mathcal{H}}$$

with $0 \le \mathcal{H} \le 1$ being the Hurst exponent. Hence, we can plot $R_n/S_n$ against $\log(n/2)$ and find a value of the Hurst exponent.

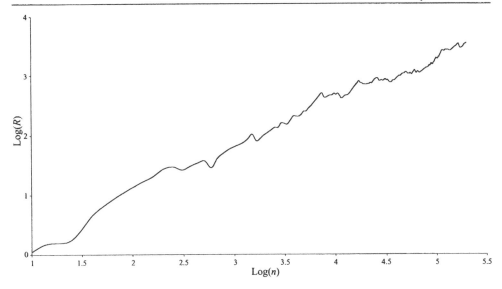

**Figure 6.4**   The Hurst test

Applying this test in Figure 6.4, we find a multiscaling behavior of the Hurst exponent. In particular, for small values of $n$, $\mathcal{H}$ is between 0.5 and 1, suggesting a persistent ($\mathcal{H} > 0.5$) fractal structure with a long memory. However, for large values of $n$, $\mathcal{H}$ exceeds 1, indicating behavior not in the framework of the fractional Brownian motion.

## 6.3   A MULTIFRACTAL FORMALISM SETTING

Let us consider the time series $T(i)$, $i = 1, 2, \ldots, N$. Vassilicos *et al.* (1993) addressed the question of whether the set of points $T(i)$, $i = 1, 2, \ldots, N$, is a fractal set on the time axis, in the sense of the presence of a scaling. If the answer is yes, then the next interesting question is whether this fractal distribution is homogeneous or whether it is a multifractal, in the sense that the different fractal scalings may apply to different times.

To answer this question in the context of the electricity price series, we calculate the generalized dimensions $D_q$ of the graph of the time series $T(i)$. Let us briefly recall this algorithm. The time axis is covered by a grid of points separated by a fixed distance $\varepsilon$ from each other. We label each interval between grid points with an integer $j$ and calculate the total number of announcements, $\mu_j$, that lie within the interval $j$. Then we compute the quantity

$$N_q\left(\varepsilon\right) = \sum_j \mu_j^q$$

and for various integers we use $q = 0, 2, 3, 4$.

When the distribution of the points is fractal in the sense of Vassilicos and Hunt (1991), then

$$N_0\left(\varepsilon\right) \sim \varepsilon^{-D_0}$$

for $\varepsilon$ small enough and $0 < D_0 < 1$. $D_0$ is called the fractal dimension and characterizes the fractal scaling structure of the set. If there exists a $D_0$ then there also exist powers $\tau_q$ such that

$$N_q\left(\varepsilon\right) \sim \varepsilon^{-\tau_q}$$

**Table 6.1**   Tests for multifractal structure

| $q$ | $\tau_q$ | $D_q$ |
|-----|----------|-------|
| $q = 0$ | 0.850 | 0.85 |
| $q = 2$ | −0.943 | 0.943 |
| $q = 3$ | −1.896 | 0.945 |
| $q = 4$ | −2.841 | 0.946 |

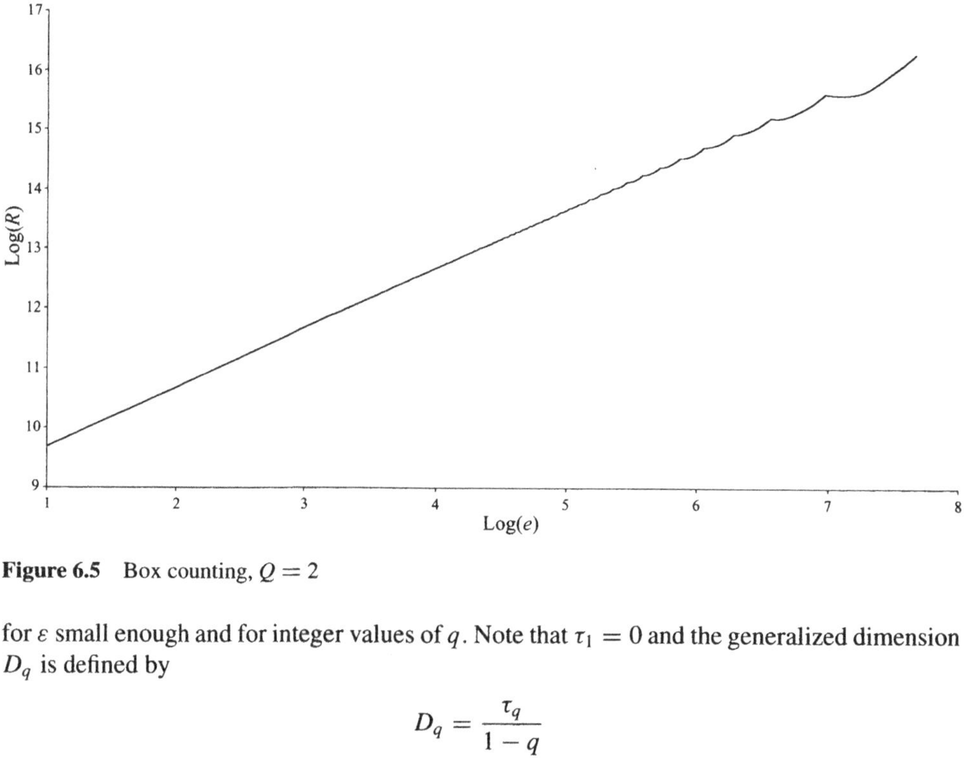

**Figure 6.5**   Box counting, $Q = 2$

for $\varepsilon$ small enough and for integer values of $q$. Note that $\tau_1 = 0$ and the generalized dimension $D_q$ is defined by

$$D_q = \frac{\tau_q}{1 - q}$$

with $1 \geq D_0 \geq D_1 \geq D_2 \geq \cdots \geq 0$.

We present the numerical results obtained by applying the previous algorithm in Table 6.1.

Clearly, these results support a homogeneous random multifractal behavior as the values of the multifractal dimension approach 1. In Figure 6.5, we present the corresponding calculations for $D_2$.

## 6.4   ON TURBULENT BEHAVIOR

Recently, Ghashghaie *et al.* (1996) have advanced the hypothesis of turbulent behavior in financial markets. Their hypothesis, however, has been criticized by Mantegna and Stanley (1996). To provide some evidence on this issue, we report a scaling behavior for the electricity price series which does not agree with the Ghashghaie *et al.* (1996) hypothesis of turbulent behavior.

**Table 6.2**  Tests for turbulence

| q | Turbulent flows | Electricity |
|---|---|---|
| $q = 1$ | 0.33 | 0.23 |
| $q = 2$ | 0.66 | 0.29 |
| $q = 3$ | 1.00 | 0.39 |

Let us define the return over $n$ time steps as $Z_n(t) = |X(t + \Delta t) - X(t)|$, where $X(t)$ is an entry of the time series and $\Delta t = 1$ is the sampling time. We have found that the moments of the distribution $Z_n(t)$ possessing a scaling behavior as a function of $n$ can be expressed as

$$\langle |Z_n(t)|^q \rangle_t \propto n^{\xi(q)}$$

where $\xi(q)$ is the self-affinity exponent. In Table 6.2, we indicate the values obtained for $q = 1, 2, 3$ for the electricity price series and compare them with the values $\xi(q) = q/3$ for turbulent flows.

Clearly, the behavior of electricity prices is not consistent with the Ghashghaie *et al.* (1996) hypothesis of turbulent behavior.

## 6.5  ON NONLINEARITY

Here we apply the Grassberger and Procaccia (1983) algorithm in order to calculate the correlation dimension. We calculate the autocorrelation function, as in Jenkins and Watts (1969):

$$A(\tau) = \frac{\sum_{i=1}^{N-l} \overline{T}(t_i)\overline{T}(t_{i+l})}{\sum_{i=1}^{N} \overline{T}(t_i)^2}$$

where

$$\overline{T}(t_i) = T(t_i) - \frac{1}{N}\sum_{j=1}^{N} T(t_j)$$

We present the autocorrelation function in Figure 6.6. Clearly, the autocorrelation coefficient never becomes zero; in all of the well-known chaotic systems a zero point of the autocorrelation function is reported. This is evidence against deterministic chaos in this electricity price series.

The evidence against deterministic chaos is further supported by the reconstruction plots in Figure 6.7. The reconstruction plot, $X(t) - X(t + \tau)$ for $\tau = 5$, is constructed using the methods of Takens (1980) and Packard *et al.* (1990). As is evident in Figure 6.7, the motion is concentrated on the first diagonal and no correlation is observed.

## 6.6  ON CHAOS

In this section we follow the recent contribution by Whang and Linton (1999) and Linton and Shintani (2003) and construct the standard error for the Nychka *et al.* (1992) dominant Lyapunov exponent for the electricity price series, thereby providing a statistical test for chaos.

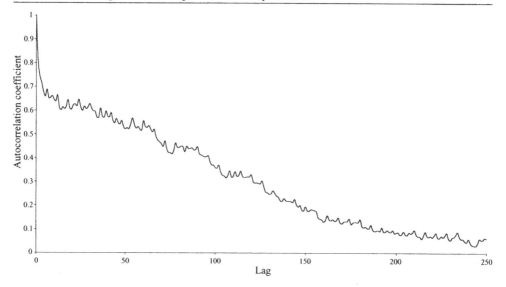

**Figure 6.6**   The autocorrelation function

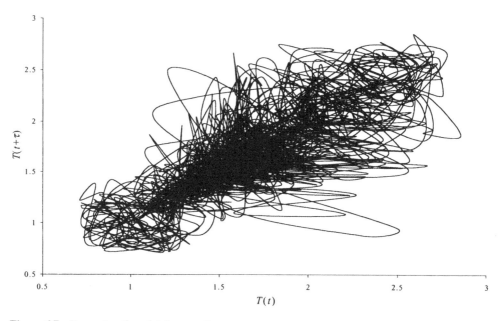

**Figure 6.7**   Reconstruction plot for $\tau = 5$

We also follow Shintani and Linton (2004) and Serletis and Shintani (2003) and report both global and local Lyapunov exponents. As argued by Wolff (1992), Bailey (1996) and Bailey *et al.* (1997), local Lyapunov exponents provide a more detailed description of the system's dynamics, in the sense that they can identify differences in short-term predictability among regions in the state space.

Let $\{X_t\}_{t=1}^T$ be a random scalar sequence generated by the following nonlinear autoregressive model:

$$X_t = \theta(X_{t-1}, \ldots, X_{t-m}) + u_t \tag{6.1}$$

where $\theta: \mathbb{R}^m \to \mathbb{R}$ is a nonlinear dynamic map and $\{u_t\}_{t=1}^T$ is a random sequence of i.i.d. disturbances with $E(u_t) = 0$ and $E(u_t^2) = \sigma^2 < \infty$. We also assume $\theta$ to satisfy a smoothness condition, and $Z_t = (X_t, \ldots, X_{t-m+1})' \in \mathbb{R}^m$ to be strictly stationary and to satisfy a class of mixing conditions – see Whang and Linton (1999) and Shintani and Linton (2004) for details regarding these conditions.

Let us express the model (6.1) in terms of a map

$$F(Z_t) = (\theta(X_{t-1}, \ldots, X_{t-m}), X_{t-1}, \ldots, X_{t-m+1})' \tag{6.2}$$

with $U_t = (u_t, 0, \ldots, 0)'$ such that

$$Z_t = F(Z_{t-1}) + U_t$$

and let $J_t$ be the Jacobian of the map $F$ in (6.2) evaluated at $Z_t$. Then the dominant Lyapunov exponent of the system (6.1) is defined by

$$\lambda \equiv \lim_{M \to \infty} \frac{1}{2M} \ln v_1(\mathbf{T}_M' \mathbf{T}_M) \tag{6.3}$$

where

$$\mathbf{T}_M = \prod_{t=1}^M J_{M-t} = J_{M-1} \cdot J_{M-2} \cdots\cdots J_0$$

and $v_i(A)$ is the $i$th largest eigenvalue of a matrix $A$. Necessary conditions for the existence of the Lyapunov exponent are available in the literature. Usually, if $\max\left\{\ln v_1\left(J_t' J_t\right), 0\right\}$ has a finite first moment with respect to the distribution of $Z_t$, then the limit in (6.3) almost surely exists and will be a constant, irrespective of the initial condition.

To obtain the Lyapunov exponent from observational data, Eckmann and Ruelle (1985) and Eckmann et al. (1986) proposed a method based on nonparametric regression which is known as the Jacobian method. The basic idea of the Jacobian method is to substitute $\theta$ in the Jacobian formula by its nonparametric estimator $\widehat{\theta}$. In other words, it is the sample analogue estimator of (6.3). It should be noted that we distinguish between the "sample size" $T$ used for estimating the Jacobian $\widehat{J}_t$ and the "block length" $M$ which is the number of evaluation points used for estimating the Lyapunov exponent. Formally, the Lyapunov exponent estimator of $\lambda$ can be obtained by

$$\widehat{\lambda}_M = \frac{1}{2M} \ln v_1(\widehat{\mathbf{T}}_M' \widehat{\mathbf{T}}_M)$$

where

$$\widehat{\mathbf{T}}_M = \prod_{t=1}^M \widehat{J}_{M-t} = \widehat{J}_{M-1} \cdot \widehat{J}_{M-2} \cdots\cdots \widehat{J}_0$$

and

$$\widehat{J}_t = \frac{\partial \widehat{F}(Z_t)}{\partial Z'} = \begin{bmatrix} \Delta\widehat{\theta}_{1t} & \Delta\widehat{\theta}_{2t} & \cdots & \Delta\widehat{\theta}_{m-1,t} & \Delta\widehat{\theta}_{mt} \\ 1 & 0 & \cdots & 0 & 0 \\ 0 & 1 & \cdots & 0 & 0 \\ \vdots & \vdots & \ddots & \vdots & \vdots \\ 0 & 0 & \cdots & 1 & 0 \end{bmatrix}$$

for $t = 0, 1, \ldots, M - 1$, $\Delta\widehat{\theta}_{jt} = D^{e_j}\widehat{\theta}(Z_t)$ for $j = 1, \ldots, m$ in which $e_j = (0, \ldots, 1, \ldots, 0)' \in \mathbb{R}^m$ denotes the $j$th elementary vector.

In principle, any nonparametric derivative estimator $D^{e_j}\widehat{\theta}$ can be used for the Jacobian method. However, in practice, the Jacobian method based on the neural network estimation first proposed by Nychka $et\ al.$ (1992) and Gençay and Dechert (1992) is the most widely used method in recent empirical analyses in economics. The neural network estimator $\widehat{\theta}$ can be obtained by minimizing the least squares criterion

$$S_T(\theta_T) = \frac{1}{T} \sum_{t=1}^{T} \frac{1}{2}(X_t - \theta_T(Z_{t-1}))^2$$

where the neural network sieve $\theta_T : \mathbb{R}^m \to \mathbb{R}$ is an approximation function defined by

$$\theta_T(z) = \beta_0 + \sum_{j=1}^{k} \beta_j \psi(a'_j z + b_j)$$

where $\psi$ is an activation function and $k$ is the number of hidden units. For the neural network estimation, we use the FUNFITS program developed by Nychka $et\ al.$ (1996). As an activation function $\psi$, this program uses a type of sigmoid function

$$\psi(u) = \frac{u(1 + |u/2|)}{2 + |u| + u^2/2}$$

which was also employed by Nychka $et\ al.$ (1992). The number of hidden units ($k$) will be determined by minimizing the BIC criterion.

Using the argument in Whang and Linton (1999), Shintani and Linton (2004) showed that under some reasonable condition, the neural network estimator $\widehat{\lambda}_M$ is asymptotically normal and its standard error can be obtained using

$$\widehat{\Phi} = \sum_{j=-M+1}^{M-1} w(j/S_M)\widehat{\gamma}(j) \quad \text{and} \quad \widehat{\gamma}(j) = \frac{1}{M} \sum_{t=|j|+1}^{M} \widehat{\eta}_t \widehat{\eta}_{t-|j|}$$

where

$$\widehat{\eta}_t = \widehat{\xi}_t - \widehat{\lambda}_M$$

with

$$\widehat{\xi}_t = \frac{1}{2} \ln\left(\frac{v_1(\widehat{\mathbf{T}}'_t \widehat{\mathbf{T}}_t)}{v_1(\widehat{\mathbf{T}}'_{t-1} \widehat{\mathbf{T}}_{t-1})}\right) \quad \text{for} \quad t \geq 2 \quad \text{and} \quad \widehat{\xi}_1 = \frac{1}{2} \ln v_1(\widehat{\mathbf{T}}'_1 \widehat{\mathbf{T}}_1)$$

Above, $\omega(\cdot)$ and $S_M$ denote a kernel function and a lag truncation parameter, respectively. Note that the standard error is essentially the heteroscedasticity and autocorrelation covariance

**Table 6.3** Lyapunov exponent estimates for the logged electricity price series

| NLAR lag ($m$) | Number of hidden units | | | | | | | | |
| --- | --- | --- | --- | --- | --- | --- | --- | --- | --- |
| | $k = 1$ | | | $k = 2$ | | | $k = 3$ | | |
| | BIC | Full | Block | BIC | Full | Block | BIC | Full | Block |
| 1 | −3.411658 | −0.115 (−8.592) [<0.001] | −0.103 (−7.970) [<0.001] | −3.409993 | −0.100 (−6.627) [<0.001] | −0.120 (−4.901) [<0.001] | −3.399690 | −0.103 (−6.811) [<0.001] | −0.119 (−5.354) [<0.001] |
| 2 | −3.454247 | −0.073 (−7.045) [<0.001] | −0.068 (−5.697) [<0.001] | −3.453167 | −0.067 (−5.775) [<0.001] | −0.062 (−5.466) [<0.001] | −3.452560 | −0.040 (−4.319) [<0.001] | −0.059 (−3.214) [<0.001] |
| 3 | −3.508542 | −0.043 (−7.266) [<0.001] | −0.041 (−13.222) [<0.001] | −3.505075 | −0.044 (−4.358) [<0.001] | −0.053 (−5.411) [0.013] | −3.501185 | −0.027 (−3.881) [<0.001] | −0.030 (−3.353) [0.034] |
| 4 | −3.509211 | −0.039 (−7.951) [<0.001] | −0.038 (−9.814) [<0.001] | −3.502282 | −0.036 (−3.876) [<0.001] | −0.045 (−4.697) [0.021] | −3.497380 | −0.022 (−5.054) [<0.001] | −0.026 (−4.267) [<0.001] |
| 5 | −3.528917 | −0.028 (−7.071) [<0.001] | −0.027 (−11.701) [<0.001] | −3.523787 | −0.016 (−4.133) [<0.001] | −0.009 (−2.811) [0.121] | −3.518989 | −0.017 (−10.076) [<0.001] | −0.014 (−7.235) [<0.001] |

*Note*: Sample size $T = 2117$. For the full sample estimation (Full), the largest Lyapunov exponent estimates are presented with $t$-statistics in parentheses and $p$-value for $H_0 : \lambda \geq 0$ in brackets. For the block estimation (Block), median values are presented; the number of blocks was set equal to 4. QS kernel with optimal bandwidth (Andrews, 1991) is used for the heteroscedasticity and autocorrelation-consistent covariance estimation.

estimator of Andrews (1991) applied to $\widehat{\eta}_t$. We employ the QS kernel for $\omega(\cdot)$ with $S_M$ selected by the optimal bandwidth selection method recommended in Andrews (1991).

Lyapunov exponent point estimates along with their $t$-statistics (in parentheses) are displayed in Table 6.3. The results are presented for dimensions 1 through 5, with the optimal value of the number of hidden units $(k)$ in the neural net being chosen by minimizing the BIC criterion. $p$-Values for the null hypothesis $H_0 : \lambda \geq 0$ are also reported in brackets. The Full column under each value of $k$ shows the estimated largest Lyapunov exponent using the full sample. The Block column shows median values for the block estimation, with the number of blocks $(B)$ being set equal to 4.

In general, the reported Lyapunov exponent point estimates are negative and in every case we reject the null hypothesis of chaotic behavior. Of course, the estimates depend on the choice of the dimension parameter, $m$. As $m$ increases, the Lyapunov exponent point estimates increase in value. The presence, however, of dynamic noise makes it difficult and perhaps impossible to distinguish between (noisy) high-dimensional chaos and pure randomness. For this reason, as in Serletis and Shintani (2003), we don't pursue the investigation of high-dimensional chaos.

## 6.7   CONCLUSION

We have used daily on-peak observations on Alberta electricity prices since 1996 and applied tests from dynamical systems theory to distinguish between a deterministic and stochastic origin for the series. We have found evidence consistent with a stochastic origin for electricity prices in Alberta's deregulated electricity market.

## ACKNOWLEDGMENTS

We would like to thank Mototsugu Shintani and Doug Nychka for help with the computer programs and Glenn MacIntyre, Asghar Shahmoradi and Richard Stokl for research assistance.

## REFERENCES

Andreadis I. (2000). "Self-Criticality and Stochasticity of a S&P 500 Index Time Series". *Chaos, Solitons & Fractals* **11**: 1047–1059.

Andreadis I. and Serletis A. (2001). "On Stochasticity and Turbulence in the Federal Funds Market". *International Journal of Systems Science* **32**: 43–52.

Andreadis I. and Serletis A. (2002). "Evidence of a Random Multifractal Turbulent Structure in the Dow Jones Industrial Average". *Chaos, Solitons & Fractals* **13**: 1309–1315.

Andrews D.W.K. (1991). "Heteroskedasticity and Autocorrelation Consistent Covariance Matrix Estimation". *Econometrica* **59**: 817—858.

Bailey B.A. (1996). "Local Lyapunov Exponents: Predictability Depends on Where You Are". In *Nonlinear Dynamics and Economics*, W.A. Barnett, A.P. Kirman and M. Salmon (eds). Cambridge University Press, Cambridge, pp. 345–359.

Bailey B.A., Ellner S. and Nychka D.W. (1997). "Chaos with Confidence: Asymptotics and Applications of Local Lyapunov Exponents". *Fields Institute Communications* **11**: 115–133.

Bak P. and Chen. K. (1991). "Self-Organized Criticality". *Scientific American* **264**: 26–33.

Barnett W.A. and Hinich M.J. (1992). "Empirical Chaotic Dynamics in Economics". *Annals of Operational Research* **37**: 1–15.

Barnett W.A. and Serletis A. (2000). "Martingales, Nonlinearity, and Chaos". *Journal of Economic Dynamics and Control* **24**: 703–724.

Barnett W.A., Gallant A.R., Hinich M.J., Jungeilges J.A., Kaplan D.T. and Jensen M.J. (1995). "Robustness of Nonlinearity and Chaos Tests to Measurement Error, Inference Method, and Sample Size". *Journal of Economic Behavior and Organization* **27**: 301–320.

Barnett W.A., Gallant A.R., Hinich M.J., Jungeilges J.A., Kaplan D.T. and Jensen M.J. (1997). "A Single-Blind Controlled Competition Among Tests for Nonlinearity and Chaos". *Journal of Econometrics* **82**: 157–192.

Eckmann J.-P. and Ruelle D. (1985). "Ergodic Theory of Chaos and Strange Attractors". *Reviews of Modern Physics* **57**: 617–656.

Eckmann J.-P., Kamphorst S.O., Ruelle D. and Ciliberto S. (1986). "Liapunov Exponents from Time Series". *Physical Review A* **34**: 4971–4979.

Gençay R. and Dechert W.D. (1992). "An Algorithm for the $n$ Lyapunov Exponents of an $n$-Dimensional Unknown Dynamical System". *Physica D* **59**: 142–157.

Ghashghaie S., Breymann W., Peinke J., Talkner P. and Dodge Y. (1996). "Turbulent Cascades in Foreign Exchange Markets". *Nature* **381**: 767–770.

Granger C.W.J. (1991). "Developments in the Nonlinear Analysis of Economic Series". *Scandinavian Journal of Economics* **93**: 263–276.

Grassberger P. and Procaccia I. (1983). "Measuring the Strangeness of a Strange Attractor". *Physica D* **9**: 189–208.

Jenkins G.M. and Watts D.G. (1969). *Spectral Analysis and its Applications*. Holden Day, New York.

Li W. (1991). "Absence of $1/f$ Spectra in Dow Jones Average". *International Journal of Bifurcation and Chaos* **1**: 583–597.

Linton O. and Shintani M. (2003). "Is There Chaos in the World Economy. A Nonparametric Test using Consistent Standard Errors". *International Economic Review* **44**: 331–358.

Mandelbrot B.B. (1982). *The Fractal Geometry of Nature*. Freeman, San Francisco.

Mantegna R.N. and Stanley H.E. (1996). "Turbulence and Financial Markets". *Nature* **376**: 587–588.

Nychka D.W., Ellner S., Gallant A.R. and McCaffrey D. (1992). "Finding Chaos in Noisy Systems". *Journal of the Royal Statistical Society, Series B* **54**: 399–426.

Nychka D.W., Bailey B.A., Ellner S. and O'Connell M. (1996). "FUNFITS: Data Analysis and Statistical Tools for Estimating Functions". *North Carolina Institute of Statistics Mimeoseries*, No. 2289.

Packard N.H., Crutchfield J.P., Farmer J.D. and Shaw R.S. (1990). "Geometry from a Time Series". *Physical Review Letters* **45**: 710–716.

Papaioannou G. and Karytinos A. (1995). "Nonlinear Time Series Analysis of the Stock Exchange: The Case of an Emerging Market". *International Journal of Bifurcation and Chaos* **5**: 1557–1584.

Provenzale A., Smith L.A., Vio R. and Murane G. (1992). "Distinguishing Between Low-Dimensional Dynamics and Randomness in Measure Time Series". *Physica D* **58**: 431–491.

Serletis A. and Shintani M. (2003). "No Evidence of Chaos But Some Evidence of Dependence in the U.S. Stock Market". *Chaos, Solitons & Fractals* **17**: 449–454.

Shintani M. and Linton O. (2004). "Nonparametric Neural Network Estimation of Lyapunov Exponents and a Direct Test for Chaos". *Journal of Econometrics*, (forthcoming).

Takens F. (1980). "Detecting Strange Attractors in Turbulence". In *Dynamical Systems and Turbulence*, D. Rand and L.S. Young (eds). Springer-Verlag, New York, pp. 366–381.

Vassilicos J.C. and Hunt J.C.R. (1991). "Fractal Dimensions and Spectra of Interfaces with Application to Turbulence". *Proceedings of the Royal Society London Series A* **435**: 505–534.

Vassilicos J.C., Demos A. and Tata F. (1993). "No Evidence of Chaos But Some Evidence of Multifractals in the Foreign Exchange and the Stock Markets". In *Applications of Fractals and Chaos*, A.J. Crilly, R.A. Earnshaw and H. Jones (eds). Springer-Verlag, New York, pp. 249–265.

Whang Y.J. and Linton O. (1999). "The Asymptotic Distribution of Nonparametric Estimates of the Lyapunov Exponent for Stochastic Time Series". *Journal of Econometrics* **91**: 1–42.

Wolff R.C.L. (1992). "Local Lyapunov Exponents: Looking Closely at Chaos". *Journal of the Royal Statistical Society, Series B* **54**: 353–371.

# 7
# Quantile-Based Probabilistic Models for Electricity Prices

SHI-JIE DENG[1] AND WENJIANG JIANG[2]

[1]*School of Industrial and Systems Engineering, Georgia Institute of Technology, GA 30332, USA.*
[2]*School of Mathematical Science, Yunnan Normal University, Kunming 650092, China.*

## ABSTRACT

We propose a quantile function based approach for modelling the unconditional distribution and the time series of highly volatile commodity prices such as the price of electricity. We construct two new classes of distributions as well as a non-Gaussian Generalized Autoregressive Conditional Heteroskedasticity model by specifying the quantile function. These quantile-based probabilistic models have tremendous flexibility in capturing stylized features of empirical financial data. Built upon closed-form quantile functions, these models are extremely fast to simulate and thus best suited for simulation-based parameter inference and simulation-intensive risk management analysis of value-at-risk and expected shortfall.

## 7.1 INTRODUCTION

Extensive empirical finance literature on stock, fixed income and foreign exchange markets (see, for instance, Eberlein and Keller, 1995; Shephard, 1996; Barndorff-Nielsen and Jiang, 1998) demonstrates that financial market data often display the following stylized facts:

- The high/low volatility returns are followed by high/low volatility returns (a.k.a., volatility clustering).
- The tails of the empirical distributions are heavier than normal distributions, but lighter than Student distributions.
- The empirical distributions have a wide spectrum of tail behaviours such as extreme fatness, left-skewness and other general unbalanced patterns.
- The heaviness of the empirical tails depends significantly on the time frequency of the return data.

As an extension to the Autoregressive Conditional Heteroskedasticity (ARCH) model (Engle, 1982), the Generalized Autoregressive Conditional Heteroskedasticity (GARCH) model developed in the 1980s (see Bollerslev, 1986; Taylor, 1986) explains empirical phenomena such as volatility clustering with great success. A classic GARCH model (i.e., Gaussian type GARCH) has the following specification:

$$X_t = \sigma_t Z_t$$

$$\sigma_t^2 = \alpha_0 + \sum_{i=1}^{p} \alpha_i X_{t-i}^2 + \sum_{j=1}^{q} \beta_j \sigma_{t-j}^2$$

where $\{Z_t, \ t = 1, 2, \ldots\}$ is a sequence of i.i.d. normal $N(0, 1)$ random variables.

The classic GARCH models with conditional normal distributions have been quite successful in modelling real data in various applications. However, their limitations in fitting unusually fat-tailed financial data are also reported in the literature (e.g. Shephard, 1996). The fact that the financial data can have very fat-tailed distributions is well known (see Mandelbrot, 1963; and Fama, 1965). More recently, the emerging electricity market furnishes another example in which the classic GARCH price model does not perform well (this is elaborated in Section 7.3). One potential reason is that the conditional distribution of classic GARCH models is not fat-tailed and the normal distributions are not flexible enough to handle the empirical data with extremely high volatility. This naturally leads to the consideration of GARCH models based on conditional distributions with fatter-than-normal tails. In particular, Student type, Generalized Error Distribution (GED) type and nonparametric type GARCH models have been investigated as alternative models for the empirical fat-tailed distributions observed in fixed-income and exchange rate markets. While these non-Gaussian GARCH models do generate fat-tailed marginal distributions, the resulting unconditional distributions may have overly heavy tails. For instance, empirical tests on the Student type GARCH models reveal that the Student distributions have a very limited capability in modelling financial return data observed at different time frequencies due to the excessive heaviness and the fixed thickness of their tails. Another modelling limitation shared by the Student type and the GED type GARCH models is the inflexibility in capturing various unbalanced tail behaviours. From a practical point of view, GED type models cannot be readily applied to value-at-risk (VaR) and expected shortfall (ES) modelling since the quantiles of GED distributions can be difficult to compute. The nonparametric type GARCH models face the same implementation challenges. In fact, all computational tasks under nonparametric GARCH models are rather expensive (i.e., time consuming). Generally speaking, parametric models are computationally faster than nonparametric ones but they often lack the flexibility in fitting real data when compared with the nonparametric models. Therefore, it is always desirable to have a class of parametric models that is flexible to be applied to various types of empirical data while preserving the fast speed in practice.

Our goals are to develop such a class of models based on quantile function modelling and to illustrate one potential application in modelling the erratic price behaviours of electricity. The wave of electricity supply industry deregulation has established the presence of electricity markets in major industrialized countries such as the United Kingdom and the United States (see Gilbert and Kahn, 1996) since the early 1990s. In a restructured electric power industry, it is crucial for all players to be able to accurately model and predict the power price behaviour in order to support trading, risk management and asset valuation tasks as illustrated in Kaminski (1997), Barz and Johnson (1998), and Deng (1998) among others. However, it is quite a challenging task to precisely model the highly volatile electricity prices. Figure 7.1 plots the historical price paths of electricity in two regions of the USA, Northern California and PJM, during the time period from 1 April, 1998 to 31 August, 2000. The historical electricity price series exhibit salient features such as mean reversion, jumps and spikes, which reflect

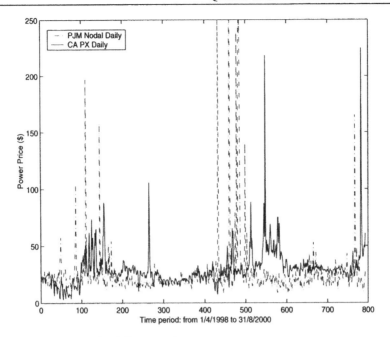

**Figure 7.1**  Historical electricity daily spot prices

the commodity nature of electricity and the unique characteristics of electricity such as non-storability, heavy reliance on the transmission networks, and characteristic steepness of the electricity supply function at high production levels. Power prices certainly have the volatility clustering feature but the clustering pattern is quite different from those seen in exchange rate or fixed-income market data. The price spikes in power prices also make it difficult for the classic GARCH models to yield a satisfying fit.

By working with quantile functions, we investigate two new classes of distributions and use them as building blocks to model the unconditional distributions and the time series of financial data. The organization of the chapter is as follows. In the next section, we introduce the concept of quantile modelling and describe the essential components of our probabilistic models. We illustrate the properties and the versatile capabilities of the two classes of quantile-defined (or quantile-based) distributions in modelling electricity price and other financial data. In Section 7.3, we propose a quantile-based GARCH model (quantile-GARCH for short) and highlight the advantages of this alternative non-Gaussian GARCH model in several financial applications. In Section 7.4, we outline a fast and effective parameter estimation scheme for fitting the quantile-based unconditional distributions and the quantile-GARCH model. We point out further research directions and conclude in Section 7.5.

## 7.2  QUANTILE-BASED DISTRIBUTIONS AND THE MODELLING OF MARGINAL DISTRIBUTIONS OF ELECTRICITY PRICE

Motivated by the wide variety of tail behaviours observed in empirical data from different research fields and the need for a model that is computationally fast for simulation studies, Jiang (2000) proposes two new classes of distributions via quantile function specification. We provide a thorough investigation of the properties of these distributions and their performance in fitting high-volatility empirical data such as electricity prices in this section.

### 7.2.1  Quantile modelling and two classes of quantile-based distributions

We formalize the concept of quantile modelling as directly specifying the quantile function (as opposed to the probability distribution function) of a probability distribution in probabilistic modelling. The quantile function of a probability distribution has the following definition.

**Definition 1 (Quantile Function).** *Suppose* $F(x)$ *is a probability distribution function of a univariate random variable X. Then the quantile function of X is the generalized inverse*

$$F^{-1}(x) = \inf\{y : F(y) \geq x\}$$

*where the infimum is taken over the range of X.*

A *quantile* function must be left-continuous and monotonically increasing on $(0, 1)$. Conversely, *any* strictly increasing continuous function defined on $(0, 1)$ must be a *quantile* function of a random variable.

Equipped with a closed-form quantile function by design, the quantile modelling has the following advantages:

- Fast sampling from a quantile-defined distribution;
- Ease of generating from a truncated quantile distribution;
- Convenient probability calculation;
- Ease of creating quantile–quantile (Q–Q) plots;
- Can be convenient for generating order statistics.

All these advantages are essentially due to an explicit quantile function. Specifically, the *inverse transform method* (see Law and Kelton, 1991) states that if a random variable $X$ has a quantile function $Q(x)$ then $Q(U)$ and $X$ are identical in distribution where $U$ is a uniform random variable over the interval $(0, 1)$. Therefore, to simulate a random variable with an explicit quantile function, it is enough to simulate a uniform random variable $U(0, 1)$ and then substitute the outcomes of $U(0, 1)$ into the quantile function. An explicit quantile function combined with sampling from a uniform random variable makes the simulation of the desired random variable almost effortless.

The following two distribution classes are constructed in Jiang (2000) using the idea of quantile modelling. We call them Class I and Class II distributions, respectively.

A **Class I** distribution is denoted by $Q_I(\alpha, \beta, \delta, \mu)$ and defined by the quantile function given below:

$$q(y; \alpha, \beta, \delta, \mu) = \delta^{\frac{1}{\alpha}} \left\{ \log \frac{y^\beta}{1 - y^\beta} \right\}^{(\frac{1}{\alpha})} + \mu \tag{7.1}$$

where model parameters $\alpha, \beta, \delta \in \mathbf{R}_+$ and $\mu \in \mathbf{R}$. The superscript "$(\alpha)$" for $\alpha > 0$ represents the operation:

$$x^{(\alpha)} = \begin{cases} x^\alpha & \text{if } x > 0 \\ 0 & \text{if } x = 0 \\ -(-x)^\alpha & \text{if } x < 0 \end{cases}$$

**Remark**: All parameters in (7.1) have intuitive interpretations: $\mu$ is a location parameter; $\delta$ functions as a scaling parameter; $\beta$ acts like a tail balance adjuster: $\beta = 1$ means a balanced tail and $\beta < (>)1$ means the left (right) tail is fatter than the right (left) tail; and $\alpha$ indicates the tail order – the smaller the value of $\alpha$, the fatter the tail of the distribution.

The cumulative distribution function and the probability density function (PDF) of $Q_I(\alpha, \beta, \delta, \mu)$ are also in closed-form. Particularly, the PDF is given by:

$$p(x; \alpha, \beta, \delta, \mu) = \frac{\alpha \cdot \frac{(x-\mu)^{(\alpha)}}{(x-\mu)} e^{-\frac{1}{\delta}(x-\mu)^{(\alpha)}}}{\delta\beta \cdot \left(1 + e^{-\frac{1}{\delta}(x-\mu)^{(\alpha)}}\right)^{1+\frac{1}{\beta}}} \tag{7.2}$$

for $x \in (-\infty, \mu) \cup (\mu, +\infty)$. We note that since a Class I distribution has closed-form probability density, a straightforward maximum likelihood estimation procedure can be employed to obtain the parameters $\alpha$, $\beta$, $\delta$ and $\mu$ in (7.1).

The **Class II** distributions are constructed to fit the extremely unbalanced tails of empirical data. We denote a Class II distribution by $Q_{II}(\alpha_-, \alpha_+, \delta_-, \delta_+, \mu)$. Its quantile function is specified as:

$$q(y; \alpha_-, \alpha_+, \delta_-, \delta_+, \mu) = -\delta_-^{\frac{1}{\alpha_-}}\left(\log\frac{1}{y}\right)^{\frac{1}{\alpha_-}} + \delta_+^{\frac{1}{\alpha_+}}\left(\log\frac{1}{1-y}\right)^{\frac{1}{\alpha_+}} + \mu \tag{7.3}$$

where model parameters $\alpha_-, \alpha_+, \delta_-, \delta_+ \in \mathbf{R}_+$ and $\mu \in \mathbf{R}$. We are mainly interested in the cases where $\alpha_- \leq 1$, $\alpha_+ \leq 1$. Similar to a Class I distribution, $\alpha_-$ and $\alpha_+$ measure the fatness of the respective tails of a Class II distribution.

A remarkable feature of a Class II distribution is its tremendous flexibility in having different tail orders at each side of the probability density function: $\alpha_-$ at the left-hand side and $\alpha_+$ at the right-hand side.

### 7.2.1.1  Properties of Class I and Class II distributions

First of all, we graphically illustrate the flexibility that Class I and II distributions have in the shape of density function through two figures. Figures 7.2 and 7.3 plot the density functions of a group of Class I and II distributions with different parameter sets (we set $\mu = 0$ in all cases). We see a broad range of tail behaviours exhibited by Class I and II distributions from these density plots.

For arbitrary constants $c$ and $d$, the following facts on Class I and II distributions are straightforward to verify:

- If $X \sim Q_I(\alpha, \beta, \delta, \mu)$ ("$\sim$" means "is distributed as"), then $cX + d \sim Q_I(\alpha, \beta, c^\alpha\delta, c\mu + d)$.
- If $X \sim Q_{II}(\alpha_-, \alpha_+, \delta_-, \delta_+, \mu)$, then $cX + d \sim Q_{II}(\alpha_-, \alpha_+, c^{\alpha_-}\delta_-, c^{\alpha_+}\delta_+, c\mu + d)$.

Several other interesting properties pertaining to Class I distributions are as follows:

- **(Multimodality)** When $\alpha > 1$, the probability density function of a Class I distribution is bimodal.
- **(Closed under powering)** Let $Q_I(\alpha, \beta, \delta)$ denote $Q_I(\alpha, \beta, \delta, 0)$, then the following holds true for $n > 0$:

$$\text{If } X \sim Q_I(\alpha, \beta, \delta) \text{ then } X^n \sim Q_I\left(\frac{\alpha}{n}, \beta, \delta\right)$$

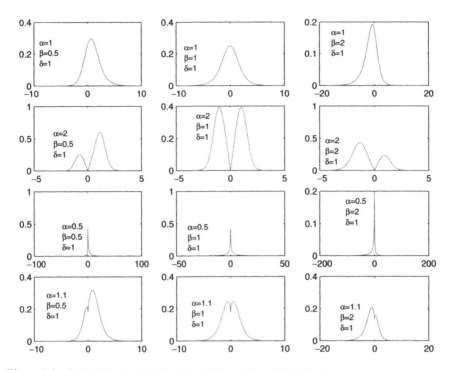

**Figure 7.2**  Probability density function: different Class I distributions

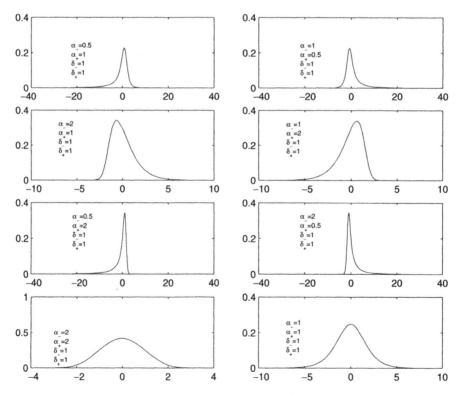

**Figure 7.3**  Probability density function: different Class II distributions

In general, if $n$ is an integer and $X \sim Q_I(\alpha, \beta, \delta, \mu)$, then $X^n$ is just a linear combination of random variables in form $Q_I(\alpha, \beta, \delta)$.

- **(The moments formulae)** Let $X \sim Q_I(\alpha, \beta, \delta, \mu)$ and $a(\alpha, \beta, \delta) \equiv \mathrm{E}[Q_I(\alpha, \beta, \delta)]$, then the $n$th moment of $X$ is given by:

$$\mathrm{E}[X^n] = \mu^n + C_n^1 \mu^{n-1} a(\alpha, \beta, \delta) + \cdots + C_n^k \mu^{n-k} a\left(\frac{\alpha}{k}, \beta, \delta\right) + \cdots + a\left(\frac{\alpha}{n}, \beta, \delta\right)$$

In particular:

$$\mathrm{E}[X] = \mu + a(\alpha, \beta, \delta)$$
$$\mathrm{Var}[X] = a\left(\frac{\alpha}{2}, \beta, \delta\right) - a^2(\alpha, \beta, \delta)$$

Note that the variance does not depend on $\mu$.

In the next two sections, we examine the performance of these two distribution classes in modelling the unconditional distributions of electricity price data and other financial data.

### 7.2.2 Marginal distributions of electricity price

As indicated earlier, it is quite challenging to get a statistical model that fits electricity price well due to the unique characteristics and the unparalleled high volatility of electricity price. To illustrate the versatile capability of Class I and Class II distributions, we employ them to fit the marginal distributions of daily log-return of electricity price.

We use data from two major US power markets for the investigation. One data set is the daily average prices at the California Power Exchange (Cal-PX) market and the other data set is the daily average prices at the Pennsylvania–New Jersey–Maryland (PJM) market – both are sampled from 1 April 1998 to 31 August 2000. The log-return of power price is fitted to a Class I or II distribution. Figure 7.4 contains the plots of the historical daily log-price differences at Cal-PX and PJM.

Let $P(t)$ denote the average electricity price over the 24-hour period on day $t$. The log-return is denoted by $X(t) \equiv \log(P(t)/P(t-1))$. We examine the marginal distribution of $X(t) = \log(P(t)) - \log(P(t-1))$ (namely, $X(t)$ is the log-price difference between the day-$t$ and the day-$(t-1)$ prices).

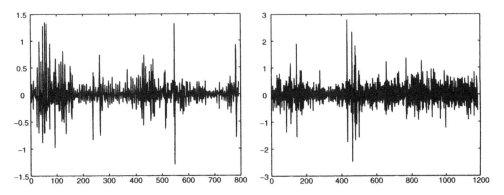

**Figure 7.4**    Historical log-price differences: Cal-PX (left) vs. PJM (right)

**Table 7.1**    Estimated parameters of Class I distributions

|          | $\alpha$ | $\beta$ | $\delta$ | $\mu$ |
|----------|----------|---------|----------|-------|
| Cal-PX   | 0.6124   | 0.8819  | 0.1901   | −0.0226 |
| PJM      | 0.7789   | 0.9765  | 0.2291   | −0.0059 |

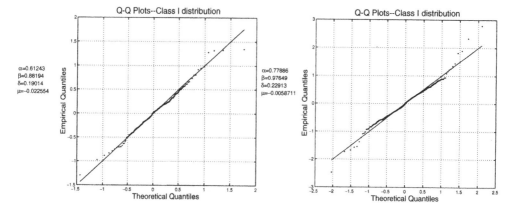

**Figure 7.5**    The Q–Q plots for fitted Class I distributions: Cal-PX (left) vs. PJM prices (right)

Employing the quantile function based parameter estimation technique described in Section 7.4, we obtain the parameters for the Class I distributions that fit the Cal-PX and PJM prices the best. Figure 7.5 illustrates the quantile–quantile (Q–Q) plots of the empirical quantiles of the Cal-PX and PJM price distributions versus their respective theoretical quantiles (the estimated parameters are shown in the two panels as well), where the theoretical quantiles are plotted on the $x$-axis and the empirical quantiles on the $y$-axis. Each of the two Q–Q plots in Figure 7.5 forms a relatively straight line, which indicates a good fit between the empirical quantile function and the theoretical quantile function, except for several outliers. The parameters are reported in Table 7.1.

For the Cal-PX data, $\beta = 0.8819$ suggests that the left tail of the Cal-PX log-return distribution is fatter than the right tail. For the PJM data, although acceptable, the fit of PJM log-return is not as good as that of the Cal-PX log-return. The Q–Q plot of the empirical quantiles of PJM data versus the theoretical quantiles deviates slightly from the 45° line (see the right panel of Figure 7.5). Similar to the Cal-PX data, the PJM price data also yields a less-than-one $\beta$ value ($\beta = 0.9765$) indicating a fatter left tail of the log-return distribution in the PJM market.

We next fit the Cal-PX and PJM daily log-returns to Class II distributions. The resulting Q–Q plots are shown in the two panels of Figure 7.6 and the estimated parameters are given in Table 7.2.

The Q–Q plot of the fitted Class II distribution on the PJM price data appears to be better than that of the Class I distribution. Moreover, $\alpha_-$ is less than $\alpha_+$ for the PJM price data implying a fatter left tail than the right tail. This is consistent with the observation made from the PJM fitting results in the Class I distribution case.

For the Cal-PX data, we restrict $\delta_+$ to be identical with $\delta_-$. The fitted Class II distribution generates a reasonably good Q–Q plot as well. The estimated $\alpha_+$ is greater than $\alpha_-$ (see

**Table 7.2**    Estimated parameters of Class II distributions

|          | $\alpha_-$ | $\alpha_+$ | $\delta_-$ | $\delta_+$ | $\mu$ |
| -------- | ------ | ------ | ------ | ------ | ------ |
| Cal-PX   | 0.5264 | 0.5907 | 0.1833 | 0.1833 | 0.0164 |
| PJM      | 0.6386 | 0.8356 | 0.2089 | 0.2423 | 0.0804 |

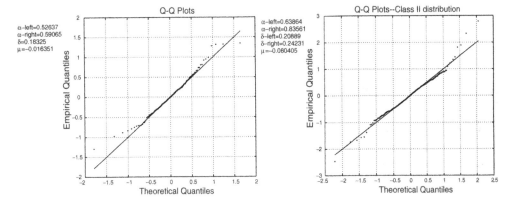

**Figure 7.6**    The Q–Q plots for fitted Class II distributions: Cal-PX (left) vs. PJM prices (right)

Table 7.2), which is again consistent with the observation of a fatter right tail than the left tail in the distribution of Cal-PX log-returns (as implied by the Cal-PX fitting results in the Class I distribution case).

### 7.2.3    Risk-neutral distribution of S&P 500 Index

In addition to electricity price, we consider the Standard and Poor 500 (S&P 500) Index return, which is one of the most commonly used sets of financial data. Instead of fitting the statistical unconditional distribution of the S&P 500 Index return, we infer the risk-neutral probability distribution of the S&P 500 Index return over fixed time intervals from the market prices of the traded index options.

It is well documented in the literature that the risk-neutral distribution of the S&P 500 Index return extracted from the option prices has much fatter tails than a normal distribution after the financial market crash in October 1987 (see Rubinstein, 1994). There has been lots of work on modelling the option-implied risk-neutral distribution by either a parametric model or a nonparametric one. For instance, Jackwerth and Rubinstein (1996) describe a nonparametric approach for inferring the unconditional risk-neutral distributions of the S&P Index return from Index option prices (see Jackwerth, 1999 for a thorough review).

In the same spirit as Jackwerth and Rubinstein (1996), we collected the market bids and ask prices of S&P 500 Index (European-style) options maturing at some fixed time $T$ and used them to recover the risk-neutral distribution of the S&P 500 Index at the chosen time $T$ parametrized by either a Class I or a Class II distribution. Specifically, we search for Class I and II distributions that can generate theoretical option prices falling in between the market bids and ask prices of the corresponding options for as many strike prices as possible.

**Table 7.3**   Estimated Class I distributions for S&P 500 Index return

|        | $\alpha$ | $\beta$ | $\delta$ | $\mu$ |
|--------|----------|---------|----------|-------|
| 14-Day | 0.9583   | 2.4322  | 0.0313   | 0.0528 |
| 30-Day | 1.0152   | 2.4130  | 0.0381   | 0.0683 |

**Table 7.4**   Estimated Class II distributions for S&P 500 Index return

|        | $\alpha_-$ | $\alpha_+$ | $\delta_-$ | $\delta_+$ | $\mu$ |
|--------|-----------|-----------|-----------|-----------|-------|
| 14-Day | 0.7825    | 1.0059    | 0.0926    | 0.0926    | 0.0215 |
| 30-Day | 0.6250    | 1.4836    | 0.1220    | 0.0278    | $-0.0395$ |

For the computational experiments, we chose $T$ to be 14 and 30 trading days. The prices of options with the same expiration date (i.e., 20 September 2002) but different strike prices are taken on 12 August 2002 (33 prices) and 3 September 2002 (34 prices). The closing quotes of the S&P 500 Index are 903.8 on 12 August and 878.02 on 3 September. Using the LIBOR rate as the risk-free rate, we successfully obtained both a Class I and a Class II distribution that price all 33 S&P 500 Index options maturing in September, traded on 12/8/2002, correctly. For the 34 option prices observed on 3/9/2002, we could match all but one of them with both Class I and II distributions.

Table 7.3 contains the resulting parameters for Class I distributions calibrated with the option prices on 12/8/2002 and 3/9/2002, respectively. We also examined the ability of the two classes of distributions in predicting out-of-sample option prices by "back" testing parameters estimated from a subset of the whole option price sample. For instance, we used 32 (out of 33 and 34) options to infer the parameters for a Class I or a Class II distribution. We then used the resulting distribution to price the one or two out-of-sample call options. The predicted theoretical prices of the out-of-sample options always fell between the market bids and ask prices. This demonstrates the robustness and the predicting power of the fitted risk-neutral distributions. Another supporting evidence for the robustness of the model is the fact that the estimated parameters using the partial data set were very close to those obtained using the entire data set.

The parameters for Class II distributions inferred from the Index option prices are shown in Table 7.4. Again, these parameters are for the risk-neutral distributions of the S&P 500 Index return over 14 and 30 trading days, respectively. We tested the model robustness and the predictive power on out-of-sample data for Class II distributions as well and found that similar observations as those in the Class I distribution case held true.

## 7.3   QUANTILE-GARCH MODELS AND THE MODELLING OF TIME SERIES OF ELECTRICITY PRICE

Having introduced and investigated the distributions defined by the quantile function, we turn to time series models based on these quantile-defined distributions. In particular, we propose a class of non-Gaussian GARCH models constructed with Class I and II error distributions and use them to model the time series of electricity price.

### 7.3.1    Quantile-based non-Gaussian GARCH model

Let $\{X_t,\ t \in \mathcal{Z}\}$ be a stationary stochastic process adapted to the filtration $\{\mathcal{F}_t,\ t \in \mathcal{Z}\}$ with $\mathcal{F}_t = \sigma(\{X_s; s \le t\})$. $X_t$ is defined as:

$$X_t = \sigma_t Z_t \qquad (7.4)$$
$$\sigma_t^2 = f\left(X_{t-1}, \sigma_{t-1}^2\right)$$

where $\{Z_t,\ t \in \mathcal{Z}\}$ is a series of i.i.d. innovations in the form of Class I or Class II; $Z_t$ is assumed to be independent of $\{X_t; s \le t\}$; and $f : \mathcal{R} \times \mathcal{R}_+ \to \mathcal{R}_+$ is a strictly positive-valued function. We call (7.4) a Class I/II quantile GARCH model. If $f$ takes the form of (7.5), then (7.4) becomes the well-known GARCH(1, 1) model:

$$f(x, \sigma^2) = \alpha_0 + \alpha_1 x^2 + \beta \sigma^2, \quad \alpha_0, \alpha_1, \beta > 0 \qquad (7.5)$$

The general GARCH type structure provides the Class I/II quantile GARCH model (7.4) with certain inherent ability in capturing the volatility clustering of empirical data. Nevertheless, the most distinctive advantages of model (7.4) are its versatility and the easy-to-simulate feature, which stem from the chosen conditional error distributions (Class I and II). We summarize the key advantages of the quantile GARCH model (7.4) as follows.

#### 7.3.1.1    Properties of the quantile GARCH model

- The conditional distribution of $X_t$ in (7.4) has fatter-than-normal tails and great flexibility in accommodating various tail behaviours as illustrated in Section 7.2.1.
- The conditional quantile function of $X_t$ is in closed-form, which leads to the fast simulation of model (7.4). This makes the simulation-based methods attractive for parameter inference and risk management applications.
- The Class I (i.e., $Q_I(\alpha, \beta, \delta, \mu)$) based GARCH model has explicit likelihood function. Thus, maximum likelihood estimation is an alternative parameter estimation approach to the simulation-based approaches highlighted in Section 7.4.

We explore several potential applications of the quantile GARCH model in the next section.

### 7.3.2    Financial risk management applications: a case with the electricity price time series

The satisfactory results achieved in fitting Class I/II distributions to the unconditional distribution of electricity price prompt for the modelling of the time series of electricity price by the quantile GARCH model. Early works of Kaminski (1997), Barz and Johnson (1998) and Deng (1998) propose several different continuous-time mean-reversion jump-diffusion models for modelling the electricity price process. While these continuous-time models are convenient for derivative pricing and risk management applications, it is often a challenging task to infer model parameters from limited electricity market data. Mount and Ethier (1998) and Alvarado and Rajaraman (2000) among others investigate alternative time series (discrete-time) price models of electricity. However, these models have not been fully demonstrated to be effective in financial applications such as derivative pricing and risk management measure computation.

Following notations defined in Section 7.2.2, we propose to model the daily electricity log-return series $\{X(t),\ t = 1, 2, \ldots\}$ by the quantile GARCH model (7.4). In particular, we adopt the GARCH(1,1) specification of (7.5) with the conditional error distributions being either

Class I or Class II and utilize the simulation-based parameter inference technique described in Section 7.4 to infer the model parameters. While the estimation procedure is straightforward, we shall demonstrate how the quantile GARCH models are ideally suited for the following applications:

- Option pricing;
- VaR and ES modelling;
- VaR or ES based portfolio selection.

### 7.3.2.1   Option pricing

As seen in Section 7.2.3, quantile-based models can be used to directly model financial asset returns under a risk-neutral probability measure. The same is true with the time series models. Let $C(X_t, t)$ denote the time-$t$ price of a financial option on some asset $X_t$ where $X_t$ represents either the asset price or the asset return at time $t$. According to the risk-neutral option pricing theory (see Harrison and Kreps, 1979), option price $C(X_t, t)$ is given by the conditional expected value of the discounted payoff of the option with respect to a risk-neutral probability measure $Q$ over the filtration $\{\mathcal{F}_t, \ t \in \mathcal{Z}\}$. Namely,

$$C(X_t, t) = E^Q \left[ \int_t^T e^{-\int_t^u r_s ds} \Phi(X_u, u) du \mid \mathcal{F}_t \right] \tag{7.6}$$

where $\Phi(X_u, u)$ is the payoff of the option (usually a function of $X_t$) at time $t$, $r_s$ is the risk-free interest rate at time $s$, and $T$ is the option expiration time.

By the Law of Large Numbers, equation (7.6) can be evaluated through simulation. Specifically, an unbiased estimator of $C(X_t, t)$ is given by

$$\widehat{C}(X_t, t) = \lim_{N \to \infty} \frac{1}{N} \sum_{i=1}^N \int_t^T e^{-\int_t^u r_s ds} \Phi(X_u(\omega_i), u) du \tag{7.7}$$

where $\{\omega_i, i = 1, 2, \ldots, N\}$ are simulated sample paths of the underlying asset process $\{X_u : t \le u \le T\}$. Having closed-form quantile functions, the conditional distributions of (7.4), thus (7.4) itself, take little time to simulate using the *inverse transform method*. Therefore, the quantile GARCH model enables fast and accurate option pricing via simulation. The extremely fast simulation speed of model (7.4) makes it even more attractive to applications of valuing path-dependent options such as American-style and Asian options where simulation is practically the only effective solution approach.

### 7.3.2.2   VaR and ES modelling

We further illustrate the advantages of model (7.4) in simulation-intensive risk management applications such as VaR and ES modelling.

Let $X$ represent the random return of a portfolio. The VaR of a portfolio $X$ at level $\alpha$ (for $0 < \alpha < 1$), denoted by $\text{VaR}^{(\alpha)}(X)$, is a quantity that equals the worst possible loss of the portfolio $X$ at the $100 \cdot (1 - \alpha)\%$ confidence level. Namely,

$$x^\alpha(X) = \sup_x \{x : P[X \le x] \le \alpha\}$$

$$\text{VaR}^{(\alpha)}(X) = -x^{(\alpha)}(X)$$

Note that

$$\mathrm{VaR}^{(\alpha)}(X) = -q(\alpha) \tag{7.8}$$

where $q(u)$ is the quantile function of $X$.

As one important risk management concept, VaR has long been utilized in practice. However, it is constantly criticized for not possessing the sub-additive property (see Artzner et al., 1999). In searching for alternative risk measures, the concepts of tail conditional expectation (TCE), conditional VaR (CVaR) and ES are put forward. Among these measures, expected shortfall, defined as the expected loss incurred within the $\alpha\%$ worst cases of the portfolio/asset return, is the most popular quantity. The ES of $X$ at level $\alpha$ can be calculated as

$$\mathrm{ES}^{(\alpha)} = -\frac{1}{\alpha} \int_0^\alpha q(u)du \tag{7.9}$$

where $q(u)$ is the quantile function of $X$.

It is clear from equations (7.8) and (7.9) that the two important risk management measures, VaR and ES, can be trivially obtained when the underlying price or return models have closed-form quantile functions. The quantile GARCH model (7.4) is one such example. In fact, if a random variable $Z \sim Q_I(\alpha, \beta, \delta, \mu)$, then for any $\sigma > 0$

$$\sigma Z \sim Q_I(\alpha, \beta, \sigma^\alpha \delta, \mu)$$

Thus, if $Z_t \sim Q_I(\alpha, \beta, \delta, \mu)$ in (7.4), then $X_t | \mathcal{F}_{t-1} \sim Q_I(\alpha, \beta, \sigma_t^\alpha \delta, \mu)$ and its quantile function is in closed-form. The same result holds true for $Z_t \sim Q_{II}(\alpha_-, \alpha_+, \delta_-, \delta_+, \mu)$.

This is a remarkably encouraging fact for the VaR or ES-based portfolio selection problems, where the evaluation of VaR and ES needs to be repeated thousands of times when solving for the optimal portfolios. If quantile GARCH models are employed for modelling asset price or return in the VaR or ES-based portfolio problems, they could significantly reduce the computational time.

## 7.4  PARAMETER INFERENCE

As mentioned earlier, Class I distributions have explicit formulae for quantile function, probability distribution function and probability density function. Therefore, maximum likelihood estimation (MLE) is a viable approach for parameter inference in both the unconditional Class I distribution model and the Class I quantile GARCH model (7.4).

On the other hand, an alternative parameter estimation scheme based on directly matching quantile functions can be employed to infer parameters for either a Class I or a Class II model. Suppose a distribution class is defined by the quantile function which is parametrized by a vector $\theta$ in a parameter space $\Theta$. Termed the Q–Q estimation method in Jiang (2000), it searches for the "best" $\theta$ by minimizing the "distance" (e.g., in $L_1$-norm sense) between the theoretical quantile function as a function of $\theta$ and the empirical quantile function. The Q–Q estimation method is a simulation-based scheme and it takes full advantage of the closed-form quantile function.

Specifically, let $\{F(x;\theta), \theta \in \Theta \subseteq R^n\}$ be a distribution class parametrized by $\theta$. A member of $F(x;\theta)$ with unknown $\theta$ generates a series of observations $Y_1, Y_2, \ldots, Y_n$. Further assume that $F(x;\theta)$ can be simulated for any given $\theta$. The Q–Q estimation method infers $\theta$ from

$Y_1, Y_2, \ldots, Y_n$ by solving the minimization problem (7.10):

$$\min_{\theta \in \Theta} f(R_1(Y), \ldots, R_l(Y); \theta, T_1(X), \ldots, T_l(X)) \qquad (7.10)$$

where $f(\cdot)$ is an appropriately chosen score function, with the most common choice being the $L_1$ or $L_2$ norm. $\{R_1(Y), \ldots, R_l(Y)\}$ and $\{T_1(X(\theta)), \ldots, T_l(X(\theta))\}$ are empirical quantiles of $Y = (Y_1, \ldots, Y_n)$ and $X(\theta) = (X_1, \ldots, X_{n'})$, respectively, meaning that $R_i(Y) = F_n^{-1}(p_i; Y)$ and $T_i(X) = F_{n'}^{-1}(p_i, X)$. $X(\theta)$ is simply a set of simulated samples of $F(x; \theta)$ for a given $\theta$; $F_n(\cdot, Y)$ denotes the empirical distribution function based on $Y$ with sample size $n$; and $(p_1, p_2, \ldots, p_l)$ denotes the set of probabilities for which the quantiles are obtained.

The reason for using quantiles to construct the score function is that empirical quantiles are robust estimators of the theoretical quantiles. Therefore the Q–Q method is expected to yield reliable estimators, a fact that is confirmed by our experimental testing on some common distributions.

For quantile-based models, since the theoretical quantiles are explicitly specified as $q(u; \theta)$, (7.10) can be rewritten as:

$$\min_{\theta \in \Theta} f(R_1(Y), \ldots, R_l(Y); \theta, q(p_1; \theta), \ldots, q(p_l; \theta)) \qquad (7.11)$$

The following sample forms of $f(\cdot)$ are used in Jiang (2000):

$$\min_{\theta \in \Theta} \sum_{i=1}^{l} w_i |R_i(Y) - F^{-1}(p_i)|$$

and

$$\min_{\theta \in \Theta} \sum_{i=1}^{l} w_i [R_i(Y) - F^{-1}(p_i)]^2$$

where $w_1, \ldots, w_l$ are suitably chosen weights. Clearly, the Q–Q estimation method is best suited for probabilistic models with quantile functions in closed-form.

Regarding parameter inference for the quantile GARCH model (7.4), with $Z_t$ being in either Class I or Class II, simulation-based methods such as the simulated method of moments (SMM) and the efficient method of moments (EMM) can be applied to estimate model parameters.[1] We briefly highlight the advantage of the quantile GARCH model in using the EMM method for parameter estimation. The EMM method consists of two main steps: the first step is to use the observation data to select a criteria function, either a quasi-likelihood function or a quasi-score function; and the second step is to search for a set of parameters such that the corresponding simulated data sample maximizes the criteria function chosen in step one. To make the EMM procedure reliable, a large number of simulated samples is required when evaluating the criteria function for optimization purposes corresponding to each parameter set in the domain of parameter space. This can be prohibitively time consuming depending on the structure of the underlying model. The quantile GARCH model is very fast to simulate by design thus making EMM an effective method to apply.

---

[1] See Ingram and Lee (1991), Duffie (1993), Bansal, et. al. (1995) and Gallant and Tauchen (1996) for details about the implementation of SMM or EMM.

# 7.5  CONCLUSION

In this chapter, we advocate the idea of quantile modelling. Particularly, we construct several quantile function based probabilistic models and demonstrate their advantages via an application in electricity price modelling. In summary, the quantile-based models are computationally fast, suitable for robust statistical inference, and versatile for modelling empirical data in a broad array of applications.

Using electricity price data from two different markets, we illustrate the versatile capability of Class I and II quantile distributions in capturing the wide spectrum of tail behaviours found in empirical power prices. The perfect fitting of the S&P 500 Index option prices by the Class I and II distributions, which implies good modelling of the risk-neutral distribution of the S&P 500 Index return, also confirms the versatility of these models.

We further develop a class of quantile GARCH models using Class I and II distribution as building blocks. With conditional distributions taken from either Class I or Class II, these GARCH models possess similar merits of having very flexible tail behaviours and being extremely conducive to simulation-oriented computational tasks. Ideally suited for simulation-based parameter inference schemes (e.g., EMM) and tailor-made for a fast and easy simulation procedure (i.e., inverse transform method), the quantile GARCH model is a promising alternative for simulation-intensive risk management applications such as VaR and ES modelling, and particularly VaR or ES constrained portfolio optimization.

# ACKNOWLEDGEMENTS

This chapter is based on an early version of working papers by the authors (Deng and Jiang, 2002a,b). Support by a Power System Engineering Research Center (PSerc) grant, NSF CAREER Award ECS-0134210 (Deng) and Yunnan Science Foundation Award 2003A0030M (Jiang) are gratefully acknowledged.

# REFERENCES

Alvarado F.L. and Rajaraman R. (2000). "Understanding Price Volatility in Electricity Markets". *Proceedings of the 33rd Hawaii International Conference on System Sciences*, Hawaii, 2000.

Artzner P., Delbaen F., Eber J. and Heath D. (1999). "Coherent Measures of Risk". *Mathematical Finance* **9**: 203–228.

Bansal R., Gallant R., Hussey R. and Tauchen G. (1995). "Non-parametric Estimation of Structure Models for High-Frequency Currency Market Data". *Journal of Econometrics* **66**: 251–287.

Barndorff-Nielsen O.E. (1998). "Processes of Normal Inverse Gaussian Type". *Finance and Stochastics* **2**: 41–68.

Barndorff-Nielsen O.E. and Jiang W. (1998). "An Initial Analysis of Some German Stock Prices". Working Papers No. 15, CAF.

Barz G. and Johnson B. (1998). "Modeling the Prices of Commodities that are Costly to Store: the Case of Electricity". *Proceedings of the Chicago Risk Management Conference*, Chicago, IL, May 1998.

Bollerslev T. (1986). "Generalised Autoregressive Conditional Heteroscedasticity". *Journal of Econometrics* **51**: 307–327.

Deng S.J. (1998). "Stochastic Models of Energy Commodity Prices and Their Applications: Mean-reversion with Jumps and Spikes". PSERC Working Paper, University of California at Berkeley.

Deng S.J. and Jiang W. (2002a). "Levy Process Driven Mean-reverting Electricity Price Model: A Marginal Distribution Analysis". Working Paper, Georgia Institute of Technology.

Deng S.J. and Jiang W. (2002b). "A Class of Quantile-based GARCH Models". Working Paper, Georgia Institute of Technology.

Deng S.J., Johnson B. and Sogomonian A. (2001). "Exotic Electricity Options and the Valuation of Electricity Generation and Transmission Assets". *Decision Support Systems* **30**(3): 383–392.

Diggle P.J. and Gratton R.J. (1984). "Monte Carlo Methods of Inference for Implicit Statistical Models". *Journal of the Royal Statistical Society, Series B* **46**: 193–227.

Duffie D. (1993). "Simulated Moments Estimation of Markov Models of Asset Prices". *Econometrica* **61**: 929–352.

Eberlein E. and Keller U. (1995). "Hyperbolic Distributions in Finance". *Bernoulli* **1**: 281–299.

Engle R.F. (1982). "Autoregressive Conditional Heteroscedasticity with Estimates of the Variance of the United Kindom Inflation". *Econometrica* **50**: 987–1007.

Fama E. (1965). "The Behaviour of Stock Market Prices". *Journal of Business* **38**: 34–105.

Gallant R. and Tauchen G. (1996). "Which Moments to Match?" *Econometric Theory* **12**: 657–681.

Gilbert R. and Kahn E. (eds) (1996). *International Comparisons of Electricity Regulation*. Cambridge University Press, Cambridge.

Harrison M. and Kreps D. (1979). "Martingales and Arbitrage in Multi-period Securities Markets". *Journal of Economic Theory* **20**: 381–408.

Ingram B.F. and Lee B.S. (1991). "Simulation Estimation of Time Series Models". *Journal of Econometrics* **47**: 197–205.

Jackwerth J.C. (1999). "Option Implied Risk Neutral Distributions and Implied Binomial Trees: A Literature Review". *The Journal of Derivatives* **Winter**: 66–82.

Jackwerth J.C. and Rubinstein M. (1996). "Recovering Probability Distributions from Option Prices". *Journal of Finance* **51**: 1611–1631.

Jiang W. (2000). "Some Simulation-based Models towards Mathematical Finance". Ph.D. Dissertation, University of Aarhus.

Kaminski V. (1997). "The Challenge of Pricing and Risk Managing Electricity Derivatives". In *The US Power Market*. Risk Publications, London, pp. 149–171.

Law A. and Kelton D. (1991). *Simulation Modeling and Analysis*, 2nd edn. McGraw-Hill, New York.

Mandelbrot B. (1963). "The Variation of Certain Speculative Prices". *Journal of Business* **36**: 394–419.

Mount T. and Ethier R. (1998). "Estimating the Volatility of Spot Prices in Restructured Electricity Markets and the Implications for Option Values". PSerc Working Paper, Cornell University.

Rubinstein M. (1994). "Implied Binomial Trees". *Journal of Finance* **49**: 771–818.

Schwartz E.S. (1997). "The Stochastic Behavior of Commodity Prices: Implications for Valuation and Hedging". *Journal of Finance* **52**: 923–973.

Shephard N. (1996). "Statistical Aspects of ARCH and Stochastic Volatility". In *Time Series Models – in Econometrics, Finance and Other Fields*, D.R. Cox, D.V. Hinkley and O.E. Barndorff-Nielsen (eds). Chapman and Hall, London: pp. 1–67.

Taylor S.J. (1986). *Modelling Financial Time Series*. John Wiley, Chichester.

# 8
# Forecasting Time-Varying Covariance Matrices in the Intradaily Spot Market of Argentina

ANGEL LEÓN AND ANTONIO RUBIA

*Departamento de Economía Financiera, University of Alicante, C.P. 03690, Spain*

## ABSTRACT

This chapter deals with modelling and forecasting intradaily volatility in electricity spot prices. The methods used here consist basically in fitting a VAR model on the conditional mean as well as several multivariate GARCH models to capture the volatility dynamics. We compare two alternative models which are selected by their parsimony and their computational convenience in modelling multivariate variance. The performance in forecasting daily conditional matrices at different horizons is assessed in the out-of-sample period. These procedures could be useful in modelling and managing risk on portfolios of daily block contracts in electricity markets.

## 8.1 INTRODUCTION

Electricity deregulation is an ongoing process that is introducing significant changes in all important aspects of the industry. One of the more important repercussions is that power energy is now traded and priced in many countries as a commodity in their competitive wholesale markets. The basic structure of these exchanges consists of a one-day-ahead spot market in which electricity is traded on the auction principle, usually taking hourly contracts as underlying assets. Because the deregulation process remains an ongoing phenomenon in the international context, new methods and trading contracts are being progressively introduced as new markets are opened and as the whole process evolves. Thus, the basic structure of a spot market has been further complemented in several exchanges with products designed to satisfy the specific needs of market participants. Examples of such products include derivative contracts, taking the electricity price as underlying asset (traded usually in OTC exchanges, but also in organized subsections of the power pool) and block contracts, traded in the spot market along with the standard hourly contracts.

In block bidding, relevant prices for participants are settled on consecutive intervals (blocks) of hours within the day. This allows market agents to trade the entire daily production by holding a portfolio on a very few daily contracts. Market agents holding such portfolios are exposed to the financial risk and uncertainty caused by the strong volatility of electricity prices. As in the case of financial markets, it would be of interest for participants to be able to measure and manage this source of risk. Value-at-risk and other well-known methods in

*Modelling Prices in Competitive Electricity Markets.* Edited by D.W. Bunn.
© 2004 John Wiley & Sons, Ltd. ISBN 0-470-84860-X.

financial econometrics require prior modelling and forecasting of portfolio risk on the basis of the estimations of the (conditional) covariance matrix of portfolios.

The aim of this chapter is to show a tractable method of fitting the covariance dynamics of portfolios onto electricity block contracts in order to forecast their future paths. We use a two-staged procedure. First, the conditional mean (predictable term) of the relevant daily series is approached in terms of the autoregressive vector (VAR) model. Then, taking the multivariate residual error series from this stage, the conditional covariance matrices are estimated and forecast by the multidimensional GARCH class of models.

The outline of the chapter is as follows. Section 8.2 estimates the VAR structure for averaged price time series. In Section 8.3 the multivariate GARCH models are presented and estimated. Section 8.4 is devoted to comparing the forecasting performance of these specifications in the in-sample and out-of-sample periods. Finally, the main conclusions and concluding remarks are summarized in Section 8.5.

## 8.2 VAR ANALYSIS FOR BLOCK BIDS

For the most part, electricity is traded on the basis of hourly auctions in organized spot markets for delivery the following day. Typically, all bids submitted by purchasers and sellers are collected and then aggregated to construct one demand and one supply curve for each of the 24 hours in the day, 365 days a year. The intersection between those curves determines the market price, also called the system price or clearing price, and the clearing volume of electricity.

With this system as the basic structure, some of the more recent power exchanges in Europe (as are those of NordPool and Leizpig Power Exchange, LPX) also allow their participants to trade energy through block contracts in the spot market, setting up constant prices for standardized blocks of connected hours within the day. Submitted block bids are integrated in an hourly auction after transforming them in independent bids for the hours concerned. When the whole process of settlement is eventually completed, block contract prices are determined as the average of the hourly clearing prices over the hours concerned. Block contracts are designed to attract trade from buyers and sellers alike, although they seem to be especially interesting for the producers of thermal power. These assets ensure an average price for a range of hours, thereby providing a more efficient handling of start-up and shut-down costs than a reliance on hourly bidding.[1]

In devising a simple method of forecasting the covariance matrix of portfolios of daily block contracts, an initial difficulty lies in the availability of relevant data. Block bidding is a recent trading alternative in those markets where it has been implemented, and typically, the correct fitting of econometric models requires a sufficiently long time series. We have taken the Argentine Wholesale Electricity Market, which carried out its progressive deregulation process early in the 1990s, as reference. Although block contracts are not actually traded in this market, there are some methodological advantages in considering a market like this as benchmark. First, it is possible to get a sufficiently long series to allow a good calibration of relevant parameters; furthermore, data are quoted in a stable and fully competitive environment, so distortions in prices that can be observed in the early years of the power exchange can be circumvented. Despite the particularities of the trading process in each market, block prices

---

[1] Note that thermal power generation is much less flexible than hydraulic power generation, and that power stations work efficiently only if they can produce an uninterrupted supply. Thus, the holding of a portfolio of block contracts is of especial interest to these sellers. For further details about this trading modality, see the official Webpage of Nordpool (http://www.norpdpool.com/products).

can be mimicked simply by averaging the hourly prices for the hours concerned, so the method we are going to show can be applied straightforwardly in other markets.

The Argentine Wholesale Electricity Market (MEM) consists mainly of an organized spot market where electricity is traded on an hourly basis.[2] Hereafter we denote $P_{jt}$ as the system price (quoted in dollars per megawatt) at each hour, $j = 1, \ldots, 24$, during the selected daily sample period $t = 1, \ldots, T$. To avoid market irregularities in the early years of this market, the sample period was restricted to the period 1/01/1996–30/06/2000, and thereby included 1643 daily observations for each hour of the day.[3]

Like other markets, the MEM recognizes different patterns in the intradaily demand, and hence in the price dynamics, related to the strong seasonal behaviour displayed by power consumption. Thus, the day is divided into three subperiods or hour blocks regarding the level of power demand. The two main blocks are those of minimum and maximum demand, including the hours from 24.00 to 5.00 and 19.00 to 23.00, respectively. We shall refer to these intervals throughout the remainder of this chapter as *off-peak block I* and *peak block*. The third block comprises the remaining hours between the above blocks, in which demand is steadier (i.e., hours from 6.00 to 18.00), which will be referred to throughout the chapter as *off-peak block II*. It is worth noting that NordPool and LPX trade three-block contracts which divide the day in the same way that MEM does, since this is a natural and widely used distinction of demand dynamics in power exchanges throughout the day.

Now let $\mathbf{Z}_t = (\mathbf{z}_{1t}, \mathbf{z}_{2t}, \ldots, \mathbf{z}_{Nt})'$ be a vector representative of the log prices of disjoint block contracts covering all the hours in the day, where $N > 1$ is the number of such assets held in the portfolio.[4] For the sake of simplicity, here only the above three contracts (i.e., $N = 3$) are considered, although the analysis could be extended straightforwardly to any case of higher dimension, including the limit case of $N = 24$. Clearly, the tractability of the problem is lower as the system dimension $N$ increases.

We consider therefore a multivariate system where $\mathbf{z}_{1t} = \ln[(P_{24t} + \sum_{j=1,5} P_{jt})/6]$ denotes the daily observation of the log transformation of the averaged hourly prices corresponding to the off-peak block I, and $\mathbf{z}_{2t} = \ln[\sum_{j=6,18} P_{jt}/13]$ and $\mathbf{z}_{3t} = \ln[\sum_{j=19,23} P_{jt}/5]$ are the representative log prices for off-peak block II and peak block, respectively. Figure 8.1 displays the graphics of these time series, showing high correlated dynamics. Of course, factors of seasonality cause these series to have different paths over the day and, as expected, prices are more volatile and show higher levels in hours of higher demand.

Initially we can use the VAR representation to fit the dynamics of $\mathbf{Z}_t$, analysing and modelling the temporal dependencies and interactions among the variables of the multivariate process. This method is valid for modelling the dynamics of a set of endogenous, covariance-stationary variables, which are assumed to be observed simultaneously. The latter statement is of particular application in data from power exchanges because clearing electricity prices are one-day-ahead prices and are settled and published at the same time. So, although block prices refer to different daily intervals, all of them are simultaneously recorded. Regarding the assumption of stationarity, the seasonal unit roots test by Hylleberg *et al.* (1990) (HEGY henceforth) was implemented to test for stationarity in the long run (zero frequency) as well as for all the seasonal frequencies related to weekly seasonality, since stylized features of daily electricity

---

[2] The electricity industry in Argentina is the most important one, after Brazil and Mexico, in the Latin American area. Thermal and nuclear resources constitute the major part of the power generation, while hydraulic resources account for about 46% of production. See Mastrángelo (2001) for further details about the organization of this market.

[3] The MEM began to operate in 1992. The latest reforms on the market were introduced in 1995. The power market is considered to have stabilized since then. The authors are indebted to Sabino Mastrángelo (CAMMESA) for his valuable suggestions about technical issues. Data are available at http://memnet2.cammesa.com:81

[4] Vectors and matrices will be denoted by boldface throughout.

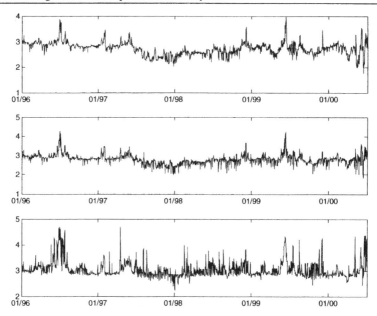

**Figure 8.1**    Off-peak I/off-peak II/peak hours average price time series

time series include a strong weekly seasonal pattern.[5] The outcomes of these tests show evidence of stationarity in both the zero and seasonal frequencies for all the series concerned.

The autoregressive vector model of order $p$, denoted VAR($p$), for a covariance stationary random vector $\mathbf{Z}_t = (\mathbf{z}_{1t}, \mathbf{z}_{2t}, \ldots, \mathbf{z}_{Nt})'$ is represented as follows:

$$\mathbf{Z}_t = \boldsymbol{\mu}_t + \sum_{j=1}^{p} \mathbf{B}_j \mathbf{Z}_{t-j} + \varepsilon_t \tag{8.1}$$

where $\varepsilon_t = (\varepsilon_{1t}, \varepsilon_{2t}, \ldots, \varepsilon_{Nt})'$ is a white noise vector with zero mean and positive-definite covariance matrix $\mathbb{E}(\varepsilon_t \varepsilon_t') = \boldsymbol{\Omega}$. The $\mathbf{B}_j$ are unknown coefficient matrices and $\boldsymbol{\mu}_t$ denotes a vector of intercepts which might include (deterministic) seasonal and nonseasonal trends. Under the stationary condition, the characteristic polynomial $\boldsymbol{\Phi}(L)$ of the above equation has all its roots outside of the complex unit circle and the system reverts to a long-run expected value of $\mathbb{E}(\mathbf{Z}_t) = \boldsymbol{\Phi}(1)^{-1} \boldsymbol{\mu}_t$. This method was firstly applied on electricity prices by Wolak (1997), estimating VAR models on hourly and half-hourly spot prices from several deregulated markets. Identification of (8.1) is usually performed through the information criteria of time-series analysis, as in the Schwartz Information Criterion (SIC), comparing plausible specifications for $\boldsymbol{\mu}_t$ and different values of $p$. SIC statistics for relevant specifications are summarized in Table 8.1.

All the specifications of $\boldsymbol{\mu}_t$ try to accommodate the seasonal regularities that daily electricity prices display through deterministic variables, which implicitly implies the occurrence of predictability in the seasonal term. It is well known that stylized features of daily electricity prices include weekly and annual seasonality related to the same patterns in daily demand,

---

[5] See Chapter 5 and references cited therein for further details on this testing procedure. The results of applying such tests are not presented here, but they are available from the authors on request.

**Table 8.1    SIC statistics VAR($p$).** SIC statistics for different
lag-orders of the VAR($p$) process (first column) and given the
following specifications for the deterministic mean of the process:

$$Z_t = \mu_{kt} + \sum_{j=1,p} B_j Z_{t-j} + \varepsilon_t; \quad \mu_{2t} = \mu_{1t} + \lambda t$$

$$\mu_{1t} = c + \sum_{j=2,7} \gamma_j D_{(day)jt}; \quad \mu_{2t} = \mu_{1t} + \lambda t$$

$$\mu_{3t} = \mu_{1t} + \alpha \cos(2\pi t/365); \quad \mu_{4t} = \mu_{1t} + \beta \cos(2\pi t/365 + \phi)$$

| $p$ | $\mu_{1t}$ | $\mu_{2t}$ | $\mu_{3t}$ | $\mu_{4t}$ |
|-----|------------|------------|------------|------------|
| 1   | −3.684     | −3.683     | −3.750     | −3.745     |
| 2   | −3.758     | −3.754     | −3.795     | −3.787     |
| 3   | −3.776     | −3.770     | −3.800     | −3.791     |
| 4   | −3.748     | −3.742     | −3.768     | −3.758     |
| 5   | −3.745     | −3.738     | −3.759     | −3.748     |
| 6   | −3.749     | −3.742     | −3.758     | −3.747     |
| 7   | −3.807     | −3.799     | −3.814     | −3.802     |
| 8   | −3.776     | −3.768     | −3.783     | −3.772     |
| 9   | −3.745     | −3.736     | −3.751     | −3.740     |
| 10  | −3.731     | −3.722     | −3.734     | −3.723     |
| 14  | −3.620     | −3.611     | −3.621     | −3.609     |
| 21  | −3.394     | −3.833     | −3.397     | −3.385     |

so we try to fit these regularities through 1/0 dummy variables on each day of the week and trigonometric functions on the annual harmonics. The results of the SIC method show that the data-generating process includes a significant weekly deterministic seasonal term. The effect of annual seasonality, however, seems to be much less important in this case, since the gain from including sinusoidal functions on the annual frequency is rather poor, though it seems to be relevant in statistical terms. Note that specifications also allow for a non-zero phase in the annual frequency, but it is not significant. Including other explanatory terms, such as a linear time trend, does not seem to be appropriate. Finally, the lag-order that gives better results after comparing the relevant alternatives is equal to seven. The intuition behind this lag-order is quite clear. Because it is not likely that weekly seasonality is fully predictable, including seasonal lags allows us to capture the seasonal pattern stochastically.[6] Hence the specification selected reflects a mean reversion behaviour which includes the effects of seasonal components in electricity prices. The complete specification of the model is therefore given by:

$$Z_t = c + \delta \cos(2\pi t/365) + \sum_{j=2}^{7} \gamma_j D_{(day)jt} + \sum_{j=1}^{7} B_j Z_{t-j} + \varepsilon_t \tag{8.2}$$

This model is then estimated by maximum likelihood (ML) under the usual assumption of normality in the error term. The goodness of fit (see Table 8.2), measured by the $\overline{R}^2$, varies from 85% in the off-peak I case to 62% in the peak hours, while the fit in the remaining hours is about 76%.

---

[6] Fitting seasonality by deterministic variables implies that this component is fully predictable. Although this supposes an easy form of adjusting this kind of regularity, it is usually rather appealing.

**Table 8.2   Estimation results of the VAR(7) model.** Main results from the estimation of the VAR(7) model:

$$Z_t = c + \sum_{j=2,7} \gamma_j D_{(day)jt} + \alpha \cos(2\pi t/365) \sum_{j=1,7} B_j Z_{t-j} + \varepsilon_t$$

| Statistics | $z_{1t}$ | $z_{2t}$ | $z_{3t}$ |
|---|---|---|---|
| $R^2$ | 0.85 | 0.77 | 0.63 |
| $\bar{R}^2$ | 0.85 | 0.76 | 0.62 |
| Std. dev. | 0.10 | 0.13 | 0.19 |
| Residuals | | | |
| Q(100) | 108.5 (0.26) | 116.8 (0.12) | 113.4 (0.17) |
| Q(200) | 216.7 (0.20) | 203.1 (0.42) | 189.2 (0.70) |
| $Q^*(100)$ | 766.9 (0.00) | 758.0 (0.00) | 249.3 (0.00) |
| $Q^*(200)$ | 950.6 (0.00) | 868.8 (0.00) | 379.69 (0.00) |

$Q(m)$ and $Q^*(m)$ refer to the Ljung–Box portmanteau statistics ($p$-values in brackets) for up to $m$th-order serial correlation in residual and squared residuals respectively.

**Table 8.3   Granger causality test statistics.** Statistics of joint significance ($p$-values in brackets) of the Granger causality test. The null hypothesis states that the $i$th variable in the first column does not Granger-cause variables in the remaining columns

| | $z_{1t}$ | $z_{2t}$ | $z_{3t}$ |
|---|---|---|---|
| $z_{1t}$ | – | 11.552 (0.00) | 1.690 (0.10) |
| $z_{2t}$ | 37.006 (0.00) | – | 1.975 (0.05) |
| $z_{3t}$ | 8.054 (0.00) | 9.795 (0.00) | – |

VAR models assume that the past of each individual variable in the system is useful in forecasting not only its own future but also the remaining variables in the system. This idea is intimately related to the concept of *causality*. Formally, it is said that a variable Granger-causes another if and only if the best linear prediction of the latter depends on the past values of the former. If it does not, VAR modelling is in fact empty of significance, and variables can be modelled simply through the univariate perspective. This premise can easily be tested by performing the Granger (1969) causality test and checking the joint significance of lags of the variable concerned in every VAR equation. As a result (see Table 8.3), it can be concluded that a clear Granger-causality relation exists among the off-peak block I and off-peak block II series in both directions. Prices in peak hours seem to be useful when forecasting the other two variables; meanwhile, the evidence that both $z_{1t}$ and $z_{2t}$ do Granger-cause $z_{3t}$ seems to be somewhat weak.

On the other hand, a look in Table 8.2 at the squared residuals resulting from regression reveals clear evidence of conditional heteroskedasticity through significant Ljung–Box statistics on the squared residuals. Conditional volatility is not a surprising phenomenon in high-frequency series, and it is well documented in financial series. Analysis of these patterns constitutes the core of this chapter and is treated in greater detail in the next section.

## 8.3    MODELLING THE CONDITIONAL COVARIANCE MATRIX

In this section we weaken the assumption of homoskedasticity in the error term from equation (8.2) and estimate alternative time-varying conditional covariance matrix models. Conditional volatility in high-frequency data is due mainly to the clustering phenomenon, so that periods of high (low) variability tend to be followed by periods of high (low) variability. This phenomenon has important implications for asset pricing and risk management, and has been modelled in univariate series mainly by means of the GARCH class of models (see, among others, Bollerslev et al., 1994 for a review of this topic). The major advantage of these models is their simplicity in explaining convincingly the empirical features of volatility returns through a fairly parsimonious model. However, an extension of these models to the multivariate case presents a collection of technical difficulties and hence is not straightforward. Thus, from a practical point of view it is necessary to establish conditions and restrictions to limit both the number of parameters to be estimated and the number of parametric restrictions to ensure positive-definite estimations, since typically they increase exponentially on the dimension of the multivariate system.

Owing to the computational complexity of estimating multivariate GARCH models, several specifications have been proposed to make the resulting model more parsimonious. We will consider two such alternative methods: the so-called orthogonal GARCH (OGARCH) model (Alexander, 2000) and a constrained multivariate GARCH (MGARCH) model proposed by Engle and Mezrich (1996). Both specifications have been developed to cope with the time-dependent volatility of portfolios which include a great number of assets in financial and capital markets. Recently, the OGARCH methodology has also been applied to electricity spot prices and future prices from NordPool in order to obtain the hedging ratio (Byström, 2000).

Let us rewrite equation (8.2) in a more general setting to recognize explicitly the time-varying conditional volatility, by assuming the vector error term to be driven by a (Gaussian) martingale difference process:

$$\mathbf{Z}_t = \mathbb{E}\left(\mathbf{Z}_t \mid \Psi_{t-1}\right) + \varepsilon_t; \quad \varepsilon_t \sim (0, \Omega); \quad \varepsilon_t | \Psi_{t-1} \sim (0, \mathbf{H}_t) \qquad (8.3)$$

where $\mathbb{E}\left(\mathbf{Z}_t \mid \Psi_{t-1}\right)$ denotes the predictable component of the process by the conditional expectation of $\mathbf{Z}_t$ on the information set $\Psi_{t-1}$ (the set containing all the relevant information up to time $t-1$). The unconditional and conditional covariance matrices of the unpredictable term (innovations) are denoted as $\Omega = \{\sigma_{ij}\}$ and $\mathbf{H}_t = \{h_{ij,t}\}$ respectively. It is worth recalling that modelling and forecasting the dynamics of the latter matrix is the main aim of the chapter.

The complete estimation of relevant parameters from the above model is performed in two stages. First, we determine the ML estimations of the conditional mean of the process by assuming conditional normality in the error term, so the results are the same as those obtained in Section 8.2. We then compute the VAR residuals and describe the CCM dynamics of the unpredictable component using both the OGARCH and MGARCH models, again applying the ML procedure. Although the assumption of conditional normality is not true in general, estimating as if the underlying distribution is normally distributed yields quasi-maximum likelihood estimations that are consistent and asymptotically normally distributed. This method is widely used, although the model is misspecified and estimations are known to be inefficient.

### 8.3.1 Orthogonal GARCH (Alexander, 2000)

Denote by $\mathbf{P}$ the $N \times N$ orthonormal matrix of eigenvectors of the unconditional covariance matrix $\Omega$. Because it is symmetrical, it is well known that the latter matrix admits the decomposition $\Omega = P \Lambda P'$, where $\Lambda$ is the diagonal matrix of eigenvalues of $\Omega$. The orthogonal GARCH method is based on the application of the principal component analysis (PCA hereafter) to identify the main sources of common variation of the multivariate system associated with each eigenvalue of $\Omega$. This allows us to generate a basis of orthogonal factors defined on the principal components whose volatility is then individually treated from the univariate perspective. The set of orthogonal factors of a multivariate system, say $Y_t = (\mathbf{y}_{1t}, \mathbf{y}_{2t}, \dots, \mathbf{y}_{Nt})'$, is just defined through the linear mapping $\mathbf{Y}_t = \mathbf{P}'\varepsilon_t$, where $\mathbb{E}\left(\mathbf{Y}_t \mathbf{Y}_t'\right) = \Lambda$ due to the orthogonal property of $\mathbf{P}$. Under the assumptions of the OGARCH model, the conditional covariance matrix of $\mathbf{Y}_t$, $\mathbb{E}_{t-1}\left(\mathbf{Y}_t \mathbf{Y}_t'\right) = \mathbf{P}'\mathbf{H}_t \mathbf{P}$, is also a diagonal matrix that we denote as $\mathbf{V}_t$. Since $\mathbb{E}(\mathbf{V}_t) = \Lambda$, we can simply estimate the CCM of $\varepsilon_t$ as $\hat{\mathbf{H}}_t = \mathbf{P}\hat{\mathbf{V}}_t \mathbf{P}'$. This conditional covariance matrix is called OGARCH when the diagonal matrix $\mathbf{V}_t$ of conditional variances for principal components is estimated by using the univariate GARCH $(1,1)$ method, i.e. when the specification

$$h_{i,t} = \omega_i + \alpha_i y_{i,t} + \beta_i h_{i,t-1}; \quad \omega_i > 0; \quad \alpha_i, \beta_i \geq 0; \quad \alpha_i + \beta_i < 1 \tag{8.4}$$

is applied on every orthogonal factor in $\mathbf{Y}_t$, recalling that $i = 1, \dots, N$.

The major advantage of this method is that the number of parameters to be estimated becomes a linear function of $N$ and, furthermore, estimations of relevant parameters involve only univariate specifications. System reduction is also possible, provided that the selected number of factors explains a sufficiently high level of variability in the system. As a drawback, however, it has to be noted that it is not possible to give a clear interpretation of the particular meaning of estimated parameters in such estimations, since orthogonal factors are not economical time series. Furthermore, assets in the portfolio have to be highly correlated in order to ensure good approximations.

The results of the PCA on the VAR residuals show that the variability of the whole system is explained mainly through three factors. The first factor, related to the highest eigenvalue, is able to forecast about 71% of the total variance, the second factor can explain about 21% more, and the last factor explains the remaining 8% of common variability. As expected, the high correlation among electricity block prices allows for the first factor to explain a large level of common volatility. Furthermore, it is worth noting that system reduction could be effectively applied here by considering only the first two factors, since by themselves they are able to explain 92% of the total variability. However, since the dimension is moderate we do not use that option but consider the whole system, estimating therefore GARCH(1,1) models on the three orthogonal factors. The main results from these estimations are summarized in Table 8.4.

### 8.3.2 Multivariate GARCH model (Engle and Mezrich, 1996)

In this subsection, we consider a GARCH-type model obtained after constraining the multivariate GARCH representation by Engle and Kroner (1995), as this is the one discussed by Engle and Mezrich (1996) and Bourgoin (2000). The key element in this model is to assume that the long-run covariance matrix equals (or can be estimated by) the sample covariance

**Table 8.4    GARCH estimations on orthogonal factors.** Main results of the GARCH(1,1) estimation on the $i$th orthogonal factor. In brackets, $p$-values from the robust estimations (Bollerslev and Wooldridge, 1992). The diagnosis of the residual shows the statistics of the normality test of Jarque–Bera (J–B test) and their $p$ values in brackets. $Q(m)$ $Q^*(m)$ refer to the Ljung–Box portmanteau statistics ($p$ values in brackets) for up to $m$th-order serial correlation in residuals and squared standardized residuals respectively

|            | Factor I        | Factor II       | Factor III      |
|------------|-----------------|-----------------|-----------------|
| $\omega_i$ | 0.04 (0.00)     | 0.001 (0.00)    | 0.000 (0.00)    |
| $\alpha_i$ | 0.231 (0.00)    | 0.094 (0.00)    | 0.088 (0.00)    |
| $\beta_i$  | 0.704 (0.00)    | 0.867 (0.00)    | 0.887 (0.00)    |
|            | **Residuals**   |                 |                 |
| Average    | 0.000           | 0.000           | 0.000           |
| Std. dev.  | 0.210           | 0.115           | 0.072           |
| Skewness   | 1.029           | 0.714           | −0.423          |
| Kurtosis   | 10.119          | 5.757           | 7.344           |
| J–B test   | 3743 (0.00)     | 656 (0.00)      | 1335 (0.00)     |
| $Q(100)$   | 102.72 (0.40)   | 138.01 (0.00)   | 114.74 (0.00)   |
| $Q(200)$   | 181.05 (0.82)   | 222.88 (0.12)   | 231.20 (0.06)   |
| $Q^*(100)$ | 62.05 (0.99)    | 124.40 (0.05)   | 107.01 (0.30)   |
| $Q^*(200)$ | 113.10 (0.99)   | 210.69 (028)    | 250.48 (0.00)   |

matrix. Under this assumption, the dynamics of the CCM can be modelled as follows:

$$\mathbf{H}_t = (1 - \alpha - \beta)\mathbf{S} + \alpha\varepsilon_{t-1}\varepsilon_{t-1}' + \beta\mathbf{H}_{t-1} \tag{8.5}$$

where $\mathbf{S}$ is the sample covariance matrix and $\alpha$, $\beta$ are non-negative parameters constrained to sum to less than one.

The major advantage of this specification is that the number of parameters is constant and always equal to 2, regardless of the dimension of $\mathbf{Z}_t$. Consequently, this method is very efficient from a computational point of view. The moderate dimension of the system here makes it possible to expect a good performance of this method. Since the assumption $\varepsilon_t|\Psi_{t-1} \sim (0, \mathbf{H}_t)$ still holds, the log-likelihood function of the model (dropping the constant term) is given by:

$$L(\alpha, \beta; \mathbf{Z}_t) = -\frac{1}{2}\sum_{t=1}^{T}(\ln|\mathbf{H}_t| - \varepsilon_t'\mathbf{H}_t^{-1}\varepsilon_t) \tag{8.6}$$

The results of the MGARCH estimation are also consistent in showing once again the strong persistence of power price volatility. The estimated parameters ($p$-values in brackets) are $\hat{\alpha} = 0.081$ (0.00) and $\hat{\beta} = 0.871$ (0.00), so that a strong persistence in variance is clear again through parameters being close to the unit boundary.

## 8.4    FORECASTING CONDITIONAL COVARIANCE MATRICES

We now compare the forecasting performance for MGARCH and OGARCH models under in-sample and out-of-sample periods. We have selected both a univariate and a multivariate metric in order to calibrate the forecasting ability of the specifications concerned. On the one

**Table 8.5  In-sample performance.** In-sample results under the $M_{1,ij}(\times 100)$ and $M_2$ metrics from the OGARCH and MGARCH models. These metrics are defined as follows:

$$M_{1,ij} = T^{-1} \sum_{t=1}^{T} (\varepsilon_{i,t}\varepsilon_{j,t} - \hat{h}_{ij,t})^2; \quad i,j = 1,2,3$$

$$M_2 = T^{-1} \sum_{t=1}^{T} \|\text{vec}(\mathbf{S}_t - \hat{\mathbf{H}}_t)\|^2$$

|          | $M_{1,11}$ | $M_{1,22}$ | $M_{1,33}$ | $M_{1,12}$ | $M_{1,13}$ | $M_{1,23}$ | $M_2$ |
|----------|-----------|-----------|-----------|-----------|-----------|-----------|-------|
| OGARCH   | 0.0587    | 0.0911    | 0.299     | 0.0601    | 0.0858    | 0.106     | 0.953 |
| MGARCH   | 0.0594    | 0.0915    | 0.290     | 0.0601    | 0.0858    | 0.105     | 0.943 |

hand, we consider the most common measure given by the mean squared error of predictions. We apply this metric, say $M_{1,ij}$, to the results from forecasting the $ij$th element of the portfolio CCM, that is:

$$M_{1,ij} = T^{-1} \sum_{t=1}^{T} (\varepsilon_{i,t}\varepsilon_{j,t} - \hat{h}_{ij,t})^2; \quad i,j = 1,2,3 \tag{8.7}$$

where $\hat{h}_{ij,t}$ is the $ij$th element of the estimated matrix $\hat{\mathbf{H}}_t$ under OGARCH and MGARCH models and $\varepsilon_{i,t}\varepsilon_{j,t}$ is the usual proxy for either the realized variance ($i = j$) or the realized covariances ($i \neq j$) among the asset returns of the portfolio at time $t$.

Second, a matrix norm to measure the distance between the estimated and realized matrices is considered. In particular, we take the Euclidean matrix norm (also called the Frobenius-norm), say $M_2$, which is not subordinated to any vectorial norm and is defined as:

$$M_2 = T^{-1} \sum_{t=1}^{T} \|\text{vec}(\mathbf{S}_t - \hat{\mathbf{H}}_t)\|^2 \tag{8.8}$$

where the vec($\cdot$) operator stacks the columns of a matrix in a column vector and $\|\cdot\|$ denotes the Euclidean norm of a vector. The matrix $\mathbf{S}_t = \varepsilon_t \varepsilon_t'$ is the realized covariance matrix at time $t$.

Results regarding the in-sample performance of models are shown in Table 8.5. Note that under the univariate metric the MGARCH model seems to perform slightly better than the OGARCH model when forecasting covariances, although not when forecasting variances. The MGARCH model seems to explain better the CCM dynamics of electricity block prices under the multivariate metric, although none of these differences seems to be very large.

The $k$-ahead OGARCH forecast of the covariance matrix at time $t$ is given by the projection $\mathbb{E}_t\left(\mathbf{H}_{t+k}^O\right) = \mathbf{P}\mathbb{E}_t\left(\mathbf{V}_{t+k}\right)\mathbf{P}'$, where the diagonal matrix $\mathbf{V}_{t+k}$ contains the $k$-ahead GARCH(1,1) forecasts of the principal components at time $t$, that is:

$$\mathbb{E}_t(v_{ii,t+k}) = \hat{\omega}_i \left[ \frac{1 - (\hat{\alpha}_i + \hat{\beta}_i)^{k-1}}{1 - (\hat{\alpha}_i + \hat{\beta}_i)} \right] + (\hat{\alpha}_i + \hat{\beta}_i)^{k-1} v_{ii,t+1} \tag{8.9}$$

where $v_{ii,t+1} = \hat{\omega}_i + \hat{\alpha}_i y_{it}^2 + \hat{\beta}_i v_{ii,t}$ is the one-ahead forecasting for the $i$th principal component.

**Table 8.6   Out-of-sample performance.** Out-of-sample results under $M_{1,ij}$ and $M_2$ metrics from the OGARCH and MGARCH $k$-ahead forecasts ($k = 1, 5, 10, 15$). These metrics are defined as follows:

$$M_{1,ij} = T^{-1} \sum_{t=1}^{T} (\varepsilon_{i,t}\varepsilon_{j,t} - \hat{h}_{ij,t})^2; \quad i, j = 1, 2, 3$$

$$M_2 = T^{-1} \sum_{t=1}^{T} \|\text{vec}(S_t - \hat{H}_t)\|^2$$

|         | $M_{1,11}$ | $M_{1,22}$ | $M_{1,33}$ | $M_{1,12}$ | $M_{1,13}$ | $M_{1,23}$ | $M_2$ |
|---------|------------|------------|------------|------------|------------|------------|-------|
| **OGARCH** |         |            |            |            |            |            |       |
| 1 day   | 0.0130     | 0.0217     | 0.08044    | 0.0137     | 0.0097     | 0.0188     | 0.1994 |
| 5 days  | 0.0142     | 0.0232     | 0.0829     | 0.0135     | 0.0095     | 0.0186     | 0.2035 |
| 10 days | 0.0131     | 0.0242     | 0.0862     | 0.0151     | 0.0097     | 0.0185     | 0.2101 |
| 15 days | 0.0155     | 0.0246     | 0.0855     | 0.0140     | 0.0095     | 0.0180     | 0.2083 |
| **MGARCH** |         |            |            |            |            |            |       |
| 1 day   | 0.0140     | 0.0224     | 0.0796     | 0.0134     | 0.0099     | 0.0193     | 0.2013 |
| 5 days  | 0.0147     | 0.0236     | 0.0805     | 0.0136     | 0.0095     | 0.0188     | 0.2028 |
| 10 days | 0.0148     | 0.0246     | 0.0832     | 0.0141     | 0.0095     | 0.0182     | 0.2062 |
| 15 days | 0.0152     | 0.0250     | 0.0852     | 0.0141     | 0.0197     | 0.0187     | 0.2103 |

The MGARCH forecasts are straightforwardly computed through the projection $\mathbb{E}_t(H_{t+k}^M)$, whose elements are:

$$\mathbb{E}\left(h_{ij,t+k}^M\right) = s_{ij} + (\hat{\alpha} + \hat{\beta})^{k-1}(h_{ij,t+1} - s_{ij}); \quad i, j = 1, 2, 3; \quad k \geq 2 \qquad (8.10)$$

and where $h_{ij,t+1}^M = s_{ij} + \hat{\alpha}\varepsilon_{i,t}\varepsilon_{,t} + \hat{\beta}h_{ij,t}$ is the one-ahead forecasting.

We consider 01/07/2000–18/09/2000 as the out-of-sample period. Forecasts are made by using a rolling scheme. This scheme takes a fixed-length window of the past 1643 observations and sets the last day of the window as the forecasting origin. Relevant parameters in equations are estimated on the fixed window and forecasts are made up to 15 days ahead. Then, the oldest observation is successively removed in an iterated process over the out-of-sample period as the fixed window is daily updated, and not used in new estimations and forecasts. Table 8.6 shows the forecasting performance under both $M_{1,ij}$ and $M_2$ metrics in the out-of-sample period for several $k$-step predictors ($k = 1, 5, 10, 15$).

As before, the analysis of the forecasting performance does not seem to find great differences between the performance of OGARCH and MGARCH models. As a result, the MGARCH model could be more suitable than the OGARCH method, since it yields quite similar results but implies a slighter computational burden.

## 8.5   CONCLUDING REMARKS

The aim of this chapter has been to forecast the multivariate conditional volatility for portfolios containing daily spot electricity block contracts. These contracts are being successfully implemented in the more recent power generation markets, since they provide a natural way of facing the uncertainty implied in electricity prices. The method proposed in this chapter could be a useful tool to manage the risk implied by the high volatility of the daily power price. We have applied some methodologies characterized as simple multivariate conditional volatility models by using the OGARCH and MGARCH models. Both models arrive at the estimation of parameters in a feasible computational way. The main conclusion of the forecasting performance between both approaches in the empirical case treated here is that they seem to yield similar results.

A priority in this chapter has been to provide an intuitive tool that could be readily implemented by practitioners approaching the risk measure of block contract portfolios, rather than to provide an "academic" model able to deal with all the complex features of electricity prices but intractable in practice. In fact, it would not be very difficult to implement all the procedures described here so that market agents could approach and forecast the market risk of their positions in a reasonably fast and accurate way. However, the price to be paid for this tractability is that the linear models proposed would be unable to accurately forecast sudden jumps in electricity prices. Although electricity jumps are not very likely to occur, and even the probability of such an event is far from being the same for every market (as it depends mainly on technical factors and the quality of the transmission grid), such a possibility should not be dismissed. Modelling spikes is by far the most difficult task in modelling electricity prices, and so sometimes it is necessary to leave out this feature in order to provide a first step in that direction (see, e.g., the models to value derivatives contracts developed in Lucia and Schwartz, 2002). We have acted in that spirit, since it is virtually impossible to provide a multivariate model that is able both to capture all characteristics of electricity prices and infrequent jumps, and at the same time be tractable. The procedures described above therefore have limitations and must be undertaken with care.

Directions in which this work could be extended straightforwardly suggest the inclusion of heavily-tailed distributions to cope with aberrant observations in the models. The main problem with this issue is that it would be necessary to estimate all parameters jointly, meaning that (i) a large number of parameters would have to be estimated in a highly non-linear specification, and (ii) proper optimization routines and hence advanced packages would be needed, so accessibility and tractability would be lost. Another interesting direction for further research includes the valuation of derivatives, such as basket options, taking block contract portfolios as the underlying asset.

## ACKNOWLEDGEMENTS

We thank Sabino Mastrángelo for his comments and insights regarding technical issues of the Argentine Market. We have also benefited from discussions with G. Fiorentini, I. Peña, G. Rubio, E. Schwartz and E. Sentana, and from suggestions of participants in a research seminar at the University Carlos III of Madrid. Support from the Spanish Department of Science and Technology through project 2002–03797 is acknowledged. An earlier version of this chapter appeared in the working paper series of the Instituto Valenciano de Investigaciones Económicas (IVIE), which is acknowledged. All the contents are the sole responsibility of the authors.

## REFERENCES

Alexander C.O. (2000). "A Primer on the Orthogonal GARCH Model". Unpublished manuscript, ISMA Centre, University of Reading, UK.
Bollerslev T. and Wooldridge J.M. (1992). "Quasi-Maximum Likelihood Estimation and Inference in Dynamic Models with Time Varying Covariances". *Econometric Reviews* **11**: 143–172.

Bollerslev T., Engle R. and Nelson D. (1994). "ARCH Models". In *Handbook of Econometrics*, vol IV, R.F. Engle and D. MacFadden (eds). North-Holland, Amsterdam.

Bourgoin F. (2000). "Large Scale Conditional Correlation Estimation". In *Advances in Quantitative Asset Management*, C.L. Dunis (ed.). Kluwer Academic, Dordrecht.

Byström H.N. (2000). "The Hedging Performance of Electricity Futures on the Nordic Power Exchange Nord Pool". Working Paper 2000:15, Lund University, Department of Economics.

Engle R.F. and Kroner K.F. (1995). "Multivariate Simultaneous Generalized GARCH". *Econometric Theory* **11**: 122–150.

Engle R.F. and Mezrich J. (1996). "GARCH for Groups". *Risk Magazine* **9**: 36–40.

Granger C.W.J. (1969). "Investigating Causal Relations by Econometric Models and Cross-Spectral Methods". *Econometrica* **37**: 424–438.

Hylleberg S., Engle R.F., Granger C.W.J. and Yoo B.S. (1990). "Seasonal Integration and Cointegration". *Journal of Econometrics* **44**: 215–238.

Lucia J. and Schwartz E.S. (2002). "Electricity Prices and Power Derivatives, 2002. Evidence from the Nordic Power Exchange". *Review of Derivatives Research* **5**(1): 5–50.

Mastrángelo S. (2001). "Legislación y Regulación del Mercado Eléctrico". En *Introducción al Conocimiento del Mercado Eléctrico Mayorista*. Instituto de Tecnología, Buenos Aires.

Wolak F.A. (1997). "Market Design and Price Behavior in Restructured Electricity Markets: An International Comparison". Working Paper PWP-051, University of California Energy Institute.

# Part III
## Spatial Price Interactions

# 9

# Identifying Dynamic Interactions in Western US Spot Markets

CHRISTINE A. JERKO[1], JAMES W. MJELDE[2] AND
DAVID A. BESSLER[2]

[1]*Commercial and Trading Group, PacifiCorp, USA*
[2]*Department of Agricultural Economics, Texas A&M University, College Station, TX 77843-2124, USA*

## ABSTRACT

Dynamic interactions among six electricity spot markets in the western United States are examined using time series analysis and directed acyclic graphs. Results show the markets to be highly integrated. The California market appears to be the driving force in contemporaneous time. There are seasonal differences in the short-run price discovery mechanisms. In the longer run, price dynamics appear to be similar between seasons. The mid-Columbia market appears to be the dominant market in the long run in both seasons.

## 9.1 INTRODUCTION

The wholesale electricity industry in the western United States is characterized by a highly interconnected transmission system and established trading regime (DeVany and Walls, 1999b). The geographic scope of this market is quite wide under most market conditions, but narrow markets may arise when transmission congestion occurs (Bailey, 1998). The magnitude of trades between wholesale spot markets has been stimulated by the recent deregulation in the industry (US Department of Energy, 1998). Deregulation of the electricity industry and its impact on prices is a subject of considerable interest, especially given the recent price spikes occurring in California and elsewhere. Weron (2000) notes deregulation is a global trend and is not limited to the United States. Further, Angelus (2001) states market structures appear to vary greatly between wholesale markets and the markets seem to be changing yearly, resulting in volatile prices.

Because electricity cannot be economically stored, demand and supply are balanced on a knife-edge with weather grid reliability, grid dynamics, transmission dynamics, and generation concentration paramount to determining price (Weron, 2000; Wagman, 2000). Weron and Przybylowicz (2000, p. 464) state, "The whole complex process of electricity price formulation results in a behavior not observed in the financial or even other commodity markets. It is extremely interesting to investigate this new world." Most studies of electricity pricing have investigated market structure and power, reasons for deregulation, or impact of deregulation on price (Joskow, 1997; White, 1996; Angelus, 2001; Deb *et al.*, 2000), but few studies have examined the dynamic nature of empirical price evolution. Further, time series analysis has been used in only a handful of studies.

*Modelling Prices in Competitive Electricity Markets.* Edited by D.W. Bunn.

Weron (2000) and Weron and Przybylowicz (2000) using price data from California and Switzerland note the process underlying electricity prices is mean reverting. Because electricity prices are mean reverting, Weron (2000) suggests Black–Scholes type models must be questioned when modeling such prices. Weron and Przybylowicz (2000) suggest an appropriate modeling technique is the Hurst R/S approach. This approach attempts to distinguish "…completely random time series from correlated time series" (Weron and Przybylowicz, 2000, p. 463). Herguera (2000), in examining spot markets in England and Wales and the Nordic countries, notes there are significant differences in the evolution of prices and volume traded. He states the data supports the theoretical result of Allaz and Villa (1993) that the introduction of futures markets leads to tougher price competition in spot markets. However, in the United States, prices may not be as transparent because most trades are bilateral and futures trading volume is limited.

DeVany and Walls (1999b) examined daily, peak and off-peak electricity spot prices during 1994 and 1996 using an error correction model on 11 regional markets in the western United States. They find spot markets are generally non-stationary and cointegrated. Peak prices at Palo Verde, however, are cointegrated with the off-peak price at only one other market, suggesting transfer capacities are limited during peak periods in this part of the western grid. DeVany and Walls (1999a) use a vector autoregressive model to obtain impulse response functions and variance decomposition. Their impulse responses indicate shocks to a market impact neighboring markets first and then more distant locations along the transmission network. Variance decompositions suggest the California–Oregon border as one of the most important spot markets in determining prices throughout the network. Unlike De Vany and Walls (1999a,b), Woo *et al.* (1997) find the presence of stationarity within Pacific Northwest spot markets. They infer the presence of pairwise cointegration based on price difference tests of their stationary price series. The results of Woo *et al.* (1997) are questionable because cointegration refers to the linear combination of non-stationary variables (Engle and Granger, 1987).

Providing information on the dynamics of power prices in the western United States is the objective of this study. In achieving this objective, price discovery and communication between different spot markets are obtained. Dynamic relationships allow the degree of interaction between wholesale spot markets to be determined. Understanding how spot markets interact allows a better understanding of the direction and extent to which price innovations reverberate through the western trading region. To meet this objective, prices from six spot markets located in the western United States are used to estimate vector autoregression. Directed graphs are used to provide identification restrictions on causal information flows in contemporaneous time for impulse response functions and forecast error variance decompositions.

## 9.2  DATA

The data consists of 643 observations of daily firm-peak spot market prices for day-ahead trades spanning the period 15 March 1999 to 24 August 2001. The data are Platts power indices provided by Logical Information Machines, Inc., Chicago, IL. Peak prices are sales with next day delivery for the hours between 6 a.m. and 10 p.m. Prices are, generally, for Monday through Friday. Starting in May 2001, peak prices for Saturday are included. Saturday peak prices are not included until May 2001, because of a high number of missing prices. Most national holidays are also excluded from the data set because of missing values. The prior day's price is used to represent any remaining missing values for a particular day and market.

**Figure 9.1**  Approximate location of the spot markets (areas Ë) and major cities (#) in the western US electricity region

The six spot markets included are mid-Columbia (MC), California–Oregon border (COB), North Path in California (NP), South Path in California (SP), Palo Verde (PV) and Four Corners (FC). The approximate locations of the markets (areas) are given in Figure 9.1. Plots of the price series are provided in Figure 9.2. The most striking features of the plots are the price spikes experienced in 2000 and 2001.

When the system is relatively unconstrained, the market price is determined by the variable costs of the marginal input. Therefore, of interest, is the capacity and main type of electricity generation near each spot market. The main source of electricity generation near mid-Columbia is hydro-generation (Ashton, 2001). Seven dams on the midsection of the Columbia River have a generating nameplate capacity of 13 475 MW (US Department of Energy, 2001). Fossil fuel generation is the primary source of power at Four Corners. This area (New Mexico and Arizona) has a collective nameplate capacity of approximately 7962 MW (US Department of Energy, 2001). Palo Verde is the site of the largest nuclear generating facility in the United States (US Department of Energy, 2001). Three reactors have a combined nameplate capacity of 4210 MW. North and South Path and the California–Oregon border are mainly transmission areas. While both the North and South Path areas have various types of electricity generating plates, the North Path is predominately hydro-generation, whereas the South Path has more oil and gas power plants (California Energy Commission, 2001b).

In addition to electricity prices, aggregate cooling and heating degree-days are used. Degree-days are units used to estimate heating and cooling requirements (Microsoft, 2001). One degree-day is defined as a difference of one degree between mean temperature ((maximum temperature + minimum temperature) / 2) and a reference temperature. For cooling degree-days the reference temperature is 75 degrees Fahrenheit (cooling degree-day = mean temperature − reference temperature), whereas for heating degree-days the reference temperature used is

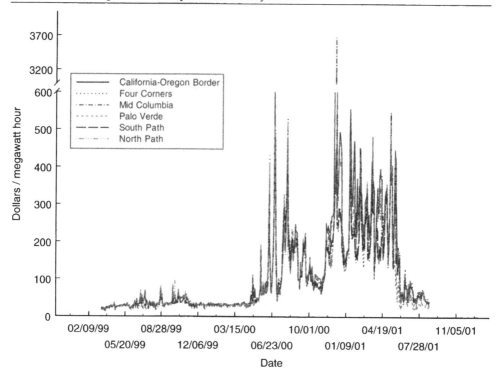

**Figure 9.2**    Daily peak electricity prices for the six western US spot markets

65 degrees Fahrenheit (heating degree-day = reference temperature − mean temperature). If either degree-day is negative, it is set equal to zero. Daily cooling and heating degree-days are calculated for the following eight western cities: Seattle, Portland, San Francisco, Los Angeles, Salt Lake, Denver, Las Vegas and Phoenix (Figure 9.1). Daily degree-days for each city are then aggregated into daily total cooling and heating degree requirements for the western United States by calculating a weighted average. Population figures from 2000 for each city are used for the weights (US Census Bureau, 2001). Temperature data is from the National Center for Environmental Prediction provided by Logical Information Machines, Inc.

## 9.3    METHODS

Because the data are observed over time, it is expected they will show correlation patterns through time, such that pairs of observations located near one another will show higher correlation than observation pairs located at distant intervals. Further, because the data are prices, it is expected that unit root (non-stationary) patterns will characterize each price series (Samuelson, 1965).

### 9.3.1    Vector autoregression

The basic engine of analysis is the vector autoregression (VAR), which allows regularities in the series to be studied without imposing many prior restrictions. For the historical electricity spot market price data, $P_t$, a six market VAR is:

$$P_t = \mu + \sum_{i=1}^{k} B_i P_{t-i} + C Z_{t-1} + e_t \tag{9.1}$$

where $P_t$ and $e_t$ are both $(6 \times 1)$ random vectors, $Z_t$ is a $(q \times 1)$ vector of $q$ non-stochastic (or strictly exogenous) variables, $\mu$ is a $(6 \times 1)$ vector of intercepts, $B_i$ and $C$ are appropriately dimensioned matrices of coefficients, $k$ is the number of lags on $P_t$ required to make the observed error $(\hat{e}_t)$ white noise, and $t$ is the particular observation from a sample of $T$ observations. The innovation term $e_t$ is assumed to be white noise, where $E(e_t) = 0$, $\Sigma_e = E(e_t \ e_t')$ is a $(6 \times 6)$ positive definite matrix. The innovations, $e_t$ and $e_s$, are independent for $s \neq t$. Although serially uncorrelated, contemporaneous correlation among the elements of $e_t$ is possible, such that the individual sources of error may move together (not orthogonal). Here, heating degree-days and cooling degrees-days in period $t - 1$ are included in each equation of the VAR, as strictly exogenous variables.

Following Bernanke (1986), we can write the non-orthogonal innovations $(e_t)$ as a function of more fundamental driving sources of variation, $\epsilon_t$, which are independent of other sources of variation:

$$e_t = A\epsilon_t \tag{9.2}$$

where $A$ is a matrix which describes how each non-orthogonal innovation $(e_t)$ is determined (or caused) by the orthogonal or driving sources of variation in each equation $(\epsilon_t)$. Zero restrictions on $A$ are investigated to obtain an identified "structural VAR". There are no easy rules for identifying $A$. For a VAR in six variables, if more than 15 parameters are to be estimated, the model is not identified. Doan (1995, pp. 8–10) suggests the following rule:

> If there is no combination of $i$ and $j$ ($i \neq j$) for which both $A_{ij}$ and $A_{ji}$ are nonzero, the model is identified.

Usual innovation accounting procedures (impulse response and forecast error decompositions) can be carried out on the transformed VAR:

$$A P_t = A\mu + \sum_{i=1}^{k} A B_i P_{t-i} + A C Z_{t-1} + A e_t \tag{9.3}$$

Directed acyclic graphs are used to provide an identifying restriction on the matrix $A$. Before discussing model results, a brief overview of directed acyclic graphs is presented.

### 9.3.2  Directed acyclic graphs

A graph is a pictorial representation of causal flow among a set of variables (vertices). Lines with arrows indicate causal flow, where the base of the arrow is placed next to the causal variable and the arrowhead is placed next to the effect variable. Given a set of variables {A, B, C, D} the following graphs can be obtained: (i) an undirected graph – contains only undirected edges (e.g., A — B); (ii) a directed graph – contains only directed edges (e.g., B → C); (iii) an inducing path graph – contains both directed edges and bi-directed edges (C ↔ D); and (iv) a partially oriented inducing path graph – contains directed edges, bi-directed edges, non-directed edges (o — o), and partially directed edges (o →), where "o" indicates the possibility of an omitted latent variable at the vertex endpoint. An undirected edge indicates causal flow, but the algorithm is unable to determine the direction of the flow, whereas a directed edge indicates the flow could be determined. A bi-directed edge indicates causal flow in both directions. Non-directed edges indicate no causal flow. Partially directed edges indicate the possibility of latent variables. A directed acyclic graph is a directed graph that contains no directed cyclic paths (an acyclic graph contains no vertex more than once). Only acyclic graphs are used here.

Directed acyclic graphs are designs for representing conditional independence as implied by the recursive product decomposition:

$$\Pr(x_1, x_2, x_3, \ldots, x_n) = \prod_{i=1}^{n} \Pr(x_i | pa_i) \qquad (9.4)$$

where Pr is the probability of vertices $x_1, x_2, x_3, \ldots, x_n$ and $pa_i$ the realization of some subset of the variables that precede (come before in a causal sense) $x_i$ in order $x_1, x_2, \ldots, x_n$. Pearl (1995) proposes $d$-separation as a graphical characterization of conditional independence. That is, $d$-separation characterizes the conditional independence relations given by equation (9.4). If a directed acyclic graph is formulated in which the variables corresponding to $pa_i$ are represented as the parents (direct causes) of $x_i$, then the independencies implied by equation (9.4) can be read off the graph using the notion of $d$-separation. Pearl (1995, p. 671) defines $d$-separation as:

> Let X, Y and Z be three disjoint subsets of vertices in a directed acylic graph G, and let p be any path between a vertex in X and a vertex in Y, where by "path" we mean any succession of edges, regardless of their directions. Z is said to block p if there is a vertex w on p satisfying one of the following: (i) w has converging arrows along p, and neither w nor any of its descendants are on Z, or (ii) w does not have converging arrows along p, and w is in Z. Further, Z is said to d-separate X from Y on graph G, written (X⊥Y | Z) G, if and only if Z blocks every path from a vertex in X to a vertex in Y.

Geiger *et al.* (1990) show that there is a one-to-one correspondence between the set of conditional independencies, X ⊥ Y | Z, implied by equation (9.4) and the set of triples (X, Y, Z) that satisfy the $d$-separation criterion in graph G. Essential for this connection is the following result: if G is a directed acyclic graph with vertex set X, A and B are in X, and H is also in X, then G linearly implies the correlation between A and B conditional on H is zero if and only if A and B are $d$-separated given H.

Spirtes *et al.* (1993) have incorporated the notion of $d$-separation into a program (TETRAD II) for building directed acyclic graphs, using the notion of sepset (defined below). TETRAD II is based on an algorithm, PC algorithm, that is an ordered set of commands that begins with a general unrestricted set of relationships among variables and proceeds stepwise to remove edges between variables and to direct "causal flow". The algorithm is described in detail in Spirtes *et al.* (1993, p. 117). More advanced versions (refinements) are described as the Modified PC Algorithm (Spirtes *et al.*, 1993, p. 166), the Causal Inference Algorithm (p. 183), and the Fast Causal Inference Algorithm (p. 188). Because the basic definition of a sepset is used in all algorithms and the PC algorithm is the most basic, the discussion is limited to the PC algorithm.

Briefly, one forms a complete undirected graph G on the vertex set X. The complete undirected graph shows an undirected edge between every variable of the system (every variable in X). Edges between variables are removed sequentially based on zero correlation or partial correlation (conditional correlation). The conditioning variable(s) on removed edges between two variables is called the sepset of the variables whose edge has been removed (for vanishing zero-order conditioning information the sepset is the empty set). Edges are directed by considering triples X — Y — Z, such that X and Y are adjacent as are Y and Z, but X and Z are not adjacent. Direct edges between triples X — Y — Z as X → Y ← Z, if Y is not in the sepset of X and Z. If X → Y, Y and Z are adjacent, X and Z are not adjacent, and there is no arrowhead at Y, then orient Y — Z as Y → Z. If there is a directed path from X to Y, and an edge between X and Y, then direct X — Y as X → Y.

In applications, Fisher's $z$ (see Spirtes *et al.*, 1993, p. 94) is used to test whether conditional correlations are significantly different from zero. Fisher's $z$ can be applied to test for significance from zero. This statistic is:

$$z(\rho(i, j \mid k)n) = 1/2(n - |k| - 3)^{1/2} \times \ln\{(|1 + \rho(i, j \mid k)|) \times (|1 - \rho(i, j \mid k)|)^{-1}\} \quad (9.5)$$

where $n$ is the number of observations used to estimate the correlations, $\rho(i, j|k)$ is the population correlation between series $i$ and $j$ conditional on series $k$ (removing the influence of series $k$ on each $i$ and $j$), and $|k|$ is the number of variables in $k$ (that are conditioned on). If $i$, $j$ and $k$ are normally distributed and $r(i, j \mid k)$ is the sample conditional correlation of $i$ and $j$ given $k$, then the distribution of $z(\rho(i, j \mid k)n) - z(r(i, j \mid k)n)$ is standard normal.

## 9.4  RESULTS

The data are divided into two periods, spring–summer and fall–winter. The spring and autumn equinox dates are used as the dividing date for winter–spring and fall–winter. Over the data set period of 15 March 1999–24 August 2001, the following partial time series are obtained. For the fall–winter period the dates are 15–19 March 1999, 21 September 1999–20 March 2000 and 21 September 2000–20 March 2001. Dates for the spring–summer period are 22 March 1999–20 September 1999, 21 March 2000–20 September 2000 and 21 March 2001–24 August 2001. The fall–winter series are spliced together using zero–one dummy variables (one for each period) for the second two periods (21 September 1999–20 March 2000 and 21 September 2000–20 March 2001). Similarly, the spring–summer period is spliced together using dummy variables for the periods 21 March 2000–14 October 2000 and 21 March 2001–24 August 2001. Three series are obtained: the entire peak price data set, fall–winter peak prices and spring–summer peak prices.

Dickey–Fuller (DF) and Augmented Dickey–Fuller (ADF) tests of unit root behavior for each individual series are given in Table 9.1. The null hypothesis is that peak prices in each market are generated by a non-stationary time series process. If the DF or ADF statistics are less than $-2.89$ the null hypothesis is rejected. The spring–summer peak prices appear to show non-stationary behavior, as the ADF test on each market is greater than $-2.89$. The DF test for each market in the spring–summer panel shows autocorrelated residuals and should not be used for inference on unit root behavior. Residuals on the ADF tests for spring–summer are better behaved – closer to the white noise benchmark. The hypothesis that peak prices in the fall–winter series are non-stationary is rejected, under both the DF and the ADF tests (these tests are the same because the optimum lag length on the ADF test is zero lags for all markets).

**Table 9.1**  Dickey–Fuller (DF), Augmented Dickey–Fuller (ADF) and associated residual tests on the null hypothesis of non-stationarity of peak electricity prices from six western US spot markets, spring–summer and fall–winter

| Market | DF | Q(36) | $p$-Value | ADF | $k$ | Q(36) | $p$-Value |
|---|---|---|---|---|---|---|---|
| | | | Spring–summer | | | | |
| COB | −3.37 | 108.19 | 0.00 | −1.72 | 6 | 32.84 | 0.62 |
| FC | −3.83 | 140.58 | 0.00 | −2.14 | 6 | 48.29 | 0.08 |
| MC | −3.27 | 110.44 | 0.00 | −1.74 | 6 | 35.55 | 0.49 |
| PV | −3.65 | 134.34 | 0.00 | −2.13 | 6 | 48.30 | 0.08 |
| SP | −3.93 | 124.93 | 0.00 | −2.18 | 6 | 44.75 | 0.15 |
| NP | −3.54 | 111.71 | 0.00 | −1.42 | 7 | 34.42 | 0.54 |
| | | | Fall–winter | | | | |
| COB | −3.76 | 21.65 | 0.97 | −3.76 | 0 | 21.65 | 0.97 |
| FC | −3.72 | 21.17 | 0.98 | −3.72 | 0 | 21.17 | 0.98 |
| MC | −3.53 | 19.05 | 0.99 | −3.53 | 0 | 19.05 | 0.99 |
| PV | −3.99 | 48.72 | 0.08 | −3.99 | 0 | 48.72 | 0.08 |
| SP | −3.70 | 38.53 | 0.35 | −3.70 | 0 | 38.53 | 0.35 |
| NP | −3.92 | 33.11 | 0.60 | −3.92 | 0 | 33.11 | 0.60 |
| | | | Entire sample | | | | |
| COB | −3.12 | 147.69 | 0.00 | −1.97 | 6 | 40.06 | 0.29 |
| FC | −3.34 | 159.49 | 0.00 | −1.91 | 7 | 34.78 | 0.53 |
| MC | −2.94 | 144.69 | 0.00 | −1.97 | 6 | 36.25 | 0.46 |
| PV | −3.29 | 148.46 | 0.00 | −1.84 | 7 | 42.45 | 0.21 |
| SP | −3.33 | 161.47 | 0.00 | −1.82 | 7 | 42.12 | 0.22 |
| NP | −3.20 | 146.15 | 0.00 | −1.76 | 7 | 41.40 | 0.25 |

*Notes:* The column under the heading "DF" refers to the Dickey–Fuller test on the null hypothesis that the price data from the market listed in the far left-hand-most column are non-stationary in levels (non-differenced data). The test for each series of price data is based on an ordinary least squares regression of the first differences of prices from each market on a constant and one lag of the levels of prices (non-differenced prices) from each market. The $t$-statistic is associated with the estimated coefficient on the lagged levels variable from this regression. Under the null hypothesis, the statistic is distributed in a non-standard $t$. Critical values are given in Fuller (1976). The 5% critical value is −2.89. We reject the null for observed $t$ values less than this critical value. The associated Q-statistic is the Ljung–Box statistic on the estimated residuals from the above-described regression. Under the null hypothesis of white noise residuals Q is distributed chi-squared with 36 degrees of freedom. The $p$-value associated with this Q statistic is given in the column immediately to the left of the Q-statistic. We reject the null hypothesis for large values of Q or for low $p$-values (i.e. $p$-values less than 0.05).

The column under the heading "ADF" refers to the Augmented Dickey–Fuller test associated with the null hypothesis that the price data from the market listed in the far left-hand-most column are non-stationary in levels (same null as above). Here, the test is of the same form as that described above, except that $k$ lags of the dependent variable are added to the right-hand side of the DF regression. The value for $k$ is determined by minimizing the Schwarz-loss metric on values of $k$ ranging from 1 to 10. The ADF regression was run with lags of the dependent variable ranging from one lag to ten lags. The Schwarz-loss metric was minimized at the value given in the column headed by the label "$k$". Again, the critical value of the $t$-statistic is −2.89 and we reject for values of the calculated statistic less than this critical value. Finally, as above, the Q-statistic is the Ljung–Box statistic on the estimated residuals from the ADF regression. Under the null hypothesis of white noise residuals Q is distributed chi-squared with 36 degrees of freedom. The $p$-value associated with this Q-statistic is given in the column immediately to the left of the Q-statistic.

Unit root tests become somewhat problematic when applied to "spliced" data as used here. The critical values were established using Monte Carlo methods on each form of the Dickey–Fuller tests (Fuller, 1976, p. 373). Here, the estimating regression is $\Delta p_t = \beta_0 + \beta_1 p_{t-1} + \delta_1 D_1 + \delta_2 D_2$, where $D_1$ and $D_2$ are dummy variables set equal to one in periods two and three. Critical values from the standard DF tests were not originally derived using such dummy variables. Accordingly, DF and AF tests without these zero–one dummy variables in the regression were conducted. In this case, both the spring–summer and fall–winter series show non-stationary behavior. The ADF test statistics for COB, FC, MC, PV, SP and NP (without the dummy variables) are: $-1.99$, $-2.13$, $-1,92$, $-2.18$, $-2.10$ and $-2.00$ (fall–winter) and $-2.07$, $-1.76$, $-1.60$, $-1.89$, $-1.82$ and $-1.72$ (spring–summer).[2]

Engle and Granger (1987) state a VAR in levels (non-differenced data) for a large number of observations will be equivalent to an error correction model (a time series model with first differences as the dependent variable). Following their result, VARs in levels are estimated. Two tests for the appropriate number of lags in the VAR are given in Table 9.2. Tests are provided for both separate VARs fit to the spring–summer and the fall–winter data and to the entire sample. Under the separate data, dummy variables associated with the dates where splicing occurs, as described above, are included. In each seasonal VAR, both the Schwarz-loss and Hannan and Quinn's M measure suggest one lag. In the VAR fit to the entire sample, Schwarz-loss again suggests a single-lag VAR, while Hannan and Quinn's loss suggests a two-lag VAR. Given these tests, the remainder of this chapter uses a single-lag VAR.

Likelihood ratio tests of the equality of VAR coefficients in the spring–summer VAR versus the fall–winter VAR are conducted. The tests are based on the relative difference in residual variance–covariance, as measured by the log of the determinant of the error covariance matrix on a VAR fit to the entire data (with no seasonal dummy shifter) versus a VAR fit to the data, allowing coefficients to vary between spring–summer and fall–winter. This is a test of 42 zero restrictions (six coefficients associated with fall–winter data in each of six equations (36), plus one intercept in each equation (9.6)). The likelihood ratio statistic is 96.25. Under the null hypothesis that these 42 coefficients equal zero, the test statistic is distributed chi-squared with 42 degree of freedom. The null hypothesis is rejected at a very low level of significance ($p$-value $< 0.000$). Accordingly, throughout the remainder of the chapter results for separate spring–summer and fall–winter VARs are provided.

Because VARs in levels are fitted to the data, which possibly are non-stationary, tests of non-stationarity of residuals (innovations) are given in Table 9.3. It is important that the innovations from each VAR equation are stationary. The null hypothesis for each row of the table is that the innovations from that equation are non-stationary. DF and ADF tests are used, only now the critical value for the 5% level of significance is $-3.40$ because the tests are using estimated innovations rather than "true" innovations (Granger and Newbold, 1986). In all cases, the augmented tests indicate stationary innovations.

Provided in Table 9.4 are the $p$-values associated with lagged coefficients of each market price in the autoregressive equation of each market price. In the COB spring–summer equation, coefficients associated with lagged price from FC, MC and the NP are significant at the 5% level, whereas in the fall–winter data, only MC has a significant influence on the COB price. FC is significant in every spring–summer equation (except its own), but FC is not a significant variable in any fall–winter market, except its own. MC is significant in every spring–summer

---

[2] Other tests of unit root behavior were investigated, both with and without the splicing dummy variables. Sims' Bayesian test (see Doan, 1995, pp. 6–20) gave probabilities of the null hypothesis of non-stationarity being true for COB, FC, MC, PV, SP and NP as follows: 0.004, 0.001, 0.006, 0.005, 0.001, 0.001 (spring–summer with dummy variables) and 0.30, 0.192, 0.403, 0.131, 0.164, 0.161 (spring–summer without dummy variables). Further, Sims' Bayesian probabilities for COB, FC, MC, PV, SP and NP are: 0.000, 0.000, 0.000, 0.000, 0.000, 0.000 (fall–winter with dummy variables) and 0.588, 0.529, 0.648, 0.492, 0.565, 0.530 (fall–winter without dummy variables). Finally, Phillips–Perron tests (Phillips and Perron, 1988) with six lags to account for covariance in residuals gave similar results. Robinson (2000) also found non-stationarity for pool electricity prices when using ADF tests.

**Table 9.2**  Schwarz-loss and Hannan and Quinn loss on 0 to 10 lags on levels vector autoregressions on daily peak electricity prices from six western US spot markets, spring–summer and fall–winter

| Number of lags | Schwarz-loss | Hannan and Quinn-loss |
|---|---|---|
| | Spring–summer | |
| 0 | −21.054 | −21.188 |
| 1 | −26.543* | −26.917* |
| 2 | −26.115 | −26.738 |
| 3 | −25.669 | −26.541 |
| 4 | −25.287 | −26.408 |
| 5 | −24.998 | −26.368 |
| 6 | −24.400 | −26.019 |
| 7 | −23.946 | −25.814 |
| 8 | −23.422 | −25.540 |
| 9 | −22.819 | −25.186 |
| 10 | −22.291 | −24.907 |
| | Fall–winter | |
| 0 | −22.877 | −23.011 |
| 1 | −27.445* | −27.818* |
| 2 | −27.089 | −27.712 |
| 3 | −26.566 | −27.438 |
| 4 | −25.992 | −27.113 |
| 5 | −25.469 | −26.839 |
| 6 | −24.907 | −26.527 |
| 7 | −24.442 | −26.310 |
| 8 | −23.960 | −26.078 |
| 9 | −23.446 | −25.813 |
| 10 | −23.028 | −25.644 |
| | Entire sample | |
| 0 | −20.212 | −20.290 |
| 1 | −26.476* | −26.694 |
| 2 | −26.428 | −26.793* |
| 3 | −26.156 | −26.667 |
| 4 | −25.919 | −26.574 |
| 5 | −25.751 | −26.553 |
| 6 | −25.442 | −26.389 |
| 7 | −25.219 | −26.312 |
| 8 | −24.929 | −26.168 |
| 9 | −24.628 | −26.012 |
| 10 | −24.391 | −25.921 |

*Notes:* Tests are Schwarz-loss (SL), Hannan and Quinn's $\Phi$ measure on lag length of a levels vector autoregression:

$$SL = \log(|\Sigma| + (6k)(\log T))/T$$
$$\Phi = \log(|\Sigma| + (2.01)(6k)\log(\log T))/T$$

where $\Sigma$ is the error covariance matrix estimated with $k$ regressors in each equation, $T$ is the total number of observations on each series, the symbol " | | " denotes the determinant operator, and log is the natural logarithm.

**Table 9.3**  Dickey–Fuller and Augmented Dickey–Fuller tests and associated residual tests on the null hypothesis of non-stationarity of innovations ($\hat{e}$) in peak electricity prices from a levels VAR on six western US spot markets, spring–summer and fall–winter

| Market | DF | Q(36) | p-Value | ADF | Number of lags | Q(36) | p-Value |
|--------|-----|-------|---------|------|------|-------|---------|
| | | | Spring–summer | | | | |
| COB | −15.84 | 107.12 | 0.00 | −9.98 | 5 | 42.89 | 0.20 |
| FC | −16.23 | 148.78 | 0.00 | −9.35 | 5 | 55.44 | 0.02 |
| MC | −15.83 | 104.30 | 0.00 | −9.95 | 5 | 45.07 | 0.14 |
| PV | −17.77 | 123.92 | 0.00 | −8.47 | 5 | 51.35 | 0.05 |
| SP | −16.57 | 127.08 | 0.00 | −8.94 | 5 | 48.92 | 0.07 |
| NP | −16.30 | 112.34 | 0.00 | −9.41 | 5 | 42.33 | 0.21 |
| | | | Fall–winter | | | | |
| COB | −18.74 | 21.02 | 0.98 | −18.74 | 0 | 21.02 | 0.98 |
| FC | −19.21 | 24.00 | 0.94 | −19.21 | 0 | 24.00 | 0.94 |
| MC | −18.68 | 21.20 | 0.98 | −18.68 | 0 | 21.20 | 0.98 |
| PV | −19.02 | 37.53 | 0.40 | −19.02 | 0 | 37.53 | 0.40 |
| SP | −19.14 | 31.46 | 0.68 | −19.14 | 0 | 31.46 | 0.68 |
| NP | −20.26 | 23.20 | 0.95 | −20.26 | 0 | 23.20 | 0.95 |

*Notes:* The column under the heading "DF" refers to the Dickey–Fuller test on the null hypothesis that the price data from the market listed in the far left-hand-most column are non-stationary in levels (non-differenced data). The test for each series of price innovation data is based on an ordinary least squares regression of the first differences of prices from each market on a constant and one lag of the levels of prices (non-differenced prices). The $t$-statistic is associated with the estimated coefficient on the lagged levels variable from this regression. Under the null hypothesis, the statistic is distributed in a non-standard $t$. Critical values are given in Fuller (1976). The 5% critical value is $-3.35$. We reject the null for observed $t$ values less than this critical value. The associated Q-statistic is the Ljung–Box statistic on the estimated residuals from the above-described regression. Under the null hypothesis of white noise residuals, Q is distributed chi-squared with 36 degrees of freedom. The $p$-value associated with this Q statistic is given in the column immediately to the left of the Q-statistic. The null hypothesis is rejected for large values of Q or for low $p$-values (i.e. $p$-values less than 0.05).

The column under the heading "ADF" refers to the Augmented Dickey–Fuller test associated with the null hypothesis that the price data from the market listed in the far left-hand-most column are non-stationary in levels (same null as above). Here, the test is of the same form as that described above, except that $k$ lags of the dependent variable are added to the right-hand side of the DF regression. Here, the value for $k$ is determined by minimizing the Schwarz-loss metric on values of $k$ ranging from 1 to 10. The ADF regression was run with lags of the dependent variable ranging from one lag to ten lags. The Schwarz-loss metric was minimized at the value given in the column headed by the label "$k$". Again, the critical value of the t-statistic is $-3.35$ and we reject for values of the calculated statistic less than this critical value. Finally, as above, the Q-statistic is the Ljung–Box statistic on the estimated residuals from the ADF regression. Under the null hypothesis of white noise residuals, Q is distributed chi-squared with 36 degrees of freedom. The $p$-value associated with this Q statistic is given in the column immediately to the left of the Q-statistic.

equation, while it is significant only for the northern markets (COB, MC and NP) in the fall–winter equation. PV is significant in the PV, SP and NP markets during spring–summer, but is significant only in the PV equation during fall–winter.

The estimated coefficients associated with aggregate heating degree-days and cooling degree-days are given in Table 9.5. Heating degree-days contribute negatively to price in the spring–summer data in all markets except MC. However, none of these heating degree-days coefficients is significantly different from zero at the 5% level. On the other hand, cooling degree-days contribute positively and significantly (at a 5% level) to price in every market in the spring–summer data. The strongest effect on price is in the FC market (0.091), whereas the weakest effect is in the PV market (0.056). In the fall–winter data, heating degree-days

**Table 9.4**  $p$-Values on coefficients on lagged prices on each of six electricity spot markets in the vector autoregressive representation of daily peak market price by season

| Market | $COB_{t-1}$ | $FC_{t-1}$ | $MC_{t-1}$ | $PV_{t-1}$ | $SP_{t-1}$ | $NP_{t-1}$ |
|--------|------|------|------|------|------|------|
| | | | Spring–summer | | | |
| $COB_t$ | 0.08 | 0.01* | 0.00* | 0.09 | 0.70 | 0.03* |
| $FC_t$ | 0.99 | 0.25 | 0.02* | 0.12 | 0.30 | 0.54 |
| $MC_t$ | 0.08 | 0.00* | 0.00* | 0.06 | 0.72 | 0.09 |
| $PV_t$ | 0.80 | 0.01* | 0.02* | 0.00* | 0.24 | 0.97 |
| $SP_t$ | 0.66 | 0.04* | 0.02* | 0.00* | 0.02* | 0.90 |
| $NP_t$ | 0.39 | 0.01* | 0.01* | 0.00* | 0.16 | 0.00* |
| | | | Fall–winter | | | |
| $COB_t$ | 0.15 | 0.38 | 0.00* | 0.75 | 0.78 | 0.14 |
| $FC_t$ | 0.93 | 0.02* | 0.53 | 0.69 | 0.01* | 0.76 |
| $MC_t$ | 0.01* | 0.37 | 0.00* | 0.88 | 0.65 | 0.22 |
| $PV_t$ | 0.75 | 0.70 | 0.22 | 0.00* | 0.90 | 0.93 |
| $SP_t$ | 0.61 | 0.94 | 0.10 | 0.97 | 0.00* | 0.92 |
| $NP_t$ | 0.33 | 0.69 | 0.03* | 0.89 | 0.88 | 0.00* |

*Notes:* Table entries are $p$-values associated with the null hypothesis that the coefficient associated with the variable in the column heading in the equation associated with the variable in the row label is equal to zero. An asterisk (*) indicates rejection of the null hypothesis at a 5% significance level.

**Table 9.5**  Estimated coefficients on aggregate heating degree-days and cooling degree-days in each VAR market equation by season

| Market | Heating degree-days | | Cooling degree-days | |
|--------|--------------|-------------|--------------|-------------|
| | Spring–summer | Fall–winter | Spring–summer | Fall–winter |
| COB | −0.001 | 0.007 | 0.065* | 0.057 |
| | (0.006) | (0.004) | (0.024) | (0.037) |
| FC | −0.005 | 0.008* | 0.091* | 0.046 |
| | (0.006) | (0.003) | (0.024) | (0.032) |
| MC | 0.001 | 0.007* | 0.068* | 0.052 |
| | (0.006) | (0.003) | (0.025) | (0.038) |
| PV | −0.008 | 0.012* | 0.056* | 0.070 |
| | (0.006) | (0.003) | (0.026) | (0.036) |
| SP | −0.008 | 0.011* | 0.066* | 0.046 |
| | (0.006) | (0.003) | (0.024) | (0.031) |
| NP | −0.005 | 0.007* | 0.068 | 0.053 |
| | (0.006) | (0.003) | (0.024) | (0.034) |

*Notes:* Estimated standard errors are in parentheses. An asterisk (*) indicates significance at the 5% level.

contribute positively to price in all markets with the strongest effects being in PV (0.012) and SP (0.011). Using a 5% significance level, these effects are different from zero for all markets, except COB. Cooling degree-days in the fall–winter data show positive effects on price in every market, although not significantly different from zero at the 5% level.

Estimated correlation matrix on contemporaneous time innovations from each market for spring–summer VAR is:

$$
corr\,(\hat{e}_{tSS}) =
\begin{bmatrix}
1.0 & & & & & \\
0.88 & 1.0 & & & & \\
0.96 & 0.85 & 1.0 & & & \\
0.83 & 0.86 & 0.80 & 1.0 & & \\
0.86 & 0.88 & 0.83 & 0.91 & 1.0 & \\
0.90 & 0.85 & 0.87 & 0.86 & 0.94 & 1.0
\end{bmatrix}
\tag{9.6}
$$

where $\hat{e}_{tSS}$ denotes innovations in the spring–summer VAR and the listing order of the lower triangular elements of innovations from each market is COB, FC, MC, PV, SP and NP. Innovations from the COB market show strongest correlations with contemporaneous innovations from the MC market (0.96) and weakest correlations with innovations from the PV market (0.83). The FC market innovations show strongest correlation with innovations in the SP market (0.88) and weakest correlations with innovations from NP and MC (0.85). MC shows the strongest correlations with innovations from COB (0.96) and weakest with innovations from PV (0.80). Innovations from PV show the strongest correlation with innovations from SP (0.91) and weakest with innovations from MC (0.80). Innovations from the SP market show the strongest correlations with innovations from NP (0.93) and weakest correlations with innovations from MC (0.83). Finally, innovations from the NP market show the strongest correlation with innovations from SP (0.93) and weakest correlations with innovations from FC (0.85).

For the fall–winter VAR, the contemporaneous time error correlation matrix is:

$$
corr\,(\hat{e}_{tFW}) =
\begin{bmatrix}
1.0 & & & & & \\
0.77 & 1.0 & & & & \\
0.97 & 0.78 & 1.0 & & & \\
0.72 & 0.85 & 0.73 & 1.0 & & \\
0.74 & 0.85 & 0.75 & 0.92 & 1.0 & \\
0.78 & 0.78 & 0.77 & 0.84 & 0.89 & 1.0
\end{bmatrix}
\tag{9.7}
$$

where $\hat{e}_{tFW}$ denotes innovations and the lower triangular elements are listed in order COB, FC, MC, PV, SP and NP. The correlations in equation (9.7) are generally smaller (although not for all markets) than the correlations given in equation (9.6). There are just two correlations in equation (9.7), which exceed their corresponding elements in equation (9.6), albeit by a very small amount. The correlation between COB and MC in the fall–winter (0.97) exceeds its corresponding value in the spring–summer (0.96). Similarly, the correlation between PV and SP (0.92) exceeds its corresponding spring–summer entry (0.91). In all other cases, the fall–winter correlations are smaller than their corresponding spring–summer correlations.

Correlations from equations (9.6) and (9.7) are inputs for the directed graph analysis of the innovations from our spring–summer and fall–winter VARs. Based on vanishing correlations and partial correlation patterns derived from these two matrices, causal flow between contemporaneous innovations from each of these six markets is assigned. TETRAD II (Scheines et al., 1994) is used to obtain the causal flows (Figure 9.3). Results are provided for each VAR (spring–summer and fall–winter) at three different levels of significance: 1%, 5% and 10%. Spirtes et al. (1993) recommend that one considers the graphical representation found using TETRAD II under several levels of significance. Further, they recommend applying an inverse

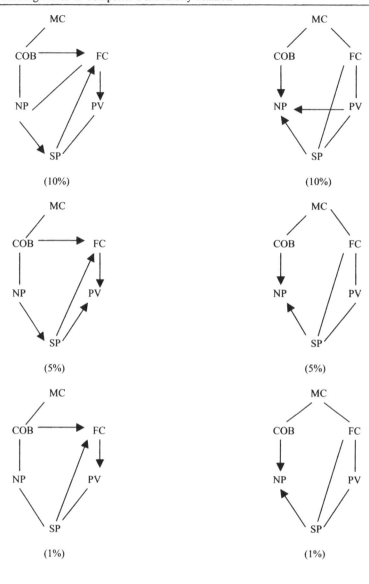

Spring–Summer 1999–2001                    Fall–Winter 1999–2001

**Figure 9.3**   Graphical patterns at 1%, 5% and 10% significance level on peak electricity price innovations from six western US spot markets

relation between significance level used and the number of observations used to calculate correlations and partial correlations. Because each VAR is estimated using 310 observations, a modestly large number, the 5% panel is used in subsequent analysis. The term "Graphical Patterns" is used in Figure 9.3, because several edges are not directed. These edges indicate possible information flow between their corresponding endpoints, however, the direction of flow is not clear.

The 5% panel of Figure 9.3 shows a pattern with the PV market acting as an information "sink" in the spring–summer period. Arrows are directed into the PV node from FC and SP, but no arrows flow out. PV's sink-like status does not hold in the 1% and 10% panels, because the edge between PV and SP is undirected in these alternative panels. The reason the edges differ between the various levels of significance is the addition or subtraction of edges between the markets. The SP market is a "link" in the causal chain running from NP to FC onto PV, via SP. Similarly, FC serves as an information link between COB and PV.

During the fall–winter period, NP is an information sink, because it receives information from SP and COB, passing nothing on to other markets (Figure 9.3). All other edges in Figure 9.3 are undirected, indicating interaction between COB and MC, MC and FC, FC and PV, and PV and SP, but no definitive direction of causal information flow.

Dynamic behavior of peak power prices using innovation accounting techniques is examined for each VAR model using the direction of causal flows defined in Figure 9.3. Many researchers have modeled the information flow between markets in contemporaneous time by performing a Choleski factorization of the innovation covariance matrix, $\Gamma = H'H$, where $\Gamma$ is the positive definite innovation covariance matrix. They then pre-multiplied the contemporaneous price vector and each autoregressive coefficient matrix by the inverse of $H$ to obtain a transformed VAR model with orthogonal residuals (innovations). This transformation of the VAR, while solving the problem of contemporaneous causality, has not been universally applauded, because the ordering of variables in the Choleski factorization is arbitrary. Researchers had little prior beliefs on which innovation came first in contemporaneous time (Cooley and LeRoy, 1985). Work by Bernanke (1986) and others has found other recursive orderings to address the arbitrariness of the Choleski form, while letting contemporaneous correlation affect the dynamic model. Another way to "deal" with contemporaneous correlation would be to ignore it. The graphical patterns given in Figure 9.3 allow the Bernanke procedure for dealing with contemporaneous correlation to be used, without having to resort to subjective or non-data-based methods.

Forecasting to horizon $t + h$ ($h$ steps ahead) at time $t$, the error between what the VAR model predicts, based on information known up to period $t$, and what actually happens, is a moving average (MA) process of order $h - 1$ (Granger and Newbold, 1986). The coefficients associated with the moving average process are found by inverting the vector autoregression, writing it as an infinite sum of weighted past innovations. The standard error of the forecast at horizon $k$ can be decomposed into shocks in each variable of the VAR. These forecast error decompositions are given for each VAR (spring–summer and fall–winter) in Tables 9.6 and 9.7 using the causal graphs in Figure 9.3. Undirected edges are ignored. Alternative dynamic relationships assuming the undirected edges are directed one way or the other in Figure 9.3 were studied. These alternative dynamic patterns are similar, but not identical, to the relationships reported here.

For spring–summer, in the long run (arbitrarily selected to be 15 days ahead), the MC market is clearly the dominant market. Over 55% (note from any panel in Table 9.6 at horizon 15, the percentage of the forecast uncertainty explained by innovations in MC is greater than 55%) of the forecast uncertainty at the 15-day horizon is explained by previous shocks in the MC price (Table 9.6). The other mover in long-run time is COB, as it explains over 20% of the uncertainty in all markets at the 15-day horizon.

In contemporaneous time (horizon zero), the sink-like behavior of price in the PV market is evident. PV peak electricity prices in contemporaneous time are explained predominately by innovations in the NP market. Innovations in the SP market price explain slightly over 9% of the variation in the PV price in contemporaneous time. The influence of price innovations from

**Table 9.6**　Forecast error decompositions from the VAR on daily peak electricity prices from six western US spot markets, spring–summer

| Step ahead | Standard error | Orthogonalized market innovations | | | | | |
|---|---|---|---|---|---|---|---|
| | | COB | FC | MC | PV | SP | NP |
| | | COB | | | | | |
| 0 | 0.24 | 100.00 | 0.00 | 0.00 | 0.00 | 0.00 | 0.00 |
| 1 | 0.27 | 79.68 | 1.12 | 13.54 | 0.27 | 0.10 | 5.28 |
| 2 | 0.33 | 56.18 | 1.99 | 34.16 | 1.02 | 0.36 | 6.28 |
| 15 | 0.90 | 28.92 | 1.19 | 64.66 | 3.52 | 0.52 | 1.18 |
| | | FC | | | | | |
| 0 | 0.18 | 35.77 | 27.40 | 0.00 | 0.00 | 4.47 | 32.36 |
| 1 | 0.22 | 24.73 | 18.94 | 9.73 | 0.31 | 4.58 | 41.71 |
| 2 | 0.27 | 18.51 | 13.47 | 27.49 | 1.18 | 3.41 | 35.93 |
| 15 | 0.74 | 23.93 | 2.57 | 63.46 | 3.93 | 0.68 | 5.40 |
| | | MC | | | | | |
| 0 | 0.24 | 0.00 | 0.00 | 100.00 | 0.00 | 0.00 | 0.00 |
| 1 | 0.40 | 8.99 | 0.59 | 88.82 | 0.16 | 0.04 | 1.40 |
| 2 | 0.54 | 14.13 | 0.86 | 83.16 | 0.44 | 0.12 | 1.29 |
| 15 | 1.17 | 24.88 | 0.78 | 71.46 | 2.21 | 0.30 | 0.35 |
| | | PV | | | | | |
| 0 | 0.23 | 1.83 | 1.40 | 0.00 | 19.75 | 9.33 | 67.66 |
| 1 | 0.29 | 1.19 | 0.95 | 6.73 | 25.67 | 7.88 | 57.55 |
| 2 | 0.35 | 1.99 | 1.04 | 19.09 | 27.00 | 5.87 | 45.00 |
| 15 | 0.87 | 20.13 | 0.88 | 57.54 | 12.49 | 1.08 | 7.88 |
| | | SP | | | | | |
| 0 | 0.24 | 0.00 | 0.00 | 0.00 | 0.00 | 12.13 | 87.87 |
| 1 | 0.28 | 0.00 | 0.38 | 6.99 | 0.92 | 11.29 | 80.41 |
| 2 | 0.32 | 1.24 | 0.89 | 20.92 | 2.30 | 8.94 | 65.71 |
| 15 | 0.75 | 20.59 | 0.94 | 59.67 | 4.72 | 1.78 | 12.27 |
| | | NP | | | | | |
| 0 | 0.23 | 0.00 | 0.00 | 0.00 | 0.00 | 0.00 | 100.00 |
| 1 | 0.27 | 0.31 | 0.66 | 7.90 | 1.02 | 0.21 | 89.89 |
| 2 | 0.31 | 0.89 | 1.42 | 23.88 | 2.51 | 0.51 | 70.79 |
| 15 | 0.80 | 20.67 | 1.12 | 62.03 | 4.63 | 0.56 | 10.98 |

*Notes:* Decompositions at each step are given for a "Bernanke" factorization of contemporaneous innovation covariance, following the flow of information summarized in Figure 9.3. The decompositions sum to 100% in any row within rounding error.

NP and SP on the PV price dampens with the influence of the MC price increasing over time, such that after 15 days the former two markets have less than a 10% combined contribution to price uncertainty in the PV market. MC explains over 57% of the uncertainty in the PV price at the long-run horizon.

For the spring–summer data, innovations from MC contribute very little or nothing to the uncertainty in price from all non-MC markets in the short run (Table 9.6). To understand short-term price variation in FC, PV, NP and SP, it is essential to understand innovations in the NP market. However, in the longer term (after two days and certainly after 15 days), price uncertainty during the spring–summer season is explained by innovations in the MC market. This apparently reflects the short-run inability of western markets to move enough power around quickly (within the day or up to two days ahead) to offset regional price differentials. However, within two weeks, such movements appear to be possible and the markets adjust. It

**Table 9.7**   Forecast error decompositions from the VAR on daily peak electricity prices from six western US spot markets, fall–winter

| Step ahead | Standard error | Orthogonalized market innovations | | | | | |
| --- | --- | --- | --- | --- | --- | --- | --- |
| | | COB | FC | MC | PV | SP | NP |
| | | | COB | | | | |
| 0 | 0.22 | 100.00 | 0.00 | 0.00 | 0.00 | 0.00 | 0.00 |
| 1 | 0.34 | 47.85 | 0.44 | 50.48 | 0.20 | 0.83 | 0.20 |
| 2 | 0.46 | 34.37 | 0.52 | 63.67 | 0.15 | 1.02 | 0.27 |
| 15 | 0.78 | 25.58 | 0.59 | 72.27 | 0.06 | 1.13 | 0.37 |
| | | | FC | | | | |
| 0 | 0.20 | 0.00 | 100.00 | 0.00 | 0.00 | 0.00 | 0.00 |
| 1 | 0.21 | 0.02 | 85.39 | 1.82 | 0.24 | 12.52 | 0.01 |
| 2 | 0.24 | 1.56 | 66.58 | 13.67 | 0.32 | 17.85 | 0.01 |
| 15 | 0.48 | 14.93 | 17.45 | 59.52 | 0.11 | 7.84 | 0.16 |
| | | | MC | | | | |
| 0 | 0.23 | 0.00 | 0.00 | 100.00 | 0.00 | 0.00 | 0.00 |
| 1 | 0.42 | 11.68 | 0.32 | 87.19 | 0.05 | 0.67 | 0.10 |
| 2 | 0.55 | 15.27 | 0.41 | 83.27 | 0.04 | 0.88 | 0.15 |
| 15 | 0.88 | 18.86 | 0.53 | 79.23 | 0.02 | 1.08 | 0.28 |
| | | | PV | | | | |
| 0 | 0.21 | 0.00 | 0.00 | 0.00 | 100.00 | 0.00 | 0.00 |
| 1 | 0.25 | 0.48 | 0.15 | 6.56 | 92.76 | 0.05 | 0.00 |
| 2 | 0.28 | 2.82 | 0.13 | 19.74 | 76.90 | 0.40 | 0.01 |
| 15 | 0.47 | 14.11 | 0.32 | 57.46 | 26.59 | 1.32 | 0.19 |
| | | | SP | | | | |
| 0 | 0.19 | 0.00 | 0.00 | 0.00 | 0.00 | 100.00 | 0.00 |
| 1 | 0.23 | 1.22 | 0.00 | 10.33 | 0.00 | 88.43 | 0.00 |
| 2 | 0.27 | 4.65 | 0.02 | 26.35 | 0.00 | 68.96 | 0.00 |
| 15 | 0.49 | 15.37 | 0.23 | 60.47 | 0.00 | 23.66 | 0.16 |
| | | | NP | | | | |
| 0 | 0.16 | 12.21 | 0.00 | 0.00 | 2.69 | 55.39 | 29.72 |
| 1 | 0.21 | 7.32 | 0.19 | 26.08 | 1.82 | 41.48 | 23.10 |
| 2 | 0.28 | 8.92 | 0.39 | 48.30 | 1.08 | 26.39 | 14.92 |
| 15 | 0.56 | 16.86 | 0.62 | 70.23 | 0.26 | 7.68 | 4.35 |

*Notes:* Decompositions at each step are given for a "Bernanke" factorization of contemporaneous innovation covariance, following the flow of information summarized in Figure 9.3. The decompositions sum to 100% in any row within rounding error.

appears all other markets eventually move to the MC market. This may reflect MC's status as a low cost producer. Two issues help contribute to the inability to move power. First, Bonneville Power Association has a more complicated point-to-point transmission structure than the rest of the Western System Coordinating Council. Second, California electricity transmission has one of the premier power bottlenecks in the USA, namely the electron pileup on Path 15 (Stouffer, 2001).

A similar set of panels for each market price from the fall–winter VAR is provided in Table 9.7. Again, the MC market price is the standard, accounting for over 55% of the price variation in all other markets at the 15-day horizon. In contemporaneous time, the fall–winter data are for the most part exogenous, as each market explains its own contemporaneous time uncertainty. The one exception to this last point is NP, where over 55% of the movement in contemporaneous time uncertainty is explained by innovations in the SP price. An additional

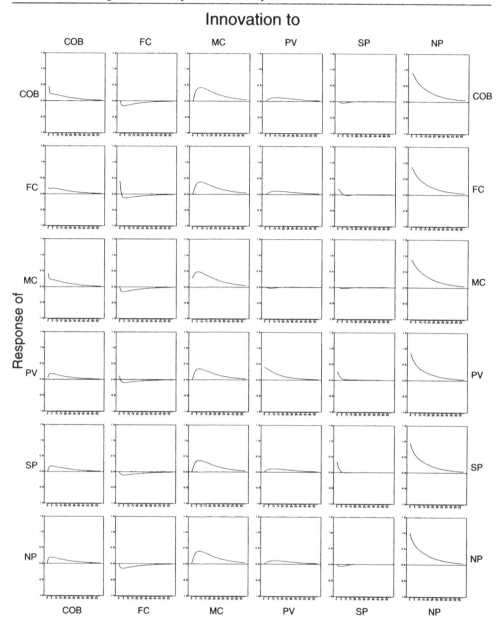

**Figure 9.4**   Normalized impulse response functions to one-time-only shocks in spring–summer peak prices from six western US spot markets

12% of the variation in the NP price is accounted for by contemporaneous time innovations in the COB market.

Impulse response functions summarizing the dynamic response of each price series to a one-time-only shock in every series for the spring–summer and fall–winter VARs are given in Figures 9.4 and 9.5. Again, the Bernanke ordering of contemporaneous correlation is used

## Innovation to

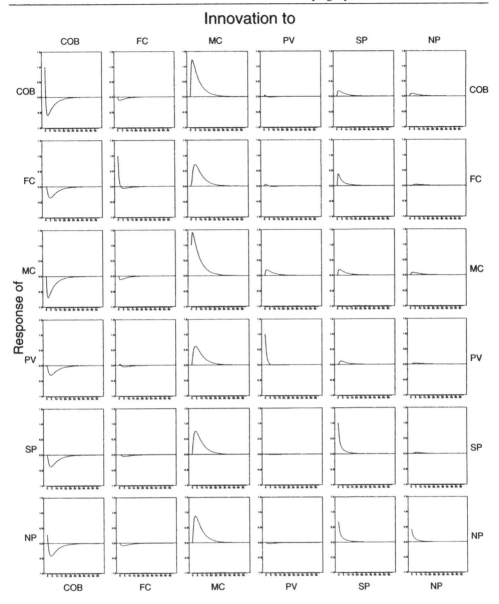

**Figure 9.5** Normalized impulse response functions on one-time-only shocks in fall–winter peak prices from six western US spot markets

following the directed edges in Figure 9.3. All responses from each VAR are provided in each figure to allow the reader to see the relative effects of each market. The horizontal axis on each subgraph is the horizon or number of days following the shock, up to 60 days. The vertical axis is the standardized response to the one-time shock in the market listed at the top of each column of graphs. This normalization is with respect to the historical standard deviation of innovations in the market listed on each row. The normalization keeps all responses within the $[-1, +1.5]$ range, allowing for comparisons of relative responses across markets.

The dynamic importance of a shock in the NP and the MC markets during the spring–summer period is shown in Figure 9.4. Such shocks are transferred as a positive impulse to all other markets, damping to zero after several weeks. However, the response of all markets to an innovation in the NP market is immediate and dampens to zero thereafter; whereas a shock in the MC price takes a few days to be felt in all other markets, thereafter it too dampens to zero. No other market shows persistently strong influences on other markets; although an innovation in the COB price does show some lasting positive influence across other markets. Interesting is the response of all markets to an innovation in the price in the FC market. Here, the dominant effect is a negative response for several days following the jump in FC price. Such responses suggest the FC market is making up for very short-run imbalances in other markets, which are quickly made up in other markets in the following few days. Innovations in the price at the PV market are transferred to prices in other markets, as small positive and damping effects – except for the MC market, were PV appears to have little effect.

The responses of each market to one-time-only innovations in fall–winter price from each market are given in Figure 9.5. Again, the responses to MC are the most notable features in this set of responses. An innovation in MC has a relatively strong, very short-run effect on each market in the fall–winter VAR, relative to its effect on the same markets in the spring–summer VAR (compare the column MC between Figures 9.4 and 9.5). The negative delayed responses of each market to a shock in the COB market price is not unlike that observed in Figure 9.4 for responses to shocks in the FC market price. FC, PV and NP show no particularly strong effects on any other market price in the fall–winter period. SP shows some short-run positive effect on price in all markets, although this effect dampens to zero quickly.

## 9.5   DISCUSSION

The results presented show the western trading region is highly integrated, which is expected because of the highly liquid nature of the market. The importance of several markets is also established, along with seasonal differences. In contemporaneous time, directed graphs show the importance of the California market; SP and NP markets appear to be a driving force for electricity prices. This is especially true in the spring–summer period. The SP market includes the Los Angeles area, the largest metropolitan area in the west. Many directional flows (edges) between the markets are undirected, however, which indicates interaction between the markets, but no definitive direction of causal information flow. As noted by several previous studies (e.g. Bailey, 1998), narrow markets can arise because of more localized supply and demand conditions. Local weather conditions, plant outages and transmission constraints contribute to these narrower markets. Narrower markets may help explain why some flows are undirected, as the information flow would vary based on the cause of the narrower markets.

Similar to Bailey (1998), we find contemporaneous correlations between prices are smaller in the fall–winter period than they are in the spring–summer period. A decrease in demand for electricity during the fall–winter period is the most likely reason for the difference in correlations. This decrease also contributes to the changes in importance of the California market. It is interesting to note the importance of the California market in the integration of the western trading region, even though California imports only approximately 18% of its electricity over the year (California Energy Commission, 2001a). This 18%, however, is not a trivial amount. Approximately 49 486 gWh of electricity are imported into California, in which 52% comes from the Pacific Northwest, 40% from the Southwest, and the remaining 8% from Mexico (California Energy Commission, 2001a). Both the directed edges and larger error correlations occur between spot markets, which are adjacent in physical terms.

Forecast error variances decomposition and impulse response functions allow for analysis of information flows over time in contrast to the directed graph analysis which is only for contemporaneous time. Again, differences between the spring–summer and fall–winter periods are found. For short time frames (periods of two days or less), the California market remains an important driver of spring–summer prices. For all markets except COB and MC, NP in the largest spring–summer period accounts for the largest component of forecast error variance at the short time frames. COB and MC are relatively exogenous at these time frames, with their own decomposition explaining most of its forecast error decomposition. Such exogeneity may be expected because MC is a winter peaking market and the close proximity of COB to MC. In the summer, demand is low and these markets have excess capacity depending on the snowpack year. During the fall–winter period, all markets are relatively exogenous (one exception may be COB) in the short run. At longer time frames, for both periods, it is clear the major market is MC. MC's influence appears to be even stronger in the fall–winter than the spring–summer period. The increase in influence in the fall–winter over the spring–summer period may be caused by demand and supply conditions. In the fall–winter period, MC is demand driven with high winter demand, but in the spring–summer period, MC is supply driven with low demand and snowpack runoff giving plentiful cheap hydropower.

During the data period of 2000 and 2001, limited snowpack may also have contributed to the demand driven fall–winter market. COB is the only other market at the longer time frame, which exerts a large influence on spring–summer prices. This influence, however, may be related to transmission of electricity from the Pacific Northwest and not COB itself. During the fall–winter period, MC remains the dominant market in the long run with COB's influence still being strong, but generally smaller than in the spring–summer. Several markets, FC, PV and SP, have some influence on their own price. The dominance of MC in the long run may be explained by this area being a low cost producer of electricity through hydropower. Further, coupling the dominance of the MC area with the recent droughts in the Pacific Northwest helps explain some of the high electricity prices experienced in recent years. Pira Energy Group (2000a,b, 2001) also suggests such a relationship.

Impulse response functions reinforce the discussion to this point. The importance of the California market is illustrated by the quick reaction of all spot market prices to a shock in the NP market in the spring–summer period. Responses to shocks to MC prices take several periods to be felt in the other markets, but all markets respond positively to shocks in this market.

Results suggest short-run price discovery varies between periods during this year. Electricity generally flows south during the summer months and north during the winter. Such changes in demand and supply conditions contribute to the differences in short-run price discovery dynamics. In the longer run, price dynamics appear to be similar between periods, with an overwhelming reliance on the MC spot market. Such dynamics in price discovery or communication have not been reported by previous studies.

Results associated with cooling and heating degree-days are as expected. Aggregate cooling degree-days are significant in the spring–summer and contribute positively to electricity prices. Any cooler days represented by heating degree-days in the spring–summer period do not significantly increase electricity prices. Similarly, aggregate heating degree-days are significant and contribute positively to electricity prices in the fall–winter. Warmer days represented by cooling degree-days in the fall–winter period do not significantly increase electricity prices.

Refinements would be to include northern and southern degree-days or individual degree-days for relevant cities. Although beyond the scope of this study, results indicate such refinements may help explain electricity prices.

# REFERENCES

Allaz B. and Villa J.L. (1993). "Cournet Competition, Futures Markets, and Efficiency". *Journal of Economic Theory* **59**: 1–16.

Angelus A. (2001). "Electricity Price Forecasting in Deregulated Markets". *The Electricity Journal* **14**: 32–41.

Ashton L. (2001). "Watching Over the Water Coordinated Management of NCW Dams Makes Most of a Precious Commodity". Northwest Newspaper Hydropower Articles, Foundation for Water and Energy Education Website, http://www.fwee.org/news/getStory?story = 555, accessed October 2001.

Bailey E.M. (1998). "Electricity Markets in the Western United States". *The Electricity Journal* **11**: 51–60.

Bernanke B.S. (1986). "Alternative Explanations of the Money–Income Correlation". *Carnegie-Rochester Conference Series on Public Policy* **25**: 49–99.

California Energy Commission. (2001a). "California's Major Sources of Energy". http://www.energy. ca.gov/html/energysources.html, accessed October 2001.

California Energy Commission. (2001b). "Map of Power Plants in California". http://www.energy. ca.gov/maps/power_plants.html, accessed November 2001.

Cooley T. and LeRoy S. (1985). "Atheoretical Macroeconometrics: A Critique". *Journal of Monetary Economics* **16**: 283–308.

Deb R., Albert R., Hsue L.L. and Brown N. (2000). "How to Incorporate Volatility and Risk in Electricity Price Forecasting". *The Electricity Journal* **13**: 65–75.

DeVany A.S. and Walls W.D. (1999a). "Cointegration Analysis of Spot Electricity Prices: Insights on Transmission Efficiency in the Western U.S". *Energy Economics* **21**: 417–434.

DeVany A.S. and Walls W.D. (1999b). "Price Dynamics in a Network of Decentralized Power Markets". *Journal of Regulatory Economics* **15**: 123–140.

Doan T. (1995). *RATS: User's Manual* 4.0. Estima, Evanston, IL.

Engle R. and Granger C.W.J. (1987). "Cointegration and Error Correction: Representation, Estimation and Testing". *Econometrica* **55**: 251–276.

Fuller W. (1976). *Introduction to Statistical Time Series*. John Wiley and Sons, New York.

Geiger D. Verma T. and Pearl J. (1990). "Identifying Independencies in Bayesian Networks". *Networks* **20**: 507–534.

Granger C.W.J. and Newbold P. (1986). *Forecasting Economic Time Series*. Academic Press, New York.

Herguera I. (2000). "Bilateral Contracts and the Spot Market for Electricity: Some Observations on the British and the Nord Pool Experiences". *Utilities Policy* **9**: 73–80.

Joskow P.L. (1997). "Restructuring, Competition and Regulatory Reform in the U.S. Electricity Sector". *Journal of Economic Perspectives* **11**: 119–138.

Microsoft. (2001). *Microsoft Encarta® Online Encyclopedia 2001*. Degree-day, http://encarta.msn.com, accessed October 2001.

Pearl J. (1995). "Causal Diagrams for Empirical Research". *Biometrika* **82**: 669–710.

Phillips P.C.B. and Perron P. (1988). "Testing for Unit Roots in Time Series Regression". *Biometrika* **75**: 335–346.

Pira Energy Group. (2001). "Market Recap: Borrowing Trouble". *Western Grid Market Forecast*, February 22, 2001.

Pira Energy Group. (2000a). "Market Recap: Sell it Forward". *Western Grid Market Forecast*, October 24, 2000.

Pira Energy Group. (2000b). "Market Recap: What Next". *Western Grid Market Forecast*, August 25, 2000.

Robinson T.A. (2000). "Electricity Pool Prices: A Case Study in Nonlinear Time Series Modelling". *Applied Economics* **32**: 527–532.

Samuelson P.A. (1965). "Proof that Properly Anticipated Prices Fluctuate Randomly". *Industrial Management Review* **6**: 41–49.

Scheines R., Spirtes P., Glymour C. and Meek C. (1994). *TETRAD II: User's Manual and Software.* Lawrence Erlbaum Associates, Inc., New Jersey.

Spirtes P., Glymour C. and Scheines R. (1993). *Causation, Prediction, and Search.* Springer-Verlag, New York.

Stouffer R. (2001). "DOE Offers 'Path' to Fix California Bottleneck". *Energy Insight*, October 25, 2001 (http://public.resdata.com.)

US Census Bureau. (2001). Table 3, Metropolitan areas ranked by population: 2000, http://www.census.gov/population/cen2000/phc-t3/tab03.pdf, accessed October 2001.

US Department of Energy. (1998). Energy Information Agency, *Monthly Energy Review*, DOE/EIA-0035(98/01).

US Department of Energy. (2001). Inventory of electric utility power plants: Table 20. Existing generating units at U.S. electric utilities by state, company, and plant, 1999, http://www.eia.doe.gov/cneal/electricity/ipp/html1/ippv1t20p11.html, accessed October 2001.

Wagman D. (2000). "Volatility May Rock California into 2002". *Energy Insight*, September 26, 2000 (http://public.resdata.com).

Weron R. (2000). "Energy Price Risk Management". *Physica A* **285**: 127–134.

Weron R. and Przybylowicz B. (2000). "Hurst Analysis of Electricity Price Dynamics". *Physica A* **283**: 462–468.

White M.W. (1996). "Power Struggles: Explaining Deregulatory Reforms in Electricity Markets". *Brookings Papers on Economic Activity, Microeconomics* **1996**: 201–250.

Woo C.K. Lloyd-Zannetti D. and Horowitz I. (1997). "Electricity Market Integration in the Pacific Northwest". *The Energy Journal* **18**: 75–101.

# 10
# Transmission of Prices and Volatility in the Australian Electricity Spot Markets

ANDREW C. WORTHINGTON AND HELEN HIGGS

*School of Economics and Finance, Queensland University of Technology,*
*Brisbane, QLD 4001, Australia*

## ABSRACT

This chapter examines the transmission of spot electricity prices and volatility among five Australian electricity markets. Both peak and off-peak prices are examined. A multivariate generalized autoregressive conditional heteroskedasticity model is used to identify the source and magnitude of price and volatility spillovers. The results indicate that the markets are not fully integrated and that lagged price information is not particularly useful for price forecasting. Shocks also appear to affect price volatility over time in these markets.

## 10.1 INTRODUCTION

The Australian National Electricity Market (NEM) encompasses generators in the eastern state electricity markets of Australia operating as a nationally interconnected grid. The member jurisdictions of the NEM thus include the three most populous states of New South Wales (including the Australian Capital Territory), Victoria and Queensland, along with South Australia. The sole non-state-based member is the Snowy Mountains Hydroelectric Scheme, which is a collaborative arrangement between the state governments of New South Wales and Victoria along with the Commonwealth (federal) government. The only eastern state not currently included in the NEM is the island of Tasmania, pending completion of an underwater interconnector that will link Tasmania's electricity supply industry with that of the mainland. Of the current member jurisdictions, the largest generation capacity is found in New South Wales, followed by Queensland, Victoria, the Snowy Mountains Hydroelectric Scheme and South Australia, while peak electricity demand is highest in New South Wales, followed by Victoria, Queensland and South Australia. With the exception of the Snowy Mountains Hydroelectric Scheme, generation is almost entirely based on fossil fuels, with coal in New South Wales, Victoria and Queensland and gas-fired plants in South Australia.

Historically, the very gradual move to an integrated national system was predated by substantial reforms on a state-by-state basis, including the unbundling of generation, transmission and distribution and the commercialization and privatization of the new electricity companies, along with the establishment of the wholesale electricity spot markets (Dickson and Warr, 2000). Each state in the NEM initially developed its own generation, transmission and distribution network and linked it to another state's system via interconnector transmission lines.

*Modelling Prices in Competitive Electricity Markets.* Edited by D.W. Bunn.
© 2004 John Wiley & Sons, Ltd. ISBN 0-470-84860-X.

These many reforms reached their culmination with the establishment of the NEM on 13 December 1998 when the five regional spot electricity markets were joined together. The main objective of the NEM is to provide a nationally integrated and efficient electricity market, with a view to limiting the market power of generators in the separate regional markets [for the analysis of market power in electricity markets see Brennan and Melanie (1998), Joskow and Kahn (2001), Wilson (2002), and Robinson and Baniak (2002)].

Within the NEM, power is transmitted between regions to meet energy demands that are higher than local generators can provide, or when the price of electricity in an adjoining region is low enough to displace the local supply. However, the scheduling of generators to meet demand across the interconnected power system is very much constrained by the physical transfer capacity of the interconnectors between the regions. The limitations of transfer capability within the centrally coordinated and regulated NEM are one of its defining features. Queensland has two interconnectors that together can import and export to and from NSW, NSW can export to and from the Snowy, and Victoria can import from the Snowy and South Australia and export to the Snowy and to South Australia. There is currently no direct connector between NSW and South Australia (though one is proposed) and Queensland is only directly connected to NSW. As a result, the NEM itself is not yet strongly integrated with interstate trade representing only some 7% of total generation. During periods of peak demand, the interconnectors become congested and the NEM separates into its regions, promoting price differences across markets and exacerbating reliability problems and the market power of regional utilities (IEA, 2001; ACCC, 2000; NEMMCO, 2002).

While the appropriate regulatory and commercial mechanisms do exist for the creation of an efficient national market, and these are expected to have an impact on the price of electricity in each NEM jurisdiction, it is argued that the complete integration of the separate regional electricity markets has not yet been realized. In particular, the limitation of the interconnectors between the member jurisdictions suggests that, for the most part, the regional spot markets are relatively isolated. Nevertheless, the Victorian electricity crisis of February 2000 is just one of several shocks in the Australian markets that suggests spot electricity pricing and volatility in each regional market are still potentially dependent on pricing conditions in other markets. Unfortunately, while some quantitative evidence exists internationally on the integration of regional electricity markets [see, for instance, De Vany and Walls (1999a,b)] and other dimensions concerning electricity markets [see Deng (2000)], none concerns Australian electricity spot markets. This is important because a fuller understanding of the pricing relationships between these markets will enable the benefits of interconnection to be assessed as a step towards the fuller integration of the regional electricity markets into a national electricity market.

At the same time, the manner in which volatility shocks in the regional electricity markets are transmitted across time arouses interest in modelling the dynamics of the price volatility process. This calls for the application of autoregressive conditional heteroskedasticity (ARCH) and generalized ARCH (GARCH) models that take into account the time-varying variances of time series data [suitable surveys of ARCH modelling may be found in Bollerslev *et al.* (1992), Bera and Higgins (1993), and Pagan (1996)]. More recently, the univariate GARCH model has been extended to the multivariate GARCH (MGARCH) case, with the recognition that MGARCH models are potentially useful developments regarding the parameterization of conditional cross-moments. Although the MGARCH methodology has been used extensively in modelling financial time series [see, for instance, Dunne (1999), Tai (2000), Brooks *et al.* (2002), and Tse and Tsui (2002)], to the authors' knowledge a detailed study of the application of MGARCH to electricity markets has not been undertaken. Since this approach captures the effect on current volatility of both own innovation and lagged volatility shocks emanating from within a given market and cross-innovation and volatility spillovers from interconnected markets it permits a greater understanding of volatility and volatility persistence in these interconnected markets. It is within the context of this limited empirical work that the present study is undertaken.

Accordingly, the purpose of this chapter is to investigate the price and price volatility interrelationships between the Australian regional electricity markets. This will permit a more thorough understanding of both pricing behaviour within each regional electricity market and the outcome of efforts to promote and sustain a nationally integrated market. The remainder of the chapter is divided into four areas. Section 10.2 explains the data employed in the analysis and presents some descriptive statistics. Section 10.3 discusses the methodology employed, while the results are dealt with in Section 10.4. The chapter ends with some brief concluding remarks in Section 10.5.

## 10.2  DATA AND SUMMARY STATISTICS

The data employed in the study are daily spot prices for electricity encompassing the period 1 July 1999 to 31 December 2002. The sample period is chosen on the basis that it represents the longest continuous series of data for all five regional markets since the establishment of the NEM. All price data is obtained from the National Electricity Market Management Company (NEMMCO) originally on a half-hourly basis representing 48 trading intervals in each 24-hour period (NEMMCO, 2002). Following Lucia and Schwartz (2001) a series of daily arithmetic means is drawn from the trading interval data. Although such treatment entails the loss of at least some "news" impounded in the more frequent trading interval data, daily averages play an important role in electricity markets, particularly in the case of financial contracts. For example, the electricity strips traded on the Sydney Futures Exchange (SFE, 2002) are settled against the arithmetic mean of half-hourly spot prices. Moreover, De Vany and Walls (1999a,b) and Robinson (2000) both employ daily spot prices in their respective analyses of the western United States and United Kingdom spot electricity markets.

In order to highlight the different volatility processes in the peak and off-peak period spot electricity markets, two separate daily average price series are constructed for each region. The peak period series is formed from the half-hourly trading intervals Monday to Friday from 7:00 to 21:00 hours resulting in 914 observations. The off-peak period encompasses the remaining Monday to Friday half-hourly trading intervals along with Saturday and Sunday. This results in a longer continuous series of 1280 observations. Categorization of peak and off-peak (or base load) period prices in this manner is identical to that employed in the NEM and as specified in the Sydney Futures Exchange Corporation Limited/d-cypha Limited (a subsidiary of Transpower Limited – owner and operator of the New Zealand national electricity grid) electricity strips for New South Wales, Victoria, Queensland and South Australia.

Table 10.1 presents a summary of descriptive statistics of the daily spot prices for the five electricity markets. Sample means, medians, maximums, minimums, standard deviations, skewness, kurtosis and the Jarque–Bera statistic and $p$-value are reported. Between 1 July 1999 and 31 December 2002, the highest peak spot prices are in South Australia (SA) and Queensland (QLD), averaging $63.42 and $56.58 per megawatt-hour, respectively. The lowest peak spot prices are in New South Wales (NSW) and the Snowy Mountains Hydroelectric Scheme (SNO), with $41.99 and $40.36, respectively. The standard deviations for peak period

**Table 10.1**   Summary statistics of peak and off-peak spot prices in five Australian regional electricity markets 1 July 1999–31 December 2002

|  | NSW | VIC | QLD | SA | SNO |
|---|---|---|---|---|---|
| Peak period |  |  |  |  |  |
| Mean | 41.9866 | 43.8923 | 56.5841 | 63.4214 | 40.3642 |
| Median | 30.9222 | 30.6250 | 35.6572 | 38.9643 | 30.6808 |
| Maximum | 585.3686 | 1658.6050 | 2204.4190 | 1880.7390 | 569.1528 |
| Minimum | 13.3610 | 4.2003 | 13.8045 | 11.3086 | 12.6614 |
| Std. deviation | 50.4305 | 75.8857 | 97.9587 | 129.2079 | 44.4959 |
| Skewness | 6.5483 | 13.3354 | 13.7997 | 9.3655 | 6.7485 |
| Kurtosis | 54.1520 | 245.0531 | 270.7784 | 103.3027 | 61.1328 |
| Coef. of variation | 1.2011 | 1.7289 | 1.7312 | 2.0373 | 1.1024 |
| Jarque–Bera | 106178.1000 | 2258382.0000 | 2759785.0000 | 396504.2000 | 135637.1000 |
| JB $p$-value | 0.0000 | 0.0000 | 0.0000 | 0.0000 | 0.0000 |
| ADF test | −8.3706 | −10.8765 | −9.9459 | −10.9847 | −8.9292 |
| Off-peak period |  |  |  |  |  |
| Mean | 26.9239 | 25.7555 | 28.3205 | 33.8922 | 26.2141 |
| Median | 23.4306 | 21.7500 | 22.2900 | 27.1358 | 23.4379 |
| Maximum | 311.4856 | 1133.9540 | 1175.5260 | 862.1242 | 311.5247 |
| Minimum | 9.6137 | 6.1663 | 12.3579 | 11.8490 | 9.2863 |
| Std. deviation | 20.7612 | 37.5718 | 41.5095 | 35.5941 | 16.0294 |
| Skewness | 8.6624 | 23.0816 | 18.3579 | 13.6055 | 8.6244 |
| Kurtosis | 98.4060 | 634.4951 | 466.9333 | 265.5773 | 120.3597 |
| Coef. of variation | 0.7711 | 1.4588 | 1.4657 | 1.0502 | 0.6115 |
| Jarque–Bera | 501464.6000 | 21382243.0000 | 11551050.0000 | 3716655.0000 | 750444.0000 |
| JB $p$-value | 0.0000 | 0.0000 | 0.0000 | 0.0000 | 0.0000 |
| ADF test | −6.5203 | −10.9899 | −9.8891 | −10.2742 | −7.2994 |

*Notes:* NSW – New South Wales QLD – Queensland SA – South Australia SNO – Snowy Mountains Hydroelectric Scheme VIC – Victoria; ADF – Augmented Dickey–Fuller test statistics; JB – Jarque–Bera test statistic. All prices are in Australian dollars per megawatt-hour. Standard deviations for skewness are 0.0810 and 0.0684 for peak and off-peak periods respectively. Standard deviations for kurtosis are 0.1620 and 0.1369 for peak and off-peak periods respectively. Hypothesis for ADF test is $H_0$: unit root (non-stationary), $H_1$: no unit root (stationary). The lag orders in the ADF equations are determined by the significance of the coefficient for the lagged terms. Only intercepts are included. ADF critical values for the peak and off-peak series are −3.4373 and −3.4352 at the 0.01 level −2.8645 and −2.8636 at the 0.05 level and −2.5684 and −2.5679 at the 0.10 level respectively.

spot electricity range from \$44.50 (SNO) to \$129.21 (SA). Of the five markets, NSW and SNO are the least volatile, while QLD and SA are the most volatile. The value of the coefficient of variation (standard deviation divided by the mean price) measures the degree of variation in spot price relative to the mean spot price. Relative to the average spot price, NSW and SNO are also less variable than SA, QLD and VIC.

In the off-peak period, the highest average price is SA with a mean of \$33.89 and the lowest is VIC with an average of \$25.76. In all instances, the mean off-peak price in each region is significantly less than the mean peak price. Off-peak prices are also less volatile, as measured by standard deviation, with QLD along with VIC being relatively more volatile, and NSW and SNO less so. The degree of variation of the off-peak spot price relative to the mean spot price, however, indicates that VIC and QLD have more variable off-peak prices than the remaining regions. In addition, average spot prices in NSW, VIC and SNO are generally lower in both the peak and off-peak periods, than in QLD and SA.

The distributional properties of both the peak and off-peak spot price series generally appear non-normal. All of the spot electricity price series are positively skewed, indicating the greater probability of large increases in prices than falls, ranging from 6.55 in peak period NSW to 23.08 in off-peak period VIC. The kurtosis, or degree of excess, in all of these electricity markets is also large, ranging from 54.15 in peak period NSW to 634.50 in off-peak period VIC, thereby indicating leptokurtic distributions. Since the sampling distribution of kurtosis is normal with mean 0 and standard deviation $\sqrt{24/T}$, and that of skewness is normal with mean 0 and standard deviation $\sqrt{6/T}$, where $T$ is the sample size, then all the estimates of skewness and kurtosis are overwhelmingly statistically significant at any conventional level.

The calculated Jarque–Bera statistics and corresponding $p$-values in Table 10.1 are also used to test the null hypothesis that the daily distribution of spot prices is normally distributed. All $p$-values are smaller than the 0.01 level of significance, suggesting the null hypothesis can be rejected. These daily spot prices are then not well approximated by the normal distribution. Lastly, each price series is tested for the presence of a unit root using the Augmented Dickey–Fuller (ADF) test. Contrary to previous empirical work by De Vany and Walls (1999a,b), which found that US spot electricity prices contain a unit root, this study concurs with Lucia and Schwartz (2001) that electricity prices are stationary in both the peak and off-peak periods across all five regions.

## 10.3  MULTIVARIATE GARCH MODEL

The following MGARCH model is developed to examine the joint processes relating to the daily peak and off-peak period spot prices for the five electricity markets from 1 July 1999 to 31 December 2002. Separate models are estimated for peak and off-peak period electricity prices. The following conditional expected price equation accommodates each market's own prices and the prices of other markets lagged one period:

$$P_t = \alpha + AP_{t-1} + \varepsilon_t \tag{10.1}$$

where $P_t$ is an $n \times 1$ vector of daily prices at time $t$ for each market and $\varepsilon_t \,|I_{t-1} \sim N(0, H_t)$. The $n \times 1$ vector of random errors, $\varepsilon_t$ is the innovation for each market at time $t$ with its corresponding $n \times n$ conditional variance–covariance matrix, $H_t$. The market information available at time $t - 1$ is represented by the information set $I_{t-1}$. The $n \times 1$ vector, $\alpha$, represents long-term drift coefficients. The elements $a_{ij}$ of the matrix $A$ are the degree of mean spillover effect across markets, or put differently, the current prices in market $i$ that can be used to predict future prices (one day in advance) in market $j$. The estimates of the elements of the matrix $A$ can provide measures of the significance of the own and cross-mean spillovers. This multivariate structure then enables the measurement of the effects of the innovations in the mean spot prices of one series on its own lagged prices and those of the lagged prices of other markets.

Bollerslev (1990) and Engle and Kroner (1995) present various MGARCH models with variations to the conditional variance–covariance matrix of equations. For the purposes of the following analysis, the BEKK (Baba, Engle, Kraft and Kroner) model is employed, whereby the variance–covariance matrix of equations depends on the squares and cross-products of innovation $\epsilon_t$ and volatility $H_t$ for each market lagged one period. One important feature of this specification is that it builds in sufficient generality, allowing the conditional variances and covariances of the electricity markets to influence each other and, at the same time, does not require the estimation of a large number of parameters (Karolyi, 1995). The model also ensures the condition of a positive semi-definite conditional variance–covariance matrix in the optimization process, and is a necessary condition for the estimated variances to be zero or positive. The BEKK parameterization for the MGARCH model is written as:

$$H_t = B'B + C'\epsilon_t \epsilon_{t-1} C + G' H_{t-1} G \tag{10.2}$$

where $b_{ij}$ are elements of an $n \times n$ symmetric matrix of constants $B$, the elements $c_{ij}$ of the symmetric $n \times n$ matrix $C$ measure the degree of innovation from market $i$ to market $j$, and the elements $g_{ij}$ of the symmetric $n \times n$ matrix $G$ indicate the volatility spillover between market $i$ and market $j$. This can be expressed for the bivariate case of the BEKK as:

$$\begin{bmatrix} H_{11t} & H_{12t} \\ H_{21t} & H_{22t} \end{bmatrix} = B'B + \begin{bmatrix} c_{11} & c_{12} \\ c_{21} & c_{22} \end{bmatrix}' \begin{bmatrix} \epsilon_{1t-1}^2 & \epsilon_{1t-1} \epsilon_{2t-1} \\ \epsilon_{2t-1} \epsilon_{1t-1} & \epsilon_{2t-1}^2 \end{bmatrix} \begin{bmatrix} c_{11} & c_{12} \\ c_{21} & c_{22} \end{bmatrix}$$

$$+ \begin{bmatrix} g_{11} & g_{12} \\ g_{21} & g_{22} \end{bmatrix}' \begin{bmatrix} H_{11t-1} & H_{12t-1} \\ H_{21t-1} & H_{22t-1} \end{bmatrix} \begin{bmatrix} g_{11} & g_{12} \\ g_{21} & g_{22} \end{bmatrix} \tag{10.3}$$

In this parameterization, the parameters $b_{ij}$, $c_{ij}$ and $g_{ij}$ cannot be interpreted on an individual basis: "instead, the functions of the parameters which form the intercept terms and the coefficients of the lagged variance, covariance, and error terms that appear in [(10.3)] are of interest" (Kearney and Patton, 2000, p. 36). With the assumption that the random errors are normally distributed, the log-likelihood function for the MGARCH model is:

$$L(\theta) = -\frac{Tn}{2} + \ln(2\pi) - \frac{1}{2} \sum_{t=1}^{T} (\ln |H_t| + \epsilon_t' |H_t^{-1}| \epsilon_t) \tag{10.4}$$

where $T$ is the number of observations, $n$ is the number of markets, $\theta$ is the vector of parameters to be estimated, and all other variables are as previously defined. The BHHH (Berndt, Hall, Hall and Hausman) algorithm is used to produce the maximum likelihood parameter estimates and their corresponding asymptotic standard errors. Overall, the proposed model has 25 parameters in the mean equations, excluding the five constant (intercept) parameters, and 15 intercept, 15 white noise and 15 volatility parameters in the estimation of the covariance process, giving 75 parameters in total.

Lastly, the Ljung–Box $Q$ statistic is used to test for independence of higher relationships as manifested in volatility clustering by the MGARCH model (Huang and Yang, 2000, p. 329). This statistic is given by:

$$Q = T(T+2) \sum_{j=1}^{p} (T-j)^{-1} r^2 (j) \tag{10.5}$$

where $r(j)$ is the sample autocorrelation at lag $j$ calculated from the noise terms and $T$ is the number of observations. $Q$ is asymptotically distributed as $\chi^2$ with $(p-k)$ degrees of freedom and $k$ is the number of explanatory variables. The test statistic in (10.5) is used to test the null hypothesis that the model is independent of the higher order volatility relationships.

## 10.4   EMPIRICAL RESULTS

The estimated coefficients and standard errors for the conditional mean price equations are presented in Table 10.2. The upper section of Table 10.2 contains the estimated coefficients for the peak period conditional mean price equations, while the lower section contains the estimated results for the off-peak period equations. Turning first to the peak period estimates, of the five electricity spot markets only VIC, QLD and SNO exhibit a significant own mean

**Table 10.2** Estimated coefficients for peak and off-peak conditional mean price equations

| | NSW ($i = 1$) | | VIC ($i = 2$) | | QLD ($i = 3$) | | SA ($i = 4$) | | SNO ($i = 5$) | |
|---|---|---|---|---|---|---|---|---|---|---|
| | Coefficient | Std error | Coefficient | Std error | Coefficient | Std error | Coefficient | Std error | Coefficient | Std error |
| **Peak period** | | | | | | | | | | |
| CONS | ***22.7000 | 6.5900 | ***29.7000 | 11.4000 | ***31.2700 | 12.3200 | ***45.8000 | 17.5000 | ***21.4000 | 5.1800 |
| $a_{i1}$ | −0.1350 | 0.2730 | −0.0032 | 0.1130 | −0.0666 | −0.0666 | −0.0043 | 0.0747 | 0.6800 | 0.2840 |
| $a_{i2}$ | −0.2660 | 1.3600 | *0.2420 | 0.1530 | −0.0104 | 0.1100 | −0.0386 | 0.0611 | 0.3400 | 1.4700 |
| $a_{i3}$ | 0.0902 | 0.7580 | −0.0561 | 0.1230 | ***0.3200 | 0.1130 | *0.0657 | 0.0435 | 0.0537 | 0.8130 |
| $a_{i4}$ | −0.1900 | 2.6500 | 0.0954 | 0.2740 | 0.0134 | 0.1640 | 0.0860 | 0.2010 | 0.1790 | 2.9000 |
| $a_{i5}$ | ***−0.2980 | 0.1030 | −0.0024 | 0.1000 | *−0.0637 | 0.0448 | −0.0008 | 0.0632 | ***−0.8320 | 0.1210 |
| **Off-peak period** | | | | | | | | | | |
| CONS | ***14.2784 | 6.0923 | 11.1588 | 13.5213 | ***15.0134 | 6.3558 | ***19.9024 | 10.5826 | ***12.6273 | 3.8003 |
| $a_{i1}$ | *0.3682 | 0.2508 | −0.0814 | 0.4045 | 0.0033 | 0.0965 | −0.0185 | 0.1507 | 0.2352 | 0.4919 |
| $a_{i2}$ | −0.1091 | 0.5181 | 0.3326 | 1.0529 | −0.0045 | 0.2878 | −0.0330 | 0.3684 | 0.4012 | 1.1411 |
| $a_{i3}$ | 0.2524 | 0.5347 | −0.0862 | 0.9557 | 0.1290 | 0.1695 | −0.0494 | 0.1837 | 0.2639 | 1.3176 |
| $a_{i4}$ | −0.0548 | 0.5361 | 0.1307 | 0.7869 | −0.0088 | 0.2035 | 0.1452 | 0.2639 | 0.2886 | 0.9979 |
| $a_{i5}$ | −0.0544 | 0.1078 | −0.0684 | 0.3113 | 0.0028 | 0.0777 | −0.0225 | 0.1232 | ***−0.6751 | 0.3141 |

*Notes:* NSW – New South Wales QLD – Queensland SA – South Australia SNO – Snowy Mountains Hydroelectric Scheme VIC – Victoria; CONS – constant; asterisks indicate significance at *0.10, *0.05 and ***0.01 levels, respectively.

spillover from their own lagged electricity price. In all cases, the mean spillovers are positive. For example, in VIC a $1.00 per megawatt-hour increase in its own spot price will Granger-cause an increase of $0.24 per megawatt-hour in its price over the next day. Likewise, a $1.00 per megawatt-hour increase in the SNO lagged spot price will Granger-cause a $0.83 increase the next day, while a $1.00 per megawatt-hour increase in the spot price in QLD will Granger-cause an increase of $0.32 over the same period. There are also a number of significant lagged mean spillovers from some of the spot markets to other markets. For example, NSW exhibits a significant own mean spillover from the lagged SNO electricity price. The estimated coefficient indicates that a $1.00 per megawatt-hour increase in the SNO price will Granger-cause a $0.30 fall in the NSW per-megawatt price over the next day. There is also a similarly significant own mean spillover effect from SNO to the QLD market, though of a smaller magnitude ($0.06).

In terms of the off-peak period estimates of the conditional mean price equations, only NSW and SNO exhibit significant own mean spillovers from their own lagged electricity price and there are no significant lagged mean spillovers from one market to another. In both cases of significant own mean spillovers the estimated coefficients are positive, suggesting that increases in today's per megawatt-hour spot price are associated with increases in the spot price over the next day. The estimated coefficients for NSW and SNO thereby associate $1.00 per megawatt-hour increases today with $0.37 and $0.68 increases over tomorrow. The general results for both the peak and off-peak period conditional mean price equations suggest that, on average, short-run price changes in any of the five Australian spot markets are not associated with price changes in any of the other spot electricity markets, seemingly despite the connectivity offered by the NEM.

The conditional variance covariance equations incorporated in the chapter's multivariate GARCH methodology effectively capture the volatility and cross-volatility spillovers among the five spot electricity markets. These have not been considered by previous studies. Table 10.3 presents the estimated coefficients for the variance covariance matrix of equations. The upper section of Table 10.3 presents the estimated coefficients for the peak period variance covariance equations and the lower section the estimated coefficients for the off-peak period equations. These quantify the effects of the lagged own and cross-innovations and lagged own and cross-volatility spillovers on the own and cross-volatility of the electricity markets. Turning first to the peak period, the coefficients of the variance covariance equations are generally significant for own and cross-innovations and for own and cross-volatility spillovers to the individual prices for all electricity markets, indicating the presence of strong ARCH and GARCH effects. In evidence, 92% (23 out of 25) of the estimated ARCH coefficients and 100% (25 out of 25) of the estimated GARCH coefficients are significant at the 0.05 level or lower.

Own-innovation spillovers in all the electricity markets are significant, indicating the presence of strong ARCH effects. The own-innovation spillover effects range from 0.0940 in QLD to 0.1031 in NSW. In terms of cross-innovation effects in the electricity markets, past innovations in most markets exert an influence on the remaining electricity markets. For example, in the case of VIC cross-innovation in the NSW, QLD, SA and SNO markets are all significant, of which SNO has the largest effect. Likewise in NSW, cross-innovations in VIC, QLD, SA and SNO all exert an effect, of which VIC is the largest and QLD the smallest. The exceptions to the overwhelming presence of strong cross-innovation effects are QLD and SA. No cross-innovations from SA influence the QLD market, and the QLD market in turn does not influence the SA market. This is consistent with the fact that there is currently no direct interconnector linkage between SA and QLD .

**Table 10.3**  Estimated coefficients for peak and off-peak variance covariance equations

| | NSW ($j = 1$) | | VIC ($j = 2$) | | QLD ($j = 3$) | | SA ($j = 4$) | | SNO ($j = 5$) | |
|---|---|---|---|---|---|---|---|---|---|---|
| | Coefficient | Std error | Coefficient | Std error | Coefficient | Std error | Coefficient | Std error | Coefficient | Std error |
| **Peak period** | | | | | | | | | | |
| $b_{1j}$ | ***231.5000 | 20.9700 | ***72.0400 | 26.8800 | ***139.0000 | 55.9100 | *88.7700 | 55.2200 | ***196.6000 | 15.5500 |
| $b_{2j}$ | ***72.0400 | 26.8800 | ***541.2000 | 50.5400 | 24.8400 | 107.2000 | ***580.1000 | 63.7000 | ***68.6700 | 25.9400 |
| $b_{3j}$ | ***139.0000 | 55.9100 | 24.8400 | 107.2000 | ***751.9000 | 136.5000 | 73.6300 | 149.8000 | ***111.2000 | 52.4700 |
| $b_{4j}$ | *88.7700 | 55.2200 | *580.1000 | 63.7000 | 73.6300 | 149.8000 | ***1480.0000 | 151.7000 | ***87.9400 | 37.0000 |
| $b_{5j}$ | ***196.6000 | 15.5500 | ***68.6700 | 25.9400 | **111.2000 | 52.4700 | ***87.9400 | 37.0000 | ***176.5000 | 13.4200 |
| $c_{1j}$ | ***0.1031 | 0.0057 | ***0.1067 | 0.0137 | ***0.0986 | 0.0160 | ***0.1016 | 0.0342 | ***0.1028 | 0.0001 |
| $c_{2j}$ | ***0.1067 | 0.0137 | ***0.0990 | 0.0195 | **0.0892 | 0.0413 | ***0.0995 | 0.0128 | ***0.1073 | 0.0132 |
| $c_{3j}$ | ***0.0986 | 0.0160 | **0.0892 | 0.0413 | 0.1079 | 0.0095 | 0.1079 | 0.0867 | ***0.0971 | 0.0155 |
| $c_{4j}$ | ***0.1016 | 0.0342 | ***0.0995 | 0.0128 | 0.1079 | 0.0867 | ***0.0994 | 0.0149 | ***0.1029 | 0.0338 |
| $c_{5j}$ | ***0.1028 | 0.0001 | ***0.1073 | 0.0132 | ***0.0971 | 0.0155 | ***0.1029 | 0.0338 | ***0.1029 | 0.0056 |
| $g_{1j}$ | ***0.8040 | 0.0055 | ***0.8102 | 0.0132 | ***0.8100 | 0.0329 | ***0.8076 | 0.0651 | ***0.8057 | 0.0002 |
| $g_{2j}$ | ***0.8102 | 0.0132 | ***0.8055 | 0.0145 | ***0.8681 | 0.0626 | ***0.8102 | 0.0108 | ***0.8058 | 0.0146 |
| $g_{3j}$ | ***0.8100 | 0.0329 | ***0.8681 | 0.0626 | ***0.8178 | 0.0262 | ***0.8500 | 0.1746 | ***0.8147 | 0.0339 |
| $g_{4j}$ | ***0.8076 | 0.0651 | ***0.8102 | 0.0108 | ***0.8500 | 0.1746 | ***0.8127 | 0.0162 | ***0.7959 | 0.0747 |
| $g_{5j}$ | ***0.8057 | 0.0002 | ***0.8058 | 0.0146 | ***0.8147 | 0.0339 | ***0.7959 | 0.0747 | ***0.8060 | 0.0054 |
| **Off-peak period** | | | | | | | | | | |
| $b_{1j}$ | *34.6953 | 16.5159 | 42.1199 | 37.9148 | 14.8932 | 24.4471 | 33.7995 | 35.8288 | **25.1052 | 11.8758 |
| $b_{2j}$ | 42.1199 | 37.9148 | ***130.1066 | 34.6883 | 11.8688 | 75.9527 | **99.6133 | 53.9567 | **44.2826 | 21.3752 |
| $b_{3j}$ | 14.8932 | 24.4471 | 11.8688 | 75.9527 | ***145.1031 | 28.2672 | 7.4207 | 48.8486 | 10.5180 | 15.2745 |
| $b_{4j}$ | 33.7995 | 35.8288 | **99.6133 | 53.9567 | 7.4207 | 48.8486 | **114.4877 | 66.4008 | *35.6695 | 21.9434 |
| $b_{5j}$ | **25.1052 | 11.8758 | **44.2826 | 21.3752 | 10.5180 | 15.2745 | **35.6695 | 21.9434 | ***24.2051 | 8.9685 |
| $c_{1j}$ | ***0.1036 | 0.0225 | ***0.1020 | 0.0203 | ***0.1054 | 0.0182 | ***0.1014 | 0.0269 | ***0.1023 | 0.0139 |
| $c_{2j}$ | ***0.1020 | 0.0203 | ***0.0998 | 0.0220 | 0.1084 | 0.1272 | ***0.0995 | 0.0089 | ***0.1002 | 0.0127 |
| $c_{3j}$ | ***0.1054 | 0.0182 | 0.1084 | 0.1272 | 0.1003 | 0.0208 | 0.1003 | 0.1872 | ***0.1021 | 0.0251 |
| $c_{4j}$ | ***0.1014 | 0.0269 | ***0.0995 | 0.0089 | ***0.1015 | 0.1872 | ***0.0994 | 0.0133 | ***0.1001 | 0.0174 |
| $c_{5j}$ | ***0.1023 | 0.0139 | ***0.1002 | 0.0127 | ***0.1003 | 0.0251 | ***0.1001 | 0.0174 | ***0.1008 | 0.0117 |
| $g_{1j}$ | ***0.8109 | 0.0209 | ***0.8058 | 0.0353 | ***0.8062 | 0.0227 | ***0.8064 | 0.0429 | ***0.8070 | 0.0119 |
| $g_{2j}$ | ***0.8058 | 0.0353 | ***0.8078 | 0.0181 | ***0.7635 | 0.2865 | ***0.8094 | 0.0088 | ***0.8061 | 0.0138 |
| $g_{3j}$ | ***0.8062 | 0.0227 | ***0.7635 | 0.2865 | ***0.8077 | 0.0317 | ***0.7980 | 0.4333 | ***0.8084 | 0.0550 |
| $g_{4j}$ | ***0.8064 | 0.0429 | ***0.8094 | 0.0088 | **0.7980 | 0.4333 | ***0.8106 | 0.0117 | ***0.8076 | 0.0164 |
| $g_{5j}$ | ***0.8070 | 0.0119 | ***0.8061 | 0.0138 | ***0.8084 | 0.0550 | ***0.8076 | 0.0164 | ***0.8047 | 0.0145 |

*Notes*: NSW – New South Wales, QLD – Queensland, SA – South Australia, SNO – Snowy Mountains Hydroelectric Scheme, VIC – Victoria. Asterisks indicate significance at *0.10, **0.05, ***0.01 level.

In the GARCH set of parameters, 100% of the estimated coefficients are significant. For NSW the lagged volatility spillover effects range from 0.8057 for SNO to 0.8102 for VIC. This means that the past volatility shocks in VIC have a greater effect on the future NSW volatility over time than the past volatility shocks in other markets. Conversely, in SA the past volatility shocks range from 0.7959 for SNO to 0.8500 for QLD. In terms of cross-volatility for the GARCH parameters in the peak period, the most influential markets would appear to include NSW and VIC. That is, past volatility shocks in the NSW and VIC electricity spot markets have the greatest effect on the future volatility in the three remaining markets. The sum of the ARCH and GARCH coefficients measures the overall persistence in each market's own and cross-conditional volatility. The fact that the sums of the ARCH and GARCH coefficients for all markets are fairly close to one indicates the strong persistence of past volatility in explaining current volatility. All five electricity markets exhibit strong own persistence volatility in the peak period ranging from 0.9045 for VIC to 0.9121 for SA and strong cross-volatility persistence spillover effects ranging from 0.8988 for SA to 0.9579 for QLD. Thus, past volatility shocks in SA persist longer in its own market as compared to volatility shocks in other markets, though it is relatively less subject to cross-volatility persistence spillover effects emanating from other markets. Moreover, these results provide strong evidence that the daily price series can be characterized by a GARCH(1,1) specification and that the current volatility of prices can usefully be explained by past volatility shocks that tend to persist over time.

The coefficients in the off-peak period conditional variance covariance equations in the lower section of Table 10.3 are also generally significant for own and cross-innovations and own and cross-volatility spillovers, thereby also indicating the presence of strong ARCH and GARCH effects. In evidence, 84% (21 out of 25) of the estimated ARCH coefficients and 100% of the estimated GARCH coefficients are significant at the 0.05 level or lower. The own-innovation spillover effects range between 0.0994 in SA to 0.1036 in NSW while the lagged cross-innovation spillover effects are also generally significant. Exceptions do exist. In the case of both VIC and SA lagged innovation spillover effects from QLD are not significant nor are lagged innovation spillover effects from these regions back to QLD. Once again, the spillover effects are closely tied to the degree of interconnection, with no direct linkage between QLD and SA or QLD and VIC.

All estimated GARCH coefficients in the off-peak period are, however, significant. For VIC, the lagged volatility spillover effects range from 0.7635 for QLD to 0.8094 for SA. This implies that past volatility shocks in SA have a relatively greater effect on future VIC volatility over time than past volatility shocks in the other regions. In terms of the cross-volatility of the GARCH parameters in the off-peak period, the most influential markets would appear to be NSW and SNO. Put differently, past volatility shocks in the NSW and SNO electricity spot markets have the greatest effect on the future volatility in the three remaining electricity spot markets; namely, VIC, QLD and SA. Once again, the sum of the ARCH and GARCH coefficients measures the overall persistence in each market's own and cross-conditional volatility. All five regional markets exhibit strong own persistence volatility ranging from 0.9055 for SA to 0.9145 for NSW. However, while the cross-volatility persistence spillover effects are significant and close to one, their magnitudes are generally less than their own volatility persistence. For instance, the cross-volatility persistence spillover effects range only between 0.8718 (VIC) to 0.9116 (NSW).

Finally, the Ljung–Box (LB) $Q$-statistics in Table 10.4 are used to test for higher-order autocorrelation in the standardized residuals. Significance of the Ljung–Box (LB) $Q$-statistics for the peak and off-peak period electricity spot price series then indicates linear dependences

**Table 10.4**  Ljung–Box tests for standardized residuals

|  |  | NSW | VIC | QLD | SA | SNO |
|---|---|---|---|---|---|---|
| Peak period | statistic | 28.9280 | 13.6750 | 6.8740 | 27.7060 | 18.0680 |
|  | p-value | 0.0040 | 0.3220 | 0.8658 | 0.0061 | 0.1136 |
| Off-peak period | statistic | 81.7840 | 17.0970 | 3.9020 | 180.1890 | 48.4720 |
|  | p-value | 0.0000 | 0.1460 | 0.9851 | 0.0000 | 0.0000 |

*Notes:* NSW – New South Wales, QLD – Queensland, SA – South Australia, SNO – Snowy Mountains Hydroelectric Scheme, VIC – Victoria.

due to strong conditional heteroskedasticity. In the peak period, the LB test statistics for NSW and SA are highly significant ($p$-values of less than 0.01) while those for VIC, QLD and SNO are insignificant ($p$-values of 0.3220, 0.8658 and 0.1136, respectively). These Ljung–Box statistics then suggest a strong higher-order linear dependence in only two out of the five peak period electricity spot markets estimated by the MGARCH model. These results are comparable to the LB tests in the off-peak period, with the exception that the test for SNO is now significant with a $p$-value of less than 0.01.

## 10.5  CONCLUSION

This chapter examines the transmission of prices and price volatility among five Australian electricity spot markets during the period 1 July 1999 to 31 December 2002. All of these spot markets are member jurisdictions of the recently established National Electricity Market (NEM). At the outset, unit root tests confirm that Australian electricity spot prices are stationary. A multivariate generalized autoregressive conditional heteroskedasticity (MGARCH) model is used to identify the source and magnitude of innovation and volatility spillovers. The estimated coefficients from the conditional mean price equations indicate that despite the presence of a national market for electricity, the state-based electricity spot markets are not fully-integrated with only three of the five markets exhibiting a significant lagged mean spillover from another regional market in the peak period and none in the off-peak period. In fact, just three of the markets experience an own mean spillover from their lagged price in the peak period and only two in the off-peak period. This would suggest, for the most part, that Australian spot electricity prices could not be usefully forecasted using lagged price information from either each market itself or from other markets within the national market.

More importantly, the results indicate the inability of the existing network of interconnectors to create a substantially integrated national electricity market and that, for the most part, the sizeable differences in peak and off-peak spot prices between most of the regions will remain, at least in the short term. This provides validation for regional interconnectors currently under construction and those that are proposed, and the anticipated inclusion of Tasmania in the national market. Nonetheless, there are generally more significant linkages in the peak period than in the off-peak period suggesting that during peak demand there is at least some tendency for spot prices to be driven together. This is somewhat contrary to De Vany and Walls (1999a) who found that there were essentially no price differentials between trading points in off-peak periods (though differentials did exist in peak periods) because they were less constrained by limitations in the transmission system.

However, own-volatility and cross-volatility spillovers are significant for nearly all markets, indicating the presence of strong ARCH and GARCH effects. Strong own and cross-persistent volatility are also evident in all Australian regional electricity markets. This indicates that while the limited nature of the interconnectors between the separate regional spot markets prevents full integration of these markets, shocks or innovations in particular markets still exert an influence on price volatility. As a general rule, the less direct the interconnection between regions, the less significant the cross-innovation and volatility spillover effects between these regions. The results also indicate that volatility innovations or shocks in all markets persist over time and that in all markets this persistence is more marked for own-innovations or shocks than cross-innovations or shocks. This persistence captures the propensity of price changes of like magnitude to cluster in time and explains, at least in part, the non-normality and non-stability of Australian electricity spot prices.

Of course, the full nature of the price and volatility interrelationships between these separate markets could be either under- or overstated by misspecification in the data. One possibility is that by averaging the half-hourly prices throughout the peak and off-peak periods, the speed at which innovations in one market influence another could be understated. For instance, with the data as specified the most rapid innovation allowed in this study is a day, whereas in reality innovations in some markets may affect others within just a few hours. The critical information in intraday price patterns suggests further work in this area. Another possibility is that the occurrence of time-dependent conditional heteroskedasticity could be due to an increased volume of trading and/or variability of prices following the arrival of new information into the market. It is well known that financial markets, for instance, can still be efficient but exhibit GARCH effects in price changes if information arrives at uneven intervals. One future application of modelling would then include demand volume as a measure of the amount of information that flows into the electricity market.

# REFERENCES

ACCC. (2000). *Infrastructure Industries: Energy.* Australian Competition and Consumer Commission, Commonwealth of Australia, Canberra.

Bera A.K. and Higgins M.L. (1993). "ARCH Models: Properties, Estimation and Testing". *Journal of Economic Surveys* 7(4): 305–366.

Bollerslev T. (1990). "Modelling the Coherence in Short-run Nominal Exchange Rates: A Multivariate Generalized ARCH Model". *Review of Economics and Statistics* 73(3): 498–505.

Bollerslev T., Chou R.Y. and Kroner K.F. (1992). "ARCH Modeling in Finance: A Review of the Theory and Empirical Evidence". *Journal of Econometrics* 52(1): 5–59.

Brennan D. and Melanie J. (1998). "Market Power in the Australian Power Market". *Energy Economics* 20(2): 121–133.

Brooks C., Henry O.T. and Persand G. (2002). "The Effects of Asymmetries on Optimal Hedge Ratios". *Journal of Business* 75(2): 333–352.

De Vany A.S. and Walls W.D. (1999a). "Cointegration Analysis of Spot Electricity Prices: Insights on Transmission Efficiency in the Western US". *Energy Economics* 21(3): 435–448.

De Vany A.S. and Walls W.D. (1999b). "Price Dynamics in a Network of Decentralized Power Markets". *Journal of Regulatory Economics* 15(2): 123–140.

Deng S. (2000). *Stochastic Models of Energy Commodity Prices and their Applications: Mean-reversion with Jumps and Spikes.* University of California Energy Institute Working Paper No. 73 Los Angeles.

Dickson A. and Warr S. (2000). *Profile of the Australian Electricity Industry.* Australian Bureau of Agricultural and Resource Economics (ABARE) Research Report No. 2000.7 Canberra.

Dunne P.G. (1999). "Size and Book-to-Market Factors in a Multivariate GARCH-in-Mean Asset Pricing Application". *International Review of Financial Analysis* 8(1): 35–52.

Engle R.F. and Kroner K.F. (1995). "Multivariate Simultaneous Generalized ARCH". *Econometric Theory* **11**(1): 122–150.

Huang B.N. and Yang C.W. (2000). "The Impact of Financial Liberalization on Stock Price Volatility in Emerging Markets". *Journal of Comparative Economics* **28**(2): 321–339.

IEA. (2001). *Energy Policies of IEA Countries: Australia 2001 Review.* International Energy Agency, Organisation for Economic Cooperation and Development (OECD) Paris.

Joskow P.L. and Kahn E. (2001). "A Quantitative Analysis of Pricing Behaviour in California's Wholesale Electricity Market During Summer 2000". *The Energy Journal* **23**(4): 1–35.

Karolyi G.A. (1995). "A Multivariate GARCH Model of International Transmissions of Stock Returns and Volatility: The Case of the United States and Canada". *Journal of Business and Economic Statistics* **13**(1): 11–25.

Kearney C. and Patton A.J. (2000). "Multivariate GARCH Modeling of Exchange Rate Volatility Transmission in the European Monetary System". *Financial Review* **41**(1): 29–48.

Lucia J.J. and Schwartz E.S. (2001). *Electricity Prices and Power Derivatives: Evidence for the Nordic Power Exchange.* University of California Los Angeles Working Paper Los Angeles.

NEMMCO. (2001). *An Introduction to Australia's National Electricity Market.* National Electricity Market Management Company Limited, Melbourne.

NEMMCO. (2002). National Electricity Market Management Company Limited, www site: <http://www.nemmco.com.au/>, accessed December 2002.

Pagan A. (1996). "The Econometrics of Financial Markets". *Journal of Finance* **3**(1): 15–102.

Robinson T. (2000). "Electricity Pool Series: A Case Study in Non-linear Time Series Modeling". *Applied Economics* **32**(5): 527–532.

Robinson T. and Baniak A. (2002). "The Volatility of Prices in the English and Welsh Electricity Pool". *Applied Economics* **34**(12): 1487–1495.

SFE. (2002). *NSW and Victoria Electricity Futures.* Sydney Futures Exchange, www site: <http://www.sfe.com.au/>, accessed December 2002.

Tai C.S. (2000). "Time-varying Market Interest Rate and Exchange Rate Risk Premia in the US Commercial Bank Stock Returns". *Journal of Multinational Financial Management* **10**(3–4): 397–420.

Tse Y.K. and Tsui A.K.C. (2002). "A Multivariate Generalised Autoregressive Conditional Heteroscedasticity Model with Time-varying Correlations". *Journal of Business and Economic Statistics* **20**(3): 351–362.

Wilson R. (2002). "Architecture of Power Markets". *Econometrica* **70**(4): 1299–1340.

# Part IV
## Forward Prices

# 11

# Forecasting Higher Moments of the Power Price Using Medium-Term Equilibrium Economics and the Value of Security of Supply

Chris Harris

*RWE Innogy, Windmill Hill Business Park, Swindon, Wiltshire SN5 6PB, UK*

## ABSTRACT

Here we examine how we can apply equilibrium microeconomics, real options and security of supply to the forward market, to develop a theoretical framework for estimating the full predictive risk-adjusted distribution of the prompt price for the medium-term future. In terms of price forecasting, we note that the first moment of price (the expectation) is insufficient for solving the long-term information requirements of generators and suppliers, and that successively higher moments become important as we consider plant whose main role is security of supply. We will see that traded options provide a highly effective mechanism for the exchange of probability information through actual transactions. Although presented in theory, all stages of the framework have proved to be separately implementable in practice. The model is designed to incorporate information about the observed prices of traded options and forward contracts.

## 11.1 INTRODUCTION

Compared to all other markets, power prices have exceptionally high volatilities, and an exceptionally granular price structure. These arise predominantly from the influence of high real-time variability in generation availability and in demand, on a market with storage that is both limited and expensive on the part of generators, consumers and purpose-built storage vehicles. The nature of the requirements and capabilities of physical market participants (generators and suppliers) are commonly expressed in terms of derivative instruments. These instruments are frequently complex and are priced using sophisticated pricing methods and sophisticated price processes involving such features as stochastic volatility, $n$-factor movement, mean reversion and regime switching.

For the purposes of pricing these instruments, the presence of particular features such as price "spikes", low forward market liquidity and the common need to contend with path dependence has tended to focus study on *prompt* price processes as opposed to *forward* price processes. However, these must ultimately be reconcilable, differing only by the cost of risk.

*Modelling Prices in Competitive Electricity Markets.* Edited by D.W. Bunn.

In a world in which the decision to maintain sufficient installed generation capacity to cost-effectively meet demand is driven by forward market prices, the *forward* price is a more useful instrument than the prompt price for the solution of problems such as asset purchase and sale, security of supply and relative investment in flexibility or reliability or reduction in fuel-to-power conversion costs. The prompt price process then is a construct of the forward price process (and, possibly deterministic, responses to exogenous signals) rather than *vice versa*. In principle, the two views of the world should be symmetrical. In practice the respective curve constructions place different emphases on different features of the price process. For example, forward price processes pay more attention to stochastic means, correlation term structures and skewness of terminal distributions relative to lognormal, and less attention to non-stationarity, spikes and regime switching than prompt processes do. The result, quite naturally, is that prompt price simulations represent actual prompt price trajectories relatively well and forward price simulations reflect actual forward market price histories well, but prompt price simulations poorly reflect actual forward price histories, and *vice versa*.

## 11.2   CONSTRUCTION OF THE MOMENTS OF PRICE

### 11.2.1   Model setup

In order to focus the conceptual presentation, we first simplify the nature of the system. The more important assumptions are:

- No annual emission limits (these have the effect of adding seasonal storage to the generation stack);
- Zero cost of starting and stopping plant;
- Demand is stochastic but inelastic;
- Simple models for the failure of all of the power plant in the stack;
- Zero transmission and distribution costs and constraints;
- Zero fuel price volatility;
- Zero government bond interest rates and zero credit risk.

We start by building the generation marginal cost stack in the usual way, approximating the planned and unplanned outage rate for the year in question by "de-rating" the effective capacity. Usually we would apply this to the series of expected system demands, arranged chronologically, but in this simple example in which the start-up costs of power stations are assumed to be zero, we simply construct an annual "demand-duration curve", and ignore the chronological sequence. It is important that the demand-duration curve is constructed for each of several past years and then averaged, rather than being constructed once from an averaged demand (Figure 11.1).

### 11.2.2   The supply stack and the offer premium X

The price-duration curve is initially constructed from the marginal cost supply stack and the demand-duration curve. It is then apparent that not all generators are compensated for their fixed costs and they would withdraw from the system. Therefore an amount X, that is deterministically related to the fixed cost, is added to the generation stack in such a manner that each generator covers its fixed costs. When looking five years forward, fixed costs will

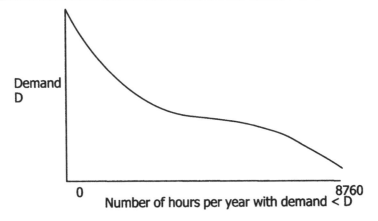

**Figure 11.1**   The demand-duration curve

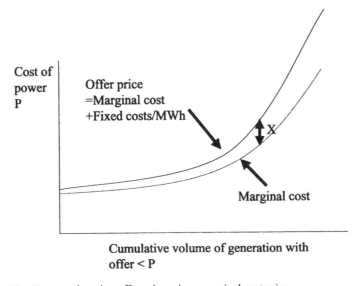

**Figure 11.2**   The X vector denoting offer price minus marginal cost price

generally include capital costs.[1] Note that we initially assume that this does not alter the order[2] of the stack (Figure 11.2). This has three health warnings.

First, there is debate amongst regulatory economists concerning the price received by generators concerning the validity of X at all, since in the absence of any market power, the market would clear at the short-run marginal cost. The offering at a finite X clearly invokes some market power, and if (as is usual) the offer price of a unit is above the marginal cost of the next unit in the merit order, some form of communication to maintain order. This chapter concentrates primarily on the X required for equilibrium and secondarily on the market power issues that affect prices.

---

[1] Note that the relevant capital cost should be based on current asset value rather than actual interest or notional interest on accounting book value of the asset.

[2] This effectively means that fixed costs fall monotonically with increasing marginal costs.

Second, in constructing two-dimensional price/volume curves, there is an implicit assumption made that the product offered is simple and that the range of productive techniques are similar, differing only in fixed and marginal costs. In practice, the power generators offer, and the consumers demand, a service more complex than simply "megawatts". Such services include flexibility and emission abatement. This introduces substantial heterogeneity to the problem and means that the curves of price versus "megawatts" are not necessarily monotonic.[3] This is manageable within the approach described here by monetizing the value of all services in such a manner that the internal commercial signal causes a response that matches the external driver. For example, the elevation of internal emission permit prices in order to stay within an annual emission limit.

Third, there is debate amongst regulatory economists concerning the extent to which the market should be used to manage the whole system. It is in fact common for some plant that is uneconomic in market terms to be supported by some form of subsidy. Here we assume that all plant can be, and is, part of the market.

The graph of Figure 11.2 shows that the X vector is strongly convex in relation to demand. For example, a baseload plant has over 8000 hours per year over which to "smear" the fixed cost recovery, but an open cycle gas turbine that runs for five hours per year will need to recover the fixed costs in five hours of generation.

Assuming that X is deterministic and not unstable due to gaming, then we can now apply the deterministic generation stack to a net demand that is stochastic due to actual variation in (annually trended) demand and variation in generator breakdown. Demand variation can be established from actuarial analysis of historic demand, noting that the stochastic nature of the daily and seasonal *phases* is an important effect. Generation variability is estimated by Monte Carlo processes for each unit on load. The process involves three "throws". The first throw is the failure interval, measured in plant running time (hours off-load count for zero, but starts count for several hours). The second throw is the failure duration in elapsed time which is then mapped back to plant running time. The third throw is the fail extent as a percentage of full load. The combination of the two processes (failure and demand) and the deterministic stack gives a terminal price distribution for each period (4-hourly resolution gives a good combination of tractability and capture of intraday peaks). Note that the distributions of each Monte Carlo throw must be carefully selected to reflect the mean, standard deviation, skewness and boundary conditions of the various aspects of the failure process.

### 11.2.3  Generator contracting strategy in equilibrium

We now consider each generating unit as a standalone business, motivated only by maximizing the revenue of the unit, and which is prepared to shut down if it does not cover its costs on an annual basis.

The iteration process for prompt price construction is this:

1. Construct short-run marginal cost stack using the known generation capacity for the year in question.

---

[3] The equilibrium argument rests on the ability of the generation sector to respond incrementally to slowly changing external value signals. The strong heterogeneity in the generation sector means that capital switching between technologies can be relatively rapid and potentially means the equilibrium can never be achieved. See Sraffa (1960) for a discussion on capital switching. It is the author's view that this problem is soluble since plant has capability to adjust the fixed/marginal cost ratio and plant services such as emission abatement can be expressed as proxy costs per megawatt, thereby simplifying the stack dimensionality.

2. Construct unit failure permutations for each period from the Monte Carlo analysis.
3. Construct expected load factors using $X = 0$ and expected demand net of plant outages.
4. Starting with the low merit plant, adjust the $X$ vector until all plant covers at least the avoidable fixed costs for the year.
5. Repeat, making adjustments to fixed and marginal costs from run schedules, as well as proxy costs such as internal permit price signals.

If there is no forward market, then each generator will estimate the offer premium $X$ above short-run marginal cost that it must use in the prompt market in order to ensure capture of fixed costs.

If there is a forward market, then each generator may sell a forward contract if it is "in merit" (minimum offer less than market price) at the forward price. Note that the longer the tenor, the greater the time available to avoid fixed costs, and hence the greater the marginal costs. In theory, if both forward and cash market clear at marginal costs then, before cost of risk considerations, the forward market should be higher.[4]

If there is an option market, then each generator may sell a fuel-to-power call option contract, struck at the marginal cost of generation. Before considerations of failure against contract, it is clear that striking the option at marginal costs means that net cash[5] flow is zero whether or not the plant is called to run. For the plant to remain on the system, the option premium should therefore at least equal the fixed costs.

Here we will assume that generators sell "firm" power options and must therefore be responsible for managing the cost of capability shortfalls. We will see that this requires the generator to make some estimates about general generation capability and demand variations. A case could be made that peaking generators sell non-firm power and leave this estimation to specialists. This question is not considered here in any detail because these two choices are, in principle, economically equivalent.[6] The general equivalence of loading costs into the production or consumption sector is described in more detail by Coase (1960),[7] but in essence we assume that all costs are recovered somewhere in the economic system. The consumer pays in the end, either directly or indirectly as a pass-through of costs incurred by the generator.

### 11.2.4 Supplier contracting strategy in equilibrium

The supply sector buys forward the expected consumption (inelastic but stochastic), and then buys options to cover demand variation.

We imagine that the supply sector can cut[8] the power to its customers for a fixed compensation that is sufficiently high for some sectors to volunteer to be cut off first. In the analytic framework

---

[4] In the presence of sufficient traders, the forward price and risk-adjusted prompt price expectation come together. This is resolved in this situation by the probability of the prompt price trading at the value of lost load after plant withdrawal from the system.

[5] Here amortized flows such as marginal plant reinvestment requirement are treated as equivalent to cash.

[6] In practice, there is generation elasticity that is most effectively accessed by the option being managed in the generation sector. The elasticity includes operational changes such as temporary plant operating reconfiguration to increase load at the expense of efficiency, and managing the timing of minor reliability events.

[7] The Coase argument is intended primarily for monolithic markets. With a strongly heterogenous supply stack, then costs incurred by generators at the margin create windfalls for generators with lower marginal costs. This windfall is funded by the consumer.

[8] Security of supply has different meanings over different time priods. In the short term it concerns wholesale price stability, in the medium term it concerns generation capacity, and in the long term it concerns energy sourcing. In this context, security of supply is a commodity related to generation capacity and price.

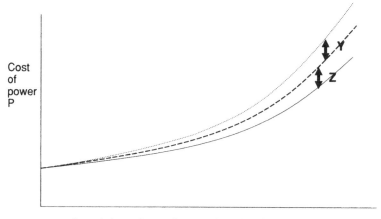

**Figure 11.3** The Y and Z vectors for options. Z represents the margin of strike price above marginal cost and Y represents the uplift of selling price required by the option buyer in order to recoup premium

described it is relatively simple to take into account the fact that the disutility of interruption is not identical for all, and that there is a stack of price versus volume which has the appearance of a generation stack.

### 11.2.5  Calculation of price distribution from option premiums

A plant will not sell options if the premium for an option struck at marginal costs plus the expected cost of reliability loss is less than the annual fixed costs, and indeed it will plan[9] to close. There is therefore a close connection between option premiums and fixed costs.

Since the option premium is the risk-adjusted integral of all probability-weighted positive payoffs of prompt price minus strike price, then before the considerations of risk adjustment, if we know the option premiums, we know the prompt price distribution, and if we know the prompt price distribution, we know the option premiums.

The iteration process for an option-based system is then this:

1. Construct the short-run marginal cost stack using the known generation capacity for the year in question.
2. Using fixed costs, calculate required premiums for call options struck at marginal costs.
3. Construct price probability distribution by recovering option[10] premiums with numerical integration.
4. Adjust X until all option buyers exactly recover option premium.
5. Repeat, making adjustments to fixed and marginal costs from option deltas.[11]

Figure 11.3 shows a generalization of this process, in which the strike price is set above marginal costs ($Z > 0$). The price uplift from the strike price, that the option buyer requires

---

[9] If there is a market price with sufficient volume and liquidity, it is always suboptimal to invest on the basis of proprietary prices. See Baxter and Rennie (1996).

[10] In the worked example, the sale of a forward contract and a put option is synthesized by the sale of a call option.

[11] The option delta is produced from the Black–Scholes option formula and represents the probability of option exercise. The delta, and an estimation of average run lengths, thereby gives a schedule estimate which in turn affects the fixed and marginal costs.

on release of power to the market to recover the option premium, is denoted by Y. For prompt prices to be unchanged by the risk transfer, $Y + Z = X$.

So, finally, we have a funded generation stack, a forward price vector and an option price matrix with vectors in both time and strike price. The forward price gives us the vector of the first moment of risk-adjusted terminal price distribution with respect to tenor. It is the option price matrix that, provided it is "complete" enough, tells us the risk-adjusted distribution of all of the higher moments of the terminal price distribution. It is common practice amongst traders to use the Black–Scholes option formula as a convenient communication vehicle, with the annualized standard deviation of price returns (or "volatility") as the principle word in the language.[12] The calculation methods are well known and not described here.

We now have the biased estimators of the moments of prompt prices. To estimate the true moments of prompt price, we must take a view on the cost of holding risk. This is discussed later.

It should be noted that the visualization of the power price world in option terms has not added new information in total, but by providing a communication vehicle in which proprietary probability information is fed into the market system and affects prices and thereby investments, the information is coordinated rather than fragmented.

## 11.3  WORKED EXAMPLE

We consider a 10-unit supply stack and a pricing year that is divided into 12 homogenous periods. Plant failure is greatly simplified; for each period, the plant is either available at full capacity or unavailable, throughout the period. Demand variation is not shown, although it can be treated as a zero-cost plant, and system capacity shortfall is modelled by load shedding at the predetermined disutility value of lost load (VOLL). See Tables 11.1 and 11.2. Then, for each period, each permutation of failure is calculated, and the price is then set by the marginal unit on load. It is immediately obvious that not all units cover their fixed costs, and the X vector is constructed to make all units do so (Figure 11.4). Table 11.3 shows the result. Note that the final profit per year does not change in a monotonic fashion.

**Table 11.1**  Demand in each priod

| Period | Demand (MW) |
|--------|-------------|
| 1      | 1300        |
| 2      | 1500        |
| 3      | 1600        |
| 4      | 1700        |
| 5      | 1800        |
| 6      | 2000        |
| 7      | 2100        |
| 8      | 2200        |
| 9      | 2400        |
| 10     | 2800        |
| 11     | 3000        |
| 12     | 3400        |

[12] Two other common words are "skew" and "smile". There are many others that describe particular features for different markets.

**Table 11.2**   Unit-by-unit data

| Unit | Marginal cost | Failrate | Capacity (MW) | Fixed costs/kw/year |
|------|---------------|----------|---------------|---------------------|
| A | 7 | 10% | 351 | 80 |
| B | 8 | 10% | 502 | 75 |
| C | 9 | 10% | 529 | 70 |
| D | 11 | 10% | 614 | 65 |
| E | 13 | 10% | 470 | 60 |
| F | 15 | 10% | 440 | 56 |
| G | 18 | 10% | 585 | 52 |
| H | 27 | 10% | 610 | 45 |
| I | 40 | 10% | 510 | 39 |
| J | 65 | 10% | 500 | 28 |
| VOLL | 2000 | 0% | 99999 | 0 |

**Table 11.3**   Annual unit profits for two X offer vectors

| Unit | X | Profit/kw/year | X | Profit/kw/year |
|------|---|----------------|---|----------------|
| A | 0 | 6 | 0 | 37 |
| B | 0 | −1 | 0 | 28 |
| C | 0 | −6 | 0 | 23 |
| D | 0 | −19 | 0 | 8 |
| E | 0 | −17 | 0 | 13 |
| F | 0 | −19 | 0 | 12 |
| G | 0 | −26 | 2 | 2 |
| H | 0 | −27 | 14 | 1 |
| I | 0 | −18 | 85 | 0 |
| J | 0 | −8 | 320 | 0 |

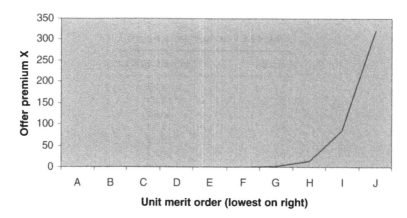

**Figure 11.4**   Offer vector required to cover the fixed costs of all units

Note that we have made some strong equilibrium assumptions: (1) each plant knows the offer premium of all other plant, the demand and the complete fail probability dataset in order to construct its offer premium; (2) each plant sticks to its offer premium. In this context, we can examine the optimality of the plant mix to serve the load. For example, consider variation

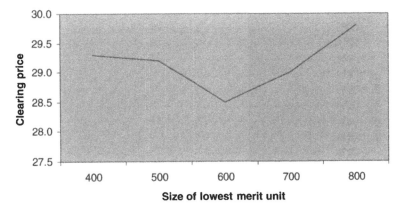

**Figure 11.5** The sensitivity of demand-weighted clearing price in relation to the amount of low merit capacity, that adjusts its offer premium X in order to cover its fixed costs

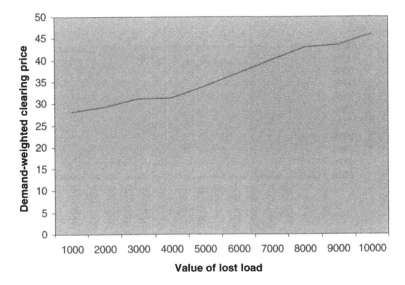

**Figure 11.6** The sensitivity of demand-weighted clearing price to the value of lost load

of the size of the lowest merit unit J (Figure 11.5). Similarly, we can calculate our sensitivity to the value of lost load (Figure 11.6).

For each period, we can calculate the probability distribution of the clearing price. Figure 11.7 and 11.8 show this for period 1 (lowest demand) and a detailed view of period 12 (highest demand).

The probability-weighted clearing prices for each period are shown in Table 11.4.

So, in the world of perfect information and perfect stable equilibrium, we know all of the moments of the expected outturn prices. If liquidity grew in a forward market, these would be the forward prices if only speculators traded and there were no hedge trades in the risk-neutral world.

Now, as the forward market grows in liquidity, the physical actors (generators and suppliers) become interested in reducing their risks (and thereby increasing their risk-adjusted net present

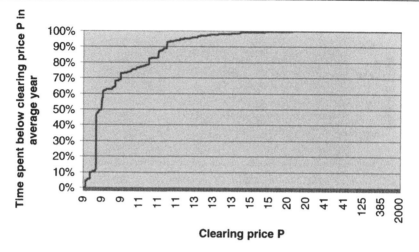

**Figure 11.7**    The terminal probability distribution for the price in the lowest demand period

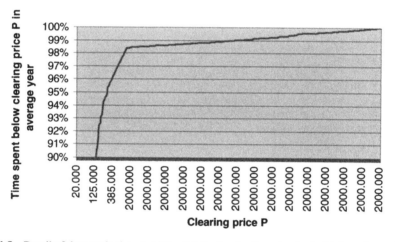

**Figure 11.8**    Detail of the terminal probability distribution for the price in the highest demand period

values) by transferring their market risk to the market. If each unit sold forward 100% of their capacity wherever the forward contract price exceeded marginal costs, then the result would be as in Table 11.5. Even before we have considered the effect of (un)reliability, we can see that the lowest merit unit J cannot enter into a forward hedging arrangement and lock in a profit. This makes financing low merit new build difficult, and hence equilibrium is hard to sustain as plants age and new build is required.

One solution is to regulate low merit plant by removing it from the market structure, scheduling it at marginal price and subsidizing its fixed costs. The subsidy then comes from an energy tax. In the example shown, dropping the offer premium of unit J from 320 to 132, adjusting all other unit bids to their lower-bound equilibrium values and subsidizing the 5.1/kw/year cash shortfall for unit J will cause the demand-weighted clearing price to drop by 0.6 before application of the energy tax of 0.1. Similarly, all plant could be regulated to offer in at marginal costs. In the example, the demand-weighted clearing price would then drop to 22.3/MWh

**Table 11.4**  Probability-weighted
clearing price in each period

| Period | Price |
|--------|-------|
| 1 | 9.7 |
| 2 | 11.8 |
| 3 | 11.9 |
| 4 | 12.1 |
| 5 | 12.2 |
| 6 | 14.8 |
| 7 | 15.3 |
| 8 | 15.7 |
| 9 | 17.6 |
| 10 | 28.4 |
| 11 | 48.2 |
| 12 | 87.7 |

**Table 11.5**  Net annual £/kw profits
that can be locked in for each unit by
forward hedging, before deduction of
reliability losses

| Unit | Hedge (at 100% reliability) |
|------|------------------------------|
| A | 67.0 |
| B | 63.3 |
| C | 59.5 |
| D | 47.9 |
| E | 39.9 |
| F | 33.8 |
| G | 28.6 |
| H | 15.9 |
| I | 1.9 |
| J | −11.4 |

before application of the energy tax of 4.1/MWh. This foreclosure of the market recycles the profits of all plant into the energy price and is in effect a fully managed market. The energy price-saving results from the capture of "windfall"[13] profits of some of the generators who gain from the price-setting activities of low merit plant. Apart from the fact that markets liberalize and reduce central control in order to incentivize cost reduction, the main difficulty of this approach is that the tax is inefficiently applied and does not incentivize peaking generation.

In brief then, equilibrium cannot be sustained in a fragmented forward-only market since there is not an effective market mechanism to sustain low merit plant.

Option markets develop as a natural result of forward markets. Since we had our price distributions for each period, then we should have the complete matrix of option premiums for all strike prices in each period. If each unit sells options struck at marginal costs (thereby

---

[13] In theory, these windfall profits disappear over time because new generation enters the area with greatest profits and the flexibility of fixed/marginal cost ratios on the other plants in the stack causes a general reshuffling that leaves all plant with small returns.

**Table 11.6**   Net annual £/kw profits that can be locked in for each unit by option hedging, before and after deduction of reliability losses and with comparison to prompt revenue with no hedging

| Unit | £/kw/year (at 100% reliability after option sales) | Reliability loss | Net | Comparison prompt revenue |
|------|------|------|------|------|
| A | 67.0 | 30.2 | 36.8 | 36.8 |
| B | 63.3 | 34.9 | 28.3 | 28.3 |
| C | 59.5 | 36.6 | 22.9 | 22.9 |
| D | 48.0 | 39.7 | 8.3 | 8.3 |
| E | 40.9 | 27.5 | 13.4 | 13.4 |
| F | 37.9 | 25.8 | 12.1 | 12.1 |
| G | 35.1 | 32.9 | 2.2 | 2.2 |
| H | 31.7 | 30.9 | 0.8 | 0.8 |
| I | 26.8 | 26.1 | 0.6 | 0.1 |
| J | 31.3 | 22.1 | 9.2 | 0.0 |

ensuring zero net cash flow after selling the options, regardless of whether the plant is called to run), then the net profits of the units in this example are as shown below, before and after reliability considerations.

We first calculate the expected cost of reliability. This is done here by assuming initially that the option purchasers release power to the prompt market using exactly the same X vector as the plant did. For example, the buyer of the call option struck at 65/MWh will offer power at 385/MWh. Then if the plant fails, it must buy back power at the offer price of the next available unit not running, and will save the marginal cost of generation. The costs are shown in Table 11.6. Note that apparently the total net revenue from the option approach is higher than that from no hedging. This is because the option sale was at full plant volume whereas in practice, the volume that the option market would purchase would reflect part loading. Therefore the premium would be the same and the volume would be less. Note also that we have assumed that plant offer prices (directly or via option traders) do not change. For example, if unit J failed against an option struck at its strike price, the market would still clear at the initial offer price of unit I despite its market power.

## 11.4   COMMENTARY

### 11.4.1   The transaction behaviour of the low load factor plant

In this example, we have seen that providing the offer structure in prompt clearing is unchanged, we can use option terminology and structure to define the generator revenues and market prices. We saw also that forced outage valuation and part loading must be factored into the option framework in order to recover the original economics of the system without options.

Since options are traded instruments that are commonly associated with traded forward markets, it is pertinent to question what effects the presence of a traded option market might have. There are four principal effects.

First, the statistical variation of annual revenue of peaking plant arising from stochastic net demand (including failure of other generators) is substantially reduced by contracting, and the risk passes initially to the market sector. This reduces the cost of risk (which is treated as a fixed cost) in the peaking generation sector.

Second, the coefficients of the practical equilibrium X vector may reduce. An independent peaking generator cannot take a long-term statistical view and must aim to capture revenue early in case it is not forthcoming later, and it does this by using what local market power it has in raising its X. If the risk moves to a sector that handles the risk differently or has a lower cost of annual statistical revenue variation, then the raising of X from this effect is lowered. A related factor is that standalone peaking generators cannot finance the analytic and risk management infrastructure to optimize risk and must therefore act conservatively and with simple rules of thumb, by raising X to the extent that market power allows.

Third, in contracting most of their revenue forward, then the economics of generators are less sensitive to the prompt offer stack than in a prompt-only market with no forwards and options. In fact the main economic importance of the prompt price outturn is in the maintenance of sufficient price level and structural stability to sustain the forward market, and therefore the incentive to game in the prompt market is much reduced.

Fourth, generators should ideally hedge their reliability risk and rehedge[14] dynamically as market prices and failure probability[15] change. If generators do this, then even in the fragmented market, the information captured in the market is the same as for the fully managed market. Information use is slightly more effective, because the stack can "flex" by using the generators' limited ability to swap fixed and marginal costs in a yearly timeframe, and physical optimization driven by the internal signals from rehedging.

In summary, the low load factor plant would prefer to migrate all of its risks to another sector and not even have to worry about the "correct" X offer. However, the need to hedge and rehedge reliability risk means that some degree of system analysis is likely to be required, particularly in relation to the value of lost load and the probability of forced consumer load shedding. We will see below that the market sector does not influence the X vector (although it does influence the stability), and generators retain a key role in maintaining a stable prompt market structure (through a stable X vector) in order to sustain the forward market.

### 11.4.2    The transaction behaviour of the supplier

By investing in generation capacity, the generator has a definite long position in fuel-to-power conversion. The supply sector risk position is different. The sector itself has the option to raise tariff, and the customers have the option to switch supplier. These options effectively mean that the aggregate supply sector "delta" risk to power prices does not equal the aggregate generation sector delta in the medium term. In common with most commodity markets, the market is structurally long[16] in the medium term, and traders may take on the long position (and the long option position) and hold it in wait for the suppliers, in return for being compensated for the risk.

Before adjustment for customer turnover, the supplier will buy forward the amount that corresponds to expected customer demand, plus call and put options to cater for increases and decreases in demand. Since a forward purchase plus put option purchase is equivalent to the purchase of a call option, then suppliers effectively buy the same instrument that generators

---

[14] The strike price is slightly above the market price conditional on it being higher than the strike, and the volume is equal to the expected fail volume multiplied by a liquidity factor read directly from the fail volume and the offer stack.

[15] Generator cost of risk is different according to the moment of risk. So, for example, a generator may have relatively high tolerance of annual variance but low tolerance to "reasonable worst case". This substantially affects the reliability hedging.

[16] Internal to itself, the market is structurally long. Since stock market prices tend to fall on upward shocks in crude oil prices, then the market in a wider context may be structurally short. This becomes relevant if the structural short is (i) known, (ii) acted on. See Ronn (2003).

sell–call options. Note that just as the options bought (in theory) by generators are at a higher strike than the options sold, the options bought by the suppliers are at a higher series of strike prices than "at-the-money" (strike price equal to current forward price). In fact, since the generation sector will ultimately fulfil the inelastic requirement of the demand sector, it is clear that it is optimal for the system as a whole for the suppliers to buy very similar instruments to those that the generators naturally have to sell.

Note that individual suppliers only have to forecast their own client demand initially, but the options will depend to some degree on the correlation between extra demand for the own clients and extra general demand on the system. Hence, as with generation, system-wide demand analysis is useful but accuracy is not critical.

### 11.4.3   The transaction behaviour of the market

To intermediate risk between sectors, the "market" has three distinct roles, which are (i) holding risk in exchange for an expectation of profit, (ii) provision of a forum for transaction execution with services such as communication and administration, (iii) analytics. Some roles can be fulfilled within the generation and supply sectors.

We have seen that at one extreme, in which each plant sells options to a single trader, the prompt market structure is identical to a centrally managed one. The single trader releases energy to market according to the X vector, calls it from the plant at marginal costs, and makes an expected return (net of premium) of zero.

At another extreme, the plants try to contract fully and flood a fragmented traded market with options. In the absence of an obviously stable prompt market, the forward and option market would dry up very quickly as premiums fell below fixed costs.

Consider instead how the market in its role as risk-taker and intermediator can interact with the generation and supply sectors. We note that what generators would ideally sell is very similar to what the supply sector would ideally buy, but that generators need to sell before suppliers need to buy. We can then see a situation in which the traders buy a small amount of options from the generators and then sell similar options later on to the supply sector. This requires intermediation, risk holding and the analytics to create a framework to fairly price options (rather than just act as broker between buyer and seller of the identical item).

We have seen that in the longer term, the risk-holding market will require compensation for taking on a long[17] forward position (first moment of price) and long option position (higher moments of price), but that the highest strike options (highest moments of price) will not be in surplus and are in fact closely related to load shedding and the value of lost load. In the shorter term, the high possible losses from short positions mean that all sectors have negative cost of risk. This causes the generation sector to undercontract, and therefore, through its retained interest in the prompt market, the generation sector retains a role in price setting. Note that it is in everyone's interest for equilibrium X to be maintained. Generators need it to sustain the forward market, the market needs it to maintain market stability, and the supply sector needs it to ensure the maintenance of an optimal generation mix on the system (which protects[18] the prompt price). Since perhaps less than 10% of economic revenue/cost is then determined by the prompt market, the incentive to capture short-term revenue by disrupting the equilibrium X vector is less than without the forward market.

---

[17] If the market requires compensation for being long, then the cost of risk is said to be positive.

[18] The supplier has a different form of risk to *expected* demand-weighted average prices and to the *risk* of high peak prices. The former can be mitigated by raising tariffs. The latter can only be protected by upstream hedging.

There is clearly some fragility in the system, since the unilateral calculations of X may not be consistent, and communication is disallowed by competition regulation. However, the problem is to some degree self-limiting. X can be calculated from fixed costs/option premium and expected load factor. Too high a prompt X will raise the option premium and thereby attract competing capacity. Too low a prompt X that schedules plant out of merit will quickly cause a fall in the prompt market from competitor response. The theoretical forward price falls but selling dries up, leaving the suppliers short. Therefore while the option-based market system does not have the stability of a monopoly market, it is more stable than a fragmented prompt and forward market and much more stable than a fragmented prompt-only market.

We must consider how option traders hedge in practice. Traders tend to form fairly discrete communities of prompt, forward, "vanilla" European options and "complex" derivatives. Option traders tend to hedge the delta[19] positions quite closely to minimize their exposure to small movements in forward prices. Therefore the purchasers of options from peaking plants will, on buying 1 MW of option, sell 1 MW times the option delta, and will continue to sell more as the market rises. When the market rises to the marginal cost of the plant, then the trader will have sold half of the option volume, and the probability of exercise will be a little under 50%. The result of this behaviour is to drive the forward price towards the option strike price. Therefore an option-based system in which option traders hedge as they do in other markets cannot work effectively unless the supply sector participates fully, so that the options are substantially sold by the traders before they reach prompt.

### 11.4.4  Cost of risk

Risk is transferred from one sector to another if both sectors gain on the basis of risk-adjusted expectation of profit. The relative paucity of pure risk-takers with no physical activity in the power sector means that costs of risk can be very high. This in turn means that all moments of the forward price can be highly biased as expectations of the prompt price. Since in a mature market it is the forward price that determines the economics of the actors, this calls into question reliance of prompt price histories in making judgements that may cause behavioural change for physical actors.

Our best source of information for the absolute cost of holding risk[20] is the equity market. The equity risk premium (approximately described as the long-run stock return minus long-run government bond return, divided by the annual variance in stock market return) gives us an equity market cost of risk which we then apply as a generic cost of risk. We use models such as the Capital Asset Pricing Model (CAPM) to determine the scaling factor for our aversion to a particular risk depending on its correlation to the stock market. Finally, since we require risk aversion to the higher moments of risk, we must employ other tools. The two industry areas that focus on the higher moments of risk are credit and reinsurance, and the pricing of corporate bonds[21] and reinsurance contracts[22] can directly reveal the cost of higher moments of risk.

---

[19] The option delta is an output from the Black–Scholes option formula and represents the units of underlying contracts that should be hedged for a unit of option contract to minimize risk to spot/forward price movements.

[20] Risk in this context is annual variance.

[21] A corporate bond can be priced theoretically by (i) making assumptions about the application of a generic credit rating transition matrix to the bond, as well as other assumptions such as recover on default, (ii) estimating the "true" credit rating and adjusting the rating agency assessment with public domain knowledge, (iii) assuming a differential cost of risk for each moment of risk, (iv) using backward induction to price the bond. Inference of cost of risk depends, amongst other things, on assumptions of the estimated recovery on default, and the "accuracy" of the credit agency ratings.

[22] These commonly use probability of ruin and modelled disutility of extreme losses.

While CAPM is a useful method for assigning an absolute value to the cost of holding "risk" under the conventions of the model, we should be circumspect in the application to the traded electricity market. The two main reasons are (i) CAPM relies heavily on the estimate of correlation of the risk to the investment portfolio (the stock market basket in this case) and correlations can be highly unstable, and (ii) CAPM considers only the second moment of return variation (variance).

A plant that sells options alters the nature of its risk position substantially. For example, (i) the sign of the correlation may change, since a completely unhedged plant would normally have positive[23] correlation to the stock market, but reduction of this exposure and retention of cost risk may leave the plant with negative[24] correlation, (ii) the variance is reduced but the higher moments of risk are increased due to the potential losses against contract on failure.

Any risk transference will in general simultaneously affect the skewness, portfolio variance and systematic correlation to the relevant market (such as the stock market). It is not an easy matter to estimate the net change in cost of risk arising from transactions. While it is not an easy matter, it is possible to estimate the cost of risk for the peaking plant. When unhedged, the distribution of return is skewed and the cost of risk can be estimated by charging a CAPM-related rate for the "normal" component of risk and a cost of risk for the skewness that is derived from the disutility of negative returns worse than one standard deviation from the mean, using techniques from the insurance industry. Similarly the cost of risk charged by the option trader can be calculated using risk denominators such as value-at-risk[25] with the option "vega" as the risk factor.

### 11.4.5  Market completeness

The lack of "completeness" in the electricity market is a common objection to the testing of theories about derivative prices in the traded market. The granularity in the power market is extreme in relation to other markets and this makes it impossible for there to be temporal continuity of quotation of a whole curve of complete granularity. The construction of an annual contract "shaped" at half-hourly granularity to a particular load profile would commonly require this degree of resolution. While a quotation for a single half-hour contract some months ahead would not be available in the open market, the same quotation is available internally in all firms who have risks in their traded books, or internal physical requirements at that granularity. To all intents and purposes then, internal markets are fully granular, and even though an external market cannot interrogate the individual "granules", it can continually access quotations that require and contain implicit granularity, and from this sense, can be regarded as being effectively complete. In the same way that we can regard the market in price to be complete, we can regard the market in probability (via options) to be complete, since the argument about granularity is the same.

## 11.5   CONCLUSIONS

1. We have seen that even a fragmented market, provided that the option market is actively used, acts as a highly effective gatherer of all available knowledge even when the knowledge

---

[23] Input prices are responsive to crude oil price (rises of which cause the stock market to fall), whereas output prices are "sticky".

[24] After fuel, the input costs are positively correlated to stock market prices. Net correlation change depends on the connection between power prices and the stock market.

[25] Cost of value-at-risk is commonly explicit within firms.

is fragmented. The efficient market hypothesis tells us that in the presence of sufficient intermediation and pure risk-taking, option[26] prices must represent the risk-adjusted expectations of all moments of prompt price.

2. The real option approach is useful in connecting equilibrium economics to security of supply. By incorporating the fixed cost of production, traded options are more effective than blanket capacity payments, and better combine plant used for energy and plant used for capacity cover.

3. Power price is a derived state variable, and the natural processes are demand variation (which is an actuarial process) and generation shortfall (which is a Poisson process with variable parameters). Market terms such as "spikes", regime switches, mean reversion, etc. are then interpretations of the features of the way that power price reflects these processes.

4. By placing volume rather than price at the centre of the econometric system (as opposed to the microeconomic system), we see that high price volatility is a natural result even when the system is in equilibrium. It is volatilities and prices created by non-equilibrium (e.g. unstable X) that are more revealing of shortcomings in the robustness of the system.

5. The demand and generation supply stack has an implicit value of security of supply at a calculable cost, according to a particular criterion for security of supply. If relatively small changes in the value of lost load have a large impact on the theoretical equilibrium price, then we could consider the market to be in shortfall. Otherwise it is in surplus. While it is hard to arrive at an explicit value for security of supply, we can make an empirical estimate from the reliability performance metrics in the regulated distribution sector (which is the sector causing most short-term losses), although it is important to recognize that transient disconnection is qualitatitively different from sustained loss of generating capacity.

6. There are dangers in the sole use of either prompt or forward prices for policy or economics. In a mature market, the economics of the actors are driven by forward prices and the dependence on the prompt market is mainly in the way that it affects the forward market. Similarly, if the net volume of transactions intermediated by the forward market is low, and hedging cannot be effected in reasonable timeframes, then it is still the prompt market and not the forward market that determines the economics of the actors.

## REFERENCES

Baxter M. and Rennie A. (1996). *Financial Calculus – An Introduction to Derivative Pricing*. Cambridge University Press, Cambridge.

Coase R. (1960). "The Problem of Social Cost". *Journal of Law and Economics* **3**: 1–44.

Ronn E. (2003). *Real Options, Capital Budgeting*. Risk Publications, London.

Sraffa P. (1960). *The Production of Commodities by Means of Commodities*. Cambridge University Press, Cambridge.

---

[26] At high resolution, the relevant option is commonly termed a caplet. While this tends to trade in separable groups in instruments called caps, and inseparable groups called swaptions, the caplet prices can be "bootstrapped" using techniques developed in the corresponding interest rate markets.

# 12
# Modeling Electricity Forward Curve Dynamics in the Nordic Market

NICOLAS AUDET,[1] PIRJA HEISKANEN,[2] JUSSI KEPPO[1]
AND IIVO VEHVILÄINEN[2]

[1] *Department of Industrial and Operations Engineering, University of Michigan, Ann Arbor, MI 48109-2117, USA*
[2] *Fortum Power and Heat, Oy, Finland*

## ABSTRACT

This chapter considers the modeling of electricity forward curve dynamics with parameterized volatility and correlation structures. We estimate the model parameters by using the Nordic market's price data and show how the model can be implemented into everyday industry practice.

## 12.1  INTRODUCTION

Electricity markets are different from the usual financial markets and many other commodity markets due to the non-storability of electricity. The spot price of electricity is set by the short-term supply–demand equilibrium, and supply and demand must be in balance at each instance. Because the demand (supply) today does not necessarily have anything to do with the demand (supply) in the future, the spot electricity today is a different asset from the spot electricity in the future. This implies that the relation between the spot price and the forward prices in the electricity markets is not as straightforward as in the usual financial and commodity markets.

In this chapter we develop a simple parameterized model for forward curve dynamics. We estimate the model parameters by using the data from the Nordic electricity market. The Nordic electricity market is hydro-dominated with roughly 50% of the electricity supply being hydro-based. The winters are cold and much of the precipitation comes as snow. In the spring the snow melts causing floods whose timing varies a lot from year to year due to the temperature. There is a significant electricity heating load while the mild summers do not require a lot of air conditioning, so that electricity demand is concentrated on the winter season. The time-dependent variation present in the demand results in a seasonal, weekly and daily profile in the electricity spot price and electricity forward curve. However, these price variations are smoothed to some extent in the Nordic market because of the hydropower production. Some hydro producers have the possibility to optimize their discharge up to one year ahead, and many have the possibility for some months ahead. The short-term, i.e. intra-week and intra-day, variations in the spot prices decrease due to the easily adjustable hydropower. On the other hand, there is high variation in the price level between different years because the total amount of

*Modelling Prices in Competitive Electricity Markets.* Edited by D.W. Bunn.

hydropower available in the market depends on the amount of yearly precipitation. The forward prices of electricity mostly reflect the market expectations on the future reservoir levels.

Stochastic modeling of the deregulated markets has concentrated on the electricity spot markets. Research is roughly divided into statistical models and fundamental models. Statistical models depend on the set of parameters that describe the properties of the spot process while fundamental electricity price models are based on competitive equilibrium models for the electricity market. Several models are presented in Wallace and Fleten (2002) and Skantze and Ilic (2001). The statistical models easily fall to over-parameterization and are often considered to be "black-boxes" while the fundamental models require a complete set of coherent historical data to be useful. Further, as mentioned earlier, because the electricity supply–demand equilibrium depends on the time of the year and on the development in the hydrological situation, the stochastic process for the spot price changes over time. Thus, it is likely that the form of the stochastic model is not constant and, therefore, the estimation of the model parameters is difficult.

There are also a few models that study the forward price behavior. The benefit from modeling the forward curve directly is that unlike with the spot models there is no problem fitting the model to the current forward curve. This is a similar advantage to when the Heath, Jarrow and Morton (1992) framework is used in interest rate markets. General statistical analysis on electricity forward prices is found in Lucia and Schwartz (2002). The similarities between the interest rate markets and electricity forward markets are studied in detail by Koekebakker and Ollmar (2001). They find that a simple Heath–Jarrow–Morton approach does not explain electricity forward curve dynamics as well as interest rate dynamics. However, we partly utilize their framework and use similar volatility parameterization but we allow the spot volatility to be time-dependent. Further, we use a parameterized correlation structure and a different estimation method. Within an infinite-dimensional Heath–Jarrow–Morton type model, Björk and Landén (2000) study the theoretical properties of futures and forward convenience yield rates in a case where the underlying asset can be non-tradable, like electricity.

In this chapter we study the dynamics of the whole forward curve. Implicitly this also gives the relationship between the spot price and the forward prices. This is important for the market participants in many business applications, such as power plant optimization, risk management and in the pricing of exotic derivative instruments [see e.g. Geman and Vasicek (2001), Keppo (2002a,b), Vehviläinen (2002), Deng et al. (2001)]. For example, the understanding of the relation between the spot and forward prices is needed when hedging electricity production with the forward contracts. In this chapter we focus on the modeling of a few key features in the forward price dynamics and they enable the combined analysis of spot and forward markets. The features that we study are the spot volatility curve, the volatility curve's maturity effect and the forward curve's correlation structure. The historical daily quotes of electricity forwards and futures as well as the historical spot prices are used in the estimation of the model parameters.

The rest of the chapter is organized as follows. Section 12.2 introduces the model while the Appendix illustrates the estimation method of the model parameters. Section 12.3 illustrates the model estimation with market data. Then Section 12.4 gives three practical examples and finally Section 12.5 concludes.

## 12.2  THE MODEL

In this section we introduce our parametric model for electricity forward curve dynamics. We consider an electricity market where forward contracts are traded continuously within a finite time horizon $[0, \tau]$. When describing the probabilistic structure of the market, we refer to an underlying probability space $(\Omega, F, P)$, along with the standard filtration $\{F_t : t \in [0, \tau]\}$. Here $\Omega$ is a set, $F$ is a $\sigma$-algebra of subsets of $\Omega$, and $P$ is a probability measure on $F$.

We denote by $f(t, T_1, T_2)$ the forward price for the time period $[T_1, T_2]$ at time $t$. That is, $f(t, T_1, T_2)$ is a constant price for the duration $T_2 - T_1$ and, therefore, it can be viewed as the average price for the period $[T_1, T_2]$. In order to get the forward curve that depends only on one maturity date, we model the following theoretical forward prices:

$$f(t, T) = \lim_{T_2 \to T} f(t, T, T_2) \quad \text{for all} \quad t \in [0, T], \; T \in [0, \tau] \tag{12.1}$$

That is, $f(t, T)$ is the forward price at time $t$ for the time period $[T, T + dt]$. In contrast to the usual financial markets, where a price process is usually given by a one-dimensional Itô process, in electricity markets the corresponding price at time $t$ is the whole forward curve $f(t, \cdot) : [t, \tau] \to \mathbf{R}_+$ [see e.g. Björk and Landén (2000)].

Note that all forward prices are in nominal terms. According to the definition of the forward price, the spot price is given by

$$S(t) = f(t, t) = \lim_{T \to t} f(t, T) \quad \text{for all} \quad t \in [0, \tau] \tag{12.2}$$

That is, the forward price converges to the spot price. Later in this chapter we use weekly average prices for electricity spot price and, therefore, at the expiration date the spot price equals the weekly future price.

The following assumption characterizes the dynamics of the forward prices, i.e., it gives our parameterized forward curve dynamics.

**Assumption 12.1.** *The forward prices follow an Itô stochastic differential equation*

$$df(t, T) = f(t, T)e^{-\alpha(T-t)}\sigma(T)dB_T(t) \quad \text{for all} \quad t \in [0, T], \; T \in [0, \tau] \tag{12.3}$$

*where the forward price* $f(t, T) = E[S(T)|F_t]$, $\alpha$ *is a strictly positive constant,* $\sigma : [0, \tau] \to \mathbf{R}_+$ *is a bounded and deterministic spot volatility curve, and* $B_T(\cdot)$ *is a Brownian motion corresponding to the T-maturity forward price on the probability space* $(\Omega, F, P)$ *along with the standard filtration* $\{F_t : t \in [0, \tau]\}$. *The correlation structure of the Brownian motions is given by*

$$dB_{T^*}(t)dB_T(t) = e^{-\rho|T-T^*|}dt \quad \text{for all} \quad T, T^* \in [0, \tau] \tag{12.4}$$

*where* $\rho$ *is a strictly positive constant.*

Assumption 12.1 captures the main elements of our model. Specifically it implies:

- Forward prices are equal to the expected future spot prices and, therefore, forward prices are martingale under the objective probability measure $P$.
- The electricity spot volatility curve $\sigma(\cdot) : [0, \tau] \to \mathbf{R}_+$ is deterministic.
- A forward price's volatility is lower than the corresponding spot volatility and the parameter $\alpha$ models this effect.
- Forward prices with maturity dates that are close to each other are significantly correlated. Parameter $\rho$ captures this effect.
- The forward prices follow lognormal distributions.

The expectation hypothesis is made for simplicity and if this is not true under the objective measure $P$, it is true under the pricing measure $Q$ [see e.g. Hull (2000)]. Thus, in this chapter we assume that $P$ equals $Q$ and, therefore, we do not estimate the expected drifts of the forward prices. According to equation (12.1) the stochastic process for a forward price follows an exponential process where $f^2(t, T)e^{-2\alpha(T-t)}\sigma^2(T)$ is the rate of change of the conditional variance of $f(t, T)$. Note that this volatility parameterization is similar to the one used in Koekebakker and Ollmar (2001). The boundedness of the volatility function guarantees the existence and uniqueness of the solution to (12.3). The deterministic spot volatility structure is quite restrictive and it is made in order to ease the estimation and implementation of the model. In practice there are uncertainties in the spot volatility curve due to the changes in the demand and supply. Therefore, the stochastic volatility models are important also in electricity markets [see e.g. Deng (1999)]. With the third and fourth bullets we model the decreasing volatility as a function of maturity and the decreasing correlation as a function of the difference between forwards' expiration dates. The errors from Assumption 12.1 are analyzed in Sections 12.3 and 12.4. Note that since in equation (12.3) we model expected values ($f(t, T) = E[S(T)|F_t]$), the spot process $S(\cdot)$ can be e.g. geometric Brownian motion or mean-reverting [see for instance Schwartz (1997)]. Further, from Assumption 12.1 we get that the distribution of $S(T)$ is given by

$$\log(S(T)) - \log(f(t, T)) = \log(f(T, T)) - \log(f(t, T))$$
$$\sim \phi\left(-\tfrac{1}{2}\hat{\sigma}^2(T - t), \hat{\sigma}\sqrt{T - t}\right) \tag{12.5}$$

where $\phi(m, s)$ is a normal distribution with mean $m$ and standard deviation equal to $s$, $T > t$, and the average volatility on $[t, T]$ is according to (12.3) given by

$$\hat{\sigma} = \frac{\sigma(T)}{\sqrt{T-t}}\sqrt{\int_t^T \exp(-2\alpha y)\,dy} = \frac{\sigma(T)}{\sqrt{2\alpha(T-t)}}\sqrt{[\exp(-2\alpha t) - \exp(-2\alpha T)]}$$

Thus, equation (12.5) implies that the electricity prices follow lognormal distributions.

In the Appendix we show how the model parameters are estimated by using a maximum likelihood method. In the next section we apply our forward model to the Nordic market.

## 12.3   FORWARD MODEL IN THE NORDIC MARKET

In this section, we estimate the model parameters by using the Nord Pool electricity exchange's market data. First we briefly discuss the forward and future contracts in this Nordic market.

### 12.3.1   Products in the Nordic power market

In the Nordic market around one-quarter of the total physical demand is traded via the Nord Pool electricity exchange and, therefore, the Nord Pool's electricity price is a credible reference index for the whole market. There is an active market for electricity forwards and futures, both in the exchange and in the OTC-markets with volumes nearly 10-fold over the size of the total physical market.

Spot prices for physical delivery are set by an equilibrium model where the supply and demand curves of all the market participants are matched day-ahead. The last-minute balance management is done after the spot market has closed.

Nord Pool's electricity futures contracts include weeks and blocks. Week contracts are traded for the nearest four to seven weeks after which there are block contracts for about one year

**Spot price (NOK/MWh)**

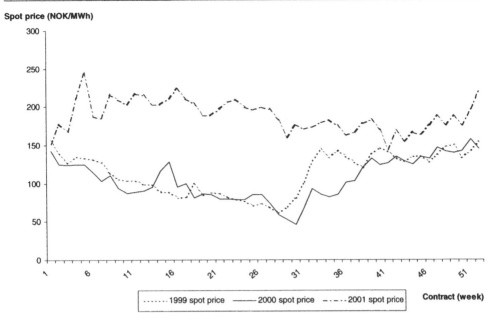

**Figure 12.1**   Weekly average for the spot price in 1999, 2000 and 2001

forward. Blocks are combinations of four weeks and split to weekly contracts as time passes. The electricity forward contracts are years and seasons that divide the year to three periods: Winter-1, Summer and Winter-2. The closest few years are traded both as seasons and as years. The difference of settlement between futures and forward contracts is ignored here because we only model nominal prices. For further information about Nord Pool see Nord Pool (2002) product information.

We estimate the volatility discount factor, the correlation discount factor and the weekly volatility structure by using Nord Pool's prices for weekly future contracts during the years 1999, 2000 and 2001. Our database consists of prices for the weekly products on each trading day. Figure 12.1 illustrates the realized electricity spot prices in different years. In the Nordic market the electricity spot price is usually high in the winter and low in the summer, as shown in years 1999 and 2000. This is due to the cold winter in the Nordic area and, therefore, high demand during winter. As can be seen from Figure 12.1, year 2001 was different since the price was all the time close to the yearly average price. The hydrological situation changed from relatively wet conditions to dry in the beginning of year 2001. The change was due to cold and relatively dry weather in the first months of 2001 and was reflected as a sharp rise in the spot price. The hydrological situation improved during the year, thus causing the spot price to fall towards autumn.

## 12.3.2   Estimation of the model parameters

The model parameters are estimated by using the maximum likelihood method. All the parameters (volatility curve, volatility and correlation parameters) are calculated in a single estimation routine. This method is illustrated in the Appendix.

The volatilities of the 52 weekly futures contracts traded during years 1999, 2000 and 2001 are shown in Figure 12.2. This figure indicates that the volatility varies inside the year and also

**Table 12.1**  Estimated volatility discount parameter as well
as its standard deviation in different years

|  | Year 1999 | Year 2000 | Year 2001 |
|---|---|---|---|
| Volatility parameter $\alpha$ | 2.31 | 6.06 | 3.67 |
| Standard deviation | 0.25 | 0.32 | 0.19 |

Annual volatility

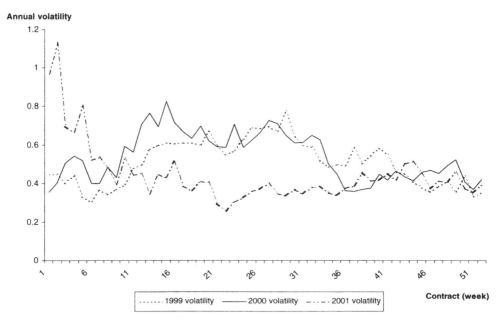

**Figure 12.2**  Volatilities of the 52 weekly contracts by using the data from 1999, 2000 and 2001

between different years. As in years 1999 and 2000, the volatility is usually high in the summer
and low in the winter. This is because in the summer the water reservoirs are usually quite
empty and, therefore, small changes in the demand can cause changes in the used production
technologies and production marginal costs. On the other hand, because in the winter mainly
condensing power is used, there are no major changes in the production marginal costs and
the winter volatility is usually lower. The winter 1999–2000 was very snowy whereas during
the winter 2000–2001 there was less snow than normally. The accumulation of snow over the
normal level during the winter 1999–2000 increased the uncertainty in the spot price level
during the possible spring flood period in 2000 and thus caused the high volatility during that
period. However, as mentioned earlier the year 2001 is different because in the beginning of
year 2001 the hydrological situation changed from relatively wet conditions to dry and this
created high spot volatility in the beginning of the year. Because in that year there was not
much snow, there was no uncertainty on the spring flood. In Figure 12.2 the average volatility
from all the volatility structures is 0.5.

Table 12.1 gives the estimated volatility discount factor and its standard deviation in different
years. According to Table 12.1 the volatility of a forward price is lower than the corresponding

**Table 12.2**   Estimated correlation discount parameter as well as its standard deviation in different years

|                              | Year 1999 | Year 2000 | Year 2001 |
|------------------------------|-----------|-----------|-----------|
| Correlation parameter $\rho$ | 3.62      | 5.30      | 4.61      |
| Standard deviation           | 0.04      | 0.26      | 0.17      |

spot volatility and the parameter $\alpha$ (volatility discount factor) models this effect. Each year the parameter is stable but due to the different annual hydro-inflow the parameter is different in different years. Since the winter 1999–2000 was very snowy it seems that during snowy years the volatility discount parameter is high. The average value is $\alpha = 4.02$ and it implies that, for instance, if the spot volatility is 50% then a one-month-maturity forward has 36% volatility. Note that similar parameter changes can be observed with the volatility estimates in stock markets [see e.g. Schwert (2002)].

Table 12.2 illustrates the estimated correlation discount factor and its standard deviation in different years. According to Table 12.2 forward prices with maturity dates that are close to each other are significantly correlated and the parameter $\rho$ (correlation discount factor) captures this effect. The average value $\rho = 4.51$ gives, e.g., that two forwards with maturity date one month apart have about a 0.69 correlation. Note that from Tables 12.1 and 12.2 we get that the volatility and correlation discount factors are correlated and their values are close to each other. Therefore, for instance, during snowy years both the parameters are high.

## 12.4   MODEL USAGE EXAMPLES

In this section we illustrate the usage of the model in everyday industry practice. We consider three cases: conditional forecasting of the forward curve when a forecast for spot price is available, the pricing of forward options and analysis on the accuracy of a forward curve model that describes the forward curve dynamics with a finite number of forward curve points.

In the conditional forecasting we update the initial forward curve with spot price predictions and study whether this kind of forecast model is suited for short or long-term planning. This conditional forecasting can be used in the production optimization and in the pricing and hedging of complex path-dependent electricity derivatives such as swing options [see e.g. Jaillet *et al.* (2001), Thompson (1995) and Keppo (2002a)].

Many options in electricity markets are options on forward prices. Therefore, the Black-76 model [see Black (1976)] is widely used. The only Black-76 model parameter not received directly from the market is the underlying forward price's average volatility during the lifetime of the option. We estimate this volatility from our forward curve model and show a few numerical pricing examples.

In the forward curve accuracy analysis we study the percentage of uncertainties described by a forward curve model that uses a finite number of forward curve points. This is important in the selection of a convenient forward curve model. For instance, frequently production optimization can be carried out by using only a rough estimate of the forward curve dynamics while in the hedging of derivative instruments better description is needed. By using the accuracy analysis the convenient model can be selected and its error can be estimated.

**Price (NOK/MWh)**

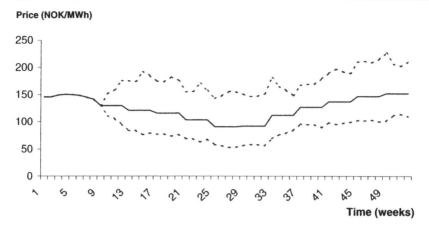

**Figure 12.3**  Updated forward curve and the corresponding 95% confidence interval

## 12.4.1  Conditional forecast for the forward curve

Our conditional prediction model uses the estimated parameters of the previous section to calculate the corresponding forward curve from a spot price scenario. In order to analyze our parameterized forward dynamics we assume that the spot price scenario is equal to the realized spot price during the year 2001. Then we compare our predicted forward curve with the corresponding realized forward curve in the market. Thus, the possible forward curve prediction error is from our forward curve model because the spot price scenario is equal to the realized spot price. We use the estimated parameters from year 2000 and test our model with independent data from year 2001. Note that based on Figures 12.1 and 12.2 spot dynamics during years 2000 and 2001 are different. Figure 12.3 illustrates the conditional forecasting. In the figure an initial forward curve has been updated with a spot price scenario during the first nine weeks.

We use 25 initial forward curves and create predictions for two-week, one-month, three-month and six-month horizons. The initial forward curves are updated weekly with the realized spot prices. For all initial forward curves and scenario horizons we compare our updated curves with the corresponding realized forward curves in the market. In measuring the differences between these curves we use the mean square error.

Since the contracts mature weekly, the number of data points in the updated forward curve decreases as our planning horizon increases and, thus, we normalize the mean square error by the number of data points. Considering all of the 25 initial forward curves, we take the average of the mean square errors for each time horizon. Figure 12.4 shows us a summary of how well our updated forward curve fits the realized forward curve. The solid line is the error term from our conditional prediction with different prediction horizons. The dotted line is the corresponding prediction error without the spot price information, i.e., prediction by using directly Assumption 12.1 and the estimated parameters in Tables 12.1 and 12.2. As expected, the dotted line is higher than the solid line because in the conditional forecast more information is used. Further, in practice prediction horizons of less than a month can be used. Thus, Figure 12.4 illustrates that even though one knows the spot price one does not know much about the forward curve. This is because there are many uncertainties in the forward curve and, therefore, knowing only one point in the curve gives an accurate situation only close to this point.

Standard deviation

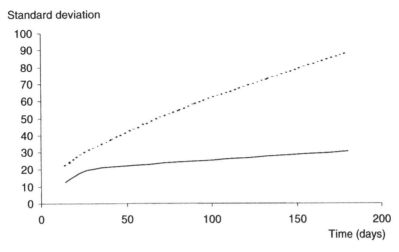

**Figure 12.4** Relationship between the forward curve prediction error and the time horizon. The solid line is the error from the conditional forecast and the dotted line is the error from the forecast without the spot price realization

### 12.4.2 Pricing of forward options

Many options in electricity markets are options on electricity forwards or futures. Therefore, the Black-76 model [see Black (1976)] is widely used in these markets. In the case of a deterministic volatility structure the Black-76 model is used with the average volatility during the lifetime of the option. Therefore, the options on an electricity forward price can be modeled as follows:

$$c(t, T_o, T) = \exp(-r(T_o - t))[f(t, T)N(d_1) - XN(d_2)]$$
$$p(t, T_o, T) = \exp(-r(T_o - t))[XN(-d_2) - f(t, T)N(-d_1)]$$

(12.6)

where $c$ is the call option price, $p$ is the put price, $T_o$ is the maturity date of the options, $f$ is the underlying forward price, $X$ is the strike price, $T$ is the maturity date of the forward, $t$ is the current time, $N(\cdot)$ is the cumulative normal distribution function:

$$d_1 = \frac{\ln\left(\frac{f(t,T)}{X}\right) + \frac{1}{2}\hat{\sigma}^2(t, T_o, T)(T_o - t)}{\hat{\sigma}(t, T_o, T)\sqrt{T_o - t}}$$
$$d_2 = d_1 - \hat{\sigma}(t, T_o, T)\sqrt{T_o - t}$$

and $\hat{\sigma}(t, T_o, T)$ is the average volatility of $f(\cdot, T)$ during $t - T_o$.

The problem with the Black-76 model is to find the correct average volatility for different maturities. Because in our model we have a deterministic volatility curve, we get from equation (12.5)

$$\hat{\sigma}^2(t, T_o, T) = \frac{\sigma^2(T)\int_t^{T_o}\exp(-2\alpha y)dy}{T_o - t} = \frac{\sigma^2(T)}{2\alpha(T_o - t)}[\exp(-2\alpha t) - \exp(-2\alpha T_o)]$$

(12.7)

We illustrate this framework through a numerical example, where we calculate the call prices with different maturities. The strike price is assumed to be equal to the underlying forward price

**Table 12.3**   Call prices on electricity forwards with
different maturities

| Maturity | Average volatility, % | Call price, % from forward price |
|----------|----------------------|----------------------------------|
| 2 weeks  | 46.4                 | 3.6                              |
| 1 month  | 42.8                 | 4.9                              |
| 3 months | 33.0                 | 6.4                              |
| 6 months | 24.9                 | 6.8                              |

and the risk-free rate equal to 5% (annual, continuous time). For simplicity, the maturity of each option is equal to the underlying forward contract's maturity. The spot volatility structure is flat and equal to 50%. Using equations (12.6) and (12.7) we calculate the call option prices and Table 12.3 summarizes the results. According to Table 12.3 the average volatility decreases as a function of maturity. However, $g(T_o) = \hat{\sigma}(t, T_o, T_o)\sqrt{T_o - t}$ is an increasing function of $T_o$ even though $\hat{\sigma}(t, T_o, T_o)$ is a decreasing function of $T_o$. Therefore, time to maturity increases the call prices in Table 12.3.

### 12.4.3   Accuracy of a forward curve model

In practice the dynamics of the forward curve are modeled by using a finite number of forward curve points. The advantage of this is that it is easier to analyze these points than the whole curve. The drawback is that we lose some accuracy because we do not model all the uncertainties in the curve, i.e., we do not model the area between the points. In this subsection we analyze this error term and similar accuracy analysis is done in Koekebakker and Ollmar (2001).

By using the correlation discount factor we estimate the percentage of the uncertainties captured with the selected forward curve points. Let us denote by $\Delta$ the time interval between the forward curve points and assume that this interval is constant. Then we get, by using the correlation parameter $\rho$, that the cumulative correlation between a forward curve point and the part of the forward curve that is closest to this point is given by

$$2 \int_{0}^{\frac{\Delta}{2}} \exp(-\rho y)dy = \frac{2}{\rho}\left[1 - \exp\left(-\rho\frac{\Delta}{2}\right)\right] \tag{12.8}$$

This is because the time interval $\left(T - \frac{\Delta}{2}, T + \frac{\Delta}{2}\right)$ is closest to the maturity $T$. Since the time length of this part is $\Delta$, we model the uncertainty proportion that the discrete model describes as follows:

$$\frac{2}{\Delta\rho}\left[1 - \exp\left(-\rho\frac{\Delta}{2}\right)\right] \tag{12.9}$$

Equation (12.9) models the correlation effect to the forward curve on $(T - \frac{\Delta}{2}, T + \frac{\Delta}{2})$ from the single forward curve point $f(t, T)$. Actually, this equation gives the lower boundary for the proportion since it ignores the independent effects from other forward curve points. However, since the closest point has the strongest correlation, for our purposes the above equation is accurate enough.

We analyze the uncertainty proportion with different discrete time interval $\Delta$ by using equation (12.9). Figure 12.5 illustrates the results. According to Figure 12.5 the longer the time interval the less we are able to model the uncertainties. For instance, if we use four

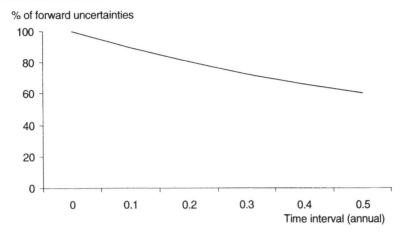

% of forward uncertainties

**Figure 12.5**   The percentage of forward curve uncertainties described by finite number of forward curve points. Time interval is the time period between the points

forward curve points (time interval 0.25, times: 0, 0.25, 0.5, 0.75) to model the whole annual forward curve dynamics we are able to capture at least 76% of the forward curve uncertainties.

## 12.5   CONCLUSION

In the electricity market the price risk is described by the whole forward curve dynamics. Therefore, the modeling of the curve dynamics is as important as the stock price modeling in the usual financial markets. In this chapter we have proposed a simple parameterized model for forward curve dynamics and estimated the parameters by using the price data from the Nordic market. According to the estimation results a forward's correlation with the spot price and its volatility decrease as a function of maturity. For instance, the volatility of a two-month-maturity future contract is about half of the corresponding spot price's volatility and the correlation between the future price and the current spot price is about 0.5.

We have shown several possible applications for our forward curve model. Firstly, we made a conditional forecast for the forward curve when a perfect forecast for the spot price is available. Secondly, we combined our volatility parameterization with a usual option pricing method. Finally, we estimated the accuracy of a forward curve model by using our correlation parameterization. Further application is, e.g., the modeling of a hydropower production. Because the market is highly competitive we can assume that the producer is a price-taker and, therefore, the power plant can be modeled as a basket of electricity options. As we have seen in this chapter, in the calculation of these option prices the forward curve dynamics are crucial. A similar example is considered in Keppo (2002a), where a power plant is modeled by using a swing option.

Our forward curve model can be extended in several ways. As was noted, there is considerable variation in the model parameters between different years. This is due to the fact that in the Nordic market the forward curve dynamics depend on the hydrological situation, i.e., the contents of the water and snow reservoirs. To develop the forward curve model further the effect of the changes in the water and snow reservoir contents into our forward curve parameters could be modeled.

## APPENDIX: ESTIMATION OF MODEL PARAMETERS

In this Appendix we show how the spot volatility curve, the maturity parameter and the correlation parameter can be estimated by using a maximum likelihood estimation method. In this estimation method, we apply an exponential weighting to give more weight to the most recent data points.

Based on Assumption 12.1 and the properties of the lognormal distribution we get

$$\ln\left[\frac{f(t+\Delta t, T)}{f(t, T)}\right] = \frac{-1}{4\alpha}\sigma^2(T)\left[e^{-2\alpha(T-(t+\Delta t))} - e^{-2\alpha(T-t)}\right]$$

$$+ \frac{1}{\sqrt{2\alpha}}\sigma(T)\sqrt{\left[e^{-2\alpha(T-(t+\Delta t))} - e^{-2\alpha(T-t)}\right]}\varepsilon \qquad (A12.1)$$

where $\varepsilon$ is a random variable that is distributed according to a standard normal distribution.

At given time $t$, one can observe a set of contracts with maturities $(T_i)_{i=n(t)}^{N(t)}$, where $n(t)$ and $N(t)$ denote the upper and lower indices of the contracts for which the price can be observed at time $t$. Note that $n(t)$ and $N(t)$ fluctuate with time and the maturities are fixed. Let $f^i(t)$ be the price of the $T_i$-maturity contract at time $t$. For our model, we will assume that there are 250 trading days and 52 weeks per year. Consequently, since we use weekly futures we define

$$\Delta t = \frac{1}{250}$$

$$T_i - T_j = \frac{i - j}{52} \qquad (A12.2)$$

Define $v^i(t) = \log f^i(t + \Delta t) - \log f^i(t)$. We know that $v^i(t)$ is Gaussian, with

$$E[v^i(t)] = -\frac{\sigma_i^2}{4\alpha}e^{-2\alpha(T_i-t)}(e^{2\alpha\Delta t} - 1)$$

$$Var[v^i(t)] = \frac{\sigma_i^2}{2\alpha}e^{-2\alpha(T_i-t)}(e^{2\alpha\Delta t} - 1)$$

$$Corr[v^i(t), v^j(s)] = \begin{cases} 0 & t \neq s \\ e^{-p|T_i-T_j|} & s = t \end{cases} \qquad (A12.3)$$

where $\sigma_i = \sigma(T_i)$. Note that the assumption of no correlation between $v(t)$ and $v(s)$ $(s \neq t)$ implies that $v(t) = (v^i(t))_{i=n(t)}^{N(t)}$ and $v(s) = (v^i(s))_{i=n(s)}^{N(s)}$ are mutually independent.

Define

$$u^i(t) = \frac{v^i(t) - E[v^i(t)]}{\sqrt{Var[v^i(t)]}} = h(v^i(t)) \qquad (A12.4)$$

Equation (A12.4) is simply a centered-reduced form of $v$ since the expected value of $u$ is 0 and its variance is 1.

We assume that we observe $u^i(t)$ on a set of dates $(\tau_j)_{j=1}^T$, with equally spaced observation time, so that $\tau_j = j \cdot \Delta t$. Denote by $u$ the vector of all the observations of all the contract maturities, i.e., the vector of $u^i(\tau_j)$ for all $i$ and $j$. Using the fact that $u^i(t)$ is Gaussian, their joint density $g_u(u)$ is given by

$$g_u(u) = \prod_{j=1}^{T} g_j(u(\tau_j))$$

$$g_j(u(\tau_j)) = (2\pi)^{-M(\tau_j)/2}|\Omega_j|^{-1/2}\exp\left(-\frac{1}{2u}(\tau_j)^T\Omega_j^{-1}u(\tau_j)\right)$$

$$[\Omega_j]_{k,l=1}^{M(\tau_j)} = \tilde{\rho}^{|k-l|}$$

$$\tilde{\rho} = e^{-\rho/52}$$

$$M(\tau_j) = N(\tau_j) - n(\tau_j) + 1$$

$$\tau_j = j \cdot \Delta t \tag{A12.5}$$

The first equation of (A12.5) is deduced from the assumption of independence of $v(\tau_j)$ and $v(\tau_k)(k \neq j)$ stated in equation (A12.3), which allows us to write the density as the product of marginal densities of the $u(\tau_j)$. The second equation simply expresses the (marginal) density of the variables $u^i(\tau_j)$ as a Gaussian density with mean zero, unit variance and a correlation given by $\Omega_j$. The third and fourth detail the values of the elements of $\Omega_j$, which are obtained from the third equation of (A12.3). The variable $M(\tau_j)$ is the number of observable contracts that are observable at time $\tau_j$.

By expanding the expression for the determinant and the inverse of the correlation matrix $\Omega_j$, it can be shown that $g_j$ may be written as

$$g_j(u(\tau_j)) = (2\pi)^{-M(\tau_j)/2}(1 - \tilde{\rho}^2)^{-\frac{M(\tau_j)-1}{2}}$$

$$\exp\left[-\frac{1}{2(1-\tilde{\rho}^2)}\left(\sum_{i=n(\tau_j)}^{N(\tau_j)-1}(u^{i+1}(\tau_j) - \tilde{\rho}u^i(\tau_j))^2 + u^{N(\tau_j)}(\tau_j)^2(1-\tilde{\rho}^2)\right)\right] \tag{A12.6}$$

We now have an expression for the density of the $u^i(\tau_j)$ as defined by equation (A12.4). The density of $v(\tau_j)$ is simply obtained by multiplying this density by the Jacobian of the transformation (A12.4):

$$d_j(v(\tau_j)) = \frac{g(h(v(\tau_j)))}{\prod_{i=n(\tau_j)}^{N(\tau_j)} \sqrt{Var(v^i(\tau_j))}} \tag{A12.7}$$

where $Var(v^i(\tau_j))$ is given by (A12.3) and, as mentioned earlier, $\tau_j = j \cdot \Delta t$. The denominator is the determinant of the Jacobian of the transformation from $v$ to $u$. It can be deduced immediately from equation (A12.4).

A maximum likelihood estimator of the parameters can be constructed by solving

$$(\hat{\alpha}_{ML}, \hat{\rho}_{ML}, \hat{\sigma}_{ML}) = \arg\max_{(\alpha,\rho,\sigma)} \sum_{j=1}^{T} \log d_j(v(\tau_j)) \tag{A12.8}$$

Unfortunately, no closed-form solution exists for these estimators and, therefore, the optimization must be carried out numerically.

In order to reduce the risk of instability in the parameters of the model, we introduce the following objective function:

$$\varphi_j(\alpha, \rho, \sigma) = \log d_j(v(\tau_j)) \cdot \exp(-\gamma(\tau_{T_j} - \tau_j)) \tag{A12.9}$$

The exponential term that is added to the likelihood function acts as a weighting factor that discounts the likelihood of the observations. This technique is a heuristic way of protecting the estimators against parameter instability.

The corresponding estimators are therefore given by

$$(\hat{\alpha}, \hat{\rho}, \hat{\sigma}) = \underset{(\alpha, \rho, \sigma)}{\arg\max} \sum_{j=1}^{T} \varphi_j(\alpha, \rho, \sigma) \tag{A12.10}$$

These estimators are exactly equal to the maximum likelihood estimators if $\gamma$ is equal to zero. In that case, the estimator is efficient in the sense that it meets the Cramer–Rao bound [see e.g. Greene (1997, pp. 133–138)]. If $\gamma > 0$, the estimator is still a member of the class of consistent and asymptotically Gaussian M-estimators [see e.g. Gourieroux and Monfort (1996, chapter 8)]. Defining $\theta = (\alpha \quad \rho \quad \sigma)^T$, the covariance matrix of our estimator is given by

$$\sqrt{T}(\hat{\theta} - \theta) \underset{T \to \infty}{\to} N(0, J^{-1}IJ^{-1})$$

$$J = E\left[\frac{\partial^2 \varphi}{\partial \theta \, \partial \theta^T}\right]$$

$$I = E\left[\frac{\partial \varphi}{\partial \theta} \frac{\partial \varphi}{\partial \theta^T}\right] \tag{A12.11}$$

and the covariance matrix is estimated as follows:

$$\hat{J} = \frac{1}{T} \sum_j \left[\frac{\partial^2 \varphi_j}{\partial \theta \, \partial \theta^T}\right]$$

$$\hat{I} = \frac{1}{T} \sum_j \left[\frac{\partial \varphi_j}{\partial \theta} \frac{\partial \varphi_j}{\partial \theta^T}\right] \tag{A12.12}$$

# ACKNOWLEDGMENTS

The authors thank the conference participants at the INFORMS Annual Meeting 2002 for helpful comments. The authors are grateful for research assistance from Gaurav Shah and for discussions with Jukka Ruusunen and Sophie Shive.

# REFERENCES

Björk T. and Landén C. (2000). "On the Term Structure of Futures and Forward Prices". SSE/EFI Working Paper Series in Economics and Finance, No. 417.

Black F. (1976). "The Pricing of Commodity Contracts". *Journal of Financial Economics* **3**: 167–179.

Deng S.-J. (1999). "Stochastic Models of Energy Commodity Prices: Mean-reversion with Jumps and Spikes". University of California Energy Institute, PWP-073.

Deng S.-J., Johnson B. and Sogomonian A. (2001). "Exotic Electricity Options and the Valuation of Electricity Generation and Transmission Assets". *Decision Support Systems* **3**: 383–392.

Geman H. and Vasicek O. (2001). "Forwards and Futures on Non-storable Commodities: The Case of Electricity". *RISK*, August.

Gourieroux C. and Monfort A. (1996). *Statistiques et Modèles économétriques*. Economica, Paris.

Greene W.H. (1997). *Econometric Analysis*. Prentice Hall, New Jersey.

Heath D., Jarrow R. and Morton A. (1992). "Bond Pricing and the Term Structure of Interest Rates". *Econometrica* **60**: 77–106.

Hull J. (2000). *Options, Futures and Other Derivatives*, 4th edn. Prentice-Hall, Englewood Cliffs, NJ.

Jaillet P., Ronn E. and Tompaidis S. (2001). "Valuation Commodity Based Swing Options". Working Paper, UT Austin.

Keppo J. (2002a). "Pricing of Electricity Swing Options". Preprint, University of Michigan, URL http://www-personal.engin.umich.edu/~keppo/swing.pdf

Keppo J. (2002b). "Optimality with Hydropower System". *IEEE Transactions on Power Systems* **3**: 583–589.

Koekebakker S. and Ollmar F. (2001). "Forward Curve Dynamics in the Nordic Electricity Market". Preprint, Norwegian School of Economics and Business Administration, URL http://www.nhh.no/for/dp/2001/2101.pdf

Lucia J.J. and Schwartz E.S. (2002). "Electricity Prices and Power Derivatives: Evidence from the Nordic Power Exchange". *Review of Derivatives Research* **5**: 5–50.

Nord Pool. (2002). Product information, URL http://www.nordpool.com

Schwartz E. (1997). "The Stochastic Behavior of Commodity Prices". *Journal of Finance* **52**(3): 923–973.

Schwert G.W. (2002). "Stock Volatility in the New Millennium: How Wacky is Nasdaq?" *Journal of Monetary Economics* **49**: 3–26.

Skantze P.L. and Ilic M.D. (2001). *Valuation, Hedging and Speculation in Competitive Electricity Markets: A Fundamental Approach*. Kluwer Academic, New York.

Thompson A.C. (1995). "Valuation of Path-dependent Contingent Claims with Multiple Exercise Decisions over Time: The Case of Take-or-Pay". *Journal of Financial and Quantitative Analysis* **30**: 271–293.

Vehviläinen I. (2002). "Basics of Electricity Derivatives Pricing in Competitive Markets". *Applied Mathematical Finance* **9**: 45–60.

Wallace S.W. and Fleten S.E. (2002). "Stochastic Programming Models in Energy". Preprint, Norwegian University of Science and Technology, URL http://www.iot.ntnu.no/~fleten/publ/fw/FletenWallace02.pdf

# 13
# The Forward Curve Dynamic and Market Transition Forecasts

SVETLANA BOROVKOVA

*Department of Applied Mathematics, Delft University of Technology, 2628 CD Delft, The Netherlands*

## ABSTRACT

We study the forward curves of energy futures. We distinguish two main types of forward curve dynamic: one characterized by alternating backwardation and contango states and another governed by seasonal effects. The first situation is typical for e.g. crude oil markets and the second for seasonal commodities such as electricity and natural gas futures and the spark spread. For these, we define the de-seasoned forward curve as the deviation of the forward curve from the seasonal component, estimated from historical data.

We address problems of predicting changes in the term structure and detecting deviations of the forward curve from the typical seasonal pattern. To do this we introduce two indicators: the first is based on the strength of the backwardation/contango market and the second on principal component analysis of the forward curve. Applying these indicators to electricity and oil futures price series shows that they reflect changes in the forward curve remarkably well. To simulate the forward curve dynamic, a smooth stationary bootstrap method is developed. It preserves the characteristic features of the futures prices and can be used for simulating the distributions and critical regions of the indicators.

## 13.1 THE TERM STRUCTURE OF COMMODITY FUTURES PRICES

*Futures* are contracts for delivery of some commodity or other financial instrument at different times in the future. These future times are called *expiry dates*, or *expiries*. Prices for futures with different expiries are recorded regularly, e.g. daily. The collection of futures prices with different expiries is called the *term structure*. The collection of the prices of futures with different expiries on a particular day (i.e. an instantaneous "snapshot" of futures prices) is called the *forward curve*.

Crude oil and oil product futures have been traded on the London International Petroleum Exchange (LIPE) and New York Mercantile Exchange (NYMEX) for many years, and futures contracts for natural gas were introduced on the LIPE in 1997. Trading in electricity futures started on NYMEX in 1996 and very recently (on 19 March 2001) on LIPE. Monthly electricity contracts are traded on LIPE for 9, 10 or 11 consecutive months. Figure 13.1 shows a series of daily Brent oil futures prices for 12 consecutive expiry months from 1994 to 2001 and

*Modelling Prices in Competitive Electricity Markets.* Edited by D.W. Bunn.
© 2004 John Wiley & Sons, Ltd. ISBN 0-470-84860-X.

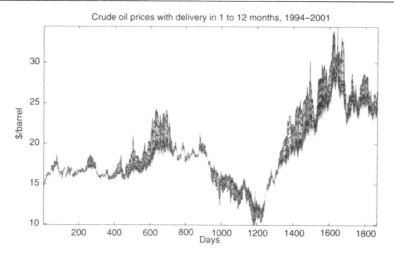

**Figure 13.1**   Brent oil daily futures prices, 1994–2001

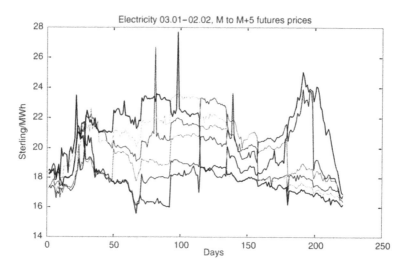

**Figure 13.2**   Electricity daily futures prices, 2001–2002

Figure 13.2 a series of daily electricity futures prices for 6 consecutive months from the start of the contract to 2002.

Forward curves play a central role in commodity markets. The relationship between prices of futures with different expiries, summarized in the forward curve, is as important as the absolute price levels. The forward prices are critical to decision making in trading, hedging, planning of energy projects and so on. The shape of the forward curve reflects market participants' perceptions of anticipated price trends and market fundamentals.

In the energy industry *inter-commodity spreads* are as important as prices. For instance, the spread between crude oil and gasoline indicates the refinery margin and the *spark spread* gives the gross-generation profit margin earned by buying natural gas and burning it to produce electricity. The forward curves for inter-commodity spreads are also of great interest to market participants.

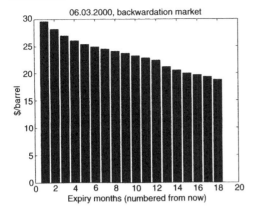 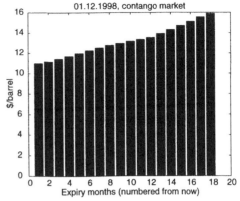

**Figure 13.3**   Backwardation and contango forward curves

It is well known that the forecasting power of forward curves for absolute prices is rather poor. The situation is slightly different for inter-commodity spreads, where forward curves have been successfully used to forecast future values of spreads.

Methods introduced here are applicable to forward curves of inter-commodity spreads as well as of futures prices.

Although the prices on futures with different expiry dates are strongly dependent, there is no exact relationship between them. This is the fundamental difference between commodities and financial futures. Recall that for futures on stocks or investment commodities, such as gold, there is a simple formula relating prices of futures with different expiries:

$$F(t + T) = F(t)e^{rT}$$

where $F(t)$ is the price of futures with expiry date $t$ and $r$ is the interest rate. So in this case the forward curve can only be rising and its precise form is determined by the spot price and the interest rate. This deterministic relationship does not hold for commodities with high and uncertain storage costs such as oil or non-storable commodities such as agricultural products. For these the relationship between futures with different expiries is largely uncertain. The situation is somewhat in between in the case of electricity and natural gas futures, where seasonal effects play an important role. For these some information is available in the form of the typical seasonal price pattern and there is only partial uncertainty about the forward curve, i.e. how the actual forward curve deviates from the seasonal pattern.

For many futures markets such as crude oil, futures with earlier expiry dates can be either cheaper or more expensive than those expiring later. This relationship defines two global market states. These states are usually referred to as *contango* and *backwardation*. The backwardation market is characterized by a falling forward curve and the contango market by a rising forward curve. These two situations are illustrated for oil futures in Figure 13.3. These market states mean that the anticipated future spot price is lower than the current one in the backwardation market and higher in the contango market. Knowing whether the market is in backwardation or contango is crucial to market participants. It influences many decisions in trading and planning, carries a lot of information about market fundamentals and often serves as an indication of future price trends.

The shape of the forward curve is determined by fundamental economic factors such as supply and demand, storage costs, "convenience" of holding a commodity, current price levels

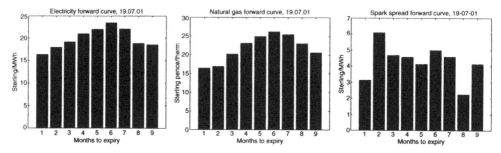

**Figure 13.4**    Electricity, NG and spark spread forward curves, 19.07.2001

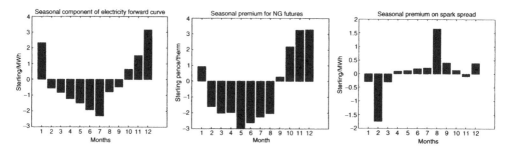

**Figure 13.5**    Seasonal components of the electricity, NG and spark spread forward curves

and in large part by the market's perception of future price trends. The forward curve changes shape as the fundamentals of the market change.

The situation is different for seasonal commodities such as electricity and natural gas. For these, the shape of the forward curve is largely determined by the seasonal demand for the commodity. Other factors, such as the overall state of the energy market, play a secondary role. For instance, in the UK there is always higher demand for gas and electricity during the winter months, resulting in a price premium for futures expiring then. Typical forward curves for LIPE electricity, natural gas futures and the spark spread[1] are shown in Figure 13.4. All curves are plotted for 19 July 2001, so the front-month contract is July. As we expect, the peak in futures prices is for the contract expiring in 6 months, i.e. in December. The spark spread is typically higher in the summer, since it is dominated by the gas price which is low then. So the peak in the spark spread is for the next-month contract, which is August.

The seasonal component dominates the shape of the forward curve and reflects a seasonal premium. To estimate this seasonal component, we first align the futures prices by delivery months (not by number of months to expiry) and then subtract the average daily levels from the historical forward curves (what is left we call the *de-centered forward curves*). Then the estimated monthly premiums are the averages across the months over the entire dataset. Figure 13.5 shows the estimated monthly premium (i.e. the seasonal component of the forward curve) for the LIPE Electricity futures, LIPE Natural Gas futures and for the spark spread.

---

[1] We computed the spark spread as the difference between the electricity price and natural gas price multiplied by the factor 0.68. This factor is obtained from converting therms into MWh and assuming 50% generator efficiency, common in the UK.

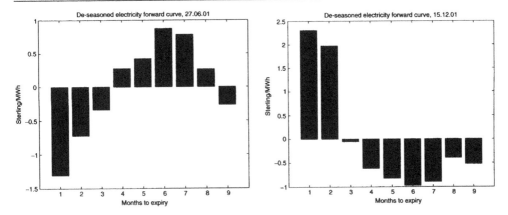

**Figure 13.6**   Examples of electricity de-seasoned forward curves

If there was no further uncertainty about futures prices, the remaining part of the forward curve would always be flat. In reality this is not the case. Figure 13.6 shows two examples of de-seasoned (and de-centered) electricity forward curves, and they are far from flat.

The market's perceptions of future price deviations from the seasonal pattern are influenced by unusual weather circumstances, unexpected demand levels and so on. These deviations are reflected in the de-seasoned forward curve (especially in its front end), and situations analogous to the backwardation/contango market states can arise.

We have examined two situations, corresponding to either seasonal or non-seasonal commodities and spreads. For the former, the typical shape of the forward curve is known in advance and the only uncertainty (apart from the absolute price levels) is the deviation from the seasonal pattern. For the latter, the forward curve can only be rising (contango) or falling (backwardation), but the state of the market is uncertain in advance. In fact, the latter situation is also characteristic of mature futures markets where seasonal effects are a factor, such as oil product futures (heating oil, gasoline). Seasonal effects can still be seen in the spot price, but the seasonal influences of supply and demand on the futures prices are hedged for a large part by e.g. oil futures.

In the next section we shall introduce a number of indicators describing the forward curve dynamic. Our goal is twofold: to forecast transitions between backwardation and contango and to detect deviations of the forward curve from the typical seasonal shape. Initially this research was motivated by the former problem, so we shall address it first. However, these indicators can also be used for the latter problem and can be successfully applied to electricity and other seasonal commodities and their spreads.

## 13.2   FORECASTING MARKET TRANSITIONS

For oil futures, changes between the backwardation and contango markets are gradual and rarely happen instantly. It usually takes from a few days to a few weeks and almost always passes through an intermediate stage, where all futures prices are approximately the same, resulting in a flat forward curve. However, a flat forward curve alone is not in itself a definite indicator of a changing market: since the market could still return to its previous state. Our goal is to detect or – better still – to forecast the switch from one market state to another as early as possible. Often, the first (and maybe the second) inter-month spreads are used for this purpose.

The transition between backwardation and contango occurs when expectations of market participants and/or market fundamentals change. Hence, information about market fundamentals can help in forecasting a transition. In practice, however, traders are interested in working with indicators derived solely from prices, such as known financial indicators (relative strength index, fast and slow moving average, etc.). This is one of the main reasons why the first inter-month spread is often used to monitor the market change. However, it can be quite inefficient since it uses only the information about the futures prices with two closest expiries, and it can be highly volatile. All this calls for a data-driven, automated procedure for forecasting the market transition, in the form of indicators that use all available futures prices and can easily be incorporated into trading programs and other software.

Here we introduce two types of change indicators that use the entire forward curve. The first indicator measures the "strength" of backwardation or contango market, i.e. the steepness of the forward curve. The second indicator is based on a principal component analysis of the forward curve.

Here we speak of "change indicators" rather than of "test statistics", since we do not formally define the null hypothesis and an alternative. We do not perform formal statistical tests here; rather we are more interested in devising early warning signals for changes in the term structure.

The main difficulty in performing any statistical analysis on term structure data is that we are dealing with multivariate strongly correlated time series. So any assumptions of independence, common in classical statistics, do not hold. Deriving formal test procedures on the basis of the indicators and their asymptotic properties is thus a challenging task, and is a subject of continuing research.

### 13.2.1  Weighted strength indicator

Let $(F(t))_t = (F_1(t), F_2(t), \ldots, F_N(t))_t$ be a series of daily futures prices, indexed by $N$ expiry dates. Let $S_k(t) = F_{k+1}(t) - F_k(t)$ $(k = 1, \ldots, N-1, \ t = 1, 2, \ldots)$ be the $k$th inter-month spread.

The first candidate for the change indicator is the quantity

$$I_1(t) = \sum_{k=1}^{N-1} w_k S_k(t)$$

where $(w_k)_{k=1,\ldots,N-1}$ is a suitably chosen collection of weights. $I_1(t)$ measures the steepness of the forward curve on the day $t$ and the following three situations can arise:

(i) $I_1(t) \gg 0 \longrightarrow$ rising forward curve (contango);
(ii) $I_1(t) \ll 0 \longrightarrow$ falling forward curve (backwardation);
(iii) $I_1(t) \approx 0 \longrightarrow$ flat forward curve (intermediate market state) and hence, possibility of an impending change.

Futures prices are highly volatile and so is the indicator $I_1$. Hence, it can get close to 0 solely as a result of a random shock. On the other hand, the transition between market states happens gradually. So only a persistent low value of $I_1$ can indicate a change in the market. Hence,

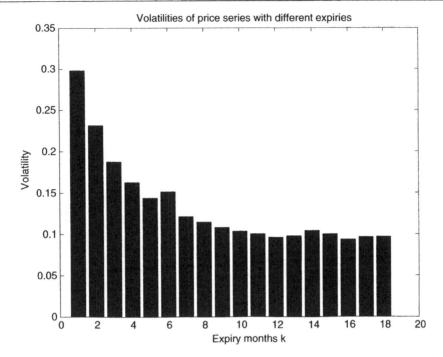

**Figure 13.7**   Volatilities of oil futures prices

instead of the "raw" indicator $I_1$, we suggest using the moving average smoothed indicator $I_1'$:

$$I_1'(t) = \frac{1}{M} \sum_{i=0}^{M-1} I_1(t-i)$$

where $M$ is the size of the moving window.

The sign of the indicator $I_1'(t)$ characterizes a particular market state and, when change takes place, $I_1'(t)$ changes sign. If the market state (and, hence, the sign of $I_1'(t)$) is irrelevant and only its change is of interest, then the following version of the indicator can be used:

$$I_1''(t) = \frac{1}{M} \sum_{i=0}^{M-1} |I_1(t-i)|$$

Then the values of $I_1''(t)$ close to 0 signal a possible change.

When choosing the weights $(w_k)$, two observations should be considered. The first is that the volatility of futures prices $(F_k(t))_{k=1,\ldots,N}$ decreases as the time to expiry $k$ increases, as Figure 13.7 illustrates for Brent oil futures. However, Figure 13.8 shows that for the inter-month spreads $(S_k(t))$ it is not always the case. The volatility of inter-month spreads with later expiries is high due to lack of liquidity.

So, first, we scale $S_k(t)$ by the corresponding sample standard deviations $s_k$:

$$\tilde{S}_k(t) = S_k(t)/s_k$$

This also allows us to apply this change indicator to incomplete data, i.e. when futures for some expiries are not traded or their prices are not available for some reason.

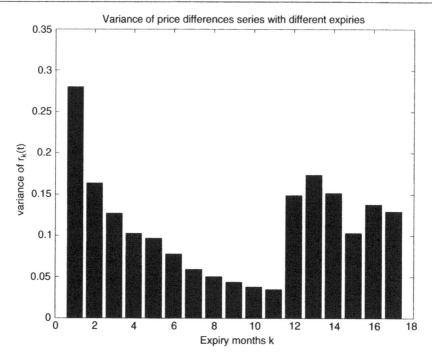

**Figure 13.8**  Volatilities of inter-month spreads

The second observation is that usually the prices for futures with closer expiries "drive" those with later expiries; so the weights must be defined to reflect this. We suggest taking weights of the form:

$$w_k = \gamma^k$$

for some $\gamma \in (0, 1)$. By this, we have a smooth way of assigning the significance of price movements on the shape of the forward curve. We give more weight to movements of the front end of the forward curve and discount price movements of futures with later expiries.

The choice of $\gamma$ for a particular price series can be data-driven, by a variant of cross-validation on the basis of historical data. Alternatively, we can assume that the correlations between inter-month spreads $\rho(k) = \mathrm{Corr}(S_1(t), S_{1+k}(t))$ decrease geometrically in $k$ and do not depend on $t$ (this assumption is realistic for many futures). Hence, we can choose $\gamma$ such that $\gamma^k$ approximates the estimated correlations $\hat{\rho}(k)$. Applying the indicator to Brent oil futures shows that values of $\gamma$ in the range 0.8–0.95 perform quite well.

The moving average window $M$ must also be chosen. Choosing $M$ too large leads to a late signal (oversmoothing), while choosing $M$ too small results in indicators that are too noisy (undersmoothing). In practice, we have to balance these two factors. For example, we can use two or more different values of $M$ ("fast" and "slow" moving averages), as is often done for price charts.

Here we introduced weights reflecting a "typical" behavior of the forward curve. In general, the choice of weights $(w_k)_k$ is a matter left to the model builder. For some commodities we may observe features of the forward curve different from those mentioned above.

Then these features can be incorporated into the weights to enhance the performance of the indicator.

### 13.2.2 Principal component indicator

Day-to-day movements of the forward curve $(F_1(t), F_2(t), \ldots, F_N(t))$ comprise three main components:

  (i) upwards or downwards movement of the entire forward curve;
 (ii) "tilting" of the curve;
(iii) change in its curvature.

    Mathematically, these three movements of the forward curve correspond to changes in the first three principal components of the $n \times N$ array of the observed series $(F_1(t), \ldots, F_N(t))_{t=1}^n$. These components are commonly referred to as *level, slope* and *curvature*. Together they describe about 95% of the variation of the forward curve. Here we are interested in movements of the second type, i.e. when the ends of the forward curve move in opposite directions.

    In studies involving a large number of observed variables, it is often convenient to consider a smaller number of *linear combinations* of these variables which summarize their main features. Principal components are such uncorrelated linear combinations. There are as many principal components as original variables and taken together, they explain all the variability in the original data. However, because of the way they are calculated, it is usually possible to consider only a few of the principal components, which together explain *most* of the original variation.

    When studying the forward curve, there are $N$ original variables (futures prices for $N$ expiry dates). But the principal component analysis allows us to concentrate on only three main combinations of these variables, which together describe virtually all possible forward curves.

    To visualize the principal components, the coefficients of these linear combinations (i.e. of the principal components) are used. They are called the *principal component loadings* and they provide a convenient summary of the influence of the original variables on the principal components, and thus a useful basis for interpretation. Figure 13.9 shows loadings of the first three principal components estimated on the historical Brent oil futures prices. From this figure it is clear why these principal components of the forward curve are called the level, slope and curvature.

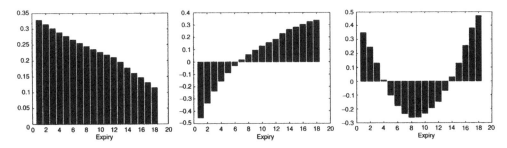

**Figure 13.9** Loadings of the first three principal components for oil futures prices

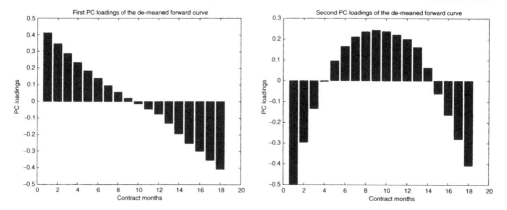

**Figure 13.10**   Loadings of the first and second principal components of the centered series

The second principal component corresponds to the slope of the forward curve, and hence it can be used to construct a change indicator.

In fact, instead of the regular forward curve $(F_k(t))_{k=1,\ldots,N}$, we shall consider the centered forward curve:

$$(\bar{F}_1(t), \ldots, \bar{F}_N(t)) = (F_1(t) - \bar{F}(t), \ldots, F_N(t) - \bar{F}(t))$$

where $\bar{F}(t)$ is the average of $F_1(t), \ldots, F_N(t)$ (i.e. the absolute price level on day $t$). Then the *first* (and not the second) principal component of the array $(\bar{F}_1(t), \ldots, \bar{F}_N(t))_{t=1,\ldots,n}$ corresponds to the slope, since absolute levels of the forward curve are removed by centering. Figure 13.10 shows the loadings of the first two principal components of this series and confirms the above conclusion.

We define the "raw" *principal component indicator* as the projection of the daily centered forward curve onto the first principal component:

$$I_2(t) = \sum_{k=1}^{N} PCL_k^{(1)} \cdot \bar{F}_k(t)$$

where $PCL_k^{(1)}$ $(k = 1, \ldots, N)$ are the first principal component loadings of the centered forward curves. Values of the indicator close to zero correspond to a flat forward curve, while high absolute values signify a strong backwardation or contango market.

The corresponding moving average smoothed indicators are then:

$$I_2'(t) = \frac{1}{M} \sum_{i=0}^{M-1} I_2(t - i)$$

and

$$I_2''(t) = \frac{1}{M} \sum_{i=0}^{M-1} |I_2(t - i)|$$

The problem of choosing $M$ can be dealt with in the same way as for the first indicator, i.e. by considering fast and slow moving averages.

### 13.2.3   Indicators for seasonal commodities

For electricity and other seasonal commodities and spreads, the dynamic of the *de-seasoned forward curve* is of interest. So we subtract both absolute levels and the seasonal component from the forward curves and then apply the weighted strength indicator or principal component analysis. It is essential that the spikes in the electricity prices are removed, since the principal components (as well as the first indicator) are very sensitive to abnormally high price changes. To remove spikes, we apply the following method: we define a "spike" as two consecutive and opposite price movements, each larger than three standard deviations of the daily price movements. Having identified a spike, we replace it by the average of the prices before and after the spike. Note that removing spikes has no negative effect on our analysis, since we are interested in gradual and persistent changes in the forward curve.

Figure 13.11 shows the first two principal components of the de-seasoned electricity forward curve dynamic. The slope and curvature components can still be identified, though perhaps not as clearly as in the case of oil futures. The two earliest expiry months have the highest first principal component loadings. This confirms that most deviations do occur in the front end of the forward curve.

We define the principal component indicator to be the projection of the de-seasoned and de-centered forward curve on the first principal component. The weighted strength indicator is defined in the same way as above, with weights reflecting particular features of a commodity. For instance, for electricity the first and second weights should be chosen significantly higher than all others. This will enable the indicator to pick up the most significant deviations in the forward curve, which occur in its front end.

The interpretation of both the principal component and weighted strength indicators for electricity and other seasonal commodities is different than for crude oil futures. Here, a typical situation is a flat de-seasoned forward curve. Hence, typically indicators' values are close to zero. So the indicators' values *far from zero* show a significant deviation of the forward curve from its seasonal shape. This information is valuable for constructing trading strategies (as we show later) as well as for detecting shifts in market fundamentals and for other applications.

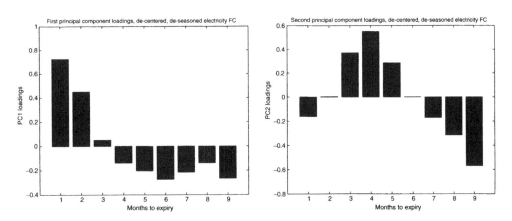

**Figure 13.11**   First and second principal components of the de-seasoned electricity forward curve

## 13.3   CRITICAL REGIONS AND BOOTSTRAP METHODS

### 13.3.1   Using the change indicators

The simplest way of using the indicators for forecasting oil market transitions is to generate a warning signal if the value of an indicator falls into some critical $\epsilon$-neighborhood of 0. For electricity, spark spread and other seasonal commodities, a warning signal should be generated if the indicator's absolute value exceeds some high threshold $\theta$. Critical values of $\epsilon$ and $\theta$ can be specified via the distributions of the indicators and their extremes under the null hypothesis of no change, or in the seasonal case, under the null hypothesis of no deviation from the seasonal pattern.

The ideas of sequential testing in change point analysis suggest another procedure (see e.g. Csorgo and Horvath (1997)). At time $t + h$, we compare the moving average indicator $I''_{1,2}(t)$ with $\frac{1}{h} \sum_{j=1}^{h} |I_{1,2}(t + j)|$, where $h$ does not have to be equal to the size of the moving window $M$. The following test statistic is then used:

$$T_{1,2}(t) = \frac{1}{h} \sum_{j=1}^{h} |I_{1,2}(t + j)| - I''_{1,2}(t)$$

and we reject the null hypothesis at time $t$ if the value of $T_{1,2}(t)$ is large (i.e. greater than some critical value). The choice of $h$ is a problem similar to the choice of $M$: if it is small, then random fluctuations can cause false signals and if it is too large, signals will be delayed. The distributions of the test statistics $T_{1,2}$ and of their maxima are again necessary to derive the critical values for such tests.

If we assume a parametric model for the futures prices, then it may be possible to compute the distributions of the indicators and the test statistics $T_1, T_2$. A widely used model is the continuous-time mean-reverting diffusion process for the spot price $P(t)$:

$$dP(t) = \alpha(\mu(t) - P(t))dt + \sigma(t, P(t))dW(t)$$

where $\mu(t)$ is a deterministic mean function (possibly containing a seasonal component), $\alpha$ is the mean-reversion parameter and $\sigma(t, P(t))$ is the volatility process. The futures prices with different expiries $T$ are then obtained from the spot price by a relationship similar to that for financial futures:

$$F_T(t) = P(t)\, e^{(r(t)+C_s(t)-C_y(t)-S(t,T))(T-t)}$$

where $r(t)$ is the interest rate, $C_y(t)$ is a stochastic convenience yield, $C_s(t)$ the marginal storage costs (for storable commodities) and $S(t, T)$ is a suitably defined seasonal premium (for seasonal commodities).

A possible parametric model in discrete time is a vector-autoregressive process (VAR) with Gaussian innovations:

$$F(t + 1) = A_1 F(t - 1) + A_2 F(t - 2) + \cdots + A_p F(t - p) + E_{t+1}$$

where $A_1, \ldots, A_p$ are the coefficient matrices and $(E_t)_t$ is a white-noise process (i.e. vectors $E_t$ are uncorrelated and each $E_t$ has a multivariate normal distribution with mean zero and covariance matrix $\Sigma$). Under some conditions this model defines a stationary process. Hence, it can be used for futures prices after subtracting all seasonal components. In fact, the autoregressive model arises if we assume the mean-reverting model in continuous time and use its discrete-time approximation by the Euler scheme.

For those interested in more detail, there is a vast literature on general term structure models (see e.g. Bjork and Landen (2000)). For a discussion on oil futures term structure models see e.g. Gabillon (1994), Schwartz (1997). The literature on realistic models for electricity futures prices is not yet very well developed, but research in this area is active.

The consequence of both vector-autoregressive and mean-reversion models is that the distribution of the price series is multivariate normal, with a given covariance matrix that can be consistently estimated from the data. All of the indicators and the test statistics introduced above are then also normally distributed, since they are linear functions of the futures prices. Their variances can be expressed via the autocovariances and cross-covariances of the original multivariate time series, and, hence, consistently estimated. However, in our case deriving the explicit as well as asymptotic formulas for these variances is very involved. So instead of computing the variances explicitly, we can fit a parametric model to the historical data and simulate the distribution of the indicators and the test statistics using a Monte Carlo method.

A major drawback of the above approach is that the parametric models, such as vector autoregression, are often unrealistic. So for practical purposes, we suggest approximating these distributions by bootstrap distributions. For this, we outline a bootstrap procedure for simulating the forward curve dynamic that takes into account its characteristic features. This bootstrap scheme can also be used in other applications where many simulations of the term structure data are required.

### 13.3.2  Smooth stationary bootstrap

The main idea of bootstrap is to obtain the sampling distribution of a certain statistic by repeatedly resampling the data and recomputing the value of this statistic on the basis of the bootstrap samples. In this way, we replace the underlying theoretical distribution of the observations by their empirical distribution. Since, by a version of the Glivenko–Cantelli theorem, the empirical distribution is close to the theoretical one, the continuity argument usually assures that the bootstrapped distribution of the desired statistic is also close to its sampling distribution.

The classical bootstrap procedure of Efron (drawing observations from the original dataset with replacement) does not work for time series data, since the dependence structure is then destroyed. Various block resampling techniques for time series data are given in the literature, such as the moving block bootstrap (Kunsch, 1989). The problem with these procedures is that the resulting bootstrapped sequence is usually not stationary. As a solution to this problem, the *stationary bootstrap* was suggested (Politis and Romano, 1994).

Here we introduce a smooth version of the stationary bootstrap, whereby we resample the historical multivariate price series $(F(t))_{t=1,\ldots,n}$ in a way that preserves its term structure properties. With the help of this procedure we can simulate the distributions of the change indicators and the corresponding test statistics.

Recall that changes in term structure happen gradually. Hence, a generated bootstrapped series $(F^*(t))$ should have the property that any next-day forward curve (a vector $(F_1^*(t+1),\ldots,F_N^*(t+1))$) is similar to the previous one $(F_1^*(t),\ldots,F_N^*(t))$.

We generate bootstrapped series $(F^*(t))_{t=1,\ldots,n}$ as follows. On the first step, we choose $F^*(1)$ from $(F(t))_{t=1}^n$ at random (with probability $1/n$). Suppose on the $i$th step we have $F^*(i) = F(k)$ for some $k = 1,\ldots,n$. Then, on the next $(i+1$st) step, with probability $p \in (0,1)$, we continue along the original series: $F^*(i+1) = F(k+1)$. With probability $1-p$, we make a "jump" to a new observation in the original series. We do it in such a way that the historical forward curves that are "close" (in some sense) to $F^*(i)$ have higher chance of being chosen than those "further away". More precisely, we let $F^*(i + 1)$ be $F(j)$, $j = 1, \ldots, n$ according to the probabilistic rule

$$P[F^*(i + 1) = F(j)] \sim \| F^*(i), F(j) \|^{-1}$$

Here $\| \cdot, \cdot \|$ is some distance between two $N$-dimensional vectors, e.g. maximum or $L_1$ or Euclidean distance. We repeat this scheme until a bootstrapped series of desired length is obtained. In this way, the "smooth" dynamics of the original centered series is preserved and no "discontinuities", such as sudden change in term structure, arise. The implementation of this probabilistic sampling algorithm is relatively straightforward.

To simulate the distribution of an indicator under the null hypothesis of no change, we can use a distance that puts an extra penalty on the pair of forward curves from opposite market states. Then, depending on $F^*(1)$, the generated price series is either always in contango or always in backwardation. This can lead to an asymmetric critical neighborhood of 0 for indicators $I'_{1,2}$, which is realistic for e.g. oil futures.

We suggest applying the smooth stationary bootstrap algorithm to the series of centered and de-seasoned forward curves $(\bar{F}(t))_t$ rather than to the original historical forward curves $(F_k(t))_t$. This is because absolute price levels are subtracted and hence, for the centered series there are more "similar" historical forward curves to choose from. The resampled series can be used directly to estimate the distributions of the change indicators, since for these neither absolute price levels nor seasonalities are relevant. For general-purpose simulations, the following three-stage resampling scheme is suggested: first, apply the smooth stationary bootstrap separately to the centered de-seasoned historical forward curves and to the historical absolute price levels. Then add the resampled forward curves and the resampled price levels to the seasonal component estimated from the historical data.

## 13.4  APPLICATION TO ELECTRICITY AND OIL FUTURES

First, we apply the principal component indicator to the series of electricity futures prices in 2001–2002 for nine consecutive expiries. We de-seasoned the historical forward curves by subtracting the estimated seasonal premium and applied principal component analysis to the de-seasoned and de-centered historical forward curves.

Figure 13.12 shows the principal component indicator together with its 90% bootstrap-generated thresholds. Recall that high (in absolute value) values of the indicator signal deviations of the forward curve from the typical seasonal shape.

The figure clearly shows a few short periods when the indicator exceeds the threshold. In these periods, there are significant deviations of the futures prices from the seasonal pattern. For instance, around the 180th observation (beginning of December 2001) the indicator exceeds the upper threshold. This means that during this period the futures with shorter expiries were significantly overpriced compared to the average December premium.

In the absence of delivery issues, the simplest speculative trading strategy during this period would be: sell short futures with closer expiries, buy futures expiring later and close all the positions as soon as the indicator returns inside the threshold bounds. Already this simple strategy generated profits when tested on the historical data for LIPE electricity and natural gas futures. More sophisticated trading strategies based on the information provided by the indicator are being developed at present.

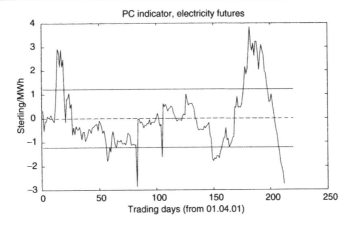

**Figure 13.12**  Principal component indicator for LIPE electricity futures

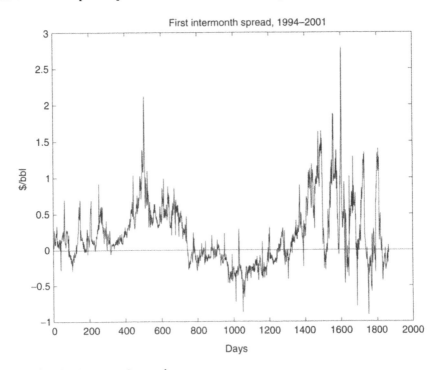

**Figure 13.13**  First inter-month spread

Next, we illustrate the performance of the indicators on the time series of daily oil futures prices. We compute the indicators $I_1'$ and $I_2'$ on the basis of 12 consecutive expiry months, with moving window size $M = 10$ (two weeks of trading days) and $\gamma = 0 : 9$.

Figure 13.13 shows the first inter-month spread, which is rather noisy. Figure 13.14 shows the principal component indicator with the first inter-month spread and the bootstrap-estimated 5%-critical region around zero (which is slightly asymmetric). The right plot shows that the

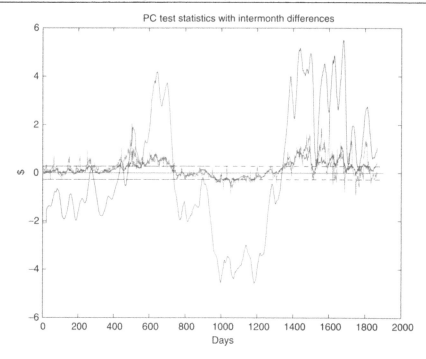

**Figure 13.14**  PC indicator

indicator enters the critical region just prior to the market transition, does not produce "false alarms" and assesses the market state more smoothly.

In Figure 13.15 the weighted strength and principal component indicators are shown together with the first inter-month spread for the same data. For clarity we show in Figure 13.16 both indicators applied to the oil futures prices of 1998–2001 (this dataset contained 18 consecutive futures prices). During this period, only one market transition took place: the contango market started shrinking around the 315th observation and then moved into strong backwardation around the 400th observation. Often the principal component indicator is slightly behind the weighted strength indicator in approaching zero. However, it produces fewer false alarms and seems to determine the market state better. The weighted strength indicator changes sign rather early, anticipating the market transition. The principal component indicator signals definite market transition just before the 400th observation. In practice, we suggest using both indicators at the same time: the weighted strength indicator for anticipating the market transition, and the principal component indicator for reinforcing the change signal.

## 13.5  CONCLUDING REMARKS

Here we have investigated the term structure of energy futures and developed new tools for detecting both changes in the forward curve and its deviations from the seasonal pattern. These tools have the form of *indicators* derived solely from futures prices. When applied to oil futures prices, the indicators forecast market transitions remarkably well.

We investigated typical seasonal patterns in the forward curves of electricity futures and the spark spread. We estimated the monthly premiums of electricity futures and the spark spread

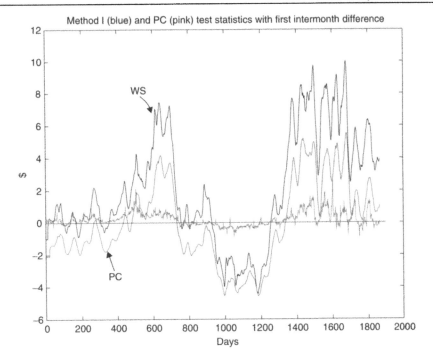

**Figure 13.15**   WS and PC indicators, 1994–2001

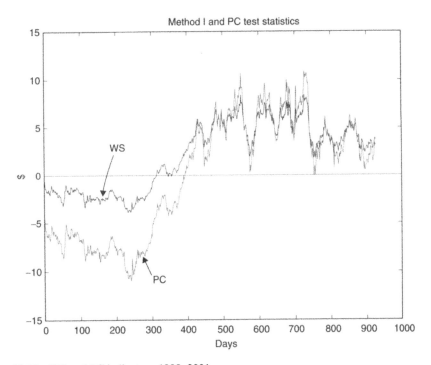

**Figure 13.16**   WS and PC indicators, 1998–2001

from the historical data and used them to de-season the forward curves. These de-seasoned forward curves were subsequently investigated by principal component analysis. We applied the indicators to the de-seasoned forward curves of electricity futures to detect significant deviations from the seasonal pattern. This leads to profitable trading strategies and greatly enhances assessment of the current market conditions. In general, all these developments open up new opportunities for making and maximizing the profits when trading in new liberalized electricity markets.

Current research in this area concentrates on developing realistic parametric models (both continuous and discrete-time) for electricity spot and futures prices (as well as for other seasonal commodities and spreads), testing these models on historical data and applying them to derivatives pricing, hedging and risk management.

# REFERENCES

Bjork T. and Landen C. (2000). "On the Term Structure of Futures and Forward Prices." *Technical Report,* Stockholm School of Economics.

Csorgo M. and Horvath L. (1997). *Limit Theorems in Change-Point Analysis.* Wiley Series in Probability and Statistics, John Wiley & Sons, New York.

Gabillon J. (1994). "Analyzing the Forward Curve." In *Managing Energy Price Risk.* Risk Publications, London.

Kunsch H.R. (1989). "The Jackknife and the Bootstrap for General Stationary Observations." *Annals of Statistics* **17**: 1217–1241.

Politis D.N. and Romano J.P. (1994). "The Stationary Bootstrap". *Journal of the American Statistical Association* **89**(428): 1303–1313.

Schwartz E.S. (1997). "The Stochastic Behavior of Commodity Prices: Implications for Valuation and Hedging". *Journal of Finance* **52**(3): 923–973.

# Part V
## Forecasting and Risk Management

# 14
# Price Modelling for Profit at Risk Management

JACOB LEMMING

*Systems Analysis Department, Risoe National Laboratory, Frederiksborgvej 399, DK-4000 Roskilde, Denmark*

## ABSTRACT

This chapter describes different approaches towards electricity price modelling and analyses how the choice of model structure and use of input data affects the solution to a simple risk management problem. Using profit at risk as the risk measure we illustrate both the separate and combined effects of price spikes and volume risk on the optimal risk management decision. Finally we illustrate that relatively small changes in the input data used to estimate a financial electricity price model can have a significant effect on the optimal risk management decision.

## 14.1 INTRODUCTION

As a consequence of market liberalization, price modelling has emerged as an important input to a wide range of decision problems in the electricity sector. Electricity prices are extremely volatile compared to prices in other commodity markets and choices concerning model structure and use of input data for parameter estimation will therefore often have a large effect on the solution to a subsequent decision problem.

When facing a risk management problem the decision maker must choose between a series of possible model structures for electricity prices and must determine a set of input data that includes as much relevant information about future price developments as possible. The aim of this chapter is to analyse the model risk that results from using financial electricity price models to create price scenarios for risk management problems in the electricity sector. To facilitate this analysis an overview of different electricity price model structures is provided and the effect of key parameters such as volume risk, price spikes and input data selection is analysed in detail.

As a case study we use a parametric financial electricity price model that includes both price spikes and seasonality and a simple risk management problem where an electricity generator hedges the income from a power plant with forward contracts to satisfy a Profit at Risk (PaR) limit. The PaR measure has received relatively limited attention in the academic literature and we therefore describe the merits of PaR compared to Value at Risk (VaR) as a risk measure in the electricity sector. Furthermore we use the case study to illustrate some counterintuitive results concerning optimal PaR levels for a portfolio consisting of a long call option and a short forward hedge.

*Modelling Prices in Competitive Electricity Markets.* Edited by D.W. Bunn.
© 2004 John Wiley & Sons, Ltd. ISBN 0-470-84860-X.

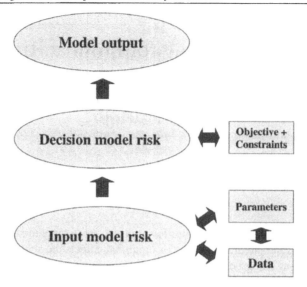

**Figure 14.1**   Elements in the modelling process that affect the solution to risk management problems

The output from risk management decision models is affected by a series of risk sources throughout the modelling process as illustrated in Figure 14.1. First of all the decision maker must formulate a risk management framework that fits the organization and translate this into a decision model in terms of objective, risk limits and input parameters.

Secondly, risk factors such as the electricity price must be modelled as input parameters. The literature on price modelling in the highly liquid and developed financial markets is extensive. To predict future price developments analysts use both technical analysis based on patterns in historical market price movements and fundamental analysis based on expectations about the development in the underlying market price drivers. Electricity markets worldwide are still in the development phase and not surprisingly there exist conflicting views about the value of tools such as technical or fundamental analysis for price modelling in electricity markets. In this chapter we show that relatively small changes in the input data set to parametric financial electricity price models can significantly affect the risk management decision. This implies a significant model risk, which must be taken into account when comparing financial price models with alternative approaches such as fundamental models.[1]

The structure of the chapter is as follows. Section 14.2 categorizes different price modelling techniques based on the input data used to estimate model parameters and describe the application of such models to electricity pricing. Section 14.3 describes a PaR-based risk management problem used as a case study and Section 14.4 describes models for the primary stochastic input parameters with emphasis on the different steps towards the construction of a parametric financial electricity price model. Section 14.5 presents experimental results that show how risk factors such as price spikes, forced outages and the choice of input data affect the solution to the PaR optimization problem. Finally Section 14.6 concludes.

---

[1] The distinction between financial and fundamental models is described in detail in Section 14.2.

## 14.2    ELECTRICITY PRICE MODELLING

A useful way of categorizing price models is to look at model structure in terms of parameters and the input data used to provide parameter estimates. In electricity markets one can distinguish between two main categories of input data:

* Market price data
* Fundamental data

With this distinction market price data comprise both historical spot prices and derivative prices such as the forward curve.[2] Fundamental data include technical and market-based information about market price drivers such as weather conditions, precipitation, production costs and other factors that affect the shape of future supply and demand curves in the market.

The distinction between fundamental data and market data sets the stage for two different approaches towards electricity price modelling. The first approach is based on econometric models such as Stochastic Differential Equations (SDE) known from financial theory. In such financial models the parametric is adapted to fit the characteristics of electricity prices and parameters are then estimated using market price data. The motivation is that of technical analysis where patterns in market data are assumed to be the most valuable predictor of future prices. The second approach is based on a technical bottom-up modelling of the electricity system where data about supply, transmission, distribution and demand is used to model future market price dynamics. The motivation here is that of fundamental analysis where the expected development in underlying price drivers is used to construct expectations about future price developments.

### 14.2.1    Financial models

In financial price models the time dynamics of market prices are driven by stochastic processes generally in the form of stochastic differential equations. As described in Clewlow and Strickland (1999b), most literature on financial price models falls into one of two main categories. The first category of models describe the spot price $P(t)$ dynamics along with other key state variables using a set of stochastic processes. These processes are generally spilt into a deterministic component $f(t)$ modelling trends and cycles and a stochastic component $S(t)$ modelling the uncertainty or distribution of prices. The second category of models use a similar set-up but focus directly on the dynamic evolution of the entire forward price curve. The two approaches are interrelated as forward prices can be derived from the risk-adjusted or risk-neutral version of a spot price process provided that an explicit solution to the stochastic differential equation governing the spot price can be obtained analytically (see Clewlow and Strickland (2000) for an example).

Applications of the spot price approach to electricity markets can be found in references such as Lucia and Schwartz (2002), De Jong and Huisman (2002), Pilipovic (1998), Deng (2000), Kellerhals (2001), Knittel and Roberts (2000), Barlow (2002) and Johnson and Barz (2000). References that apply the forward price approach to electricity pricing include Clewlow and Strickland (1999b), Koekebakker and Ollmar (2001), Clewlow and Strickland (1999a) and Joy (2000).

---

[2] The term forward curve refers here to the term structure of electricity prices, i.e. the forward price as a function of the time to maturity.

The main strength of financial models lies with the use of realized market prices, which include information about less tangible factors such as speculation, market power and the general psychology of traders. The main weakness is the potential lack of predictive power in historical data, especially in the new and dynamically developing electricity markets.

## 14.2.2  Fundamental models

Fundamental models constitute a category of engineering models based on a technical bottom-up modelling of the production, transmission and consumption parts of the system. This form of modelling tends to be rather complex, since it requires an accurate description of a large technical system including factors such as production capacity, production costs, transmission constraints and consumption patterns. Modelling the development of such factors over time is generally a data-intensive task and the large amount of stochastic fluctuations place an even higher demand on the amount and quality of input data required.

In fundamental models price spikes and seasonal variations are a direct result of movements in a set of underlying variables that must be modelled with a considerable degree of accuracy. The number of such underlying price-driving variables far exceeds the number of variables used in any financial model. As a result no two fundamental models will generally be based on the exact same data set, making them much harder to verify and compare than financial models.

In addition to the complex technical modelling the main challenge with fundamentally based price modelling lies with the translation of modelling results into credible market price scenarios. The preferences of suppliers and consumers must be accurately reflected through the modelling, which is a difficult task.

## 14.2.3  Combined approaches

The problems sketched above with financial and fundamental models explain why practitioners often prefer models that combine the two model types. Fundamental data contains invaluable information about short-term weather-related changes in supply and demand, which generally cannot be found in market data. Also, in the very long term, market data will tend to be insufficient. This is because the number of yearly observations required to statistically estimate how fluctuations in annual hydrological conditions (wet years vs. dry years) affect average annual prices would lack predictive power by the time it became available. On the other hand, market price data such as forward price curves represent important information about the comprised expectations and risk aversion of market players. This kind of data cannot be modelled from technical factors in any meaningful way.

An approach that combines the two types of models can be formed by using a bottom-up model to construct price scenarios and then calibrate these such that expected prices in the set of scenarios fit the observed forward price curve in the market.[3] If desired such calibration can include extrapolation of patterns found in historical data or parameters inferred from other derivative prices, e.g. volatilities from options.

---

[3] If arbitrage restrictions are imposed this approach is equivalent to the forward price curve construction approach suggested in Fleten and Lemming (2003).

## 14.3    A PROFIT AT RISK RISK MANAGEMENT MODEL

The primary goal of this chapter is to illustrate how the structural choices concerning electricity price modelling affect the output from risk management decision problems in the electricity sector. To analyse such aspects we use a simple case study where a power producer wishes to hedge the annual PaR of a portfolio with a physical long position in a thermal power plant and a short position[4] in an annual forward contract. In the absence of any start-up costs, a power plant can be seen as a series of spark spread options[5] for each day in the annual time period considered. With fixed variable costs $VC$ these options can be simplified to a set of European call options on electricity. This effectively means that the decision problem illustrates the effect of hedging a series of call options (a caption) to a certain PaR level using a forward contract.

The PaR measure is a variant of the VaR measure known from the financial industry. PaR describes the worst expected operational profit to a specified confidence level over a given time period. In the above example an annual €10 million 95% confidence PaR describes a setting where the power producer estimates that there is a 5% chance of incurring an annual profit of less than €10 million on the portfolio. The scarce amount of literature on PaR includes (Stulz, 2002), Henney and Keers (1998) and Ku (2001), where the latter two focus explicitly on electricity markets.

In non-financial industries market value tends to be an insufficient statistic for corporate risk management decisions. This does not mean that maximizing shareholder value is not the relevant optimization criterion, but rather that additional factors not reflected in market prices affect shareholder value. Especially in non-financial markets operational profit should be considered an important variable, because this form of liquidity can create value for shareholders (Stulz, 2002). Unlike financial assets, physical assets such as a power plant are not liquidly traded in any market and cannot be sold on short notice to raise cash without large transaction costs. Avoiding the cost of financial distress, the inability to pursue strategic investments or bankruptcy are all aspects that can create shareholder value in non-financial industries and profit is therefore a relevant unit for risk measurement in the electricity sector.

Speculation and hedging should generally be conducted as separate activities to avoid accidental speculation in a risk management context. As described in the previous section forward prices can be seen as an estimate of expected spot prices under certain assumptions about the amount of hedgers and speculators in the market. To avoid speculation the price scenarios used as input for PaR calculation should be calibrated to fit any credible (liquidly traded) part of the electricity forward price curve. In this sense PaR comes to resemble VaR, however it correctly expands on the amount of information used in the model by including the effect of additional risks factors not priced in the market, e.g. volume risk and liquidity risk.

For annual profit risk management the average annual electricity price is an essential input variable. This does not imply however that there is no additional gain from high-frequency modelling of input data such as an hourly or daily time resolution. The added value from such high-frequency modelling comes from potential relations between electricity prices and other

---

[4] A short position implies a negative amount of assets and hence a position that profits from decreasing prices. A short position in a forward contract means that the holder has agreed to sell the underlying product at the forward price at some specified time in the future.

[5] See e.g. Frayer and Ulundere (2001) or Hsu (1998) for a description of how power plants can be modelled as spark spread options.

risk factors such as cost and volume. We choose a daily time resolution and model price and volume as the only two state-dependent variables in calculation of profit $PR$ as:

$$PR(Q_F, t) = \max \left[ P(t) - VC(t), 0 \right] Q_P(t) + (P(t) - F(T_0, T_1, T_2)) Q_F \qquad (14.1)$$

where $P(t)$ is the electricity spot price, $VC(t)$ is the variable cost of operation, $F(T_0, T_1, T_2)$ is the price level defined in the forward contract for delivery during $[T_1 - T_2]$ signed at some previous point in time $T_0$, $Q_P(t)$ is the volume produced at time $t$ and $Q_F$ is the volume of forward contracts with a positive value indicating a long position and a negative value indicating a short position.

Risk measures such as PaR can be seen either as an objective or as a set of constraints imposed by management. In either case the decision variable is the short position $Q_F$ necessary to obtain some PaR level. In this chapter we consider both a case where the PaR value $PV$ is maximized at a specified percentile $\alpha$ as an objective, and a case where $PV$ and $\alpha$ are specified as exogenous constraints and the objective is to minimize the forward position. This type of minimization problem can be desirable for a number of reasons such as transaction costs $TC(Q_F)$ or risk/reward preferences directed towards staying open for potential large profits. Given a set of scenarios $i \in I$ for spot price $P^i(t)$ and production volume $Q_P^i(t)$ the minimization and maximization problems can be formulated as follows.

**TC minimization with PaR constraints:**

$$\min_{Q_F} TC(Q_F)$$

s.t.

$$\sum_{t=1}^{365} PR^i(Q_F, t) \geq PV - q^i M \quad \forall i \in I$$

$$\sum_{i=1}^{N_i} q^i \leq \alpha N_i$$

$$q^i \in \{0, 1\} \quad Q_F \in [-1, 0]$$

**PaR maximization:**

$$\max_{Q_F} PV$$

s.t.

$$\sum_{t=1}^{365} PR^i(Q_F, t) \geq PV - q^i M \quad \forall i \in I$$

$$\sum_{i=1}^{N_i} q^i \leq \alpha N_i$$

$$q^i \in \{0, 1\} \quad Q_F \in [-1, 0]$$

where $PV$ is the profit at risk limit defined in the PaR measure with a confidence level $\alpha$. $M$ is a suitably large constant that combined with a binary variable $q^i$ equal to one allows a violation of the PaR level $PV$ in a given scenario $i$. To ensure that this happens only in a fraction $\alpha$ of the total number of scenarios $N_i$ a second constraint limits the sum of the binary variables $q^i$. In MC simulation all simulated scenarios are weighted equally, however, if the problem were solved using probabilities these would be used to weight the $q^i$ variables. $PR^i(Q_F, t)$ is as defined in equation (14.1).

Both formulations yield mixed integer programming problems due to the non-convex structure of the PaR measure. Such problems are difficult to solve in the general case where $PV$ (or $TC$) can have more than one inflection point, i.e. several local maxima (minima) in addition to the global maxima (minima). However due to the simple structure of the problems $PV$ is a

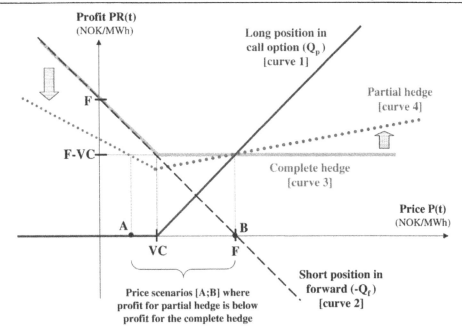

**Figure 14.2** Payoff diagrams for portfolio combinations of a short forward position and a long call option

simple convex function of $Q_F$ and $TC$ is a simple concave function of $Q_F$. This can be explained by examining the payoff or profit diagrams for the portfolio illustrated in Figure 14.2. The payoff diagram for a long position in the call option is illustrated as curve 1 (representing the ownership of a power plant), the short position in the forward contract is shown as curve 2, and finally a combined portfolio with equal weights of both contracts is shown as curve 3 (representing the completely hedged position where the amount of forward equals the amount of options).

The figure shows that in a completely hedged portfolio (curve 3) profit will always be at least $F - VC$ in all scenarios. The x-axis illustrates price scenarios and with profit equal to at least $F - VC$ in all scenarios one can see that the PaR level $PV$ will be at least $F - VC$ regardless of the $\alpha$ used in the PaR measure.

Comparing the open call option position (curve 1) with the completely hedged position (curve 3) it is clear that the former obtains a lower profit whenever the electricity price $P(t)$ is below the forward price $F$ illustrated as point B. Unless more than $(1 - \alpha)100\%$ of all electricity price scenarios lie above the forward price $F$ and hence point B, which is highly unlikely if the forward price is an estimate of expected spot prices, then $PV$ will be higher for the completely hedged portfolio than for the open portfolio. This is intuitively as expected, i.e. that hedging reduces the PaR by increasing $PV$.

By decreasing the amount of forward contracts shorted (sold) compared to a completely hedged position, i.e. $-Q_F < Q_P$, we move from the curve 3 shape towards the curve 1 shape and obtain a payoff structure like the one shown in the dotted curve 4. To understand why a decrease in the short forward hedge yields a shape as shown in curve 4 we divide the x-axis into segments using electricity prices equal to $F$ and $VC$ as the main fixed points.

At a price equal to $F$ forward contracts will have a payoff of zero and the portfolio will therefore obtain a profit of $F - VC$ regardless of the hedge. At prices above $F$ the short forward hedge loses money, but because the forward position is smaller than the call option position in a partial hedge (curve 4) the total portfolio profit will be above $F - VC$. At prices between $VC$ and $F$ the short forward contract provides a profit but in a partial hedge this profit will not outweigh the reduction in profit from the option and total profit therefore drops below $F - VC$. This effect continues at electricity prices below $VC$, however here the decrease in profit from the call option ceases to increase due to the non-linearity of the option payoff. As a result total profit therefore begins to increase directly with the increased profit from the forward contract at prices below $VC$. At some point the increasing profit from the short hedge drives total portfolio profit for the partial hedge back above the level $F - VC$.

The profit diagram for the partial hedge illustrated as curve 4 is interesting, because it explains why a complete hedge does not generally provide the optimal or lowest PaR level $PV$. When the amount of shorted forward contracts used to hedge the call option is decreased from a complete hedge $Q_F = Q_P$, a number of price scenarios illustrated by the interval [A,B] will fall below $F - VC$. However as long as this amount of scenarios is less than the fraction $\alpha$ the portfolio will have a $PV$ level higher than $F - VC$ due to the increase in profit for all price scenarios above $F$. The optimal point in terms of the lowest PaR or highest $PV$ occurs at the point where the point A has been shifted so far to the left that the fraction of electricity price scenarios in the interval [A,B] equals $\alpha$.[6] From this point on $PV$ will then decrease as $Q_F$ approaches zero.

## 14.4  MODELLING INPUT PARAMETERS

This section describes in detail a financial model for the electricity price along with a set of simple models for volume, cost and dependencies between factors. Though the main use of these models are as reference cases for sensitivity analysis in Section 14.5, the detailed description of the process for the construction of an electricity price model provides valuable insight for the analysis of interaction between input models and decision model.

### 14.4.1  Electricity price modelling

In the risk management case study described above profit is highly dependent on developments in the electricity price. Since this parameter is also highly volatile it is likely to be the input parameter where structural model choices will have the largest effect on the output from the risk management problem. Choosing a model structure for electricity prices is therefore crucial and valuable insight is gained from a review of the choices involved in the construction process.

**Type of price model**: Based on the categorization of approaches for electricity price modelling described in Section 14.2 an initial decision involves the choice between either a fundamental, a financial or a combined approach. As demonstrated through the analysis in Section 14.5 financial models are generally not the most suitable approach for constructing input scenarios to risk management problems such as the case study used here. We choose, however, to focus solely on financial spot price models here because the detailed nature of input data

---

[6] Notice as a special case that PaR will have a maximum at $Q_F = Q_P$ if more than $\alpha$ of all scenarios lie in the interval $[VC, F]$. Graphically this can be illustrated by noting that curve 3 cannot be tilted (as in curve 4) marginally without creating more than $\alpha$ profit scenarios below $F - VC$ and hence decreasing PaR.

required for fundamental models makes it virtually impossible for others to reproduce results and conclusions.

**Amount and type of input data used**: To estimate parameters in the spot price model we use historical prices from the spot market on the Scandinavian Nord Pool power exchange. Choosing a cut-off point for historical data must be based on a qualitative evaluation of how the information value of the historical data set deteriorates. We choose to include data from the time of writing 01-10-2002 and back to 01-01-1996 where a significant change occurred as the then solely Norwegian exchange Nord Pool was expanded to include Sweden. The choice of a spot price model as opposed to a forward price model implies that forward prices are not required in the estimation process.[7]

**Parametric structure**: Electricity prices are driven by fundamental factors such as temperature, hydrological conditions, demand patterns and plant availability. Even in financial models based solely on market data these factors serve as inspiration to the structural choices concerning parameters. In the Scandinavian market, rising demand in the winter period combined with an annual hydrological cycle where reservoirs of hydropower plants are filled during spring leads to a strong seasonal component in spot prices. To model cyclic price variations we follow the structure suggested in Lucia and Schwartz (2002) with a deterministic component $f(t)$ modelling of seasonal variations and demand-driven weekend effects, and a stochastic component $S(t)$ that includes the mean-reversion term $\kappa$ characteristic for commodity prices. Using a well-documented model is desirable for the experiments in this chapter, because it provides a credible reference for our analysis of how parametric changes in the price modelling affect the solution of the subsequent decision problem.

Electricity prices exhibit spikes as a result of both extreme weather conditions and unexpected forced outages of power plants. Though a jump-diffusion process with mean reversion can be used to capture such spike behaviour, such processes will generally require extremely high values of mean reversion, which in turn will have the undesirable effect of essentially removing all additional stochastic variation in the data besides the jumps. We choose instead to follow the approach of De Jong and Huisman (2002) by adding a regime shift component to the model, which encompasses both price spikes and price jumps as special cases.

Negative prices can occur in electricity markets due to start/stopping costs of power plants and other technical constraints. However, as our data is in the form of daily averages, i.e. a sum of 24 hourly prices for a system price comprising all Scandinavian price areas, negative electricity prices are not plausible. We therefore choose to work directly with the logarithm of price $\mathrm{Ln}(P_t)$ with a base case model of the form:

$$\mathrm{Ln}(P_t) = \begin{cases} f(t) + \mathrm{Ln}(S_t^N) & \text{if } T_t = N \\ f(t) + \mathrm{Ln}(S_t^S) & \text{if } T_t = S \end{cases} \tag{14.2}$$

where

$$\mathrm{Ln}(S_t^N) = (1 - \kappa)\mathrm{ln}(S_{t-1}^N) + e_t^N \qquad e_t^N \sim N(0, (\sigma^N)^2) \tag{14.3}$$

$$\mathrm{Ln}(S_t^S) = u^S + e_t^S \qquad e_t^S \sim N(0, (\sigma^S)^2) \tag{14.4}$$

$$f(t) = \sum_{i=1}^{N_D} \beta_i D(i) + \sum_{i=1}^{N_M} \gamma_i M(i) \tag{14.5}$$

---

[7] Forward prices can however be included in the estimation process by deriving spot price expectations under the risk-neutral measure for the chosen spot price processes as described in references such as Lucia and Schwartz (2002) or Deng (2000). Alternatively one can use forward price data for model verification.

Here $S_t^N$ and $S_t^S$ describe the stochastic part of the price process in respectively the normal regime $N$ and the spike regime $S$. The parameters $\mu^S$ and $\sigma^S$ represent the expected value and standard deviation of price spikes respectively, and $e_t^N$ and $e_t^S$ are independent noise components. $M(i)$ and $D(i)$ are 0–1 dummy variables describing $N_M$ monthly and $N_D$ daily effects through parameters $\beta_i$ and $\gamma_i$.[8] The two stochastic processes $S_t^N$ and $S_t^S$ run in parallel and transition between the two states $T_t = N$ and $T_t = S$ is governed by a transition matrix:

$$T_{t|t-1} = \begin{bmatrix} p_{N_t|N_{t-1}} & p_{N_t|S_{t-1}} \\ p_{S_t|N_{t-1}} & p_{S_t|S_{t-1}} \end{bmatrix}$$

For simplicity we model regime shifts as spikes of a single day duration, i.e. a shift from the normal state to the spike state is always followed immediately by a shift back to the normal regime, $p_{S_t|N_{t-1}} = 1$ and $p_{S_t|S_{t-1}} = 0$. With this formulation the frequency of spikes $F_{spikes}$ is equal to:

$$F_{spikes} = \frac{p_{S_t|N_{t-1}}}{p_{N_t|S_{t-1}} + p_{S_t|N_{t-1}}} = \frac{1}{p_{N_t|S_{t-1}} + 1} \tag{14.6}$$

**Estimation:** The parameters of the model (14.2)–(14.5) above can be estimated through maximum likelihood procedures as described in De Jong and Huisman (2002). However, as noted in Clewlow and Strickland (2000) electricity prices tend to have several spike components and maximum likelihood procedures tend to converge to high-frequency spike components in the data. This is undesirable with the model setup above because the primary function of the spike regime should be to capture the large low-frequency spikes that would not occur in the normal regime.

The time series of logarithmic spot prices used here (see Figure 14.3) contain both high and low-frequency spike components of different duration and sign. Because of this complexity a modified version of the recursive filter used in Clewlow and Strickland (2000) was therefore constructed to estimate parameters of the spike regime. These data points were subsequently removed and parameters in the normal regime were then estimated on the remaining part of the data using simple non-linear regression.

In the normal regime of equation (14.2) the absolute difference of log prices $d\text{Ln}(P_t)$ is normally distributed and Clewlow and Strickland (2000) therefore suggest an iteration procedure where values more than three empirical standard deviations from the mean are removed from the data in each iteration.[9] The standard deviation of the sample without these spikes is then recalculated and the procedure is repeated until convergence. As the choice of three standard deviations is somewhat arbitrary we choose instead to modify the spike criteria of the filter by using the difference between the observed kurtosis in the sample $K(\text{sample})$ and the kurtosis of a normal distribution $K(\text{normal})$ with the same mean and variance as the sample.

Table 14.1 shows the result of running this procedure on the data with a kurtosis-based stopping criteria defined as:

$$\Delta K = \frac{K(\text{sample})}{K(\text{normal})} = \frac{E[X^4] - 4E[X^3]E[X] + 6E[X^2]E[X]^2 - 3E[X]^4}{3(E[X^2] - E[X]^2)^2} < C \tag{14.7}$$

Here $E[X^N]$ represents the $N$th moment and the constant $C$ terminates the recursive filter

---

[8] Alternatively one can use sinusoidal functions such as suggested in Lucia and Schwartz (2002), Pilipovic (1998) and Fleten and Lemming (2003).

[9] In a normal distribution such observations would occur with a probability of less than 0.0003, i.e. only one observation out of every 3333 observations.

**Table 14.1** Iterations in recursive filter based on kurtosis criterion with $C = \Delta K = 1.5$

| $N_{spikes}$ | $F_{spikes}$ | $E_{spikes}$ | $S_{spikes}$ | $K$(normal) | $K$(sample) | $\Delta K$ |
|---|---|---|---|---|---|---|
| 5 | 0.002 | 0.910 | 0.216 | 2.77E-04 | 1.02E-03 | 3.682 |
| 10 | 0.004 | 0.749 | 0.226 | 2.25E-04 | 6.35E-04 | 2.818 |
| 15 | 0.006 | 0.671 | 0.215 | 2.02E-04 | 5.09E-04 | 2.514 |
| 20 | 0.008 | 0.628 | 0.203 | 1.92E-04 | 4.49E-04 | 2.333 |
| 25 | 0.010 | 0.588 | 0.198 | 1.70E-04 | 3.62E-04 | 2.127 |
| 30 | 0.012 | 0.555 | 0.196 | 1.61E-04 | 3.28E-04 | 2.031 |
| 35 | 0.014 | 0.527 | 0.194 | 1.50E-04 | 2.93E-04 | 1.947 |
| 40 | 0.016 | 0.505 | 0.191 | 1.39E-04 | 2.58E-04 | 1.852 |
| 45 | 0.018 | 0.487 | 0.187 | 1.33E-04 | 2.38E-04 | 1.791 |
| 50 | 0.020 | 0.469 | 0.185 | 1.27E-04 | 2.19E-04 | 1.731 |
| 55 | 0.022 | 0.454 | 0.183 | 1.24E-04 | 2.11E-04 | 1.698 |
| 60 | 0.024 | 0.442 | 0.180 | 1.20E-04 | 2.04E-04 | 1.696 |
| 65 | 0.027 | 0.430 | 0.178 | 1.12E-04 | 1.84E-04 | 1.640 |
| 70 | 0.029 | 0.419 | 0.176 | 1.05E-04 | 1.70E-04 | 1.615 |
| 75 | 0.031 | 0.414 | 0.172 | 1.03E-04 | 1.71E-04 | 1.653 |
| 80 | 0.033 | 0.406 | 0.169 | 9.71E-05 | 1.53E-04 | 1.575 |
| 85 | 0.035 | 0.397 | 0.168 | 9.19E-05 | 1.42E-04 | 1.549 |
| 90 | 0.037 | 0.391 | 0.166 | 8.93E-05 | 1.36E-04 | 1.524 |
| 95 | 0.039 | 0.383 | 0.164 | 8.58E-05 | 1.28E-04 | **1.498** |

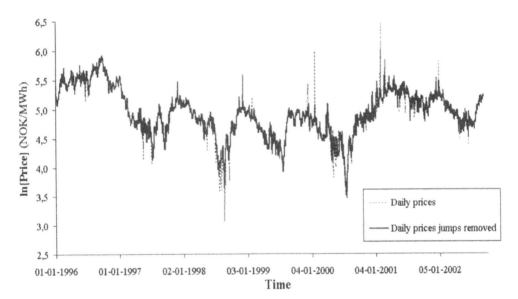

**Figure 14.3** Nord Pool spot price data 01/01/96 to 01/10/02 before and after spikes are removed with a recursive filter

when the sample kurtosis is less than $(C - 1)100\%$ higher than what a normal distribution would dictate. Optimally one would continue iteration with the filter until $C = 1$, however this attempt to force normality upon data would lead to similar problems as the maximum likelihood estimation. A significant part of the data would simply be moved to the spike regime where the problem of non-normality would be re-encountered.

Table 14.1 shows the recursive iteration used to calculate an estimate of the spike frequency $F_{spikes}$, the expected value of spikes $\mu^S$ and standard deviation of spikes $\sigma^S$. In Table 14.1, $N_{spikes}$ represents the number of spikes removed and $F_{spikes}$ is the resulting frequency. $E_{spikes} = \mu^S$ and $S_{spikes} = \sigma^S$ are respectively the mean value and standard deviation of the $N_{spikes}$ price spikes that have been removed. Finally we illustrate the effect of removing spikes in Figure 14.3 where the time series of historical spot prices is compared with the data series after spikes have been removed.

**Comments**: Before testing the model we note that an important effect has been left out of the model. In an electricity market such as the Scandinavian one, there is a significant stochastic variation in the annual price average due to the large amount of hydropower on the production side. The large variation in energy production between dry and wet years has a large effect on the annual price as illustrated by an average system spot price on Nord Pool of 258 NOK/MWh (app. €35/MWh) in the very dry year of 1996 compared to an average price of 106 NOK/MWh (app. €15/MWh) in the very wet year of 2000. As mentioned earlier this characteristic is important for the annual risk management problem. To correctly estimate the uncertainty of annual average prices one would however need a large amount of realized annual price averages spanning the entire possible range of hydrological conditions. This type of data set will generally not become available and we therefore note that models based on market data will tend to lack an important source of information. This is not just problematic because of the annual time horizon. The fact that the distribution of wet and dry years is incorrectly represented in the sample means that seasonal components and other model parameters will be biased. The extent of this problem is examined in more detail in Section 14.5.

### 14.4.2  Modelling volume risk

To model the volume risk associated with the long position in a power plant we use a two-dimensional transition matrix simulating a Markovian 0–1 point process. The matrix is fully described by two probabilities, e.g. the probability $p_{1|0}$ of a plant being unavailable in hour $t$ given that it was available at $t - 1$ and the probability $p_{0|1}$ of returning to availability state in $t$ given that the plant was out in $t - 1$:

$$Q_{t|t-1} = \begin{bmatrix} p_{1|1} & p_{1|0} \\ p_{0|1} & p_{0|0} \end{bmatrix}$$

### 14.4.3  Additional factors

Additional factors include variable costs and start-up costs. For simplicity we choose to model unit variable cost as a constant $VC$ independent of time and production volume. Furthermore we exclude start-up costs. Both factors are easily included but are left out here to keep the focus on the effect of electricity price modelling in the risk management problem.

To model correlation between plant outages and price spikes the transition matrices $Q$ for the volume process and $T$ for the price process are simulated as dependent. The dependency is modelled by expanding the transition matrix $T$ for prices to be a matrix of conditional probabilities depending not only on the previous price state but also on the state of the volume process.

**Table 14.2**   Parameters estimates for base case simulation based on Nord Pool
data. Significant parameter estimates are indicated with*

| Input factor | Parameter | Value | Parameter | Value |
|---|---|---|---|---|
| Electricity price | $\kappa$ | 0.0123* | $\alpha_{jul}$ | 4.921* |
|  | $\sigma_N$ | 0.0611* | $\alpha_{aug}$ | 4.937* |
|  | $\alpha_{sun}$ | −0.083* | $\alpha_{sep}$ | 4.958* |
|  | $\alpha_{sat}$ | −0.057* | $\alpha_{oct}$ | 4.967* |
|  | $\alpha_{jan}$ | 5.000* | $\alpha_{nov}$ | 4.997* |
|  | $\alpha_{feb}$ | 4.985* | $\alpha_{nov}$ | 4.997* |
|  | $\alpha_{mar}$ | 4.996* | $\alpha_{dec}$ | 5.017* |
|  | $\alpha_{apr}$ | 4.974* | $F_{spikes}$ | 0.039 |
|  | $\alpha_{may}$ | 4.915* | $E_{spikes}$ | 0.383 |
|  | $\alpha_{jun}$ | 4.856* | $S_{spikes}$ | 0.164 |
| Volume process | $q_{1|0}$ | 0.07 | $q_{1|1}$ | 0.93 |
|  | $q_{0|1}$ | 0.90 | $q_{0|0}$ | 0.10 |
| PaR | $\alpha$ | 0.05 | $PV$ | 6500 |
| Variable cost | $VC$ | 4.87 |  |  |
| Forward prices | $F(T_0, T_1, T_2)$ | 4.92 |  |  |

## 14.5   EXPERIMENTAL RESULTS

The framework described in the previous sections is now used to examine how the structural modelling of electricity prices affects the optimal solution to the PaR risk management problem. In particular we examine the effect of:

- Parametric modelling of price spikes and forced outages (both as dependent and independent variables).
- The general choice of a financial model for electricity price modelling in PaR risk management.

As a base case we use the parameters shown in Table 14.2 to generate electricity price scenarios based on historically observed values for seasonal variation and price spikes.[10] Table 14.2 also includes parameters for the volume process, variable costs (in NOK/MWh) and the PaR measure.

The base case model is solved both for the case with $PV$ maximization and for the case where $Q_F$ is minimized given an exogenous limit on $PV$. Output in the form of P/L (profit/loss) histograms, the optimal amount of forward contracts $Q_F$ and the optimal $PV$ value in the maximization case (top figure) is illustrated in Figure 14.4. All simulations are based on $I = 5000$ scenarios each consisting of 365 daily prices.

**The effect of volume and price spike risk**: To examine the effect of price spikes and volume risk the base case minimization problem is solved for price spike frequencies $F_{spikes}$ in the interval $[0, 0.1]$ and forced outage frequencies $F_{outages}$ in the interval $[0, 0.15]$.

The frequency of price spikes should only affect the optimal amount of forward contracts if the shape of the annual price distribution is changed. If the prices spike frequency is increased

---

[10] Though the data contained both up and down-spikes we model only up-spikes as these are expected to dominate future prices. We will assume that downward price spikes are the result of market abnormalities and consider an actual analysis of whether or not they are a persistent phenomenon outside the scope of this chapter.

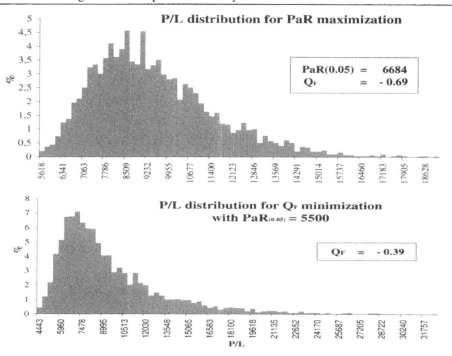

**Figure 14.4**  Profit/loss histograms for the minimization (bottom) and maximization (top) problems in the base simulation

without any additional adjustments to the data set then the total average price will also increase. This shift in average will distort the shape effect that we are looking for and we therefore adjusted each simulation so that the total average of all $365 \times 5000$ daily prices equals the exogenously defined forward price $F(T_0, T_1, T_2)$.[11]

Figure 14.5 illustrates the somewhat counterintuitive result that the required amount of forward contracts decreases as the number of spikes is increased. To understand this result we go back to the payoff diagrams in Figure 14.2. The worst case scenario in the open position (curve 1) is an annual profit of zero, which occurs only if all prices in the series of 365 daily prices lie below the variable cost of production. An increased frequency of price spikes will decrease the likelihood of such scenarios and as a result the $PaR_\alpha$ level $PV$ will increase. In the minimization problem this means that fewer short forward contracts are needed to obtain the desired $PV$ level.

The effect is illustrated in the left part of the histogram in Figure 14.6. The figure compares P/L histograms for the upper ($F_{spikes} = 0.1$) and lower limit ($F_{spikes} = 0$) used for price spikes in the case with no volume risk. The number of low-profit scenarios is larger for the case without price spikes and as a result the portfolio is more risky in terms of a lower PaR level $PV$.

Introducing volume risk adds a new factor that affects the optimal amount of forward contracts in the minimization problem. During a forced outage the portfolio will consist only

---

[11] The sample mean is divided by the desired mean (exogenous forward price) to obtain a regulation factor $RF$. All prices including the spikes are then subsequently divided by this regulating factor.

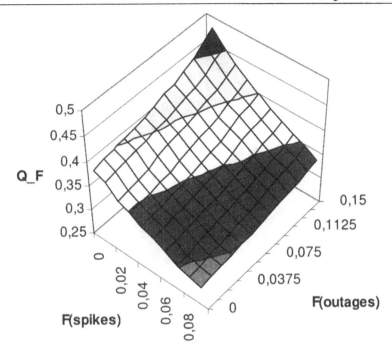

**Figure 14.5** Optimal (minimization) short position in forward contracts (positive value is a short position) for different combinations of price spikes frequency and frequency of forced outages

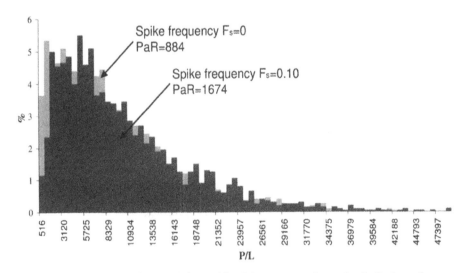

**Figure 14.6** P/L histograms for simulations with minimum or maximum level of price spikes

of the short forward position and if the electricity price is simultaneously above the forward price, e.g. in case of a price spike, then the portfolio will incur a loss proportional to the amount of forward contracts in the portfolio. The combination of volume risk and price spikes will therefore create increasingly large negative profit scenarios as the amount of shorted

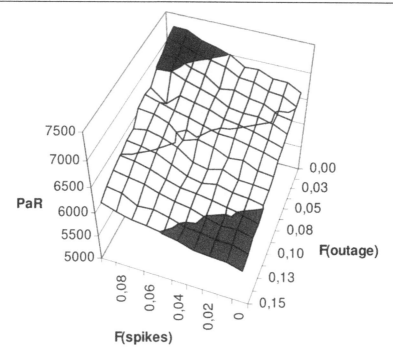

**Figure 14.7**   Optimal (maximization) PaR level *PV* for different combinations of price spikes frequency and frequency of forced outages

contracts is increased. This has a negative effect on the optimal amount of shorted forward contracts as illustrated in Figure 14.5. The figure shows that the decrease in optimal shorted forwards that occurs from increasing price spikes from $F_{spikes} = 0$ to $F_{spikes} = 0.1$ is increased from $\Delta(Q_F) = 0.102$ to $\Delta(Q_F) = 0.147$ when volume risk is increased from $F_{outages} = 0$ to $F_{outages} = 0.15$.

The isolated effect of volume risk is to decrease the amount of forward contracts required to obtain a given PaR$_\alpha$ limit $PV$. The largest decrease of 0.087 that occurs in the case without price spikes is however modest compared to the relatively large variation of 0% to 15% used for expected amount of forced outages.

Performing a similar set of simulations for the maximization problem we find no obvious trends in the amount of optimal contracts. However, as illustrated in Figure 14.7 the optimal PaR level follows the same pattern as in the minimization problem.

The optimal PaR level decreases (in absolute terms) as the amount of volume risk increases and increases[12] as the amount of price spikes is increased.

To understand why no clear effect is found for the optimal amount of contracts in the maximization problem, we illustrate the optimal PaR$_\alpha$ level $PV$ as a function of $Q_F$ for a series of selected simulations in Table 14.3.

Starting from the left in the table by comparing columns 1 and 2 we see that PaR$_\alpha$ is improved for smaller forward positions $Q_F$ when the frequency of price spikes is increased

---

[12] An increase in the PaR level in absolute terms, e.g. from 5000 to 7000, is a decrease in the amount of risk exposure.

**Table 14.3**  PaR as a function of $Q_F$ for upper and lower bound cases in the set of simulations

| $Q_F$ | 1<br>$F_s = 0, F_o = 0$ | 2<br>$F_s = 0.1, F_o = 0$ | 3<br>$F_s = 0, F_o = 0.15,$ | 4<br>$F_s = 0.1, \rho = 0$ | 5<br>$F_o = 0.15, \rho = 1$ |
|---|---|---|---|---|---|
| 0.00 | 813 | 1399 | 638 | 1133 | 571 |
| 0.05 | 1548 | 2388 | 1349 | 2067 | 1580 |
| 0.10 | 2281 | 3435 | 2101 | 2998 | 2312 |
| 0.15 | 3014 | 4090 | 2803 | 3594 | 2923 |
| 0.20 | 3695 | 4645 | 3379 | 4067 | 3365 |
| 0.25 | 4265 | 5117 | 3863 | 4544 | 3715 |
| 0.30 | 4760 | 5577 | 4265 | 5009 | 4078 |
| 0.35 | 5209 | 6079 | 4600 | 5330 | 4338 |
| 0.40 | 5567 | 6540 | 4942 | 5623 | 4398 |
| 0.45 | 5950 | 6849 | 5114 | 5706 | 4422 |
| 0.50 | 6274 | 7075 | 5217 | 5723 | 4313 |
| 0.55 | 6412 | 7265 | 5223 | 5703 | 4168 |
| 0.60 | 6562 | 7357 | 5122 | 5470 | 3907 |
| 0.65 | 6661 | 7368 | 4918 | 5202 | 3554 |
| 0.70 | 6669 | 7314 | 4594 | 4776 | 2917 |
| 0.75 | 6565 | 7137 | 4095 | 4070 | 2167 |
| 0.80 | 6405 | 6856 | 3422 | 3087 | 1122 |
| 0.85 | 6271 | 6541 | 2588 | 2020 | 30 |
| 0.90 | 5973 | 6087 | 1638 | 921 | −1115 |
| 0.95 | 5520 | 5475 | 794 | −255 | −2202 |
| 1.00 | 4696 | 4564 | −256 | −1399 | −3367 |

from $F_{spikes} = 0$ to $F_{spikes} = 0.1$. Based on the argument above this is to be expected, since the likelihood of a very low annual profit (due to 365 daily scenarios with low or zero profit) decreases as the frequency of spikes is increased. In the completely hedged position $-Q_F = Q_P$ the increase in spike frequency has no effect because the portfolio profit is constant for all electricity prices above $VC$ regardless of the price spike frequency.

Looking at the effect of forced plant outages by comparing columns 1 and 3 the table shows that an increase in volume risk has two effects on optimal PaR. First of all there is a general decrease in the optimal PaR and secondly there is a skewed effect that biases PaR more significantly downwards at higher levels of $Q_F$. The skewed effect occurs because plant outages combined with prices above the forward price leads to low profit scenarios.

Columns 4 and 5 illustrate the results of the simulation with the maximum values for both price spike and outage frequencies. In column 4 the two effects are assumed uncorrelated. Compared to column 2 we can see how the introduction of volume risk has a general decreasing effect on PaR at all levels of short forward positions $Q_F$. The column also illustrates that the skewed effect increases when price spikes and volume risk are both present. In this case it is the increase in price spike frequency that causes the effect by increasing the probability of a combined outage and high price above the forward price.

Finally we see that correlation increases the skew effect. Again this is due to the increase in the probability of scenarios with a combined price spike and forced outage caused by the introduction of correlation.

**Using a financial model based on market data for electricity price modelling**: Having examined the effect of parametric choices in the financial electricity price model we turn to

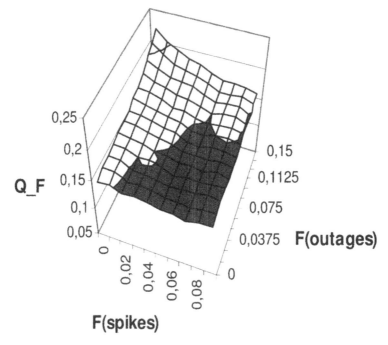

**Figure 14.8**  Difference between optimal solution in the minimization problem based on original sample vs. a sample with an additional dry year

the more general question of how the choice of a financial model based on a specific sample of market data affects the output of the risk management model. The electricity price model used here is based on 6 years of data for the Nord Pool spot market where there is a large variation between yearly average prices due to the large share of hydropower production. The 6 years of annual average prices are clearly not a sufficient representation of the hydrological distribution, i.e. the distribution of wet and dry years, and to examine the effect of rather small changes in the data sample a forecast for 2003 (as a dry year with 1996 prices) is added to the data set. After re-estimating the price model with this new 7-year data set, the simulation is repeated for the PaR minimization problem and optimal solutions are compared to those found in Figure 14.5. Figure 14.8 shows the difference between the optimal solution with the original data set and the data set with an additional dry year added for 2003.

The figure clearly shows that adding a single year of realistic data can have a significant effect.[13] The optimal amount of forward contracts is approximately halved in all scenarios and the effect is larger than both the volume and price spike effect. This shows how the lack of market data, for a sufficiently accurate measurement of variations in the annual average electricity price, can have a strong effect on the solution to the risk management problem. Moreover we see that in this case study the effect is so strong that it outweighs the importance of structural choices concerning parametric modelling of the essential input parameters such as electricity prices and volume risk.

---

[13] One could also add a very dry year to the sample. The very dry year was chosen for illustrative purposes here simply because it had the largest effect.

## 14.6  CONCLUSIONS

This chapter has illustrated how electricity price modelling can affect the optimal solution to a risk management problem in the electricity sector. Though a simple case study has been used, the considerations related to the choice of price model and parametric choices within a certain model category can be generalized to a broader context.

The analysis and experiments with the risk management problem have illustrated that generally one will not optimize the PaR level by constructing a complete forward hedge of the call option representing the physical power plant. The optimal PaR level will be located at an intermediate short position in forward contracts somewhere between the fully closed position ($Q_F=Q_p$) and a completely open position ($Q_F = 0$).

Increasing the frequency of price spikes was seen to have a positive effect on the attainable PaR level in the absence of volume risk. As volume risk was introduced, the combination of volume risk and price spike risk was seen to cause a skewed negative effect on the PaR level depending on the size of the forward position. Finally correlation between the two factors was seen to increase the negative effect of volume risk, although only moderately compared to the relatively large levels of volume risk and price spike risk examined.

The historical data set used to estimate the parameters in a financial spot price model was seen to affect the optimal solution significantly compared to the parametric choices concerning input parameter modelling, i.e. price spike modelling and volume risk modelling. Therefore we conclude that one should be careful when using financial models of the electricity price to form input to electricity risk management problems. Sensitivity analysis with input data should be performed. If, as in Figure 14.8, the results from such analyses show that small changes in the input data set can have a large effect on the optimal solution, then either the model structure or the amount of market price data available is insufficient. In both situations a fundamental or a combined approach should be adopted instead.

## REFERENCES

Barlow M. (2002). "A Diffusion Model for Electricity Prices". *Mathematical Finance* **12**(4): 287–298.

Clewlow L. and Strickland C. (1999a). "A Multi-factor Model for Energy Derivatives". Working Paper, School of Finance and Economics, Technical University of Sydney.

Clewlow L. and Strickland C. (1999b). "Valuing Energy Options in a One Factor Model Fitted to Forward Prices". Working Paper, School of Finance and Economics, Technical University of Sydney.

Clewlow L. and Strickland C. (2000). *Energy Derivatives: Pricing and Risk Management*. Lacima Publications, London.

De Jong C. and Huisman R. (2002). "Option Formulas for Mean-reverting Power Prices with Spikes". Working Paper, Rotterdam School of Management at Erasmus University, Rotterdam.

Deng S. (2000). "Stochastic Models of Energy Commodities Prices and their Application: Mean-reversion with Jumps and Spikesnote". Working Paper, POWER, University of California Energy Institute, Berkeley, CA.

Fleten S. and Lemming J. (2003). "Constructing Forward Price Curves in Electricity Markets". *Energy Economics*. (Forthcoming).

Frayer J. and Ulundere N. (2001). "What Is It Worth? Application of Real Options Theory to the Valuation of Generation Assets". *Electricity Journal* **October**: 40–51.

Henney A. and Keers G. (1998). "Managing Total Corporate Electricty/Energy Market Risks". *Electricity Journal* **October**: 36–46.

Hsu M. (1998). "Spark Spread Options Are Hot". *Electricity Journal* **March**: 28–39.

Johnson B. and Barz G. (2000). "Selecting Stochastic Processes for Modelling Electricity Prices". In *Energy Modelling and the Management of Uncertainty*. Risk Books, London, pp. 3–21.

Joy C. (2000). "Pricing Modelling and Managing Physical Power Derivatives". In *Energy Modelling and the Management of Uncertainty*. Risk Books, London, pp. 45–58.

Kellerhals B.P. (2001). "Pricing Electricity Forwards under Stochastic Volatility". Working Paper, POWER, Department of Finance, College of Economics and Business Administration, Eberhard-Karls-University, Tubingen.

Knittel C.R. and Roberts M. (2000). "Financial Models of Deregulated Electricity Prices I: discrete Time Models". Working Paper, Department of Finance and Economics, Boston University.

Koekebakker S. and Ollmar F. (2001). "Forward Curve Dynamics in the Nordic Electricity Market". Working Paper, Agder University College, Norway.

Ku A. (2001). "Value at Risk: Variations on a Theme". *Global Energy Business* **May/June**: 12–19.

Lucia J.J. and Schwartz E.S. (2002). "Electricity Prices and Power Derivatives: Evidence from the Nordic Power Exchange". *Review of Derivatives Research* **5**(1): 5–50.

Pilipovic D. (1998). *Energy Risk: Valuing and Managing Energy Derivatives*. McGraw-Hill, New York.

Stulz R. (2002). *Risk Management and Derivatives*, 1st edn. Southwestern Publishing.

# 15

# Forecasting Weather Variable Densities for Weather Derivatives and Electricity Prices

JAMES W. TAYLOR

*Saïd Business School, University of Oxford, Oxford OX1 1HP, UK*

## ABSTRACT

Weather derivatives allow electricity companies to hedge against changes in demand. Density forecasts of weather variables are needed for pricing weather derivatives. Weather ensemble predictions are generated from atmospheric models and consist of multiple scenarios for the future value of a weather variable. This study investigates the accuracy of density forecasts generated from 1 to 10-day-ahead ensemble predictions. Studies that have considered the use of ensemble predictions for weather derivative pricing and electricity demand modelling are briefly described.

## 15.1 INTRODUCTION

Weather variable density forecasts provide an understanding of the uncertainty in weather variables, which is useful for the many industries exposed to weather risk. Weather ensemble predictions are a new type of weather forecast. They are generated from meteorological models of the earth's atmosphere and consist of multiple scenarios (51 in our specific case) for the future value of a weather variable. The scenarios are known as ensemble members. The ensemble prediction, therefore, conveys the degree of uncertainty in the weather variable. The distribution of the scenarios can be used as a forecast of the conditional density of the weather variable. Weather variable density forecasts are important for pricing weather derivatives because they can be used to forecast the density of the payoff (see Cao and Wei, 2000). The mean of the payoff density is the fair price of the derivative, and the distribution about the mean provides information regarding the uncertainty, which is useful for risk management purposes, such as value-at-risk (see Duffie and Pan, 1997).

This study compares density forecasts based on ensemble predictions with those generated using univariate time series models for lead times from 1 to 10 days ahead. More specifically, we consider the forecasting of the quantiles of the conditional density. The $\theta$ quantile of the conditional density of a variable $y_t$ is the value, $Q_t(\theta)$, for which $P(y_t \leq Q_t(\theta)) = \theta$.

We analyse temperature, wind speed and cloud cover recorded at Birmingham, Bristol, Heathrow, Leeds and Manchester. These variables, recorded at these locations, are the main weather variables used in the electricity demand forecasting models at National Grid Transco,

---

*Modelling Prices in Competitive Electricity Markets.* Edited by D.W. Bunn.
© 2004 John Wiley & Sons, Ltd. ISBN 0-470-84860-X.

which is the company responsible for electricity transmission in England and Wales. Since hedging electricity load is one of the main uses for weather derivatives, the series that we analyse are obvious candidates for underlying reference in derivative contracts (see Torró et al., 2001). From an energy perspective, wind speed is a particularly interesting variable because it influences both demand and generation. Indeed, wind generation of electricity is currently receiving a lot of attention in Europe because of subsidies for renewable energy.

Weather ensemble predictions are described in Section 15.2. In Section 15.3, we review the literature on univariate modelling of temperature time series before presenting models for our weather data. In Sections 15.4, 15.5 and 15.6, we compare point and quantile forecasts from the different methods. Sections 15.7 and 15.8 briefly review studies that have evaluated the benefit of using ensemble predictions for weather derivative pricing and electricity demand modelling, respectively. The final section provides concluding comments.

## 15.2   WEATHER ENSEMBLE PREDICTIONS

The weather is a chaotic system. Small errors in the initial conditions of a forecast grow rapidly, and affect predictability. Furthermore, predictability is limited by model errors due to the approximate simulation of atmospheric processes in a numerical model. These two sources of uncertainty limit the accuracy of traditional single point forecasts, generated by running the model once with best estimates for the initial conditions.

The weather prediction problem can be described in terms of the time evolution of an appropriate probability density function in the atmosphere's phase space. An estimate of the density function provides forecasters with an objective way to gauge the uncertainty in single point predictions. Ensemble prediction aims to derive a more sophisticated estimate of the density function than that provided by the distribution of past atmospheric states. Ensemble prediction systems generate multiple realisations of numerical predictions by using a range of different initial conditions in the numerical model of the atmosphere. The frequency distribution of the different realisations, which are known as ensemble members, provides an estimate of the density function. The initial conditions are not sampled as in a statistical simulation because this is not practical for the complex, high-dimensional weather model. Instead, they are designed to sample directions of maximum possible growth (Molteni et al., 1996; Palmer et al., 1993; Buizza et al., 1998).

The benefit of using ensemble predictions is illustrated in Figure 15.1. $pdf_0$ represents the initial uncertainties. From the best estimate of the initial state, a single point forecast is produced (bold solid curve). This point forecast fails to predict correctly the future state (dashed curve). The ensemble forecasts (thin solid curves), starting from perturbed initial conditions, can be used to estimate the probability of future states. In this example, the estimated probability density function, $pdf_t$, is bimodal. The figure shows that two of the perturbed forecasts almost correctly predicted the future state. Therefore, at time 0, the ensemble system would have given a non-zero probability of the future state.

Since December 1992, both the US National Center for Environmental Predictions (NCEP, previously NMC) and the European Centre for Medium-range Weather Forecasts (ECMWF) have integrated their deterministic prediction with medium-range ensemble prediction (Palmer et al., 1993; Toth and Kalnay, 1993; Tracton and Kalnay, 1993). The number of ensemble members is limited by the necessity to produce weather forecasts in a reasonable amount of time with the available computer power. Traditional single point forecasts are produced using a

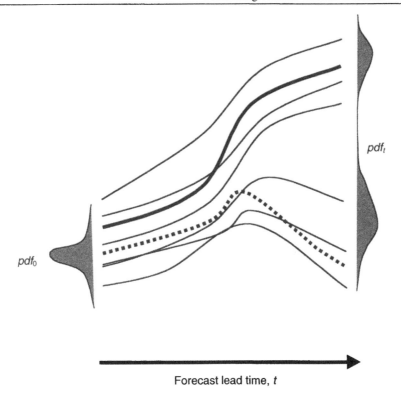

$pdf_t$

$pdf_0$

Forecast lead time, $t$

**Figure 15.1**  Schematic of ensemble prediction. Bold solid curve is the single point forecast. Dashed curve is the future state. Thin solid curves are the ensemble of perturbed forecasts
Reprinted from International Journal of Forecasting, Vol 19, Taylor *et al.*, Using weather ensemble predictions in electricity demand forecasting, pp. 57–70, Copyright 2003, with permission from Elsevier.

high-resolution grid spacing of 40 km. In December 1996, after different system configurations had been considered, a 51-member system with a horizontal grid resolution of 120 km at mid-latitude was installed at ECMWF (Buizza *et al.*, 1998). The 51 consist of one forecast started from the unperturbed, best estimate of the atmosphere initial state plus 50 others generated by varying the initial conditions. Stochastic physics was introduced into the system in October 1998 (Buizza *et al.*, 1999). This aims to simulate uncertainties due to random model error. In November 2000, the resolution of the ECMWF ensemble system was further increased to a grid spacing of 80 km at mid-latitudes.

During the period spanned by the data used in this study, ensemble forecasts were produced every day, at midday and midnight, for lead times from 12 hours ahead to 10 days ahead. The archived weather variables include both upper level variables (typically temperature, wind speed, humidity and vertical velocity at different heights) and surface variables (e.g. temperature, wind speed, precipitation, cloud cover). In our work, we used ECMWF ensemble predictions for midday temperature, wind speed and cloud cover, recorded from 1 January 1997 to 1 July 2000 at the five UK locations specified in Section 15.1. Temperature was recorded in degrees Celsius (°C) at the standard height of 2 m. Wind speed was recorded in metres per second (m/s) at the standard height of 10 m, which is high enough to avoid turbulence and dissipative effects caused by the earth's surface. Cloud cover is measured as a percentage ranging from 0% for clear sky to 100% for totally cloudy sky.

## 15.3   UNIVARIATE TIME SERIES MODELLING OF WEATHER VARIABLES

### 15.3.1   Review of models for temperature time series

Franses *et al.* (2001) estimate and evaluate a univariate model for weekly mean Dutch temperature data. Their preliminary analysis revealed four features of the time series: a yearly seasonal pattern in the mean; a yearly seasonal pattern in the volatility; large absolute deviations from the mean tend to cluster, as do small deviations; and the impact of temperatures lower than expected on conditional volatility is different from the impact of temperatures higher than expected, and this impact is seasonal. Since volatility clustering is also evident in high-frequency financial returns, Franses *et al.* consider generalised autoregressive conditional heteroskedastic (GARCH) models (Engle, 1982; Bollerslev, 1986), which have become widely used for modelling financial volatility. The simple GARCH(1,1) model is given by

$$\sigma_t^2 = \omega + \alpha \, \varepsilon_{t-1}^2 + \beta \, \sigma_{t-1}^2 \tag{15.1}$$

where $\sigma_t$ is the conditional standard deviation (volatility), $\varepsilon_t$ is a stochastic error term and $\omega$, $\alpha$ and $\beta$ are parameters. Tol (1996) uses a GARCH(1,1) model for the volatility in daily mean Dutch temperature data, and an autoregressive (AR) model for the mean. He addresses the seasonality issue by estimating separate models for the summer and winter. By contrast, Franses *et al.* try to capture all of the four features that they had observed in their weekly data by estimating the following AR-GARCH model:

$$y_t = s(\mu, t) + \sum_i \phi_i y_{t-i} + \varepsilon_t$$
$$\varepsilon_t = \sigma_t \eta_t \tag{15.2}$$
$$\sigma_t^2 = s(\omega, t) + \alpha \, (\varepsilon_{t-1} - s(\gamma, t))^2 + \beta \sigma_{t-1}^2$$

where $y_t$ is the temperature variable, $\eta_t$ is an i.i.d. error term and $\mu$, $\omega$ and $\gamma$ are vectors of parameters. The seasonality term, $s(\mu, t)$, appears in the equation for the mean along with just a first-order autoregressive term. Similar terms, $s(\omega, t)$ and $s(\gamma, t)$, are employed to model the seasonality in the volatility, and the asymmetric seasonal impact of temperatures lower and higher than expected on conditional volatility. Franses *et al.* model the seasonality as a quadratic function:

$$s(\lambda, t) = \lambda_0 + \lambda_1 w(t) + \lambda_2 w(t)^2$$

where $w(t)$ is a repeating step function that numbers the weeks from 1 to 52 within each year.

Campbell and Diebold (2002) estimate AR-ARCH time series models for average daily US temperature data. By contrast with the model of Franses *et al.*, Campbell and Diebold do not include either the lagged variance term, $\sigma_t^2$, or the asymmetric seasonality term, $s(\gamma, t)$, in the variance model of expression (15.2), leaving a symmetric ARCH formulation. In addition, Campbell and Diebold use a low-ordered Fourier series to model the seasonality, instead of a quadratic function. A second-order Fourier modelling of seasonality has the

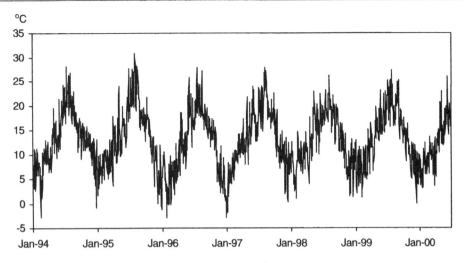

**Figure 15.2** Daily midday temperature observations at Heathrow

form:

$$s(\lambda, t) = \lambda_0 + \lambda_1 \sin\left(2\pi \frac{d(t)}{365}\right) + \lambda_2 \cos\left(2\pi \frac{d(t)}{365}\right)$$
$$+\lambda_3 \sin\left(4\pi \frac{d(t)}{365}\right) + \lambda_4 \cos\left(4\pi \frac{d(t)}{365}\right) \qquad (15.3)$$

where $d(t)$ is a repeating step function that numbers the days from 1 to 365 within each year. Campbell and Diebold removed 29 February from each leap year in order to maintain 365 days in each year. Torró *et al.* (2001) fit an AR-GARCH model to daily Spanish temperature data. In order to try to model the seasonality in the variance, they use a GARCH(1,1) model, as in expression (15.1), multiplied by a power function of lagged temperature.

### 15.3.2 Temperature models for the UK locations

Figure 15.2 shows a plot of the Heathrow temperature series. As one would expect, there is strong within-year seasonality in the mean of the series, and a reasonable degree of variation about that seasonal pattern. If there is seasonality in the variance, it is far less pronounced than in the Dutch data of Franses *et al.* and the US data of Campbell and Diebold.

We used the first five years (1994 to 1998) of each of our series to identify and estimate AR-GARCH models. In Sections 15.4 and 15.5, we use the remaining 18 months for post-sample forecast comparison.

We estimated AR-GARCH models, as in expression (15.2), for our five daily UK temperature series using the standard approach of maximum likelihood to estimate parameters under the assumption that $\eta_t$ was Gaussian. Autoregressive terms of order greater than one and moving average (MA) terms of all orders were not significant for any of our five series. This was also the conclusion of Franses *et al.* for their Dutch data. We found that Campbell and Diebold's Fourier series modelling of seasonality gave a better fit than quadratic modelling, which was used by Franses *et al.* We did not find significant Fourier terms of order more than two in any of the three seasonal features of the model in expression (15.2). We therefore used the seasonal function in expression (15.3) to represent seasonality. We followed Campbell and Diebold in removing 29 February from each leap year in our sample.

**Table 15.1**   Parameter estimates for the temperature AR-GARCH model in expression (15.2) with seasonality modelled using Fourier terms as in expression (15.3). Parentheses contain parameter $t$-statistics. Models estimated using daily data from 1994 to 1998, inclusive

| Parameters | Model | | | | |
|---|---|---|---|---|---|
| | Birmingham | Bristol | Heathrow | Leeds | Manchester |
| Equation for mean | | | | | |
| $\mu_0$ | 3.37 | 3.40 | 3.61 | 3.31 | 3.49 |
| | (16.80) | (15.81) | (15.98) | (16.93) | (16.53) |
| $\mu_1$ | −0.75 | −0.72 | −0.75 | −0.78 | −0.81 |
| | (−8.99) | (−9.12) | (−9.10) | (−9.16) | (−9.37) |
| $\mu_2$ | −1.89 | −1.73 | −1.87 | −1.90 | −1.93 |
| | (−14.92) | (−15.69) | (−14.72) | (−14.65) | (−15.00) |
| $\mu_3$ | 0.33 | 0.24 | 0.26 | 0.32 | 0.35 |
| | (4.49) | (3.76) | (3.69) | (4.16) | (4.65) |
| $\mu_4$ | | | | | |
| $\phi_1$ | 0.71 | 0.72 | 0.72 | 0.71 | 0.70 |
| | (42.47) | (43.29) | (42.37) | (41.19) | (38.43) |
| Equation for variance | | | | | |
| $\omega_0$ | 0.85 | 0.49 | 1.40 | 0.70 | 1.32 |
| | (3.06) | (1.83) | (2.94) | (1.62) | (3.43) |
| $\omega_1$ | | | | | |
| $\omega_2$ | 0.68 | | | 0.93 | 0.74 |
| | (2.96) | | | (2.16) | (3.10) |
| $\omega_3$ | | | | | |
| $\omega_4$ | | −0.42 | | | |
| | | (−2.28) | | | |
| $\alpha$ | 0.08 | 0.07 | 0.08 | 0.05 | 0.09 |
| | (4.30) | (4.21) | (3.29) | (2.33) | (4.49) |
| $\beta$ | 0.62 | 0.60 | 0.50 | 0.66 | 0.52 |
| | (9.88) | (8.80) | (4.27) | (8.09) | (5.83) |
| $\gamma_0$ | −1.60 | −0.04 | −0.40 | −3.09 | −1.65 |
| | (−3.48) | (−0.11) | (−0.93) | (−2.32) | (−3.80) |
| $\gamma_1$ | | | | | |
| $\gamma_2$ | 3.04 | 4.66 | 3.37 | 3.22 | 3.02 |
| | (4.29) | (5.00) | (3.36) | (2.17) | (4.45) |
| $\gamma_3$ | | | | | |
| $\gamma_4$ | | | | | |
| Diagnostics | | | | | |
| LB Q(7) for $\hat{\eta}_t$ | 8.17 | 15.98 | 10.23 | 5.85 | 7.69 |
| LB Q(7) for $\hat{\eta}_t^2$ | 9.14 | 7.91 | 3.83 | 5.32 | 7.62 |
| Adj $R^2$ (%) | 86.5 | 88.0 | 87.7 | 86.1 | 85.6 |
| SBC | 4.41 | 4.16 | 4.32 | 4.23 | 4.43 |

In Table 15.1 we present our preferred model for each of our five temperature series. We selected models using the Schwartz Bayesian Criterion (SBC) to judge fit. For each model, the table presents each parameter with its $t$-statistic, adjusted $R^2$, SBC and Ljung–Box Q-statistic to test for autocorrelation in standardised residuals ($\hat{\eta}_t = \hat{\varepsilon}_t/\hat{\sigma}_t$) and squared standardised residuals. The only significant Q-statistic is for the residuals from the Bristol model (critical

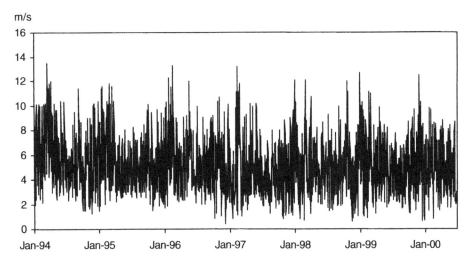

**Figure 15.3**   Daily midday wind speed observations at Heathrow

value is 12.59). This value is not significant at the 1% level (critical value is 16.81), and since we could not find a simple alternative model with better residuals, we decided to use this model. Table 15.1 shows that, for all but the Heathrow model, we found significant parameters within the seasonal GARCH function, $s(\omega,t)$. Interestingly, with all five series, when fitting GARCH models we found significant parameters in the asymmetric seasonal variance function, $s(\gamma,t)$.

The AR-GARCH models enable predictions to be made for the mean and variance at a given forecast horizon. A density forecast can then be constructed using a Gaussian assumption or the empirical distribution of standardised residuals (see Granger *et al.*, 1989).

### 15.3.3   Wind speed models for the UK locations

We are not aware of any studies that have attempted to fit AR-GARCH models to wind speed data. Figure 15.3 shows a plot of the Heathrow series. There does seem to be some indication of seasonality in the series but one might question whether the seasonality is not in the mean but, instead, in the variance. This motivates consideration of the seasonal GARCH models proposed by Franses *et al.* and Campbell and Diebold.

We estimated AR-GARCH models, as in expression (15.2), for our five daily UK wind speed series using daily observations from 1994 to 1998, inclusive. We found that lagged wind speed terms up to order seven were needed in the equation for the mean in order to satisfactorily model the autocorrelation. Fitting MA terms, in addition to the AR terms, did not lead to improvements in the model for any of the five series. As with our temperature series, we found that Fourier series modelling of seasonality gave a better fit than quadratic modelling. We did not find significant Fourier terms of order more than one in any of the three seasonal features of the model in expression (15.2). We did not find, for any of the wind speed series, significant parameters in the asymmetric seasonal volatility function, $S(\gamma,t)$. In Table 15.2, we present our preferred model for each series. Although the Q-statistic for the squared standardised residuals from the Heathrow model is marginally significant at the 5% level, we decided to use this model, as we could not find a better simple alternative model.

**Table 15.2**  Parameter estimates for the wind speed AR-GARCH model in expression (15.2) with seasonality modelled using Fourier terms as in expression (15.3). Parentheses contain parameter $t$-statistics. Models estimated using daily data from 1994 to 1998, inclusive

| Parameters | Model | | | | |
|---|---|---|---|---|---|
| | Birmingham | Bristol | Heathrow | Leeds | Manchester |
| Equation for mean | | | | | |
| $\mu_0$ | 2.61 | 3.01 | 2.78 | 2.51 | 2.17 |
| | (11.85) | (12.96) | (13.05) | (11.27) | (10.30) |
| $\mu_1$ | 0.18 | 0.16 | 0.19 | 0.18 | 0.16 |
| | (2.51) | (2.25) | (2.65) | (2.33) | (2.17) |
| $\mu_2$ | 0.16 | 0.24 | 0.16 | 0.18 | |
| | (2.30) | (3.33) | (2.35) | (2.36) | |
| $\phi_1$ | 0.37 | 0.40 | 0.40 | 0.36 | 0.38 |
| | (14.97) | (15.81) | (15.69) | (15.04) | (15.31) |
| $\phi_2$ | | | | | |
| $\phi_3$ | 0.07 | | | 0.05 | 0.06 |
| | (2.51) | | | (2.03) | (2.12) |
| $\phi_4$ | | | | | |
| $\phi_5$ | | | | 0.07 | 0.06 |
| | | | | (2.77) | (2.36) |
| $\phi_6$ | | | 0.07 | | |
| | | | (2.54) | | |
| $\phi_7$ | 0.09 | 0.06 | | 0.09 | 0.10 |
| | (3.78) | (2.66) | | (3.90) | (4.21) |
| Equation for variance | | | | | |
| $\omega_0$ | 0.07 | 0.08 | 0.07 | 0.02 | 0.10 |
| | (0.94) | (1.15) | (1.08) | (0.68) | (1.51) |
| $\omega_1$ | | | | −0.03 | |
| | | | | (−3.91) | |
| $\omega_2$ | | | | | |
| $\alpha$ | 0.03 | 0.04 | 0.04 | 0.02 | 0.05 |
| | (2.29) | (3.04) | (2.91) | (2.43) | (3.34) |
| $\beta$ | 0.96 | 0.94 | 0.95 | 0.98 | 0.93 |
| | (40.26) | (41.48) | (44.37) | (115.75) | (41.05) |
| Diagnostics | | | | | |
| LB Q(7) for $\hat{\eta}_t$ | 7.41 | 5.60 | 6.50 | 5.42 | 6.14 |
| LB Q(7) for $\hat{\eta}_t^2$ | 5.17 | 5.05 | 11.26 | 4.78 | 3.46 |
| Adj $R^2$ (%) | 19.8 | 19.4 | 19.8 | 21.0 | 22.1 |
| SBC | 4.26 | 4.28 | 4.20 | 4.45 | 4.27 |

The significance of the Fourier terms in the equation for the mean provides evidence of seasonality in the mean. We found significant Fourier terms in the variance equation for all five series, indicating statistically significant seasonality in the variance. However, for four of the series, the inclusion of these Fourier terms resulted in an insignificant ARCH parameter, $\alpha$. Removal of the GARCH terms resulted in autocorrelation in the squared standardised residuals. Therefore, for these four series, we opted to remove the Fourier terms from the variance equation, and include only a pure GARCH(1,1) model. This delivered more satisfactory squared standardised residuals. For forecasting variance up to a year ahead, the Fourier terms would be

Cloud cover %

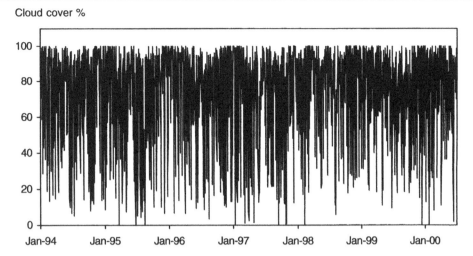

**Figure 15.4**    Daily midday cloud cover observations at Heathrow

preferable to the GARCH(1,1) terms. However, we are interested in forecasting up to 10 days ahead, so the inclusion of GARCH terms to pick up short-term autocorrelation is important.

### 15.3.4    Cloud cover models for the UK locations

In Figure 15.4, we show a plot of the Heathrow cloud cover series, which is clearly dominated by variation. There is a suggestion of seasonality in that there tends to be clusters of values of 100% cloud cover around each January. Unfortunately, we are unable to fit a GARCH model to the cloud cover series because the series is bounded above and below. Although some authors have developed AR-GARCH models for related issues, such as censoring (e.g. Wei, 2002), we are not aware of any that have been developed for data that is naturally bounded. This is presumably because this is not an issue for the financial variables for which AR-GARCH models are usually considered. It is worth noting that, although wind speed is also bounded below, this bound is never reached in our dataset, as shown in Figure 15.2 for the Heathrow series. Therefore, we elected to ignore this issue for our AR-GARCH modelling of wind speed.

## 15.4    EMPIRICAL COMPARISON OF WEATHER POINT FORECASTS

A point forecast is a prediction of the mean of the density. Evaluating its accuracy gives an understanding of the accuracy of the central location of a density forecast. We used data from 1 January 1999 to 1 July 2000 for post-sample evaluation for lead times from 1 to 10 days.

### 15.4.1    Point forecasting methods

Methods P1 to P4 are univariate time series approaches. The first uses the well-specified AR-GARCH models, while Methods P2 to P4 are naïve benchmark approaches. Methods P5 and P6 use predictions from an atmospheric model.

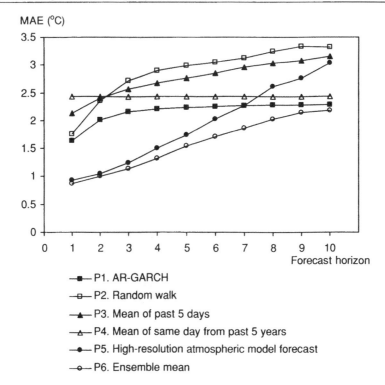

**Figure 15.5** MAE for each of the different approaches to point forecasting applied to the Heathrow temperature series

*Method P1* – The AR-GARCH models in Tables 15.1 and 15.2 were used to produce point forecasts for the temperature and wind speed series, respectively.

*Method P2* – Random walk forecasting, where the forecast for all 10 lead times is the most recent period's observed value.

*Method P3* – Average of the observed values on the same day in each of the previous five years.

*Method P4* – The average of the observed values on the five most recent days was used as the forecast for all 10 lead times.

*Method P5* – Traditional meteorological point forecasts generated by running the atmospheric model once at high resolution with best estimates for the initial conditions.

*Method P6* – The mean of the 51 ensemble members. This has been found to be more accurate than the traditional high-resolution point forecast (Leith, 1974; Molteni *et al.*, 1996), indicating that the ensemble contains information not captured by the traditional forecast.

## 15.4.2   Results

In Figures 15.5, 15.6 and 15.7, we present the mean absolute error (MAE) results for the three weather variables at Heathrow. The relative rankings of the methods for the other four locations were very similar to those shown in these three figures.

Figure 15.5 shows that for the temperature series the method that outperforms all others, at all forecast horizons, is the mean of the 51 ensemble members, Method P6. The MAE for the

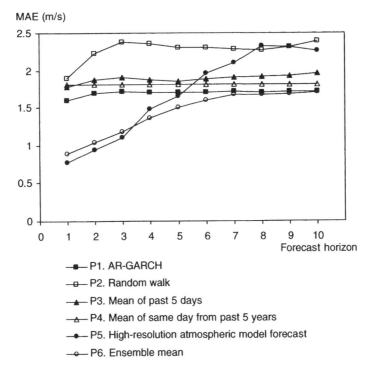

**Figure 15.6** MAE for each of the different approaches to point forecasting applied to the Heathrow wind speed series

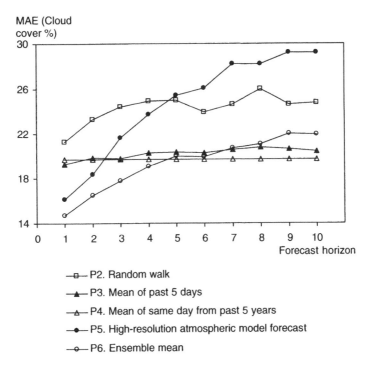

**Figure 15.7** MAE for each of the different approaches to point forecasting applied to the Heathrow cloud cover series

ensemble mean is substantially lower than that for the AR-GARCH model, Method P1, for all but the longest two lead times. The results for the ensemble mean approach are also impressive in Figure 15.6 for the wind speed series, although beyond six days ahead there is little separating the method from AR-GARCH and two of the naïve benchmark methods, Methods P3 and P4. For the cloud cover series, in Figure 15.7, the ensemble mean is dominant for the first four lead times but, beyond this, the method is unable to beat the benchmark methods P3 and P4.

For all three weather variables, the superiority of the ensemble mean over the high-resolution atmospheric model forecasts, Method P5, increases with the lead time. The deterioration of the high-resolution forecast is particularly alarming for wind speed and cloud cover. For wind speed, beyond six days ahead, the high-resolution method is substantially outperformed by two of the naïve benchmark methods, Methods P3 and P4. For cloud cover, the high-resolution method is substantially outperformed by the same two benchmark methods beyond just two days ahead and, beyond five days ahead, it is even beaten by the random walk, Method P2.

## 15.5   EMPIRICAL COMPARISON OF WEATHER QUANTILE FORECASTS

In this section, we evaluate forecasts of the following nine quantiles: 1%, 2.5%, 5%, 25%, 50%, 75%, 95%, 97.5% and 99%. We selected six quantiles in the tails of the density because this part of the distribution is of great importance from a risk management perspective. We compare post-sample quantile forecasts from four methods for lead times from 1 to 10 days for the same 18-month post-sample period considered in Section 15.4. Before introducing the methods, we briefly present quantile regression, which is used in three of the methods.

### 15.5.1   Quantile regression

If the conditional $\theta$ quantile, $Q_t(\theta)$, of a variable $y_t$ is a linear function of explanatory variables, we can write $Q_t(\theta) = x_t\beta(\theta)$, where $x_t$ is a vector of explanatory variables and $\beta(\theta)$ is a vector of parameters dependent on $\theta$. Koenker and Bassett (1978) showed that the *quantile regression* minimisation in (15.4) delivers parameters that asymptotically approach $\beta(\theta)$. Note that for computational convenience this minimisation can be formulated as a linear program:

$$\min_{\beta} \left( \sum_{t|y_t \geq x_t\beta} \theta\,|y_t - x_t\beta| + \sum_{t|y_t < x_t\beta} (1-\theta)\,|y_t - x_t\beta| \right) \tag{15.4}$$

### 15.5.2   Quantile forecasting methods

Method Q1 is a pure univariate approach. Method Q2 constructs quantiles using the ensemble mean and a univariate model for the variation about the mean. Methods Q3 and Q4 base estimation on the quantiles of the distribution of ensemble members.

*Method Q1* – AR-GARCH with empirical distribution. We used the AR-GARCH models in Tables 15.1 and 15.2 to produce mean and variance forecasts for temperature and wind speed, respectively. Quantiles were constructed separately using the empirical distribution of standardised residuals.

*Method Q2* – Ensemble mean with quantile autoregression. An alternative to the pure univariate time series AR-GARCH approach is to forecast the density using the ensemble mean as the estimate of the mean with a univariate model for the uncertainty. We use the ensemble mean here because it performed so well in Section 15.4. The $k$-step-ahead estimator for the conditional quantile of the weather variable, $y_{t+k}$ is then:

$$\hat{Q}_{t+k|t}(\theta) = \mu_{t+k|t}^{ENS} + \hat{Q}_{t+k|t}^{e}(\theta)$$

where $\mu_{t+k|t}^{ENS}$ is the mean of the 51 $k$-step-ahead ensemble members and $\hat{Q}_{t+k|t}^{e}(\theta)$ is the univariate estimator of the conditional quantile of the $k$-step-ahead forecast error, $e_{t+k|t} = y_{t+k} - \mu_{t+k|t}^{ENS}$. We estimated $\hat{Q}_{t+k|t}^{e}(\theta)$ using the following quantile autoregression approach devised by Engle and Manganelli (2002) for modelling the quantiles of financial returns:

$$\hat{Q}_{t+k|t}^{e}(\theta) = \hat{Q}_{t-1+k|t-1}^{e}(\theta) + \gamma_k(\theta) \left[ \theta - I \left( e_{t|t-k} \le \hat{Q}_{t|t-k}^{e}(\theta) \right) \right] \qquad (15.5)$$

$I(\cdot)$ is an indicator function taking a value of one when the expression in parentheses is true and zero otherwise. The parameter $\gamma_k(\theta)$ was estimated separately for each of the nine quantiles, $\theta$, and 10 lead times, $k$, using the quantile regression minimisation in expression (15.4). The expected value of the expression within the square brackets is zero if the probability of the error falling below the $\theta$ quantile estimator is $\theta$. The indicator function has the effect of reducing the next quantile estimate if, in the current period, the error is less than the estimated error quantile. If the error exceeds the quantile estimate, the next estimate is increased. We used an extensive grid search to initialise the parameters, prior to numerical non-linear optimisation.

*Method Q3* – Ensemble quantiles debiased using quantile regression. The distribution of the 51 ensemble members can be viewed as a density forecast. Preliminary analysis showed that this tends to underestimate the true uncertainty. In view of this, we used quantile regression to debias the ensemble quantiles with the weather variable as dependent variable and the ensemble quantile as regressor (see Granger, 1989). We used ensemble predictions from 1 January 1997, the earliest date in our ensemble dataset, to 31 December 1998, the final date in our estimation sample. The form of the resultant estimator is:

$$\hat{Q}_{t+k|t}(\theta) = a_k(\theta) + b_k(\theta) Q_{t+k|t}^{ENS}(\theta)$$

where $Q_{t+k|t}^{ENS}(\theta)$ is the quantile of the $k$-step-ahead 51 ensemble members, and $a_k(\theta)$ and $b_k(\theta)$ are parameters. The debiasing was performed separately for each quantile, $\theta$, and lead time, $k$.

*Method Q4* – Ensemble quantiles debiased using TVP quantile regression. In view of the developments in the ensemble generating system, such as the introduction of stochastic physics in October 1998, there is some appeal to debiasing the ensemble quantiles using the following time varying parameter (TVP) quantile regression approach:

$$\hat{Q}_{t+k|t}(\theta) = a_{t+k|t}(\theta) + b_{t+k|t}(\theta) Q_{t+k|t}^{ENS}(\theta)$$

where

$$a_{t+k|t}(\theta) = a_{t-1+k|t-1}(\theta) + \alpha_k(\theta)[\theta - I(y_t \le \hat{Q}_{t|t-k}(\theta))]$$
$$b_{t+k|t}(\theta) = b_{t-1+k|t-1}(\theta) + \beta_k(\theta)[\theta - I(y_t \le \hat{Q}_{t|t-k}(\theta))]$$

$y_t$ is the weather variable, and $\alpha_k(\theta)$ and $\beta_k(\theta)$ are parameters. The structure of the TVP parameters, $a_{t+k|t}(\theta)$ and $b_{t+k|t}(\theta)$, is based on the quantile autoregression models of Engle and Manganelli (2002). The effect of the indicator function is to reduce $a_{t+k|t}(\theta)$ and $b_{t+k|t}(\theta)$ if, in the current period, the observed value for the weather variable is less than the estimated quantile. Conversely, if the observed value exceeds the quantile estimate, the parameters are increased.

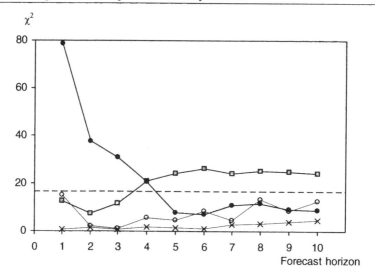

Figure 15.8   Unconditional coverage chi-squared statistic for the different approaches to forecasting the quantiles for the Heathrow temperature data. The statistic summarises performance across all nine quantiles

## 15.5.3   Results

### 15.5.3.1   Unconditional coverage

The unconditional coverage of a $\theta$ quantile estimator is the percentage of observations falling below the estimator. Ideally, the percentage should be $\theta$. To summarise unconditional coverage across the nine quantiles, we calculated chi-squared goodness-of-fit statistics for each method, at each lead time, for each weather series. We calculated the statistic for the total number of post-sample observations falling within the following 10 categories: below the 1% quantile estimator, between each successive pair of quantile estimators, and above the 99% quantile estimator. Figures 15.8, 15.9 and 15.10 show the resulting chi-squared statistics for the three weather variables measured at Heathrow (lower values are better). The dashed horizontal line in each figure is the bound of the acceptance region for the 5% significance test. The relative performances of the methods for the other four locations are very similar to those for Heathrow.

The best results for all three variables are achieved with Method Q2, which uses the ensemble mean with quantile autoregression. Performance for ensemble quantiles debiased using quantile regression, Method Q3, is particularly poor for the first three forecast horizons for the temperature and wind speed series in Figures 15.8 and 15.9, respectively. The results in Figure 15.10 show that this method performs poorly for the cloud cover series. Interestingly, TVP quantile regression debiasing, Method Q4, offers substantial improvement for the temperature and cloud cover series. The temperature results in Figure 15.8 show that the AR-GARCH

$\chi^2$

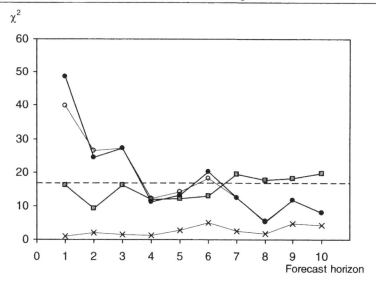

—□— Q1. AR-GARCH with empirical distribution

—×— Q2. Ensemble mean with quantile autoregression

—●— Q3. Ensemble quantiles debiased using quantile regression

—○— Q4. Ensemble quantiles debiased using TVP quantile regression

**Figure 15.9**  Unconditional coverage chi-squared statistic for the different approaches to forecasting the quantiles for the Heathrow wind speed data. The statistic summarises performance across all nine quantiles

approach, Method Q1, is the poorest beyond the early lead times. For wind speed, in Figure 15.9, this method performs well for the first seven lead times, but is the poorest beyond that.

### 15.5.3.2  Dynamic quantile test statistic

Testing for unconditional coverage is insufficient, as it does not assess the dynamic properties of the quantile (Christoffersen, 1998). Engle and Manganelli (2002) test for *conditional coverage* by jointly testing whether the following hit variable is distributed i.i.d. Bernoulli with probability $\theta$, and is independent of the value of the quantile estimator:

$$Hit_t \equiv I(y_t \leq \hat{Q}_{t|t-k}(\theta)) - \theta$$

A similar hit variable was used in the quantile autoregression in expression (15.5). For an ideal quantile estimator, the hit variable has zero unconditional and conditional expectations. Engle and Manganelli's *dynamic quantile* test statistic corresponds to the testing of the null hypothesis of the constant and both coefficients being zero in the following OLS regression:

$$Hit_t = \delta_0 + \delta_1 Hit_{t-k} + \delta_2 \hat{Q}_{t|t-k}(\theta) + u_t$$

When judged by the dynamic quantile test statistic, there was no clear pattern of superiority amongst the quantile forecasting methods for any of the three weather variables. For this reason, we do not report detailed results for this measure here.

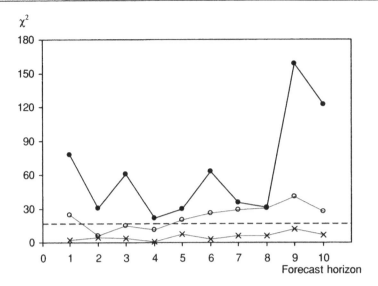

$\chi^2$

-x- Q2. Ensemble mean with quantile autoregression

-•- Q3. Ensemble quantiles debiased using quantile regression

-o- Q4. Ensemble quantiles debiased using TVP quantile regression

**Figure 15.10**  Unconditional coverage chi-squared statistic for the different approaches to forecasting the quantiles for the Heathrow cloud cover data. The statistic summarises performance across all nine quantiles

### 15.5.3.3 Informational content

Koenker and Machado (1999) propose a measure of in-sample goodness-of-fit for quantile estimators, which they refer to as $R^1(\theta)$. It is the quantile regression analogue of the OLS regression $R^2$. Instead of using a sum of squares cost function, $R^1(\theta)$ uses the quantile regression cost function given in expression (15.4). In view of the popularity of $R^2$ for evaluating the informational content of post-sample volatility forecasts, Taylor (1999) proposes the use of $R^1(\theta)$ to evaluate post-sample quantile forecasts. $R^1(\theta)$ is recorded for the quantile regression performed using post-sample data with the quantile estimator as sole explanatory variable. The measure assesses the degree to which the estimator co-varies with the true quantile, and unlike the dynamic quantile statistic, it controls for unconditional coverage by first debiasing the estimator using quantile regression.

The $R^1(\theta)$ results for the 5% quantile for the three variables at Heathrow are presented in Figures 15.11, 15.12 and 15.13 (higher values are better). The relative performance of the methods for the other quantiles and locations was similar to those presented in these three figures. Figures 15.11 and 15.12 show that the AR-GARCH results are poor relative to those based on the ensemble predictions, particularly for the wind speed data. This difference is likely to be at least partially due to the superiority of the ensemble-based methods in forecasting the mean of the series. However, it is interesting to note that for the temperature data, in Figure 15.11, the methods based on ensemble quantiles, Methods Q3 and Q4, outperform Method Q2, which is based on the ensemble mean with a univariate method for the uncertainty.

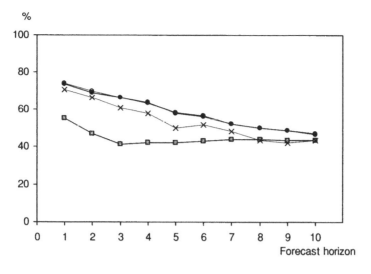

**Figure 15.11** $R^1(\theta)$ for the different approaches to forecasting the 5% quantile for the Heathrow temperature data. The results for Methods Q3 and Q4 are almost identical

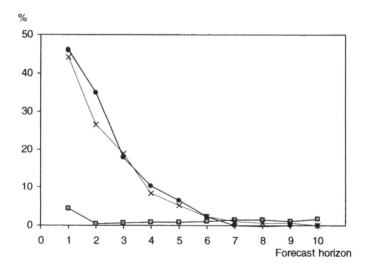

**Figure 15.12** $R^1(\theta)$ for the different approaches to forecasting the 5% quantile for the Heathrow wind speed data. The results for Methods Q3 and Q4 are almost identical

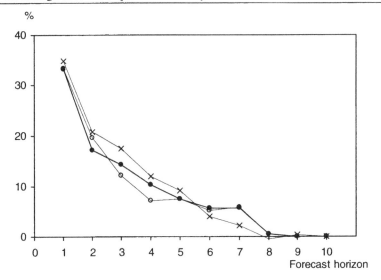

%

Forecast horizon

—×— Q2. Ensemble mean with quantile autoregression

—●— Q3. Ensemble quantiles debiased using quantile regression

—○— Q4. Ensemble quantiles debiased using TVP quantile regression

**Figure 15.13** $R^1(\theta)$ for the different approaches to forecasting the 5% quantile for the Heathrow cloud cover data

This shows that there is informational content in the distribution of the 51 ensemble members that is not captured by the ensemble mean with univariate modelling of the uncertainty. Figure 15.13 shows that, in terms of $R^1(\theta)$, there is little to choose between the three methods applied to the cloud cover series.

## 15.6  SUMMARY OF THE ANALYSIS OF TEMPERATURE, WIND SPEED AND CLOUD COVER

Our results for temperature, wind speed and cloud cover at five locations in the UK confirmed that the mean of the 51 ensemble members is a more accurate point forecast than the traditional high-resolution point forecast from an atmospheric model. The temperature and wind speed results showed that the ensemble mean also outperformed the point forecast from the AR-GARCH models for all lead times considered.

To evaluate quantile forecasts, we used unconditional coverage and two measures which aim to assess the dynamic properties of the estimator, the conditional coverage dynamic quantile statistic and the informational content $R^1(\theta)$ measure. For all three weather variables, the ensemble mean with quantile autoregression produced excellent results in terms of unconditional coverage. However, the method that performed consistently well across the different measures for all three series used TVP quantile regression to debias the quantile of the 51 ensemble members. It seems that this approach provides a good synthesis of univariate and ensemble information. For temperature and wind speed, we found that quantiles produced from the AR-GARCH method did not match the quality from the ensemble-based methods. A GARCH model could not be fitted to the cloud cover data because it is bounded above and below. Further details regarding the analysis of the temperature data can be found in Taylor and Buizza (2004).

## 15.7    FORECASTING THE PAYOFF DENSITY FOR A WEATHER DERIVATIVE

### 15.7.1    A temperature put option

The weather derivatives market is dominated by energy utilities. Due to the importance of temperature in modelling electricity and gas demand, about 90% of the weather derivatives currently traded are based on temperature (Weather Risk Management Association, 2002). The simplest and most common hedging transaction for energy providers is a put or a call option (Dischel and Barrieu, 2002). Protection against periods with lower than expected heating demand can be achieved by using a cumulative heating degree-day (HDD) put. An HDD is a measure of demand due to heating. It is defined for each day as the amount by which temperature falls below a specified benchmark, usually taken to be 18°C. This is considered to be the approximate temperature at which users switch their heating on or off. In the remainder of Section 15.7, we briefly describe a study that considered the use of weather ensemble predictions in point and density forecasting for the HDD put option with the following payoff, $P_t$:

$$P_t = \max(S_t - W_t, 0) \quad \text{where} \quad W_t = \sum_{i=0}^{9} \max(18 - y_{t-i}, 0) \quad (15.6)$$

where $y_t$ is the temperature, $W_t$ is the 10-day cumulative HDD weather index and $S_t$ is the strike price. For simplicity, we set the tick rate (payment per unit of weather index) to be one and we did not cap the payoff. As in the work of Cao and Wei (2000), we set the strike price, $S_t$, to be equal to the seasonal average of $W_t$. For the UK data in this study, there is on average only about three weeks in the year when $W_t$ is zero, and so for simplicity we considered forecasting for each day of the year. In order to be consistent with the lead times for the weather ensemble predictions, we consider a 10-day contract duration commencing in the period immediately following the forecast origin. Our analysis has relevance for longer contracts because improved forecasting over the first 10 days implies an improvement over the full duration of a longer contract. Furthermore, 10-day-ahead prediction is precisely what is required for pricing longer contracts when one is just 10 days from the expiration date.

### 15.7.2    Empirical comparison of forecasts

We used the period 1 January 1999 to 1 July 2000 to compare post-sample forecasts of the mean and quantiles of the density of the payoff in expression (15.6) for the five UK temperature series used in Sections 15.3 to 15.6. We produced forecasts for each 10-day rolling window in the post-sample period. The forecast origin was the day immediately prior to the 10-day period.

Since the expected value of a non-linear function of random variables is not necessarily the same as the non-linear function of the expected values of the random variables, it would be a mistake to forecast the expected payoff simply by substituting temperature point forecasts into expression (15.6). Instead, the standard approach is to simulate different scenarios from a model for temperature, and, using expression (15.6), create multiple realisations for the payoff (e.g. Cao and Wei, 2000; Davis, 2001). The mean of the payoff realisations is then the forecast of the expected value of the payoff, and the distribution of the realisations is the payoff density forecast. We compared the payoff mean and density forecasts from two different approaches to generating the temperature scenarios: a univariate time series model and an atmospheric model.

*Method D1* – The AR-GARCH models in Table 15.1 were used to produce mean and variance forecasts for 1 to 10 days ahead. Using these forecasts and the empirical distribution of standardised AR-GARCH residuals, 10 000 values were simulated for temperature for each lead time. Substituting these into expression (15.6) delivered 10 000 payoff realisations.

*Method D2* – As we had found that the distribution of the 51 temperature ensemble members tends to underestimate the true uncertainty, we applied a simple rescaling transformation to each ensemble member. This enabled 51 temperature ensemble members to be maintained for each lead time, from which to produce 51 realisations for the 10-day derivative payoff. (Alternatively, a form of debiasing as in Section 15.5 could be applied to ensemble-based payoff quantiles.) The following transformation was applied to $\hat{T}^i_{t+k|t}$, the $i$th ensemble member for $k$-step-ahead prediction from forecast origin $t$:

$$\mu^{ENS}_{t+k|t} + \lambda_k \left( \hat{y}^i_{t+k|t} - \mu^{ENS}_{t+k|t} \right) \quad \text{where} \quad \lambda_k = \sqrt{\frac{\sum\limits_{j} \left( y_{j+k} - \mu^{ENS}_{j+k|j} \right)^2}{\sum\limits_{j=1}^{m} \left( \sigma^{ENS}_{j+k|j} \right)^2}}$$

$\mu^{ENS}_{t+k|t}$ and $\sigma^{ENS}_{t+k|t}$ are the mean and standard deviation, respectively, of the 51 ensemble members. The rescaling inflates the deviation of each ensemble member from its mean by a factor $\lambda_k$, which is the square root of the ratio of historic error variance to the average historic ensemble variance. $\lambda_k$ decreases with lead time. For the Heathrow data, $\lambda_k$ ranged from $\lambda_1 = 3.35$ to $\lambda_{10} = 1.15$. Using expression (15.6) and the 51 rescaled ensemble members for lead times from 1 to 10 days, 51 realisations were generated for the derivative payoff.

We found that the mean of the ensemble-based payoff realisations comfortably outperformed the mean of payoff realisations produced from an AR-GARCH model. The results for Heathrow were typical with MAE for the AR-GARCH approach being 6.2°C and for the ensemble-based approach 4.3°C. We evaluated post-sample forecasts of the quantiles of the payoff density using the three quantile evaluation measures used in Section 15.5. The unconditional coverage and informational content results for the Heathrow series are shown in Tables 15.3 and 15.4. Overall, the quantiles produced from the simulation of the AR-GARCH model do not match the quality of those from the ensemble-based methods. Further details regarding this analysis can be found in Taylor and Buizza (2003b).

**Table 15.3** Post-sample unconditional coverage percentages for the Heathrow payoff quantiles. The chi-squared statistic summarises performance across the quantiles

|  | 1% | 2.5% | 5% | 25% | 50% | 75% | 95% | 97.5% | 99% | ChiSq |
|---|---|---|---|---|---|---|---|---|---|---|
| D1. Simulated AR-GARCH – empirical | **0.3** | 0.8* | 1.7* | 11.9* | 36.5* | 72.4 | 94.1 | 96.9 | 98.0* | 71.9* |
| D2. Substituted rescaled ensembles | 2.2* | **3.7** | **5.7** | **25.5** | **51.3** | **78.6** | **95.9** | **98.4** | **98.7** | **17.5*** |

\* Significant at 5% level.
Bold indicates best performing method for each quantile.

**Table 15.4**   Post-sample $R^1(\theta)$ percentages for the Heathrow payoff quantiles

|  | 1% | 2.5% | 5% | 25% | 50% | 75% | 95% | 97.5% | 99% |
|---|---|---|---|---|---|---|---|---|---|
| D1. Simulated AR-GARCH – empirical | 0.0 | 69.6 | 0.0 | −2.2 | 7.7 | 17.3 | 16.3 | 18.4 | 19.6 |
| D2. Substituted rescaled ensembles | **4.0** | **71.0** | **5.0** | **27.0** | **43.0** | **50.0** | **48.0** | **46.0** | **39.0** |

Bold indicates best performing method for each quantile.

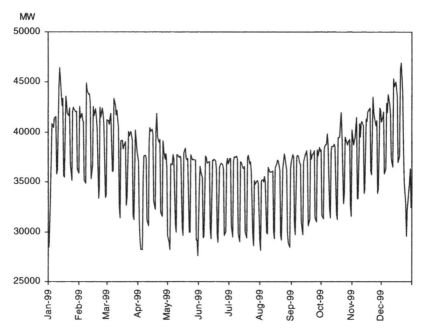

**Figure 15.14**   Demand for electricity at midday in England and Wales in 1999
Reprinted from International Journal of Forecasting, Vol 19, Taylor *et al.*, Using weather ensemble predictions in electricity demand forecasting, pp. 57–70, Copyright 2003, with permission from Elsevier.

## 15.8   ELECTRICITY DEMAND MODELLING

### 15.8.1   Modelling weather-related demand

Accurate demand prediction and an assessment of forecast uncertainty are needed by utilities in order to manage the system load efficiently and by those wishing to trade electricity. Weather variables are widely used to model electricity demand for 1 to 10-day-ahead prediction. In this section, we briefly report on a study that considered the use of weather ensemble predictions in forecasting demand. We used the demand forecasting methodology of National Grid Transco (NGT) as a basis for our analysis.

We focused on predicting demand in England and Wales at midday. This is an important period in many summer months because it is often when peak demand occurs. Figure 15.14 shows a plot of midday demand in England and Wales for each day in 1999. As in many other studies of electricity demand, we smoothed out special days, such as bank holidays, as their inclusion is likely to be unhelpful in analysing the relationship between demand and weather.

At NGT, demand is modelled using three weather variables: effective temperature, cooling power of the wind and effective illumination. These variables are constructed by transforming standard weather variables in such a way as to enable efficient modelling of weather-induced demand variation (Baker, 1985). We used the following standard weather variables for which ensemble predictions were available: temperature $(T_t)$, wind speed $(W_t)$ and cloud cover $(CC_t)$. This meant us replacing effective illumination by cloud cover, and using spot temperature, instead of the average of temperature for the previous four hours, to construct effective temperature and cooling power. *Effective temperature* $(TE_t)$ for day $t$ was defined as:

$$TE_t = \tfrac{1}{2}T_t + \tfrac{1}{2}TE_{t-1} \tag{15.7}$$

*Cooling power of the wind* $(CP_t)$ aims to describe the draught-induced load variation:

$$CP_t = \begin{cases} W_t^{\frac{1}{2}}(18.3 - T_t) & \text{if} \quad T_t < 18.3°C \\ 0 & \text{if} \quad T_t \geq 18.3°C \end{cases} \tag{15.8}$$

We followed the practice of NGT by constructing $T_t$, $W_t$ and $CC_t$ using a weighted average of weather readings at Birmingham, Bristol, Heathrow, Leeds and Manchester. The weighted average aims to reflect population concentrations in a simple way by using the same weighting for all the locations except Heathrow, which is given a double weighting. The resulting weather variables, $TE_t$, $TE_t^2$, $CP_t$ and $CC_t$ are used as explanatory variables in a regression model for electricity.

### 15.8.2 Empirical comparison of forecasts

We used daily data from 1 January 1997 to 31 October 1998 to estimate models, and 18 months of daily data from 1 November 1998 to 30 April 2000 to evaluate the post-sample point forecasts from the following four methods for lead times from 1 to 10 days ahead.

*Method E1* – A set of benchmark demand forecasts was produced from a univariate time series model that did not include any weather variables.

*Method E2* – Demand forecasts were produced by using traditional high-resolution weather point forecasts in the demand regression model.

*Method E3* – The 51 ensemble members for temperature, wind speed and cloud cover were substituted into expressions (15.7) and (15.8), which were then substituted into the demand regression model to produce 51 scenarios for demand. Demand point forecasts were produced using the mean of the 51 scenarios.

*Method E4* – To establish the limit on accuracy that could be achieved with improvements in weather prediction, we produced an unattainable set of benchmark demand "forecasts" by using actual observed weather in the demand regression model.

The mean absolute percentage error (MAPE) results in Figure 15.15 show that using weather ensemble predictions, instead of traditional high-resolution weather point forecasts, led to improvements in accuracy for all 10 lead times. These improvements increased with the lead time. We also considered the estimation of the demand forecast error uncertainty, which is likely to vary in magnitude over time due to weather and seasonal effects. The distribution of the 51 demand scenarios from Method E3 provides information regarding the uncertainty. However, this distribution tends to underestimate the demand forecast uncertainty because it does not accommodate demand model uncertainties and because the ensemble predictions tend to underestimate the uncertainty in the weather. In view of this, we recalibrated measures of variance and quantiles taken from the scenario distribution. Comparison with univariate

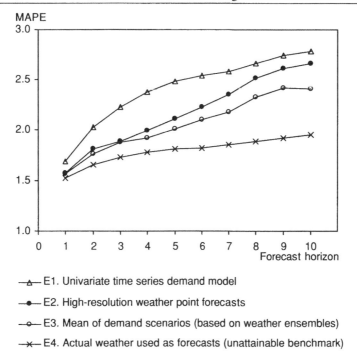

—△— E1. Univariate time series demand model

—●— E2. High-resolution weather point forecasts

—○— E3. Mean of demand scenarios (based on weather ensembles)

—✕— E4. Actual weather used as forecasts (unattainable benchmark)

**Figure 15.15**    MAPE for electricity demand point forecasts for post-sample period, 1 November 1998 to 30 April 2000
Reprinted from International Journal of Forecasting, Vol 19, Taylor *et al.*, Using weather ensemble predictions in electricity demand forecasting, pp. 57–70, Copyright 2003, with permission from Elsevier.

volatility forecasting methods showed that the ensemble-based approaches performed well in terms of informational content but did not dominate in terms of unconditional coverage. Further details and related work can be found in Taylor and Buizza (2002, 2003a).

## 15.9   CONCLUDING COMMENTS

We have evaluated the quality of point and quantile forecasts, produced using ensemble-based and univariate time series methods, for the three weather variables of greatest relevance to energy modelling in the UK. We have also described studies that have applied these approaches to weather derivative pricing and electricity demand prediction. A general finding is that the ensemble predictions enable more accurate point forecasting. In all the applications, the ensemble-based methods produced quantile forecasts with the greatest informational content. The fact that our methods were not always able to convert this informational content into clearly superior quantile coverage performance motivates research into the development of new ensemble-based quantile forecasting methods.

## REFERENCES

Baker A.B. (1985). "Load Forecasting for Scheduling Generation on a Large Interconnected System". In *Comparative Models for Electrical Load Forecasting*, D.W. Bunn and E.D. Farmer (eds). Wiley, Chichester, pp. 57–67.

Bollerslev T. (1986). "Generalized Autoregressive Conditional Heteroskedasticity". *Journal of Econometrics* **31**: 307–327.

Buizza R., Petroliagis T., Palmer T.N., Barkmeijer J., Hamrud M., Hollingsworth A., Simmons A. and Wedi N. (1998). "Impact of Model Resolution and Ensemble Size on the Performance of an Ensemble Prediction System". *Quarterly Journal of the Royal Meteorological Society* **124**: 1935–1960.

Buizza R., Miller M. and Palmer T.N. (1999). "Stochastic Simulation of Model Uncertainties". *Quarterly Journal of the Royal Meteorological Society* **125**: 2887–2908.

Campbell S. and Diebold F.X. (2002). "Weather Forecasting for Weather Derivatives". Working Paper 02-046, Penn Institute for Economic Research, Department of Economics, University of Pennsylvania.

Cao M. and Wei J. (2000). "Pricing the Weather". *Risk Magazine* **May**: 67–70.

Christoffersen P.F. (1998). "Evaluating Interval Forecasts". *International Economic Review* **39**: 841–862.

Davis M. (2001). "Pricing Weather Derivatives by Marginal Value". *Quantitative Finance* **1**: 1–4.

Dischel R.S. and Barrieu P. (2002). "Financial Weather Contracts and their Application to Risk Management". In *Climate Risk and the Weather Market*, R.S. Dischel (ed.). Risk books, London, pp. 25–41.

Duffie D. and Pan J. (1997). "An Overview of Value at Risk". *Journal of Derivatives* **4**(Spring): 7–49.

Engle R.F. (1982). "Autoregressive Conditional Heteroscedasticity with Estimates of the Variance of United Kingdom Inflation". *Econometrica* **50**: 987–1008.

Engle R.F. and Manganelli S. (2002). "CAViaR: Conditional Autoregressive Value at Risk by Regression Quantiles". Department of Economics Discussion Paper, University of California, San Diego.

Franses P.H., Neele J. and van Dijk D. (2001). "Modeling Asymmetric Volatility in Weekly Dutch Temperature Data". *Environmental Modelling and Software* **16**: 131–137.

Granger C.W.J. (1989). "Combining Forecasts – Twenty Years Later". *Journal of Forecasting* **8**: 167–173.

Granger C.W.J., White H. and Kamstra M. (1989). "Interval Forecasting: An Analysis Based Upon ARCH-Quantile Estimators". *Journal of Econometrics* **40**: 87–96.

Koenker R.W. and Bassett G.W. (1978). "Regression Quantiles". *Econometrica* **46**: 33–50.

Koenker R. and Machado J.A.F. (1999). "Goodness of Fit and Related Inference Processes for Quantile Regression". *Journal of the American Statistical Association* **94**: 1296–1310.

Leith C.E. (1974). "Theoretical Skill of Monte Carlo Forecasts". *Monthly Weather Review* **102**: 409–418.

Molteni F., Buizza R., Palmer T.N. and Petroliagis T. (1996). "The New ECMWF Ensemble Prediction System: Methodology and Validation". *Quarterly Journal of the Royal Meteorological Society* **122**: 73–119.

Palmer T.N., Molteni F., Mureau R., Buizza R., Chapelet P. and Tribbia J. (1993). "Ensemble Prediction". Proceedings of the ECMWF Seminar on *Validation of Models Over Europe: Vol. I*, ECMWF, Shinfield Park, Reading, UK.

Taylor J.W. (1999). "Evaluating Volatility and Interval Forecasts". *Journal of Forecasting* **18**: 111–128.

Taylor J.W. and Buizza R. (2002). "Neural Network Load Forecasting with Weather Ensemble Predictions". *IEEE Transactions on Power Systems* **17**: 626–632.

Taylor J.W. and Buizza R. (2003a). "Using Weather Ensemble Predictions in Electricity Demand Forecasting". *International Journal of Forecasting* **19**: 57–70.

Taylor J.W. and Buizza R. (2003b). "Density Forecasting for Weather Derivative Pricing: A Comparison of GARCH and Atmospheric Models". Unpublished Working Paper, University of Oxford, UK.

Taylor J.W. and Buizza R. (2004). "Density Forecasting of Daily Temperature Using Ensemble Predictions and GARCH Models". *Journal of Forecasting*, forthcoming.

Tol R.S.J. (1996). "Autoregressive Conditional Heteroscedasticity in Daily Temperature Measurements". *Environmetrics* **7**: 67–75.

Torró H., Meneu V. and Valor E. (2001). "Single Factor Stochastic Models with Seasonality Applied to Underlying Weather Derivatives Variables". Manuscript, University of Valencia.

Toth Z. and Kalnay E. (1993). "Ensemble Forecasting at NMC: The Generation of Perturbations". *Bulletin of the American Meteorological Society* **74**: 2317–2330.

Tracton M.S. and Kalnay E. (1993). "Operational Ensemble Prediction at the National Meteorological Center: Practical Aspects". *Weather and Forecasting* **8**: 379–398.

Weather Risk Management Association. (2002). "The Weather Risk Management Industry: Survey Findings for April 2001 to March 2002". Report by PriceWaterhouseCoopers.

Wei S.X. (2002). "A Censored-GARCH Model of Asset Returns with Price Limits". *Journal of Empirical Finance* **9**: 197–223.

# Index

Note: Page references in *italics* refer to Figures; those in **bold** refer to Tables

*Index compiled by Annette Musker*

Printed and bound by CPI Group (UK) Ltd, Croydon, CR0 4YY

23/04/2025

14660967-0005